清代外務部
中外關係檔案史料叢編
——中美關係卷

·中國第一歷史檔案館 北京大學 澳大利亞拉籌伯大學 編·

第八册·綜　合

中華書局

目録

軍務兵器

慈善賑濟

治安社黨

軍，自較熟悉，且亦係歸入版圖之人，可以由中國節
制，與他項外國人有間，惟其平日為人若何，其管帶
兵丁情形若何，以華爾較之，優劣若何，務望悉心公
商，但能於海口一帶防務有益，不致別滋後患，即可
令其管帶，並詢法思爾德是否與白齊文同為華爾生
前得力裨將，亦望查覆等語。嗣據李鴻章奏稱：常勝
軍除前調赴甯波現留松江者，按吳煦稟共有四千
五百餘名，向由華爾教練，口糧極重，每月需餉不下
七萬兩，惟華爾新亡，一時未便遣散，經臣與吳煦再
四商議，自當仍令該關道會同統帶，其白齊文、法思
爾德，應由該道妥酌是否勝任，如不能如前得力，即
將人數口糧酌量裁減，亦責成該道秉公核辦等。
上諭：常勝軍素稱得力，第前據薛○等奏稱募足三
千名，何以此次留駐松江者，有四千五百餘名？是此
軍為數不少，白齊文能否勝任，將來能否就我範圍，
不可不預行籌及，恐積漸遷就，日後轉成尾大不掉

乾興號

之勢，徒靡餉項，不如交中國大員管帶，易為駕馭。或
一時無此勝任之員，仍須暫交白齊文接統，其衆以
示羈縻，著薛○、李鴻章悉心察度，毋貽後患等因。欽
此。英國水師提督何伯之自煙台赴滬也，因該國陸
路提督士禮佛（後均作士乳佛立）必攜帶白齊文來李鴻章營晤商。何
伯面稱白齊文材勇可任，無庸令法思爾德會帶，以
一事權，並與李鴻章議明，剋日會攻嘉定縣城。鴻章
據以入告。（見李鴻章奏稿）奉
上諭：何伯推薦白齊文，自應暫為允准，令其統帶，剋
日進攻嘉定，即可察其材力是否足勝管帶之任，以
收實效等因。欽此。是年十月薛○、李鴻章覆奏略云：上海所練常勝一軍，自副將華爾戰沒後，亟須妥籌接帶之人。臣鴻章前據英國提督何伯面保舉華爾部將白齊文材勇可任，毋庸由英國派員接管，且毋庸令法思爾德會帶等語，業經陳奏，并聲明此後果能調遣，以及得力與否，再行隨時察看在案。白齊文、法思爾德均係美理駕國人，法思爾德夏間在青浦被賊擄去，後歸，現在會帶之說，既寢，可毋庸議。白齊文現據蘇松太道吳煦極力保薦，後經英國提督何伯推誠相屬，此外又驟無可任之人，祇得暫交接管，其能否勝任，以及就我範圍之處，一時難窺底蘊，仍應隨時察看，據實奏聞。華爾之

乾興號

華爾〇在中華係吳煦受丁憂蘇松糧道楊坊力薦任以教練兵勇之事，是以臣煥前在此撫任內，奏明將常勝軍飭令吳煦督帶，楊坊會同華爾管帶，其統率之任，本歸中國大員。臣鴻章復經檄飭署江南提標中營參將李恒嵩協同管束，現以白齊文接帶。此軍所有調遣鈐制一切事宜，應仍責成吳煦、楊坊轉飭遵照，不准原薦力保之人置身事外，倘有違令犯升一切情弊，亦惟吳煦、楊坊是問，李恒嵩協同管束，亦令隨時稽查，倘久而相習，再行酌籌。又此軍臣煥前奏約計共三千人，旋即交卸撫篆，迨閏八月臣鴻章接據吳煦查報，除前調赴甯波之外，留松江共四千五百餘人，面詢其故，則以華爾自行添募為詞。查華爾初練僅數百人，實稱勁旅，嗣經逐次加增，則技藝不能盡精，習氣亦漸獷悍，若飭吳煦等督率認真操練鈐束，並就現存實數截止，不准再行增添，倘或不能得力，應如臣鴻章前奏，即將人數口糧酌量裁減，俾再任意添募，或有不遵約束，否即將吳煦、楊坊二員奏參治罪。九月蒲安臣（美國公使）函稱：英法兩國兵及前常勝軍共四千餘人，將江蘇佔據嘉定之長髮逆賊戰退，欣喜以此好音寄語。先是蘇、崑、太股逆匪屢由嘉定竄犯滬防，英國水師提督何伯每以上次西兵退出為憾，迭赴李鴻章營籌商進剿，并約定克城後由李鴻章派兵防守，隨經李鴻章調派白齊文管帶常勝軍一千五百名直抵嘉定城外，西兵連宵築成砲台，連環開放炸砲，賊以鎗砲抵死回

拒我軍，輪流環擊，計歷三時之久，轟倒南門城墻十餘丈，賊勢不支，我軍分布雲梯一擁而上，西兵同時登城，擊殺守堞悍賊，大隊一律入城，當將嘉定縣城克復。該縣為蘇滬門戶，我與賊所必爭，中外將士同心輯睦，分路進攻，崇朝而下堅城，其神速尤不易得。見李鴻章奏稿

四江口之圍未解，賊勢甚熾，白齊文帶常勝軍一千人由松江馳往截剿，至杜村進白鶴港，圍攻賊巢，環開鎗砲，斃賊極多，擒斬千餘名。詳李鴻章奏稿

金陵援賊攻撲官軍營壘，偽忠王李秀成率領各股逆眾上犯，蔓延甚廣，李鴻章以白齊文接管常勝軍攻克嘉定之後，激發其力，該軍四千餘人打仗向稱奮勇，所有西洋炮大炮各利器，購備頗多，施放亦便。因曾國藩咨調程學啟一軍前往救援，而松滬賊勢亦迫，未遑赴救，乃飭署藩司吳煦、前蘇松督糧道楊坊督同白齊文提款籌撥行裝，駛往金陵協同援應。見李鴻章奏稿

李

上諭：李鴻章奏派員督帶常勝軍赴金陵等語。李鴻章飭吳煦、楊坊督率白齊文接管華爾之常勝軍洋槍隊四千餘人，添備船隻，駛往援應，可資得力。白齊

文以外國人隸帰中國出力剿賊亦具真心此軍到
金陵後曾國藩即督飭曾國荃等善為籠絡駕馭仰
可用其力以剿賊亦可使觀吾軍師律之盛以折其
心吳煦楊坊二員向與此軍相習李鴻章令其督同
前往最為合宜并著飭令該二員妥為督帶奮勉立
功欽此十月奉
上諭曾國藩奏常勝軍雖非該大臣所願調然既已
赴援即須加意籠絡俾人思感奮自能所向有功如
其情形驕悍即嚴飭吳煦等妥為鈐束俟解圍後應
否仍留金陵著曾國藩隨時酌度辦理欽此初曾國
荃被圍緊急李鴻章飭派白齊文往援吳煦楊坊均
願告奮勇復飭馳赴九洑洲合力進攻據報常勝軍
四千名共租借大小輪船十七隻聲勢尚壯嗣李鴻
章接曾國藩書不願該軍赴救曾國荃解圍後亦兩
次函止鴻章以撥調在前未便朝令夕改且吳煦与
洋商雇定輪船已付價銀七万餘兩又添製軍裝數

乾興號

萬兩若常勝軍不去船價勢難退回因催令調齊人
數兼程進發乃始以輪船難雇軍裝未備為詞既拟
起程又因寧波嘱總兵阻留遲延時日（事詳江蘇境助剿案）十
月下旬吳煦督帶頭隊輪船駛抵鎮江俟大隊到齊
定期進攻維時白齊文已至自寧波託病未行吳煦
在鎮江株守旬餘後隊杳不見到不得已折回催隊
白齊文先已由滬回松閉城門輒以餉銀未發縱
親勇搶劫松江府知府方傳書同參將李恆嵩設
法勸諭多勇一鬨而散吳煦至滬時楊坊并悉白齊
文任意延宕聲稱不願前赴金陵請辭差使楊坊責
以大義白齊文怫然回松復率洋槍隊數十人趕至
上海楊坊寓中將楊坊鼻額胸膛打傷吐血不止又
將豫備發餉之洋銀四万餘元強行劫去蓋自何伯
回國後英國駐滬提督領事繙譯各官均与白齊文
交往親密白齊文恃有袒護日漸肆橫遂尔逞凶滋
事李鴻章據實奏聞奉

乾興號

上諭白齊文毆傷監司大員劫奪餉銀數逾鉅萬實
屬不法已極該員已隸中國版圖自應照中國法
律治罪著即革去三品頂戴交李鴻章嚴拏按照中
國制度相機妥辦定擬具奏等因欽此李鴻章於白
齊文滋事後即照會英國提督士迪佛立（因原薦之何伯已回國士迪佛立與閔保薦者）係派英國兵官麥蓋理馳赴松江將白
齊文押解來滬由英國水師兵船看管白齊文藉口
先後經買軍火帳未算清須料理欠帳等情總理衙
門迭接江蘇巡撫李鴻章咨報先又照會美國駐京
公使蒲安臣並照會英國駐京公使卜魯斯同治二
年美國公使蒲安臣照覆以白齊文係美國人除美
國欽差官他人不能治白齊文之罪除美國之律別
國之律亦不能治白齊文之罪語多悖謬（詳白齊文滋事案）
並呈出白齊文自訴單及長勝軍法官保狀內白齊
文致蒲安臣書有李鴻章是我對頭向來諸多不肯
幫助反為掣肘並不用我欽常勝軍則常勝軍一定

要壞等語因尤荒謬不具錄二月李鴻章等議暫頓
常勝軍附片陳奏奉
上諭此軍所需經費向由中國發給無為數甚鉅均
由白齊文自行支用中國何從派員會算代償已諭
總理衙門照會駐京公使妥為剖辨仍著李鴻章據
理折斥飭將白齊文迅速交出毋得仍前含糊了事
致後來外國接統常勝軍者紛紛效尤挾制益難措
手等因欽此是月署三口通商大臣董○探得白齊
文有搭輪船來京之事即函商照總理衙門正在查
辦江蘇巡撫李鴻章咨文亦至內云正月廿九日晚
間有不知姓名外國武弁十餘人護送白齊文於上
輪船（聞往天津）船名揚子巡防弁丁正欲拘拏外國武弁各持
手槍嚇放弁丁人數無多眾寡不敵無從下手是白
齊文必於潛往都門請由該公使就近拘拏解審俾
免漏網等情（詳白齊文滋事案）未幾果入京城潛住美館先
後接據英美兩國照會歷述白齊文悔過之意仍求

帶罪圖功以贖前愆總理衙門核其情節稍予自新
飭令提究回滬駐旗查辦先是美國公使蒲安臣進
函會并代遞白齊文奏摺一件總理衙門以中國友
員三品虛衔尚且不准專摺況白齊文業已革職豈
能擅遞專章將原摺擲回并聲明中國辦事於執法
之中每留原情之地白齊文究屬生長外國如能自
出悔罪投案江蘇巡撫詳訊必準情酌理稍寬一綫之
路等語並是白齊文抵京理應訊究姑可將免兩國
公使為之懇請情願回滬遂不敢別萌他念云旋經
總理衙門派出賫送布國條約委黄惠庭順道伴送
白齊文赴津後由署三口通商大臣董。派五品銜
把總楊保安接送回滬名為護送實押解也三月白
齊文到滬謁李鴻章於行營鴻章諭以常勝軍現另
有外國人管帶不能令其接管白齊文因未委用復
附舟北來見三口通商大臣崇厚來函李鴻章亦致書總理衙門
略云白齊文前犯之罪均在鑒原之中毋庸置辯特

因其籍隸外洋人非安分既難以律相繩又不可疾
之已甚鈞諭將計就計飭鴻章酌辦冀其出於感奮
稍收後效並如白齊文自去冬造肆後舉國目為惡
人一聞復將任用中外駭然軍心惶惑鴻章接晤美
國提督士迪佛立伯郎兩酋聞及此多慨然歎惜恐
將來白齊文敗壞貽誤致不敢與共事是時白齊文
到滬與前次撤換諸小兵頭狂言交煽意氣甚張稅
務司赫德適過滬聞而不平呈書鴻章力持大義鴻
章參之諸說仰窺酌量辦理之諭頗有定見故於白
齊文來營叅謁峻拒之令往謁巡撫以折其氣次日
復來經鴻章傳見嚴詞斥責白齊文惟極口認罪並
有先此誤聽人言目下已全明白願遵令投效之語
鴻章復斥其前次罪犯過重現經總理衙門咨令酌
量辦理原係格外施仁寬待此外國人之意如能悔
過自新可人力保而接管常勝軍戈登現在辦了甚
妥不應撤退諭令從緩靜候云云詳白齊文歸了案白齊文

之再由津來京也總理衙門給英國參贊威妥瑪函
云白齊文並不領取執照擅自入都且本係犯罪之
人來去自由不能核辦實屬任意妄為難再予姑
容已照會美國公使蒲安臣另行辦理等情嗣接英
國公使卜魯斯照覆總理衙門以白齊文建功受誣
不為昭雪又美國公使蒲安臣函稱白齊文被參之
款冤枉甚多往復辯論較前此尤狡總理衙門覆之
云查白齊文從前出力中國曾給賞犒數已不少且

乾興號

保舉二次酬其勞苦之人無中外試問美國食餉
之武員不遵調遣貽誤軍情律以外國之例當得何
罪該革員咎自立甘願切結投隸中國其結內又叙
手書押有案可查本應照中國例辦理今既屢代說
情姑亦不為已甚俟該
旨將白齊文革出中國版圖不再收用飭令回國由
美國領來云云六月總理衙門將續辦情形具奏奉
旨知道了欽此七月李鴻章奏稱白齊文回滬闖密

投蘇賊招募外國流氓百餘人陸續偷往並有代購
外洋槍炮情事英國文武各官皆走相告雖由臣劄
行美領事西華訪拏解辦並商令戈登程學啟等嚴
為防備通飭前後營壘一體查拏而有此波折自應
益加穩慎臣惟激勵將士同心協力以制狡謀等
上諭白齊文已逐出中國版圖既有投賊情事自應
嚴密拏辦該外國人於理屈之事亦不能再行嘵辯
也欽此白齊文既招雇外國流氓潛赴蘇州助賊叛

乾興號

迹顯著法領事穆布孫英領事馬安商同美俄布各
國領事會銜刊刷告示遍貼曉諭禁止各外國人駐
從前往以敦和好復經李鴻章通行曉示四路官兵
實力兜拏務獲捆解正法未咨凡李鴻章嗣訪得白齊文
潛行到滬并聞黃浦內有廣快船一隻裝有軍火欲
往吳淞搶奪往來寧波輪船投入賊境經新到廈門
兵船前往查辦并英法美三國領事添派巡捕協拏
白齊文聞風遁逸當將廣快船并外國人十名水手

張阿華一名軍火兩箱捜獲投張阿華供稱在虹
口地方被外國人硬拉上船乞其搖到吳淞又洋涇
濱對面停有白殼船一隻掛有美國旗號裝有軍
火函役馳往拏獲據水師官云即白齊文所坐之
船蓋白齊文糾合黨羽私運軍火并圖搶奪輪船兇
狡已極（見李鴻章來咨）九月李鴻章奏稱我軍進規無錫將
對蘇州咽喉賊日危蹙偽忠王李秀成偽侍王李侍
賢皆率大股自金陵回援并勾合逆酋白齊文黨眾
來敘炸砲輪船多方狡逞必欲攻破大橋角營壘直
入常熟太倉擾我後路擊我兵勢計極狡毒本將士
用命苦戰連旬轉危為安李鶴章訊生擒賊供忠逆
以兩偽王及次子之死涕泣而去白齊文中炮折傷
膀臂又傷亡夷人太多古党灰心又換戈登宰稱白
齊文敗後直欲投誠為忠逆所覺鎖押城內臣先接
英國繙譯官梅輝立函稱白齊文對求率眾洋人投
誠臣姑允之而嚴備之密飭戈登毋為所賣今復隨

忠逆攻我大橋角營壘竟未得逞彼在賊中屢戰不
利賊亦不能深信計窮求降似已無能為役此後各
國係該管不敢再入投賊和白齊文聲言將為賊覓
購輪船李鴻章揚言若急不敢來滬購辦遂在黃浦
泖澱狙伺劫奪適值本營鑄炮兵官英人麦格理所
坐高橋小輪船回松江砲局行至松江城外豆腐濱
麦格理以事登岸白齊文率數十人竄上輪船搶駛
而去八月白齊文隨忠逆大股撲犯大橋角先以炸
砲燬我師船七隻奪去十餘隻遂圍攻陸營李鶴章
自張涇橋急行四十里往援營官周壽昌拚死伏岸
下以火箭射入輪船藥艙立焚其船即前所搶去之
高橋輪船也燒斃洋人數十名賊大敗遁忠逆疑白
齊文為官軍作奸細然而因之旋逃出戈登及英國
繙譯官梅輝立皆以准降在先為之解免鴻章當[illegible]
各領事白齊文既悔罪來歸赦其已往宜速勒令回
國嚴加管束毋任逗留上海（見李鴻章來函）冬白齊文投降

回滬藏匿不出，有捕盜局改裝小輪船甫將開駛赴蘇，白齊文從岸旁覷見，率同洋匠駕直登船，言在搶劫。是日並有戈登常勝軍租僱洋行之小輪船，名飛而復來者，亦在上海被洋匠劫去，傳云亦係白齊文所為。經炮船圍住，立將白齊文拏獲，李鴻章飭令美領事速押回國，英法各領事亦以謂先行監禁，候有美國船回船，即行解回。未幾白齊文復潛往東洋。見李鴻章來函

總理衙門據李鴻章函報，照會美國公使蒲安臣，並

乾興號

責美領事袒庇白齊文，不行飭令回國，致有東洋之逃等語。十一月，李鴻章咨報，據美領事申呈，白齊文已於十月廿四日坐埃登輪船前往日本，令其不再來中國可也。並定於何日押回本國，另難定期云云。同治三年三月，白齊文並又自東洋來滬，稅務司[illegible]德呈報總理衙門，當即照會美國公使蒲安臣，往復辯論。旋准蒲安臣照會，白齊文業經押禁，因無兵船，現已送於民間火輪貨船，俾離中土。而江蘇地據李鴻章亦

於四月間函報白齊文業經閩道，將伊交美領事勒令出洋矣。

乾興號

二

交際門

優待類

美艦來華在廈門接待案

駐美大臣伍廷芳致外務部電 光緒三十四年二月二十日

美遣水師艦隊游歷環球澳洲政府特請前往日本亦請赴横濱等處我政府似應照請

外務部致南洋大臣電 二月二十一日

美艦隊游歷既有澳洲政府日本等國邀請我國亦當照請前來游歷除電復伍使照會美外部代為邀請外希轉薩提督酌量何地相宜預備接待

南洋大臣致外務部電 二月二十四日

准薩提督電美艦隊來華如以煙台為接待之地最爲相宜請酌定示復

外務部致南洋大臣電 二月二十七日

當經電致伍使向外部商請茲准復允並約在煙台接待希轉薩提督

外務部致駐日本大臣李家駒電 二月二十九日

美遣艦隊游歷聞日本邀請赴横濱等處我國定在煙台接待希探詢日本如何接待詳復以備參酌

駐日本李大臣致外務部電 三月初三日

遵詢海軍外務兩省據云美艦東來已由駐美日使邀請預定横濱為歡迎地現距期尚遠所有接待方法先期三月始能議及

駐美伍大臣致外務部電 三月二十二日

前擬在煙台接待美艦頃美外部面稱總統與水師大員商議因艦隊游行各埠煙台未免迂道擬居冬令順赴廈門接待不必太優等語

美使臣柔克義致外務部照會 四月初一日

美國水師提督伊摩利帶領第二隊裝甲戰鬥艦八隻於西十月二十九號開至廈門停泊六日

外務部致南北洋大臣暨閩浙總督信 四月二十六日

美艦到廈約在九月初間現擬派司員謙豫麥道信堅迅赴福建並由閩派員會同往廈相度情形估計用款應需各項事宜會同該處地方官分投備辦所有用款由閩估定後電奏飭部籌撥核實用款作正開銷約在四十萬兩上下薩提督應先期赴廈指揮各員籌辦一切預計美艦到廈三箇月前在海關人員內派美國人馬而芬暨在閩美領事館當差人員一二名同往廈門商議接待辦法一面由南北洋海軍內挑選快船數艘赴廈照料並就近考查選派陸軍一標到廈以壯軍容地方街道應即預為修理潔淨凡寺觀名勝足供游覽之區均加修葺彈壓居民臨時勿形喧擾美艦應需火食甜水等物均須接濟又操場運動場各處亦須預備所有該處官商應備彩棚彩坊並修整埠頭以備歡迎又多掛形色畫一之龍旗以彰國徽而壯觀瞻

外務部致陸軍部信 四月二十六日

美艦約華歷九月初來廈現由部派員赴閩稟商閩督籌辦一切並電薩提督先期赴廈指揮布置接待事宜一面由南北洋挑選快船前往照料並就近考查選派陸軍一標赴廈以壯軍容

外務部致度支部信 四月二十六日

美艦於本年九月間赴廈游歷所有接待用款約在四十萬兩之譜俟閩省估定奏明由貴部籌撥作正開銷希備案

度支部致外務部信 四月三十日

接待美艦用款約在四十萬兩之譜本部自當照籌應付

惟該款於何時需用撥給何處請示知遵辦

外務部致度支部信 五月初四日

接待美艦用款即先撥二十萬兩交由閩督發庫存儲備用餘款隨時續撥

度支部致外務部文 五月初八日

接待美艦用款擬在江海關結存洋稅項下先撥銀二十萬兩解閩備用

外務部致南北洋大臣暨閩浙總督信 五月十三日

接待美艦用款度支部在江海關結存洋稅項下先撥二十萬兩解閩備用

閩浙總督致外務部電 五月十三日

接待美艦事廈門一島雖為各國通商口岸局面甚小地方街道逼窄附近既無名勝亦無寬展宴客之所限於地勢必須早為設法布置除電催薩提督外請飭所派部員早日來閩以便委員會合商辦

司員謙豫麥道信堅致外務部電 七月二十一日

抵廈後應辦各事粗有眉目前派之美稅司馬爾芬聞已不來美領署亦無繙譯乞飭總稅司另派美員速來并飭各稅司將此事所辦物料一體免稅

外務部致南洋大臣電 八月初一日

美艦抵廈屆期擬請

旨派皇族一員外部堂官一員前往接待

戊申年交涉要覽 篇 卷 門 類

又致閩浙總督電 八月初一日

麥道等請另派美員速來並所辦物料免稅一節已商准稅務處另派美員所需物料應於購運時報該關監督發給免稅專照希轉知

又致閩浙總督電 八月初九日

署稅務司擬派該署四等幫辦莫瀾前往廈門襄助繙譯事宜不日起身

又致麥道信堅電 八月二十九日

美艦到廈每艦應贈大小銀杯各一件大件贈本船小件贈船主杯面鏨文如下大清國政府特贈大美國某船某船主以為軍艦到華之記念光緒某年某月日贈於廈門

等字布照製
銀杯鏨字應用華文並配英文已與美使商定即照辦

又電 九月初二日

又發閩浙總督電 九月初三日

本日奉
旨美國海軍將於十月初間游抵廈門著派貝勒毓朗外務部右侍郎梁敦彥前往勞問欽此特電達

又致美公使柔克義照會 九月初五日

光緒三十四年九月初三日軍機大臣面奉
諭旨美國海軍將於十月初間游抵廈門著派貝勒毓朗外務部右侍郎梁敦彥前往勞問欽此布轉達貴國政府

戊申年交涉要覽　篇　卷　門　類

又致閩浙總督電 九月初八日

朗貝勒梁侍郎九月十四日乘快車赴漢口二十邊到滬乘海圻兵輪至廈門請轉諭麥二員將接待章程電部

又致閩浙總督電 九月初八日

美使派本館武隨員都司黎富斯抵廈為代表

閩浙總督致外務部電 九月初八日

美艦來廈接待事宜已妥為備辦惟廈口離省海道二日壽屆時應否前往乞代奏請
旨

外務部致閩浙總督電 九月初九日

奉
旨松壽電奏悉著該督屆時前往廈門督率印委各員接待照料欽此

又發司員謙豫麥道信堅電 九月十二日

此次朗貝勒赴廈美提應先來拜不知已與議定否頃見洋文禮單第一日美領請宴若美提不先來拜美領宴排在第一日似有不便不如改由中國先請第一日宴日本禮單第一日亦係日本先請頃晤美柔使亦謂美提應先拜貝勒中國係地主應先請宴請帖用名正具隨員係外務部郎中曾述棨主事聯治直隸候補道嚴廷璋廣東候補府周重候選知縣唐國安縣丞胡有良

司員謙豫等致外務部電 九月二十五日

戊申年交涉要覽　篇　卷　門　類

頃美報接提督電美艦改期初六日抵廈

駐日本大臣胡惟德致外務部電 九月二十六日

美兵艦十六日遞信艦一水師官約五百人兵約一萬二千五百人於二十四日到橫濱擬留七天日政府派海軍中將率兵艦十六遞信艦三為接待艦隊美司令官及參謀均住離宮艦長士官住旅館皆日政府供應司令參謀覲見日皇并賜讌內閣總理外務陸海各大臣暨海軍司令部長東京市長神奈川知事以及民間各團體均排日設讌歡迎東京橫濱徧懸燈彩專開大車電車以供來往導游附近名勝概不收費

閩浙總督致外務部電 九月二十七日

美艦不日抵厦，已委藩司尚其亨先行赴厦照料，壽亦即
遵
旨前往。

貝勒毓朗等致外務部電 十月初七日

美艦八艘初六日上午八鐘抵厦，下午二鐘美提督伊摩
利等來見，晚七鐘請該督及各士官計一百二十七人、水
兵三十人在接待場讌飲，彼此演説頌詞，表明中美兩國
交誼，美官盡皆鼓掌稱快感頌
皇仁。今午答拜美提，並在美艦讌飲，晚仍在接待場請讌，場所
内外巡查周至，地面亦極安静，請代奏。

外務部致朗貝勒等電 十月初八日

初七日電已進呈，美艦抵厦，中外歡騰，應由尊處傳
旨勞問。

美公使柔克義致外務部信 十月初十日

本國來厦水師提督伊摩利來電恭祝
皇太后聖壽無疆，並於本日懸旗敬礮，此次兵艦來華，蒙
特派親貴大臣遠迎接待，一併附電鳴謝。

外務部復美柔使信 十月十一日

貴國伊摩利提督恭祝
皇太后萬壽之電業經代爲奏
聞，
上意甚爲嘉悦。此次貴國兵艦遠道來華，特
派朗貝勒、梁侍郎赴厦傳
旨勞問，優加接待，中外聯歡，益臻款洽。兹承貴國水師提督電
謝，具徵親睦之忱，本爵大臣同深欣佩。

外務部致朗貝勒等電 十月十一日

美提督伊莫利電祝
皇太后萬壽，並謝特派大臣勞問，又美艦隨員專電恭祝，均經本
部奏聞，
上意甚爲嘉悦。此次美艦來華，情誼周浹，該提督及船主、兵官
等自應請
旨特賞寶星以示優獎，希先傳知，並開單送部奏請頒給。

朗貝勒等致外務部電 十月十二日

美艦在厦連日款待宴會，贈賞品物，自提督以次均極歡
洽，臨别同聲贊戴，據稱除將中國優待情形詳細報知本
國政府外，務懇代爲奏謝等語。該艦隊於本日上午十鐘
開行，臣毓朗仍乘海圻兵輪於十七日北旋，臣敦彦前面
奉
恩旨事竣
賞假一箇月回籍省親，同日回粤，乞代奏。

朗貝勒等奏請
賞給美艦人員寶星摺 宣統元年二月初四日

奏爲美艦來華，懇
恩賞給寶星，繕單呈
覽，恭摺仰祈

聖鑒事光緒三十四年九月初三日軍機大臣面奉
諭旨美國海軍將於十月初間游抵厦門著派貝勒毓朗外務部
右侍郎梁敦彥前往勞問欽此欽遵行知前來臣等當即跪聆
聖訓陛辭後於十月初二日馳抵厦門美艦隊八艘士官二百餘
員兵丁七千餘人於是月初六日辰刻抵厦十二日辰刻
啟行連日接待適宜情形歷經臣等會同閩浙總督松壽
先後電達外務部代
奏在案伏查美國海軍以中美邦交篤厚不憚波濤萬里展
駕來游迥非尋常交誼可比該艦隊海軍副提督伊摩利
施羅達等親見中國款待慇懃情文並至每至讌會之頃
必蹈揚
聖德稱頌
皇仁甚至率同各長官暨各軍士望
闕嵩呼跂踵鼓掌具感激懽愉之狀實有出於至誠難以形
容擬議者進退揖讓聯敦槃玉帛之歡賓主綢繆極劍珮
衣冠之盛蹌蹌濟濟來享來王查該艦隊所至之國均承
贈給寶星此次游歷來華既經格外優待我
皇上纘承
前烈惠逮遠人允宜仰懇
恩施
頒給寶星以示優異而昭榮寵臣等謹就該艦隊長官各職任
詳加核擇按照定章從優酌擬等第繕具清單恭呈

戊申年交涉要覽 篇 卷 門 類

御覽如蒙
俞允恭候
命下即咨由外務部照製頒發所有美艦來華懇
恩賞給寶星緣由是否有當理合恭摺具陳伏乞
皇上聖鑒謹
奏
宣統元年二月初一日奉
旨着照所請外務部知道單併發欽此
謹將請
賞美艦隊寶星銜名繕單恭呈
御覽
美國前任統領艦隊海軍副提督伊摩利
美國統領艦隊海軍副提督施羅達
以上二員擬請
賞給頭等第三寶星
美國戰艦艦長鼎爾思
美國戰艦艦長侯獲
美國戰艦艦長愿爾思
美國戰艦艦長褒若
美國戰艦艦長沙菩
美國戰艦艦長赫勤士
美國戰艦艦長畢立

美國戰艦艦長戴義
美國駐京使館海軍隨員統帶官鄧格地
以上九員擬請
賞給二等第二寶星
美國駐廈門領事官阿訥爾
以上一員擬請
賞給二等第三寶星
美國艦隊中軍旗官韓德孫
美國艦隊中軍旗官允烈文
美國駐京使館衛隊統帶官吉司黎富思
美國陸軍體操員守備威芬
以上四員擬請
賞給三等第一寶星
宣統元年二月初一日奉
旨覽欽此

戊申年交涉要覽 篇 卷 門 類

三

照錄給美使田貝照會十月二十五日

為照會事現因中日失和貴國國家篤念邦交
願照咸豐八年中美約章第一款從中善為調
處中國國家亦願由貴大臣直向日本說合中
國允許朝鮮自主並酬日本兵費按公定議數
目貴大臣既有說合之權應請將中日兩國主
見互為傳述商定以期早息兵爭仍歸和好庶
不負貴國國家及貴大臣美意須至照會者

啟者中日一事頃已面交照會一件想
貴大臣業經閱悉惟
貴大臣甫自
貴國而來恐於此中原委尚未能盡知底蘊茲特
縷細函佈
台端溯自朝鮮為我之藩服垂三百年既已著之
憲典又載於約章附文各國亦從無異議本年
夏間朝鮮全羅道民變該國王一再乞師請平
亂黨我中國
大皇帝俯念藩封不忍重違所請因照章派去兵士
祗二千人亂即敉平正擬撤回閒詎日人已陸
續興兵直入鮮境不赴全羅道而逕抵漢城數
日之間已至萬餘之數是以當時有彼此撤兵
之議而日人不即允從旋又有兵士駐紮之處
均略為退讓免生衅端之議而日人又不允從
中國遂事婉商無不準情酌理即派兵以平亂
黨亦係分所應為非獨無思據其地之意亦並
無與日人生衅之心正在百計圖維力籌和局
未幾而高陞被擊之事出又未幾而牙山失守
之信聞凡此數端皆日人先為之倡中國遂不
得不整我戎行也惟是中國兵制與各國異各
國皆備有防兵戰兵各有專責中國所有兵士
不過藉平寇盜自安境內兵無所謂防更無所
謂戰也日人自明治維新後事事效法泰西兵

法一門已得要領以致此次交戰而我兵不甚得力者職是故耳夫東方之國中日為大尤宜和好永敦以全鄰誼今日人徒以朝鮮之故與輔車相依之國妄啟兵端縱令獲勝而彼此均不免傷殘是以當平壤戰後我即復有願商之舉蓋因同處亞洲中不必自相殘害且又素為有約之國日與我國别無嫌隙而我亦並無使其有嫌隙可乘詎日人仍復侈其兵力不肯允從是真索解不得矣現舉衆已渡鴨緑江將為窺伺東三省之計並有犯我京畿之謡第兵家勝負不常正未可逞其所欲我中國總以用兵之事最為危險但能了結之處無不曲全以免

生靈塗炭雖戰端並非自我而啟和議要無不可自我而成誠以怨結兵連一切外患内憂固與我大有關繫即東方戰爭日久於

貴國亦多所關繫緣兵衅久開通商各口岸

貴國商旅恐不能安居樂業即内地各教士亦深恐保護不周致生他變轉非所以重

友誼而示懷柔是以中國

大皇帝與

貴國

大伯理璽天德深願永敦和好亦不願與日本大

啟兵端且

貴國條約載明若他國有何不公輕藐之事一

經照知必須相助從中善為調處以示友誼等

語中國現時難處自應照知

貴大臣可否由

貴國居中設法調處早息干戈以同享太平之

福則中國幸甚各國幸甚

五

照會美康使高陞船案擬請派涂德為公正人電請美國政府轉電查照由

二品銜太常寺正堂袁 正月 日

候補三品京堂聯 正月 日

俄國股

呈為照會事案查高陞輪船一案中國現與英國政府商明延請公正人評斷茲據出使英國羅大臣電稱英國政府擬舉

貴國駐英頭等使臣涂德為公正人惟須由中英政府請

美國政府准辦等語中國

國家意見相同為此照會

貴大臣電請

貴國政府允准涂大臣為此案之公正人以憑公斷並希

見覆可也須至照會者

美康使

光緒二十六年正月 日

文　五月十七日

咨

兵部為咨行事接准美國礮廠商人格利司倭函稱新創防海巨礮密法兩種願售與貴國專利其用請選派精於製礮能員來敝處閱看並將製礮合同底稿呈送等因前來　查該商人所稱創製新礮願售與中國利用事關與外洋交涉之件本部無從辦理相應鈔錄譯函並原洋文信咨送

貴衙門查照謹請酌核施行須至咨者

右　咨

計鈔函洋信各貳紙

欽命總理各國事務衙門

光緒貳拾柒年伍月　拾柒　日

附件一

致中國兵部函

兵部大臣鈞鑒敬啟者愚新創防海巨礮
密法兩種願售與
貴國專利其用
一係製造半動活機後膛巨礮法口徑寬
大裝放甚捷用之足可制勝
一係新創之法用之不但能造大礮並可
求精惟需費大有分差造法甚屬便
捷
以前兩法合用為宜分用亦可依此新法無
論何樣新式槍礮均可製造
貴國可選派精於製礮能員來敝處閱看兩法
圖樣惟須先立英文合同兩紙其式即照信內所附奉者刊印
請
貴國所派承立合同人員並駐紐約領事與愚
彼此簽押各執一分然後出示圖樣為該員詳
細講明其圖樣每種每分價值一百元倘兩
種均購每種每分減價二十五元共一百五十
元如蒙聘愚至
貴國傳授此法每月須薪水五百元並隨
帶幫辦一人月須薪水二百五十元其薪水自愚等
由敝處起程之日起至回敝國之日止按月照算
專此佈達並頌日祉速
賜回音
再啟者如用前法製造槍礮不逾五尊
之數無須另給花費五尊以外須按
合同照辦
美國紐卓塞省英格里烏城中創礮法人
格里司倭謹啟外附合同式樣一分

西五月初四日

附件二

合同

美國紐卓塞省英格里烏城人格利司倭新創製造槍礮秘法二種情願授與中國專用應與中國特派承立合同人員彼此商訂批立合同二紙各執一分為據

立合同人美國格利司倭中國承辦人某商訂將新創製礮秘法二種售與中國惟用此法造礮其數在五尊以內一切專利加利各項開銷概免五尊以外每法應給專利銀五萬元此外尚應給加利銀其給加利銀之法按照礮之口徑面積尺寸計算每方米厘美特給加利銀百分之一五此兩法合用製礮之例也若兩法分用（不論專用那一法）每礮須用其口徑面積尺寸 每方米 厘 美 特給加利銀百分之一其給加利銀之利須由第六尊礮造成之日起扣至十七年限滿止在此限內中國之礮凡用此法造成者須按歷年礮數口徑面積尺寸如例給與加利

中國所派承立合同人員於西歷正月內將前一年所造礮數以及礮式尺寸所用何法抑或自創新法製造等節詳細具一清册寄送敝處其歷年加利銀兩亦須隨同歷年清册一併匯寄匯票須通用紐約倫敦巴黎三處者

礮法圖說須由出售人購辦人與駐紐約領事官公同籤押俾免朦混

立合同人彼此均須籤押蓋印以昭信守

中歷西歷 年 月 日立合同人承辦人某 押
美國格利司倭

附件三

63 Prospect Street City of Englewood.
State of New-Jersey, U-S.A. ~~April~~ March 1st.1901.

To His Excellency,
The Minister of War.

Dear Sir:-

The undersigned (an American) has two separate secret inventions, pertaining to heavy ordnance for coast defence that he would be pleased to sell to your Government for its own use.

One is a semi-automatic breech-loading cannon that can be made of large caliber and loaded and fired rapidly-a condition that often wins a battle.

The other is a new process of manufacturing, by which not only larger, but superior guns can be made at a great difference in cost, and with less extensive appliances.

The two inventions should go together, but it is not imperative, as my cannon can be made by any other process, and my Process can be used in the manufacture of any other style of gun.

That your Government may better judge of what I claim, I will show to any expert representative that you may name, copies of drawings of both inventions and explain them to him, but to protect myself, I shall before doing so, require that you make duplicate agreements in English, (similar to enclosed type-written sample) duly signed by such officer as has power to make such contracts, and countersigned by your Consul in New-York, at which time I will also sign them.

If after inspecting my drawings should your representative desire a copy of each to send to you, I will sell them to him for one-hundred dollars ($100.oo.)for each invention, and if both are taken, then a discount of 25% (net $150 for the two).

Furthermore in case you purchase the inventions and desire that I should go to your country and instruct your men, will do so on payment to me of a salary of Five hundred dollars ($500.oo). per month to myself, and Two hundred and fifty dollars ($250.oo).per month to my assistant, actual expenses of both from date of departure to time of return to New-York, the same to be paid monthly.

Awaiting an early reply, I am,

Yours respectfully,

Merritt W. Griswold.

P. S. By the inclosed form of contract you will notice you have no bonus or royalties to pay unless you make more than five guns?

附件四

Whereas, Merritt W. Griswold of the City of Englewood, in the State of New Jersey, U. S. A., has two inventions: one an improved process of manufacturing heavy ordnance, and the other, a breech-loading cannon, which two inventions he is desirous of selling to the Government of *China* for its own use, now, therefore:

This Agreement, made in duplicate, and entered into between the said Merritt W. Griswold as "Party of the First Part", and the Government of *China* through who is duly authorized to make such contracts, as "Party of the Second Part", Witnesseth: That for and in consideration of the covenants hereinafter mentioned, the said "Party of the First Part" agrees to, and he does hereby allow the "Party of the Second Part" to make and use either or both of his said inventions in connection with five (5) guns, but only to the extent of said five (5) guns, free of charge of any bonus, or royalty, or payment whatever. In consideration of which the "Party of the Second Part" agrees that: In case they make, have made, or use either one of said inventions in, upon, or in connection with more than the five (5) guns, as above freely permitted, they, the "Party of the Second Part", will then pay to the said Merritt W. Griswold, or to his legal representatives, a bonus-sum of *Fifty* Thousand Dollars ($*50,000.00*) for each invention made or used, and in addition to this bonus-sum, will also pay a royalty of one and one-half cents ($0.015) on and for each square millimeter in the area of the bore, in each and every gun made or used, wherein both his design of gun, and his process of manufacture are used conjointly in the same gun, but if either invention is used separately and independently of the other, then the "Party of the Second Part" shall pay one cent ($0.01) per square millimeter of bore-area for each invention thus made or used, said royalties to be paid on all guns made or used during a period of seventeen (17) years from the date of the completion of the sixth gun.

The intention of this agreement is: That the "Party of the First Part" in addition to the bonus-sum, shall be paid a royalty, for seventeen (17) years, of one cent ($0.01) per square millimeter of the bore-area in each gun, for each invention, when said inventions are made or used separately, but only one and one-half cents ($0.015) per square millimeter of the bore-area for the two, when they are used conjointly in the same gun.

Annual detailed reports shall be made and forwarded by the "Party of the Second Part" to the "Party of the First Part" during the month of January of each and every year, of all guns made by his process during the year previous, stating the style of gun to, or in which his process of manufacture was applied, also of his style of gun made by any process other than his.

Payments for royalties must accompany each and every annual report, by sight drafts on New York, London or Paris.

Copies of the drawings and specifications of both inventions, to be signed (for identification) by both the "Party of the First Part" and the representative of the "Party of the Second Part", or its Consul residing in the City of New York.

In Witness Whereof, the parties hereto have affixed their respective signatures and seals on the respective date of signing.

---------------------------- Witness)
for Merritt W. Griswold at New York : ---------------------- (Seal)
this day of 1901.)

---------------------------- Witness)
for at : ---------------------- (Seal)
this day of 1901.)

七

十二月初六日到

已具

天卅一

標下統帶武衛右軍右翼步隊第一營花翎記名提督壯勇巴圖魯張勳為呈報事竊據卑營右隊領官張永成

呈稱十一月三十日下午五點鐘大清門有洋人二名乘馬馳至云與

皇上送信必須進內面見當由值班看守該門之左六正目楊寶魁詰阻告以有信必回稟始能

放進該洋人等旋即走去又十二月初三日早八點鐘東長安門有東洋兵三名身帶刺

刀要進門內遊玩亦經值班之左二正目白鳳春再三詰阻告以有我等在此不准闖進

該洋兵遂即旋去又據前隊領官張士造呈稱十二月初三日晨有英國洋人二名

美國洋人一名至西三座門云往煤山繪圖經值看門左哨哨長朱信山攔阻不准

進去該洋人即均馳去各等情前來標下覆查屬實除飭該管官兵均各認真

稽查防範外理合具單呈報伏乞

中堂鑒核須至呈者

光緒二十七年十二月初四日呈

八

欽差出使美日秘國大臣伍　為

咨呈事光緒二十七年十二月初三日欽奉電

旨朕欽奉

慈禧端佑康頤昭豫莊誠壽恭欽獻崇熙皇太后懿旨上年拳匪之變禁門一帶承美國兵官嚴飭弁兵極力保護洵屬睦誼可風深宮甚為感悦著伍廷芳

轉達美外部傳旨向總統申謝欽此冬又十二月二十七日欽奉電

旨朕欽奉

慈禧端佑康頤昭豫莊誠壽恭欽獻崇熙皇太后懿旨本月二十三日各國使臣夫人等入覲宫廷均為款洽美國使臣康格之妻前曾與各國使臣夫人同班覲見此次惟伊在京垂詢情形尚稱佳善良用欣慰每念去年拳匪之變各公使參隨

及諸内眷皆受驚恐時繫於懷現在均已回國一切起居諒皆安吉著各出使
大臣傳旨慰問以紓廑注欽此敬各等因當即欽遵恭譯兩次均親詣美外部
敬謹傳
旨申謝慰問訖除電達外理合將奉到電
旨日期備文咨呈
貴部謹請察照備案須至咨呈者
右　咨　呈

欽命外務部

光緒二十八年正月初四日

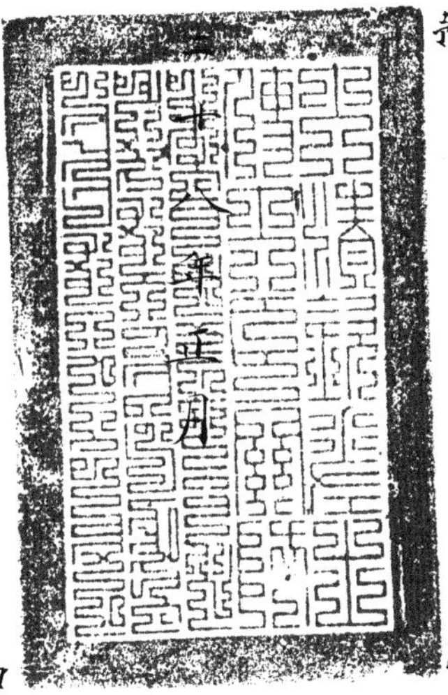

頂用 空白

九

逕啟者本國marked提督定於下禮拜一即中歷十八日起程回船是以
覲見日期必須定於禮拜六抑或禮拜日又於明日尚欲至萬壽山瞻仰
可否前往即希
貴大臣請示
慶王爺或給何據或派人同往務希於本日
見復以便早為預備明日前往是荷特此泐布即頌

日祉

名另具五月十四日

康格

一〇

逕啓者，茲有本國水師統領、管帶亞細亞一帶戰艦、頭等提督軍門裴哲恩，帶有隨員，於昨日來京，欲代美國
政府、恭誠
覲見，是以本大臣請
貴親王奏請
大皇帝、允其

覲見、表明兩國友睦之誼、以望兩有裨益、近有俄國水師提督、已蒙
大皇帝允其
覲見、想於本國水師提督、亦肯
俞允、無不願其入
覲、惟提督在京不能日久、越兩日即須回船理事、即希
貴親王入

奏請早定期
大皇帝若允婁提督
覲見知本國
政府必爲欣悦也特此泐布，即頌
爵祺，附送洋文
名另具 五月十四日

康格

附件

F.O.No. 398.

LEGATION OF THE UNITED STATES OF AMERICA,
PEKIN, CHINA.

June 19th, 1902.

Your Highness:

Admiral Fred Rodgers, Commander-in-Chief of the Asiatic Squadron of the United States Navy, arrived with his staff in Peking Yesterday, and is desirous as a friendly act on the part of his Government to pay his respect to His Imperial Majesty. I therefore respectfully request that Your Highness will properly memorialize the Throne for the favor of an Imperial audience for this purpose. This will be an additional evidence of the friendship existing between our two Governments, and I trust prove of mutual benefit.

The recent audience given to His Excellency, the Russian Admiral, assures me of the willingness of His Majesty to grant this request.

The Admiral must soon return to his duties at sea; hence I venture to hope that as early a date as possible may be fixed upon.

Thanking your Highness in advance, and being confident that the audience asked for will be pleasing to my Government, I avail myself of this occasion to assure

Your

Your Highness of my highest consideration.

E. H. Conger

Envoy Extraordinary and

Minister Plenipotentiary

of the United States.

To His Highness,

Prince of Ch'ing,

President of the Board of Foreign Affairs.

和會司
呈爲照會事前准
貴大臣函請帶領
貴國裏提督
覲見等因本爵大臣業已入奏本日面奉
諭旨著於本月十九日午初刻在乾清宮覲見欽此相應恭錄
諭旨知照
貴大臣并轉致
裏提督欽遵並將禮節單一併照送
查照可也須至照會者附禮節單
美康使

覲見禮節单

屆期本部派弁導引

貴大臣偕

婁提督乘轎進

東華門隨員繙譯等在

上駟院外下轎馬步從至

景運門外

貴大臣

婁提督換乘内務府所備之椅轎至

乾清門外堦前下椅轎步行進

乾清門中門至

尚書房少坐候屆十一點鐘時

皇太后
皇上升殿本部大臣帶領
貴大臣
婁提督暨隨員繙譯等至
殿中門一鞠躬進
殿數武一鞠躬至
納陛前一鞠躬
貴大臣
婁提督口奏頌詞繙譯譯畢
皇太后
皇上答詞本部王大臣傳述繙譯恭譯
貴大臣

殿
殿
尚
乾
景
上

婁提督聽畢一鞠躬退後數武一鞠躬至
門一鞠躬禮成率隨員繙譯由
左門側身退出仍至
書房少憩出
清門中門坐椅轎出
運門下椅轎乘轎隨員繙譯等步行至
駟院外均乘轎馬回館
光緒二十八年五月　日

一二

逕復者：本月二十三日准
貴部來函，以
貴王大臣擬請
旨賞給前年守護
禁城本國兵官寶星，以酬睦誼，並請查明銜名，轉請本國
政府允行等因。本大臣茲已照録
來函轉送本國外部諒必轉達兵部按所應行者斟酌辦理也。
特復，即頌
日祉。附送洋文。

名另具。十月二十五日

附件

F.O. No. 2843.

LEGATION OF THE UNITED STATES OF AMERICA,
PEKIN, CHINA.

Nov. 24th. 1902.

Your Highness:-

I have the honor to acknowledge the receipt of Your Highness' note of the 22d. inst. proposing to memorialize the Throne and request the bestowal of decorations upon the military officers of the United States Army who had charge of the Forbidden City year before last, as a recognition of their friendly offices, and requesting me to make inquiries as to their names, titles etc. and ask permission of my Government for said officers to receive the decorations etc.

I have the honor to reply that a copy of Your Highness' despatch has been forwarded to the State Department, which will refer the matter to the War Department for the necessary action.

I avail myself of the opportunity to renew to Your Highness the assurance of my highest consideration.

E. H. Conger

Envoy Extraordinary and

Minister Plenipotentiary of

the United States.

To His Highness Prince of Ch'ing,

President of the Board of Foreign Affairs.

一三

十一月廿三日

照會

大亞美理駕合衆國欽命駐劄中華便宜行事全權大臣康　爲

照會事茲有美國節制通國陸軍頭等提督軍門麥

勒思越一二日來京游歷不過擬住數日深以得能恭

覲

大皇帝爲欣幸是以照會

貴親王查照請爲

奏請允准麥勒思軍門

覲見並請酌於二十八、二十九、三十三日之內定期入

覲可也須至照會者、附洋文

右 照 會

大清欽命全權大臣便宜行事總理外務部事務和碩慶親王

一千九百二年拾貳月貳拾貳日

光緒貳拾捌年拾壹月貳拾叁日

LEGATION OF THE UNITED STATES OF AMERICA CHINA

一四

逕啟者適接美國麥軍門來電內稱明日由秦王島乘火車晚間

準至北京請

貴親王即為

奏請務於本月二十八二十九三十三日之日請

旨定期准其入

覲望早知照又本使臣夫人麥軍門夫人另日

覲見
皇太后一節亦希即爲
奏請如蒙
俞允更爲欣感至前所云麥軍門欲閱姜軍之操可否之處並希
示悉爲荷特此即頌
爵祺
名另具 十一月二十五日

康格

一五

逕啟者茲將明日
覲見頌詞繕就一分附函呈送即希
貴親王查照是荷順頌
爵祺

名另具 十二月二十七日

一六

和會司

呈為照會事光緒二十八年十一月二十三日接准

照稱美國陸軍提督麥勒思來京游歷照請帶領

覲見等因本部業經具奏奉

旨著於十一月二十八日巳正二刻覲見欽此相應

恭録

諭旨知照

貴大臣暨

麥提督欽遵並將禮節單一併照送查照可也

須至照會者　附禮節單

美國康使

覲見禮節單
屆期本部派弁導引
貴大臣偕
麥提督乘轎進
東華門隨員繙譯等在
上駟院門外下轎馬步從至
景運門外
貴大臣
麥提督換乘內務府所備之椅轎至
乾清門外階前下椅轎步行進
乾清門中門至
上書房少座候屆十點鐘時

皇太后
皇上升殿本部大臣帶領
貴大臣
麥提督暨隨員繙譯等至
殿中門一鞠躬進
殿數武一鞠躬至
納陛前一鞠躬
貴大臣
麥提督口奏頌詞繙譯譯畢
皇太后
皇上答詞慶親王傳述繙譯恭譯
貴大臣

殿

麥提督聽畢一鞠躬退後數武一鞠躬退至

殿

門一鞠躬禮成率隨員繙譯由

上

左門側身退出仍在

乾

書房少憩出

景

清門中門坐椅轎出

上

運門下椅轎乘轎隨員繙譯等步行至

駟院門外均乘轎馬回館

光緒二十八年十一月　日

一七

逕啟者茲值美國節制陸軍頭等提督麥軍門來京現駐本
館本大臣訂於十一月三十日下午五點鐘在本館潔備盃樽
藉圖晤敘奉請
貴大臣屆時惠臨幸勿見却並希
示復爲荷特此即頌
日祉
名正具

康格

一八

具奏美國提督麥勒思來京請
旨定期覲見由

奏 署左侍郎那
十一月二十六日

奏 署右侍郎聯
十一月二十六日

謹
奏為美國陸軍提督来京籲懇
覲見請
旨定期恭摺仰祈
聖鑒事竊臣等接據美國使臣康格照稱本國陸軍
提督麥勒思到京懇請

覲見
皇太后
大皇帝應請代奏定期
覲見等因臣等查各國提督來京經臣部奏請
覲見奉
旨允准有案茲美國陸軍提督麥勒思來京籲懇
覲見自應請
旨定期准由該使臣帶同入
覲以遂其瞻就之忱伏候
命下臣部即知照欽遵屆期由臣部帶領
覲見謹繕摺具陳伏乞
皇太后
皇上聖鑒訓示謹
奏

光緒二十八年十一月二十七日具奏奉
硃批着於本月二十八日巳正二刻覲見欽此

一九

具奏美使康格帶領提督麥勒思之妻等覲見蒙頒賞字畫食物代奏謝恩由

奏

奏

署左侍郎那

十二月初二日

署右侍郎聯

奏

十二月初二日

謹

奏為據情代奏謝

恩恭摺仰祈

聖鑒事竊臣等接據美國使臣康格函稱十一月二十九日本使臣帶領使臣之妻與提督麥勒思之妻等

覲見蒙

皇太后頒賞使臣康格
御筆著色松靈畫一軸福壽字一分康格之妻
御筆水墨葡萄畫一軸福壽字一分麥勒思之妻
御筆著色葡萄畫一軸福壽字一分瑪斯之妻衛理之妻剛姑娘
魏姑娘若士得之妻葛翰章之妻繙譯衛理各蒙
賞福壽字一分均即敬謹祇領麥勒思之妻與瑪斯之妻回國並蒙
特傳溫諭又各蒙
恩頒給食物八色不勝銘勒請將感
恩之忱代為具奏等因前來理合據情代奏伏乞
皇太后
皇上聖鑒謹
奏光緒二十八年十二月初三日奉
硃批知道了欽此

二〇

逕復者昨接

來函以

皇上大祀

祈穀壇十四日

駕御齋宫請轉知衛隊統領諭飭兵丁於十四十五兩日暫勿前往操演等因本大臣茲已轉達該衛隊統領知照矣相應函復

貴親王查照可也特此即頌

爵祺附送洋文

名另具 正月十三日

附件

F.O. No. 462,

LEGATION OF THE UNITED STATES OF AMERICA,
PEKIN, CHINA.

February IOth. 1903.

Your Imperial Highness:-

I have the honor to acknowledge the receipt of Your Imperial Highness' note of yesterday's date, requesting me to inform the Commander of our Legation Guard that the Emperor will go to the Hall of Fasting on the IIth. inst. and will offer sacrifice at the Altar of Prayer for Harvest on the I2th. inst. and requesting also that he will order his soldiers on the two days named to refrain from visiting the drill ground west of the Temple of Agriculture.

In reply I have the honor to say that I have forwarded your request to the Commander of the United States Legation Guard as desired.

I avail myself of the opportunity to renew to Your Imperial Highness the assurance of my highest consideration.

E. H. Conger

Envoy Extraordinary and
Minister Plenipotentiary of
the United States.

To His Imperial Highness, Prince of Ch'ing,
President of the Board of Foreign Affairs.

二一

逕啟者，茲有本館衛隊統帶擬派兵九十名赴長城一帶練習行操，約於西四月初二、三日隨帶行裝帳房開隊前往，首日至沙河歇宿，次日至南口，三日至長城，四日回轉南口，五日至明陵，六日至湯山，七日旋京，其意無他，不過為整齊步伐，切望經過沿路地方無所阻滯，用特函請貴親王查照，希即行飭經過沿路地方官知照，囑即轉諭百姓毋得驚疑可也。此布，即頌

爵祺。附送洋文

名另具 三月初二日

二二

外務部 刂

三月初四日收

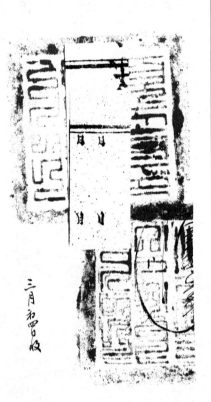

順天府為咨覆事光緒二十九年三月初三日准
貴部文開准美康使函稱茲有本館衛隊統帶擬派兵九十名
赴長城一帶練習行操約於西四月初二三日隨帶行裝帳房開隊
前往首日至沙河歇宿次日至南口三日至長城四日回轉南口五日至
明陵六日至湯山七日旋京其意無他不過為整齊步伐切望經
過沿路地方無所阻滯用特函請查照即行飭經過沿路地方
官知照轉諭百姓毋得驚疑等因前來本部查美國使館衛
隊於西歷四月初二三日即中歷三月初五六日起程前赴長城一帶

練習行操往返約計七日除函知姜提督選派妥弁屆時偕同
前往外相應劄行順天府府尹迅即徧行出示曉諭並轉飭地方
官妥為彈壓照料俾沿路居民如常安堵勿任宵小造言生事
致涉驚疑是為切要仍將辦理情形即日聲復本部以便轉
覆該使等因到府准除請由貴部函致姜提督選派妥弁護送美
弁前往沿途照料本衙門不復派弁護送外所有經過地方本衙門當即出
示徧行曉諭並飛飭大宛兩縣北路同知昌平州親自彈壓照料
勿任宵小生事俾附近居民安堵無恐相應咨覆

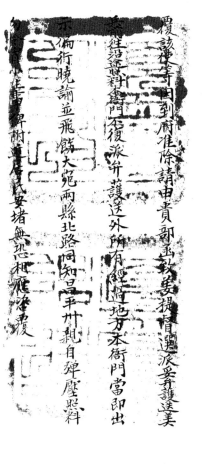

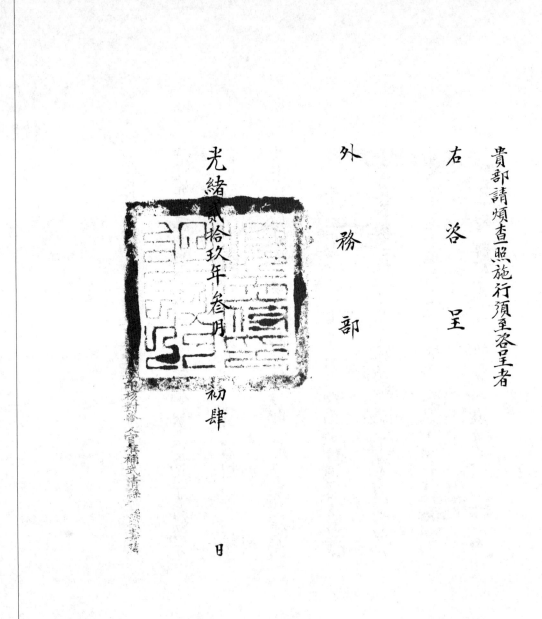

貴部請煩查照施行須至咨呈者

右咨呈

外務部

光緒貳拾玖年叁月初肆日

印務對發 官生補武清縣 書

F.O. No. 1176,

LEGATION OF THE UNITED STATES OF AMERICA,
PEKIN, CHINA.

April Ist. I903.

Your Imperial Highness:-

I have the honor to acknowledge the receipt of Your Highness' note of yesterday's date, informing me that the Emperor would visit the Temple of Agriculture on the 5th. inst. and requesting me to notify the Commander of the U.S.Legation Guard so that he might issue orders to his men to refrain from visiting the drill ground at the rear of the Temple upon that day.

I have the honor to reply to Your Imperial Highness that I have notified the Commander of the U.S.Legation Guard as requested.

I avail myself of the opportunity to renew to Your Imperial Highness the assurance of my highest consideration.

E. H. Conger

Envoy Extraordinary and
Minister Plenipotentiary of
the United States.

To His Imperial Highness, Prince of Ch'ing,
President of the Board of Foreign Affairs.

附件

外務部收

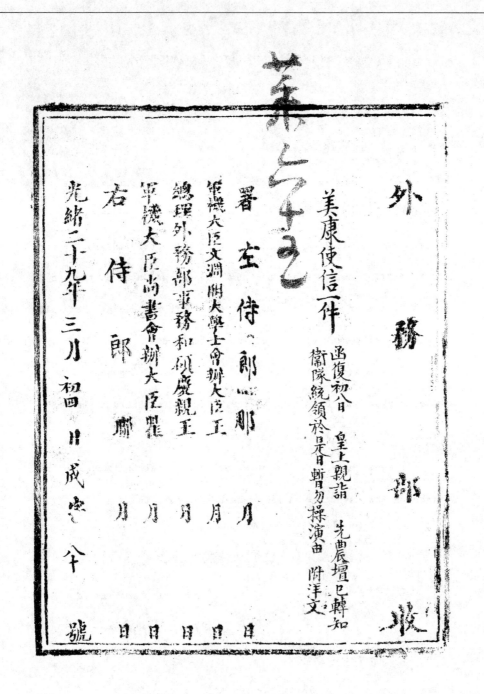

美康使信一件 函復初八日皇上親詣先農壇已轉知衛隊統領於是日暫勿操演由 附洋文

署左侍郎 那 月 日

軍機大臣文淵閣大學士會辦大臣王 月 日

總理外務部事務和碩慶親王 月 日

軍機大臣尚書會辦大臣瞿 月 日

右侍郎 聯 月 日

光緒二十九年三月初四日戌字八十號

二四

片

步軍統領衙門為片覆事准外務部咨稱光緒二十九年三月初二日准美康使函稱兹有本館衛隊統帶擬派兵九十名赴長城一帶練習行操約於西四月初二三日隨帶行裝帳房開隊前往首日至沙河歇宿次日至南口三日至長城四日回轉南口五日至明陵六日至湯山七日旋京其意無他不過為整齊步伐切望經過沿路地方無所阻滯用特函請查照即行飭經過沿路地方官知照轉諭百姓毋得驚疑等因前來本部查美國使館衛隊於西歷四月初二三日即中歷三月初五六日起程前赴長城一帶練習行操往返約計七日除函知姜提督選派妥弁屆時偕同前往外相應咨行貴衙門迅即編行出示曉諭並由順天府府尹轉飭地方官妥為彈壓照料俾沿途居民如常安堵毋任宵小造言生事致涉驚疑是為至要仍將辦理情形即日聲覆本部以便轉復該使等因前來除飭該管營汛徧行出示曉諭派撥官兵妥為彈壓照料外相應片覆

貴部查照辦理可也須至片者

右片行

外務部

光緒貳拾　年　月初伍日

二五

逕啟者，兹據美國管帶衛隊守備韋伯爾函稱，前數日該衛隊兵丁赴長城及明陵一帶演習行操，經過各地方均有官員接待照料，其尤為格外照料者則係昌平州牧，懇為轉請代謝照料之文武各官，並深謝昌平州牧等因，相應函達

貴親王查照，希即將韋伯爾申謝之意代為轉知是荷。特此奉布，即頌

爵祺。附送洋文

名另具 三月十四日

二六

逕啟者：茲接本國外部所發通行知照之函，内將海部大臣所送總理海軍事務局官員所具之禀，囑將該禀内之意轉達

貴親王，茲將該禀之意列下：本局擬如有外國兵船或他式國家官船欲進美國海口與所轄之口，有六處須先由該國駐華盛頓欽使請美外部轉請海部大臣允准，方可進口。該

六海口係弗羅利達之他爾圖嘎斯口庫力伯拉之葛雷德哈
爾伯口意係大海口古巴之閔他那磨口哈歪伊即檀香山之佩而洛口即珍珠意
瓜嗎島口非獵濱之素壁隔海灣口除此各口外本局擬准各
國兵船及各官船隨便進出美國海口與所轄之口不必先請
允准並不問船數若干與任該口若干日不過於欲入美國
造船廠與有船塢之口仍須先行請允方可前往等因相應按

照本國外部所囑照譯函送
貴親王查照可也此布即頌
爵祺附送洋文
名另具三月二十日

康格

附件

F.O. No.650.

W. LEGATION OF THE UNITED STATES OF AMERICA,
PEKIN, CHINA.

May 5th. 1904.

Your Imperial Highness:-

I have the honor to inform Your Imperial Highness that I am in receipt of a circular from the Department of State at Washington directing me to communicate to Your Highness' Government the following Report of the General Board of the Navy which had been received from the Secretary of the Navy:-

"The General Board is of opinion that with the exception of the ports named below, no restriction should be placed on the visits of foreign men-of-war or other public vessels, either as to number or period of stay, in ports within the United States or under their control; neither should it be required that previous permission must be obtained.

"The General Board is further of the opinion that before visiting any of the following-named ports all foreign men-of-war or public vessels should be required to ask permission from the Secretary of the Navy, through their respective ministers and the State Department:-

"Tortugas, Florida,
"Great Harbor, Culebra,
"Guantanamo, Cuba,
"Pearl Harbor, Hawaii,
"Guam,
"Subig Bay, Philippine Islands.

"It is of course understood that any foreign vessel, before entering the actual limits of a navy-yard in any port of the United States, would first apply for permission."

I have the honor, therefore to communicate the above report as instructed, and avail myself of the opportunity to renew to Your Imperial Highness the assurance of my highest consideration.

E. H. Conger

U.S.Minister.

To His Imperial Highness, Prince of Ch'ing,
President of the Board of Foreign Affairs.

二七

照會美康使英國高陞船案現已了結美政府前代請公斷之人甚為感謝由

行　　行

軍機大臣文淵閣大學士會辦大臣王　行　四月十六日

軍機大臣外務部尚書會辦大臣瞿　行　四月十六日

照會美康使英國高陞船案現已了結美政府前代公斷之人甚為感謝由

行　　行

署左侍郎那　四月　日

署左侍郎右侍郎聯　行　四月十六日

照會美康使英國高陞船案現已了結美政府前代請公斷之人甚為感謝由

行

署右侍郎顧　行　四月十八日

榷算司

呈為照會事案查英國高陞輪船索賠一事前曾商允

貴國政府訂請

貴國駐英大臣滌德柬公剖斷備承關照維持至為紉佩嗣經英國薩大臣商請以英金三萬三千四百餘鎊作為結案本部以所開數目較之原索之數減去一半即允通融了結當飭上海道如數撥結茲於本年四月十六日准英國壽署大臣照稱接奉本國外部來文款已照收即希查照銷案等因前來查此案久承

貴國政府關懷現經已和平商結相應照會

貴大臣查照即將本爵大臣等感謝之意代達

貴國政府暨

滌大臣為荷須至照會者

美康使

光緒二十九年四月　日

二八

逕啟者，早數日有美國小兵輪名非勒拉博，前往鄱陽湖，意要欲保護居住該處一帶之美民財產性命。九江道因而函致駐漢口美國總領事官云：美國兵輪不應前往該處一帶地方等因。查他國兵船常至該處與别處地方，其欲保護其國人民之意，見與美兵船無異。是以請貴親王查照轉囑各處地方官不必於美兵船如此辯駁攔阻，須與他國兵船一律相待。如此辦理，可免有何處滋生事端，俾兩國交涉更得愈睦也。特布，即頌爵祺。附送洋文

名另具 六月十二日

附件

F.O.No.527.

LEGATION OF THE UNITED STATES OF AMERICA,
PEKIN, CHINA.

August 4th, 1903.

Your Highness:

I have the honor to bring to the attention of Your Imperial Highness, that in consequence of a visit of the United States Gunboat "Villalabos" recently made to the Poyang Lake district, with a view to looking after and providing for the protection of the lives and property of American citizens living in that vicinity, the Taotai of Kiukiang has written a letter to the Consul General at Hankow, protesting against such visits on the part of United States Men-of-War.

In view of the fact that gunboats of other foreign Powers have been visiting this and other localities for a like purpose, I respectfully request Your Imperial Highness to give such orders to the local Officials as will prevent further protests of this nature, and insure the war vessels of the United States the same treatment as has been accorded to those of other Powers; thus local troubles may be avoided, and cordial and harmonious relations strengthened.

I seize the occasion to reiterate to Your Imperial

Highness

Highness the assurance of my highest consideration.

E. H. Conger

Envoy Extraordinary and

Minister Plenipotentiary of

The United States of America.

To His Imperial Highness, Prince of Ch'ing,

President of the Board of Foreign Affairs.

二九

具奏請賞美國武員寶星由

左侍郎聯

右侍郎顧

奏 七月十二日

奏 七月十二日

奏

謹

奏為請

旨賞給美國武員寶星恭摺仰祈

聖鑒事竊查光緒二十七年十二月初一日欽奉

懿旨上年拳匪之亂禁城以内經美國兵官嚴飭弁兵

竭力保護洵屬睦誼可風深宫實為感悦著伍廷芳

轉達美廷傳旨申謝等因欽此經臣部恭錄電知前
出使美國大臣伍廷芳欽遵轉達在案彼時因美
國國例美員非經國會議准不得領受他國寶星是
以未經奏請
恩施嗣准美國使臣康格面稱該國武員知日本守護
禁城員弁已蒙
恩賞寶星該武員等亦已得邀
賞賚為榮請臣等將此意函致該使以便據函轉請該國政
府允行臣等即經備函達知去後茲准該使臣來函
經本國外部將在事各員銜名開送前來臣等查該
武員等當聯軍入城之時守衛
禁城極為嚴謹日本守護各員既蒙

頒賞寶星美員事同一律自應奏請一體
賞給寶星以廣
皇仁謹將該將弁等六員分别酌擬等第繕具清單恭呈
御覽伏候
命下即由臣部照章製造送由該國使臣轉給祇領所有請
賞美國武員寶星緣由理合恭摺具陳伏乞
皇太后
皇上聖鑒謹
奏
光緒二十九年七月二十八日奉
硃批依議欽此

御覽

謹將美國武員銜名並酌擬寶星等第繕單恭呈

美國都司約翰西格卧而特
美國第一守備柯理非屯克尼
美國第一守備邊阿閔哈爾次合爾尼
美國第二守備保羅古得瑞奇
美國第二守備阿連司米特
美國第二守備桑伯爾題克拉爾克

以上六員均擬請

賞給

三等第三寶星

三〇

逕啓者西本月二十四日接收

貴親王來函論及東三省情形云中俄兩國全權大臣定立交收東三省條約載明將東三省俄國所駐各軍分三期撤退第一期應撤兵隊業已如期撤退第二第三兩期迄未照撤又云此係有碍各國公論並係與美國利益相關在中美條約第一款首載若他國有何不公輕藐之事一經照知必須相助從中善爲調處故

貴王爺專函請本大臣轉達本國政府善爲調辦切商俄國照約撤兵以昭公誼並將俄國索辦與

貴部照復各節抄送查閱等因本大臣接到此函赶即照電

本國外部俟接有外部大臣回電再行函復

貴親王查照可也特復即頌

爵祺 附送洋文

名另具 九月初九日

附件

F.O. No.

Legation of the United States of America,
Pekin, China.

October 28th. 1903.

Your Imperial Highness:-

I have the honor to acknowledge the receipt of Your Imperial Highness' note of the 24th. inst. reviewing the situation in Manchuria, stating that plenipotentiaries of China and Russia had agreed upon a Convention arranging the terms upon which Russia was to restore to China the Manchurian provinces and withdraw her troops therefrom, but that, although the troops to have been withdrawn at the close of the first period mentioned in the Convention had been so withdrawn, those which ought to have been withdrawn at the close of the second and third periods had not yet been taken away; that such delay was injurious to the interests of all the Treaty Powers and especially to those of the United States; that it is provided in the Treaty between the United States and China that," Should any other nation act unjustly or oppressively, information being given of the same, there shall be mutual assistance by the use of good offices to effect a settlement of the difficulty"; that you therefore urgently request me to inform my Government of the situation and ask it to use its good offices with Russia, urging her to withdraw her troops in compliance with treaty stipulations, so as to preserve the entente cordiale. Your Highness

also

(F.O. No.)

also sent copies of the Russian demands and the replies made by the Board of Foreign Affairs.

I have the honor to inform Your Imperial Highness in reply that immediately upon the receipt of your note I telegraphed its contents to the Secretary of State. As soon as I receive a reply I shall inform Your Imperial Highness of its purport.

I avail myself of the opportunity to renew to Your Imperial Highness the assurance of my highest consideration.

Envoy Extraordinary and

Minister Plenipotentiary of

the United States.

To His Imperial Highness, Prince of Ch'ing,

President of the Board of Foreign Affairs.

三一

逕啟者日前將
貴親王請本國調處中俄事之函已轉電本國外部茲接回
電云已將西本月二十五號貴大臣所發電函呈
大伯理璽天德閱視在
大伯理璽天德心中實想中政府若覩本國於此三年中所行
辦法以援救中國脫於艱難自必確信不疑本國主係仍接友
誼襄助中國本國復時常用盡心力為使中國得以保全不失
地段並助中國政府整頓庶務使黎民得以乂安更使各國人
自由來往中華有平等通商權利此數事均經各大國照允
惟於現在情形想不出有何調處善法俾中國得依倚以成
功本國
總統現未十分明晰俄向中國所索者何事亦未悉中政府已允
讓俄國利益若干是以難於設定何法俾各所盼望者能以成
就外部海大臣發字云云茲將此回電照譯轉達
貴親王查照可也特此即頌
爵祺附送洋文

名另具九月十一日

附件

F.O. No.

Legation of the United States of America,
Pekin, China.

October 30th. 1903.

Your Imperial Highness:-

I have the honor to inform Your Imperial Highness that I have just received the following reply to my telegram of the 25th. inst. conveying Your Highness' request that my Government would use its good offices to adjust the present difficulties between China and Russia:-

"Washington, Oct. 28th. 1903.

I have submitted to the President your telegram of the 25th inst. He is sure that, in view of the efforts constantly exerted by this Government during the last three years to assist the Chinese Government in its present difficulties and trials, there can be no doubt of his sincere disposition to afford every possible friendly service to that Government. We have steadily kept in sight and used all our influence in maintaining the territorial integrity of China, the restoration of peaceful and orderly government and the freedom of impartial access to the commerce of all countries, objects to which all the principal nations of the earth are solemnly pledged, but in the present emergency, the President is at a loss to see in what way his good offices could practically be made available. He is not sufficiently aware of the nature of the claims of Russia against China nor of the concessions already made by the Chinese Imperial Government to be able to decide what steps on his part would contribute to the end so much to be desired.

(Signed) Hay.

In forwarding to Your Imperial Highness this telegraphic

reply

(F.O. No.)

reply of my Government, I avail myself of the opportunity to renew to Your Imperial Highness the assurance of my highest consideration.

Envoy Extraordinary and

Minister Plenipotentiary of

the United States.

To His Imperial Highness, Prince of Ch'ing,

President of the Board of Foreign Affairs.

三二

逕復者、昨接
貴親王函告以俄將多日所撤退奉天省城之兵、復又折回佔據衙署、把守城門、禁阻來往密電、請再電本國政府設法善為調處、俾中俄事和平了結等因。本大臣茲已將俄所撤退奉天之兵復又折回、電達本國政府。前兩日
聯大人來館面告以該處情形、曾與
聯大人當時商議妥定、本大臣應將該省現時情形、電知本國
外部、
貴親王亦須電囑出使本國
梁大臣往見本國外部大臣、請其轉請本國
總統將此事善為調停、此係向來常辦之法、並係於
貴親王所言辦法更能有濟也。特此泐復、即頌
爵祺。附送洋文

名另具 九月十四日

附件

F.O. No.

Legation of the United States of America,
Pekin, China.

Nov. 2d. 1903.

Your Imperial Highness:-

I have the honor to acknowledge the receipt of Your Imperial Highness' note of yesterday, informing me that the Russian troops which were withdrawn some time ago from Moukden had been taken back to that city, that they were in possession of the public offices and in charge of the city gates, and that Russian officials were preventing the passage to and fro of cipher telegrams and Your Imperial Highness asks me to telegraph again to my Government and request its good offices to secure a peaceable settlement of the difficulties between China and Russia.

I have the honor to inform Your Highness in reply that I have already telegraphed to my Government the facts concerning the re-occupation of Moukden by Russia. When His Excellency Mr.Lien-fang called two days ago to acquaint me with the situation I arranged with him that I should telegraph the facts to my Government but that you should telegraph to your Minister at Washington, Sir Liang Cheng, and direct him to make the request that the President should use his good offices in the matter. This is the usual course and will be more effective than that suggested by Your Imperial Highness.

I avail myself of the opportunity to renew to Your Imperial Highness the assurance of my highest consideration.

Envoy

(F.O. No.)

Envoy Extraordinary and

Minister Plenipotentiary of

the United States.

To His Imperial Highness, Prince of Ch'ing,

President of the Board of Foreign Affairs.

三三

榷算司

呈為咨行事光緒三十年三月二十一日准美康使函稱接本國外部所發通行知照之函内將海部大臣所送總理海軍事務局官員禀擬如有外國兵船或他式國家官船欲進美國海口與所轄之口有六處須先由該國駐華盛頓欽使請美外部轉請海部大臣允准方可進口該六海口係弗羅利達之他爾圖嘎斯口庫力伯拉之葛雷德哈爾伯口（意係大海口）古巴之闊他那磨口哈歪伊（即檀香山）之佩而洛口（即珍珠意）瓜嗎島口非獵濱之素壁隔海灣口除此各口外本局擬准各國兵船及各官船隨便進出美

國海口與所轄之口不必先請允准並不問船數若干與住該口若干日不過於欲入美國造船廠與有船塢之口仍須先行請允方可前往等語譯送查照前來相應咨行

貴部大臣查照轉飭各海關暨各海軍知悉可也須至

咨者

商部

南北洋大臣

梁大臣

光緒三十年三月　日

三四

逕復者。西本月二十日接准

貴親王函，以江西撫轉據九江道電稱，有美國兵艦名

威力路博，入内地游歷，難免百姓驚疑，恐滋事端，請轉

達飭知。在九江兵艦嗣後勿再入内地游歷。本部查

内地非通商口岸之處，各國兵艦駛入深恐驚擾居民，

請即行電飭九江兵艦，嗣後勿再駛入内地等因。查美

國兵船從未無故駛入内地、
貴親王諒亦深悉、向日駛入内地或係欲保護美國人民、
抑或欲查考住該處美國人情形、亦係按和約准行之
事、一千八百五十八年中英約第五十二款、與一千八百
六十九年、與斯馬加所立約第三十四款、均載有兵船若非
另懷别意或因捕盜可隨便駛入中國無論何口、又一切

買取食物甜水、修理船隻地方官妥爲照料、船上水師
各官與中國官員平行相待等語、況迭次各國兵船駛入
内地、有係
貴國允准駛入、亦有係任意駛入者、本國海部常囑水師
官員、必須小心按理而行、本大臣甚可相信、地方官如能
向百姓解説明白美國兵船、係按交誼而來、並無他意、該

百姓等自必不致驚疑、且使兩國更加敦睦也。此復，即頌

爵祺。附送洋文。

名另具。四月初十日

康格

附件

F.C. No.660.

W.

LEGATION OF THE UNITED STATES OF AMERICA,
PEKIN, CHINA.

May 23d. 1904.

Your Imperial Highness:-

I have the honor to acknowledge the receipt of Your Imperial Highness note of the 20th. inst. communicating to me the contents of a telegram received by the Board of Foreign Affairs from the Customs Tao-t'ai at Kiukiang, as follows:-

> "An American gun-boat by the name of 'Villalobos' has been cruising in the interior districts, and it is difficult to prevent the people from becoming frightened and suspicious. It is to be feared that they may create disturbances. Please inform the U.S.Minister and ask him to send telegraphic instructions to the officers of the said gun-boat at Kiukiang telling them not to cruise among the ports of the interior hereafter."

Concerning this telegram Your Imperial Highness states that when foreign war vessels enter inland ports which are not open to international trade there is very great cause for fear lest the people become frightened and disturbed, and Your Highness requests me to telegraph the officers of the said gun-boat at Kiukiang, instructing them not to cruise in the inland districts hereafter.

Your Imperial Highness is aware that it is not the custom of war vessels of the United States to visit the interior of China without good reason. They generally go either for the purpose of giving protection to citizens of the United States or to gain informa-

tion

(F.O. No.   )

tion concerning them. For this they have ample warrant of Treaty provision. Article LII of the Treaty of 1858 between Great Britain and China, which is reproduced in Article XXXIV of the Treaty with Austria-Hungary of 1869, says:-

"British ships of war coming for no hostile purpose, or being engaged in the pursuit of pirates, shall be at liberty to visit all ports within the dominions of the Emperor of China, and shall receive every facility for the purchase of provisions, procuring water, and, if occasion require, for the making of repairs. The Commanders of such ships shall hold intercourse with the Chinese authorities on terms of equality and courtesy."

This privilege moreover is one that has often been granted the war vessels of other Powers or exercised by them. Our naval officers are instructed to use great care and discriminating judgment in this matte and I am therefore inclined to believe that if the friendly presence of such vessels be duly explained to the people by the local officials, nothing but good can result from their visits to the interior ports.

I avail myself of the opportunity to renew to Your Imperial Highness the assurance of my highest consideration.

U.S.Minister.

To His Imperial Highness, Prince of Ch'ing,

President of the Board of Foreign Affairs.

三五

逕啟者本年三月二十日曾將本國總理海軍事務局所擬定美國六處海口、如有外國兵船及他式國家官船、欲進該六口者、須先由該國駐華盛頓欽使請美外部轉請海部大臣允准、方可駛入業經照譯各口名函達在案、兹復准知照之函、續將在阿曾申内基斯喀島所有之各海口與泊船之處添入於須先請允海部大臣、方可進口之内、等因相應函達

貴親王查照轉行知照可也此泐即頌
爵祺附送洋文
名另具四月三十日

康格

附件

F.O. No. 669.

LEGATION OF THE UNITED STATES OF AMERICA,
PEKIN, CHINA.

June 11th 1904.

Your Imperial Highness,

I have the honor to state that upon the Fifth day of May of the present year, in response to instructions from the Department of State, I transmitted to Your Imperial Highness a list containing the names of six ports, to enter which, foreign men-of-war must first obtain permission.

I have the honor to state that I am now in receipt of further instructions from the Department of State to the effect that the ports and anchorages of the Kiska Islands in the Aleutian Archipelago are added to the above list.

I trust that Your Imperial Highness will take note of the fact and transmit the information to the proper authorities.

I avail myself of the opportunity to renew to Your Imperial Highness the assurance of my highest consideration.

E. H. Conger

Envoy Extraordinary and
Minister Plenipotentiary
of the United States.

To His Imperial Highness, Prince of Ch'ing,
President of the Board of Foreign Affairs.

敬啟者，本月十四日肅布美字第五十九號函，詳言中立事，度邀
堂鑒。十七日奉
鈞電，各節適遇星期，當於十八日譯送美外部，請其轉達海約翰。以
來電於俄人誣指各事，認真駁斥，又將俄犯中立各條，逐一臚列，謂能以義正詞嚴之舉，爲摘奸伐謀之策，極爲欣佩。同日駐京固署使電文亦到，遂呈由總統

核閱轉復俄使照會頗為切實並引俄逃艦入滬一案為中國能守中立之確據又謂宜舉萬國公會判決曲直所有各節經於十九二十二等日馳電奉聞二十三日日使高平小五郎晤海約翰將小村外部電文面交其駁斥俄人各款與我原電大畧相同昨據美外部將往來文電彙刷寄來謹將原件配譯漢文附呈用備

省覽此次俄人藉端誣指確為將來生事地步幸

代回

邸堂列憲鑒核訓示專肅敬請

均安

梁誠頓首

光緒三十年十二月二十八日

美字第六十號

附漢洋文鈔件各一分

附件一

THE TERRITORIAL INTEGRITY OF CHINA.

CIRCULAR TELEGRAM.

To the American Ambassadors to Germany, Austria, Belgium, France, Great Britain, Italy, and Portugal.

DEPARTMENT OF STATE,
Washington, January 13, 1905.

It has come to our knowledge that apprehension exists on the part of some of the powers that in the eventual negotiations for peace between Russia and Japan claim may be made for the concession of Chinese territory to neutral powers. The President would be loath to share this apprehension, believing that the introduction of extraneous interests would seriously embarrass and postpone the settlement of the issues involved in the present contest in the Far East, thus making more remote the attainment of that peace which is so earnestly to be desired. For its part, the United States has repeatedly made its position well known, and has been gratified at the cordial welcome accorded to its efforts to strengthen and perpetuate the broad policy of maintaining the integrity of China and the "open door" in the Orient whereby equality of commercial opportunity and access shall be enjoyed by all nations. Holding these views the United States disclaims any thought of reserved territorial rights or control in the Chinese Empire, and it is deemed fitting to make this purpose frankly known and to remove all apprehension on this score so far as concerns the policy of this nation, which maintains so considerable a share of the Pacific commerce of China and which holds such important possessions in the western Pacific, almost at the gateway of China.

You will bring this matter to the notice of the Government to which you are accredited, and you will invite the expression of its views thereon.

JOHN HAY.

NOTE.—Replies to this circular telegram have, so far, been received from the Governments of Germany, Austria-Hungary, France, Great Britain, and Italy, entirely agreeing with the position taken by the Government of the United States and declaring their constant adhesion to the policy of the integrity of China and the "open door" in the Orient.

JANUARY 23, 1905.

附件二

附件 二月十三

照譯美外部海約翰致美國駐德奥比法英義葡等國公使通電 光緒三十年十二月初八日 一千九百五年正月十三日

近聞各國有以將來俄日議和中立各國或將索中國土地爲慮者大總統以爲和局速成人所共盼若牽及不關涉東方戰國相爭之事徒致兵連禍結不利大局故未嘗深以爲慮惟美國素以保存中國疆土大開東方門户俾

通商利益萬國同沾為公共善策理宜永遠遵辦歷經通告
各國幸得慨然允從美國既向有此定見總無侵中國土地主
權之意自當特此聲明以釋疑慮查中國太平洋之商務美
國現已居多數而迫近中國之南洋要島亦有歸美國管
轄美國之謀不在中國也希告外部請抒所見賜覆

海約翰押

按以上通電業已接到德奥法英義五國政府覆文
均與美國政府意見相同皆允力賛保全中國疆土
以及闢開東方門戸之意並無異辭

附件三

THE OBSERVANCE OF NEUTRALITY BY CHINA.

CORRESPONDENCE BETWEEN THE RUSSIAN AMBASSADOR AND THE SECRETARY OF STATE.

I.

The Russian Ambassador to the Secretary of State.

[Translation.]

At the beginning of the war, being guided by humane considerations, the Imperial Government agreed to the proposition of the Washington Cabinet, having in view the localization of the military operations and the neutralization of the Chinese territory, and it made its decision known to the powers by circular telegram of February 5/18 of last year. As the essential conditions of said neutralization, Russia had laid down a strict observation on the part of China of the duties imposed by neutrality, as well as an honest attitude on the part of Japan with regard to this engagement, which was undertaken in principle.

An experience of eleven months, which have elapsed since the beginning of the war, has demonstrated in an obvious manner that China was neither capable nor desirous of living up to her pledges.

Without mentioning incidents, such as that of the torpedo boat *Ryeshitelni,* it would be easy to cite a whole series of cases where the duties imposed by neutrality have been violated by China to the benefit of Japan. Thus, it has been ascertained many times that bands of hoonhoozes (Hunghutse) operating on neutral territory were commanded by Japanese officers, just as whole detachments of these hoonhoozes have been enrolled in the Japanese army and are in the pay of the Tokyo Government, while Japanese instructors are constantly admitted among the Chinese troops stationed along the northern boundary of the Province of Chili.

It has been established, moreover, that since the beginning of the campaign the Japanese have been using the Miao-Dao Islands as a basis for their naval operations; that they import into Dalny, without hindrance, a great quantity of contraband of war coming from Chefoo and other ports on the Chinese coast; and that the Government shops of Hanian (Hanyang) furnished cast iron to the Japanese army.

To all the representations and protests of the Imperial Government on occasions of this kind the Chinese ministers confined themselves to giving vague promises or to answering evasively.

Reports recently received indicate that the Chinese are no longer content with violations of neutrality of the character aforementioned, and that they are making serious preparations with the apparent intention of taking an active part in the military operations. A feverish excitement, dangerous to all whites alike, reigns among the Chinese people, and is being constantly fomented.

The Imperial Government finds it impossible not to draw the attention of the powers to the facts above mentioned, which demonstrate clearly that their efforts toward assuring the neutrality of China have not been successful, owing to the manner of acting of the Japanese and to their intimidating pressure on the Peking Government.

Russia would, thorefore, in case the present situation should continue, be obliged to consider the said neutrality from the standpoint of her own interests.

WASHINGTON, *January 13, 1905.*

II.

The Secretary of State to the Russian Ambassador.

No. 253.]

DEPARTMENT OF STATE,
Washington, January 17, 1905.

EXCELLENCY: In accordance with your excellency's request, I have communicated to our Minister in China the complaint of the Russian Government in regard to the various incidents which it considers as a violation of neutrality on the part of the Government of China; and have instructed him to make known to the Foreign Office in Peking the earnest hope of the President that China will scrupulously observe her neutral obligations, any departure from which would seriously embarrass not only China, but also the powers interested in limiting the area of hostilities.

I willingly took advantage of this occasion, as I have of similar occasions in the past, to make proof of the frank and loyal friendship which has always existed between our two nations. But I feel that I ought, with the same frankness, to call your excellency's attention to the fact that the Chinese Government declare with great earnestness that they have constantly observed that strict neutrality in the present war which is imposed upon them not only by their solemn engagements, but also by the very necessity of their independent existence; and that the Government of Japan insist that they have kept and intend to keep inviolate the pledges they made at the beginning of the war to respect the neutrality of China within the limits then agreed upon.

The President directs me to express to your excellency his earnest hope and confidence that there may not be, on the part of either belligerent, nor of a neutral power, any breach of the neutrality which the whole civilized world has agreed to respect, the violation of which could only be disastrous to all the powers concerned.

I am, my dear Count Cassini, with assurances of profound regard and esteem,

Faithfully yours, JOHN HAY.

III.

The Russian Ambassador to the Secretary of State.

[Translation.]

IMPERIAL EMBASSY OF RUSSIA,
Washington, January 18, 1905.

DEAR EXCELLENCY: I have had the honor to receive your letter dated January 17, relative to the memorandum of the Imperial Government dealing with acts contrary to the neutrality which the Chinese Government had promised to observe.

You are pleased to tell me in your letter that the Chinese Government has declared that it has constantly performed in the present war the duties imposed upon it, from its standpoint, by strict neutrality, and that it denies the existence of the facts contrary to such neutrality that are laid to its charge. No other answer could assuredly be expected from the Chinese Government, but I shall take the liberty of asking you to notice that this denial of China is met by the Imperial Government with the presentation of a full series of facts, for the most part matters of public knowledge, which the foreign representatives at Peking—those at least who wish to reach a conscientious appreciation of the true condition of things—can not fail to know and to report to their respective Governments.

The present aspect of the situation is as follows: On the one hand, a series of acts, unquestionably contrary to the neutrality of China and incited by Japan; on the other, denials unsupported by any evidence. I beg to take up, among the facts cited in the Russian memorandum, the *Ryeshitelni* incident at Chefoo, which has attracted so much attention that no one can be supposed not to know of it. This incident showed to the world what heed Japan paid to the neutrality of China and the inability or unwillingness of the latter, intimidated by Japan, to enforce the neutrality of which she had assumed the obligations. The United States and Europe saw fit to close their eyes upon that flagrant breach of neutrality of China, as well as upon the deplorable attitude the latter assumed on that occasion. I took the liberty at the time to draw your attention to the probable consequences that would attend, in the future, the leniency evinced in that case toward both China and Japan. Finding encouragement in that attempt, both those powers persevered in that objectionable course which placed upon Russia, scrupulously true to the promises made, the necessity of noticing, at every moment, the encroachments of China, encouraged by Japan, upon the duties of the neutrality which had been imposed upon her in her own interest and in that of the whole world. Russia surely is as much interested as the other powers, and perhaps even more, in the maintenance of the neutrality of China as long as this neutrality is strictly and loyally observed. Engaged as Russia is in a serious war, it is obviously not to her advantage to complicate the situation by creating additional difficulties, but it is impossible, I must say it again, for her to admit for an instant that while she is herself observing her duties of neutrality, China, influenced and intimidated by Japan, may commit acts contrary to her neutral obligations and detrimental to the interests of Russia.

I highly appreciate and shall not fail to transmit to the proper quarter the words which the President has directed you to transmit to me, but I venture to remark that a favorable solution of the question depends at this time much more on China and Japan than on Russia, who, as I have already said, has heretofore scrupulously observed her duties of neutrality towards the Celestial Empire.

Be pleased to accept, dear Excellency, the assurances of my sincere devotion.

CASSINI.

IV.

The Secretary of State to the Russian Ambassador.

No. 254.] DEPARTMENT OF STATE,
Washington, January 23, 1905.

EXCELLENCY: I have given careful attention to your excellency's note of the 18th instant, in rejoinder to the note I addressed to you on the 17th, by which I informed you that I had communicated to the American Minister at Peking the complaint you addressed me on the 13th instant in regard to the course of China as a neutral, and communicated to you the declaration, elicited from the Government of China, that they have constantly observed that strict neutrality in the present war which is imposed upon them alike by their solemn engagements and by the very necessity of the independent existence of China.

Your excellency now states that the declaration of China is met by the facts adduced by the Imperial Russian Government as matters of public knowledge, and you specifically cite the case of the *Ryeshitelni* at Chefoo as an instance of the disregard of Chinese neutrality by Japan and of the inability or unwillingness of China to enforce the neutrality of which she had assumed the obligations.

It does not seem incumbent upon me to take up the question your note appears to present, touching the asserted inaction of the United States and Europe on that occasion or the consequences of what you term the leniency evinced both to China and Japan. So far as the course of the United States is concerned, the correspondence exchanged at the time shows that the seizure of the refugee torpedo boat in the port of a neutral by one of the belligerents found no encouragement whatever; while our attitude when the *Askold* and her companion vessels subsequently took refuge at Shanghai was in full encouragement of the efforts and eventual success of China in enforcing neutrality.

The interests of so many powers being deeply affected by the continuance and observance of the neutrality of China, and their keen solicitude for the maintenance of that neutrality and its observance by both the belligerents having been so conspicuously manifested on many occasions, the Government of the United States does not at this moment feel that it is called upon to express an isolated judgment or to consider the adoption of an individual course of action looking to the conservation of that neutral status which we all desire. It would, on the other hand, seem that this general solicitude of all the interested states would make it expedient and proper that the matters concerning which the Russian Government raises an international issue should be considered in a conference of the powers.

Accept, Excellency, the renewed assurance of my highest consideration.

JOHN HAY.

INSTRUCTIONS TO THE AMERICAN CHARGÉ D'AFFAIRES AT PEKING AND ANSWER OF THE CHINESE GOVERNMENT.

I.

[Telegram.—Paraphrase.]

DEPARTMENT OF STATE,
Washington, January 14, 1905.

Mr. Coolidge is informed that the Russian Government declares that China persistently violates obligations of neutrality. The Russian Government cites alleged enlistment of hoonhoozes (Hunghutses) by Japanese, Japanese instructors preparing Chinese army, use of Miao-Dao Islands by Japan, exportations of contraband from Chefoo into Dalny, the furnishing of cast iron to Japan by Hanian (Hanyang) Government shops; and alleges that China is making serious preparations to take part in military operations. The Department instructs Mr. Coolidge to advise Chinese Foreign Office that this Government earnestly hopes China will scrupulously observe neutral obligations, any departure from which would seriously embarrass not only China, but also the powers interested in limiting the area of hostilities.

II.

Translation of telegram from the Waiwu Pu, Peking.

[Received January 21, 1905, at noon.—Copy handed to the Secretary of State January 23, 1905.]

PEKING, *January 21, 1905.*

CHINESE MINISTER LIANG, *Washington.*

The American Minister officially states that the Russian Government has brought to the attention of the United States Government certain alleged violations of neutrality by China. There are five charges.

The first is that Japan has been permitted to enlist in Manchuria Hunghutse (hoonhoozes) bandits as regular soldiers.

Bands of Hunghutse bandits were first called into service by Mataldof (?) and other Russian officers, and organized into frontier guards. They were employed against the Japanese army. If, as it is alleged, they are in the pay of Japan and under the command of Japanese officers, this only makes one of the belligerents responsible for their employment. Moreover, China has not troops enough in the seat of war to keep her subjects there under perfect control. Whenever it was known that any Hunghutse bandits had crossed over into neutral territory the local authorities repeatedly effected their capture and punishment. The law of nations does not hold a neutral government responsible for the acts of its subjects or citizens or retired officers, who may choose to take sides as individuals in any conflict.

The second charge is that the Imperial Government employs Japanese officers as instructors for its foreign-drilled troops.

There are no Japanese officers employed in any capacity with the foreign-drilled troops in the north. It may be mentioned in this connection that the provincial college at Pauting has a number of Japanese employed as translators. But these secured their positions before the war, and after the war broke out they all gave their word of honor that they would have nothing to do with the conflict. They stand on the same footing with those subjects of Russia who have positions in the various educational institutions and in the maritime customs service. The law of nations does not prohibit the employment by a neutral government of the subjects or citizens of a belligerent power. This is a matter which a belligerent is not justified in making a subject of complaint.

The third charge is that the Imperial Government permits the use by Japan of the Miao-Dao Islands.

All through the year the cruiser *Haiki* has been under orders to cruise in the neighborhood of the Miao-Dao Islands, and the prefect of Tengchow has in addition commissioned the gunboat *Haipau* to patrol the adjacent waters. No attempt whatever on the part of any Japanese or any Japanese war vessel to land is reported. It is needless to say that no permission to use those islands has ever been given.

The fourth charge is that contraband goods have been carried from Chefoo to Talienwan (Dalny).

Strict orders have from the beginning been given prohibiting the shipment of contraband goods to the seat of war. No ship from Chefoo has taken a cargo to Talienwan with the knowledge of the customs authorities, which have absolutely refused to issue clearance papers for such a voyage.

The fifth charge is that the Government iron works at Hanyang (Hanian) have sold pig iron to Japan.

The iron ore from Tayeh is mined and shipped by a private company, which is entirely distinct from the management of the Hanyang iron works. In 1900 and 1903 certain contracts were made between this company and some Japanese firms. Those transactions took place before the war. Viceroy Chang had nothing to do with them; and Sheng Kungpao only acted for and in behalf of the company, which had no official character. The said transactions did not need the approval of the Government. Moreover, pig iron is not a contraband article, according to the law of nations. The subject-matter of those contracts is iron ore before the crude metal is extracted by the smelting process. Under such circumstances, it is doubly inadmissible to treat the article as contraband. It is an article of commerce, and should be properly treated as such.

It is also asserted that China is making extensive preparations with the view of taking an active part in the war. Now, the object of maintaining a military establishment is to secure the peace and tranquillity of the country. It is a part of the internal administration. What country on the surface of the globe is not using its best efforts to increase the efficiency of its military service? Why should suspicion be thrown on a step taken by China in this direction as an indication of a desire on her part to join the conflict?

The Russian circular note you cabled mentions the case of the Russian torpedo boat captured at Chefoo as evidence of a strong prepossession in favor of Japan. The fact is that the act mentioned was entirely unexpected. For this reason, Admiral Shah did not succeed in preventing it. There was no connivance whatever at the capture. The Imperial Government has already instituted an inquiry into the conduct of Admiral Shah and demanded from the Japanese Minister the restitution of the torpedo boat. Although the incident is not yet closed, everything that can be done has been done.

Moreover, Russia has not refrained from committing acts in violation of neutral rights. The following instances may be mentioned:

1. The Russians have on territory west of the Liao River built bridges and quartered troops.

2. The Russians have at Siaokulun and Sinmintun used force to compel the sale to them of cattle and provisions, and secretly carried off supplies for the army.

3. At Peitaiho, Kalgan, and Fengtai, Russians have been arrested for smuggling rifles, guns, and ammunitions concealed in merchandise.

4. The captain of the Russian vessel sent under escort from Chefoo to Shanghai secretly made his escape at Wusung.

These violations of neutral rights have repeatedly put China in a difficult position. China is determined not to swerve a tittle from the faithful maintenance of a strict neutrality. The earnest endeavors of the local authorities to preserve order and the peaceful attitude of the people have long been appreciated by the great powers. When a belligerent seeks a pretext to find fault without any reason, it is incumbent upon China to give an answer and let the truth be known. The Government of the United States, which is thoroughly familiar with the whole situation, can not fail to uphold justice with results not only fortunate for China, but also beneficial to the world. A note to the above effect is being addressed to the American Chargé d'Affaires, Mr. Coolidge. You will communicate the same to the Secretary of State, and report any expression of views he may make thereon.

WAIWU PU.

THE OBSERVANCE OF NEUTRALITY BY CHINA.

PART II.

NOTE VERBALE HANDED TO THE SECRETARY OF STATE BY THE JAPANESE MINISTER, JANUARY 28, 1905.

LEGATION OF JAPAN,
Washington.

Telegram from Baron Komura to Mr. Takahira.

You are hereby instructed to hand to the Government to which you are accredited a verbal note to the following effect:

The attention of the Imperial Government has been drawn to the communication recently addressed by Russia to the powers on the subject of the neutrality of China. The duty of defending China against the accusations of Russia does not devolve upon the Imperial Government, but so far as those accusations call in question the good faith and loyalty of Japan to her engagements, they feel bound to repel them.

(1) Russia indirectly suggests that the capture of *Reshitelinui* (*Ryeshitelni*) involved a violation of Chinese neutrality on the part of Japan. The capture in question was, on the contrary, nothing more than the just and inevitable measures of self-defense made necessary by the prior disregard of China's neutrality by Russia. The facts of the case were fully explained by the Imperial Government at the time, and it is consequently unnecessary to repeat them in the present context.

(2) It is next asserted in the Russian communication that it has been ascertained many times (*a*) that the bands of the Chunchuses (Hunghutses) operating in the neutral territory were commanded by Japanese officers, (*b*) that a whole detachment of those Chunchuses have been enrolled in the Japanese army and are in the pay of the Japanese Government, and (*c*) that Japanese military instructors are constantly admitted among the Chinese soldiers stationed along the northern boundaries of Chili. These allegations, which it is asserted, have been repeatedly ascertained are one and all without any foundation whatever. Consequently, the Imperial Government deny them, absolutely and without qualification, and declare that Russia can not produce any evidence worthy of credence to support their so-called ascertained charges.

(3) It is next stated it has been established that the Japanese have been using Miaotao Islands as a naval base of operations. Nothing of the kind has been established—nothing of the kind can be established—for the sufficient reason that the accusation is destitute of truth. As a matter

to the action of the Japanese and to their intimidating pressure on the Government at Peking.

It is difficult to imagine how it would be possible to frame charges more mischievous or more remote from actual facts than these. That the Chinese are making preparations with the intention of taking part with the Japanese in the hostilities, is entirely destitute of truth. That there is at the present moment in China any antiforeign movement or increase in the antiforeign feeling is equally unfounded. That Japan has attempted to draw China into the conflict, or to cause a recrudescence of antiforeign sentiment in China, is precisely contrary to facts which are, the Imperial Government believe, within the knowledge of all the powers. At the beginning of the war the Imperial Government agreed to the localization of warlike operations, and engaged to respect the neutrality of China outside of the belligerent zone, provided Russia, making similar engagements, should in good faith fulfill conditions of such engagement. The Imperial Government loyally and in good faith kept their engagement and they have no other intention than to continue to do so. They have at all times, since the outbreak of hostilities, watched with utmost vigilance the course of events in China and they have repeatedly, whenever occasion arose, advised the Chinese Government, in as strong a manner as possible, to maintain an attitude of strict neutrality and take all necessary steps to protect the lives and property of foreigners. They will feel bound to pursue the same course in the future, if the situation in China at any time become such as to make similar action necessary or desirable. The conclusion of the Russian communication makes it abundantly clear that the motive of the Russian Government, in formulating the baseless accusations which it contains, was to relieve themselves of an engagement the terms of which, with the progress of the war, no longer inured mainly to their advantage.

At the same time you deliver the foregoing verbal note, you will present a statement to the following effect:

STATEMENT OF SOME OF THE MORE CONSPICUOUS INSTANCES IN WHICH RUSSIA HAS VIOLATED THE NEUTRALITY OF CHINA.

(1) It is a notorious fact that Russia frequently dispatches her troops to Mongolia for the purpose of imposing military requisitions, and that she appropriated to military use horses, provisions, etc., thus collected from that province.

(2) In October last Russia chartered at Tientsin a German merchant steamer, *Fooping*, and loaded her there with arms, ammunition, provisions, etc. The vessel was placed under control and direction of a Russian military officer—Capt. Wasulyurle Wichessekalt—and was to run the blockade at Port Arthur. On her way to Port Arthur, however, she was captured by one of the imperial men-of-war off Pehuangcheng Tao and taken to Sasebo prize court, where the foregoing facts were disclosed upon examination.

(3) In December last Russia attempted to forward from Kalgan to Port Arthur 3,600,000 rounds of small-arm cartridges, concealed in 2,330 sheepskin packages, which were seized by the Chinese authorities at Fengtai. The latter also seized at Kalgan and other places about 4,000 packages of the same description and 3,200 sets of saddles at Hsuanhuafu, all of

of fact, however, those islands were used by Russia as a naval base until the blockade of Liaotung Peninsula was proclaimed, and thereafter until the fall of Port Arthur. They were made use of as a place of call for military junks employed by Russia in smuggling military stores through the blockade into Port Arthur from the Shantung Province. During this latter period Japanese men-of-war, it is true, cruised in the neighborhood of those islands, as it was deemed necessary to keep watch on the movements of these junks in question, but that a naval base in any sense of the word was ever created there by Japan is absolutely denied. It may be added, it was within the territorial waters of this Miaotao group that in March last the Japanese merchant steamer *Hanei-maru*, neither owned nor operated by the Imperial Government, was fired on and sunk by a Russian man-of-war.

(4) It is further charged that the Japanese are importing into Dalny from Chefoo and other Chinese ports, without hindrance, a great quantity of contraband of war. The Imperial Government do not deny that they have obtained from Chefoo and other Chinese ports through private persons supplies for their forces in the field. Neither do they deny that those articles, having in view their destination, were contraband of war; but they do deny that their action constituted a breach of China's neutrality on the part of either Japan or China. Trade in contraband is not interdicted by international law. It is carried on subject to right of hostile capture. The fact that Russia is not now in a position to exercise that right is not sufficient to make the trade illicit, which would be otherwise entirely licit. That Russia did not regard trade with China in contraband as violative of China's neutrality so long as she was in the possession of Port Arthur and was able to benefit by it, is shown by the fact that during the siege she drew a large portion of her military supplies for Port Arthur from China. Some idea of the extent of the traffic may be gathered from the fact that no less than half a dozen steamers and many tens of junks were captured in the attempt to pass the blockade. Besides, we know of several instances in which Russia, unlike the Japanese army, which obtained supplies from private individuals, herself fitted out vessels at several Chinese ports and transported contraband goods in them in flagrant violation of China's neutrality.

(5) The complaint that the Government shops at Hanyang are furnishing cast iron to the Japanese army stands practically on the same footing as the charge just referred to. The facts of the case are as follows:

About four years ago a private firm in Japan entered into contract with the Hanyang foundry for the supply of a certain quantity of pig iron. The Imperial Government was not a party to the contract, neither had they anything to do with the transaction. The due fulfillment of the contract in question furnishes the only foundation for the accusation under this head.

(6) It is finally alleged in the Russian communication that the Chinese, no longer satisfied with a violation of the neutrality in the directions indicated, are making serious preparations with the apparent intention of taking an active part in military operations, and that a feverish excitement, dangerous alike to all Europeans, prevails among the Chinese people and is being constantly fomented. This condition of things, it is asserted, is due

which had been forwarded by Russia. Judging from the manner of packing as well as from the enormous quantity, it is evident that these articles were intended for military purposes to be used at the theater of war.

(4) In June last wireless telegraphic apparatus were installed within the compound of the Russian consulate at Chefoo and at some other places, whereby telegraphic communication was established with the Port Arthur fortress, and in utter defiance of the repeated protests from the Chinese authorities the apparatus were maintained and communication continued.

(5) It is a well-known fact that the *Manjour*, a Russian gunboat which was lying in the port of Shanghai at the outbreak of the hostilities, unwarrantably refused to leave the port for several weeks after the demand for the immediate departure had been made by the Chinese authorities, and it was only after prolonged negotiations that the commander of the vessel finally agreed to disarm her. In consequence of the naval engagement of August 10 last, *Askold* and *Grozovoi* took refuge at Shanghai and their commanders refused, under various pretexts, either to leave the port or disarm the men-of-war, and it was only after several zealous negotiations that they eventually effected disarmament.

(6) When in November last members of the crew of the *Reshitelinui* were on their way from Chefoo to Shanghai to be interned there, the commander of the vessel illicitly left the transport at Woosung, on a pretense of paying a visit to the Russian consulate, and escaped to Europe on board a steamer which sailed on the same day. This act was in total disregard of the internment enforced on him by the Chinese Government, and, as if in approval of his action, he has since been decorated by the Emperor of Russia. Later on the crew of the *Rastorpny* were also to be interned at Shanghai. The commander of the said man-of-war, Powel Mikhailowich Plen, and Sublieutenant Klawdy Balentinowich Seliow, secretly found their way to a merchantman, *Negretia*, and attempted to escape to Vladivostok in the disguise of freight agents. They were captured by the Imperial Japanese navy and confessed the above fact at the Sasebo prize court.

(7) In December last Lieutenant-Commander Mizzenowff (second in command of *Poltava*), and seven others, including a naval officer, reached Chefoo in a small sailing vessel from Port Arthur. Whereupon the Chinese local authorities opened negotiations with the Russian consul at Chefoo, demanding that these Russians be interned in China, but the Russian consul, falsely pretending that they were merchants, allowed them to escape to Tientsin and other localities.

(8) With a view to limit the area of hostile operations in the present war to as small a zone as possible, the Imperial Government have invariably respected China's neutrality in the region west of Liao-ho, but Russia has repeatedly violated it and is now stationing a large force of her army in that region.

In presenting the foregoing statement you will explain that the Imperial Government have adopted this course of procedure because, while they wish to bring actual facts contained in the statement to the full appreciation of the Government to which you are accredited, they are still more anxious to exclude any intention inconsistent with a loyal adhesion to their engagement concerning the neutrality of China.

附件四

附件二月十三日

照譯駐美俄使喀希尼致美外部說帖（西一千九百五年正月十三日 光緒三十年十二月初八日）

溯查俄日宣戰之始

美國政府垂意於戰事布置之地界及中國境土之中立將所定辦法於上年西二月五日（俄歷）六日（西歷）通電各大國知照辦理我帝國政府承其指導和平為念曾於所議表示同情我國以上關中立一節關繫甚大所有中國應守中立之職務及日本重視中立之誠意均經按理嚴密伺察開戰至今十一閱月矣我所經歷已有確據顯見中國既無此能力復無此願念以勉盡其中立之責任凡不虞之事如來施帖尼雷艇（在烟台被日軍拋去）等案即不具論而中國破壞中立職務以便日本之事連類枚舉固甚易易姑舉數端為證如紅鬍子匪隊在中立境地歸日本兵官統帶而紅鬍子之投充日本陸軍受東京政府糧餉者甚多直隸省北界所駐華軍恆有日本教習在內又自開戰之初日本即用廟島為水師經畫之根本地又有大幫禁貨由烟台及中國濱海別口運入大連灣並無攔阻又漢陽官局將鑄鐵供給日軍疊經我帝國政府陳說聲詰而中國各大臣總以虛言允諾或以遁詞見復近又探得中國不特違犯中立

如上開各節而且嚴密預備顯示意指將以實行干預戰事激動之意徧於民間近且益加煽起凡有白種皆將受害我帝國政府按以上各節實情已見各國擔認中國中立之舉絕無成效實緣日本行為之不合及其壓力施於北京政府為已甚也此不得不為各國正告者也倘現在情事仍然不改俄國須將前議中立一節就本國關繫情形另行酌辦矣

照譯美外部復俄使文 西一千九百五年正月十七日 光緒三十年十二月十二日

為照復事本大臣按照

貴大臣來件所請業經將

貴國政府所指視為中國政府違犯中立各事咨行本國

駐華公使請其告向北京外務部畧謂我國

大總統切望中國嚴守中立責任倘有違犯不特中國為難即曾認限戰界之各國亦多不便等語本大臣前因此事屢經證明俄美兩國坦白誠篤之交誼今得此良機復向

貴大臣申明此意實所願也然本大臣尤有不得不以此坦白之意復為

貴大臣明告者中國政府屢經切實聲明彼之嚴守中立不特為勉踐原約之義且為自立圖存之要日本政府亦力任不違開戰所定之約束以尊原認中國中立之位我國

大總統特飭本大臣代將切望和平之意代達

貴大臣凡交戰之國或局外之國不至將全球文化之國所公詞認許之中立規約逕行違犯以致關涉之國同受大害則我

大總統之厚望也

海約翰押

照譯駐美俄使喀希尼致美外部文 西一千九百五年正月十八日 光緒三十年十二月十三日

為照復事准

貴大臣正月十七日來文內開俄國政府以中國政府違約不守中立列款聲告一事據中國政府聲覆此次兩國爭戰向無不循法堅守中立所開各款並無其事等情中國政府如此照復實在意中惟俄國所開各節其事皆人所共知亦各國駐京使臣所必聞若係明達事理之人有聞必報本國政府今兩國政府既各執一詞一面則將中國為日本主使明犯中立各事逐層開列一面則徒託空言不肯承認似此孰是孰非不難決斷試舉俄國節畧所開來施帖尼雷艇在烟台失事一節言之此事遐邇傳聞人所共知足見日本視中國中立之義為何物亦可見中國為日本所迫既不能循法守中立之道亦不肯行中立之道美國與歐洲各國明知日本犯中國中立之義而中國亦難辭其咎詎料均視若罔聞當時本大臣曾告

貴大臣若此事寬視中日兩國定必貽害將來該兩國於此事見無所禁忌從此仍舊橫行令俄國不得不時常防中國為日本所誘不守中立以致自誤而傷大局查中國處中立之地如能堅守不移此俄國之所深願較諸他國愈加關切因俄國現既急於軍務豈欲另多生事致招不便然俄國既自遵中立之道斷不許中國為日本所誘迫背中立之道任意妄為致礙俄國權利也茲

貴大臣奉
大總統諭旨將其意旨轉告本大臣查照感激無既自當
代達本國惟俄國向來於中國中立一事無不小心循法
辦理故善將來之辦法責成中日兩國應過於俄也為此
照復須至照會者

照譯美外部致俄公使喀希尼文 西一千九百五年正月二十三日 光緒三十年十二月十八日

為照會事前准
貴大臣本月十三日照會指中國不守中立數端當即電
飭美國駐華公使轉告中國政府隨接中國政府聲復謂
此次俄日搆兵中國一向按約辦法視自主之宜堅守中
立等情業於本月十七日照會
貴大臣在案茲准
貴大臣本月十八日照覆謂中國一面之辭不足抵敵俄
國政府所指人所共知之實事因特舉來施帖尼雷艇在
烟台失事一端為日本輕視中國中立亦為中國不能或
不肯如約守中立之明證至若
貴大臣提及美國與歐洲各國均於此案視若罔聞甚至
寬待中日兩國致遺後患一節本大臣刻下未便置辯特
就美國而論試查當時來往文牘足見該雷艇在中立口
岸避難為敵國搶去一事美國毫無偏袒隨後亞士哥勒
得兵艦帶同各艦駛入上海躲避賴美國力贊中國堅守
中立故事終得妥協查中國處中立之地關係各國甚重
各宜遵守不移是以每有因此為慮而兩戰國亦曾屢次
遵行因是之故美國政府未便為大局計獨出己見擅行

設法妥籌保全中國中立之方惟俄國特指各端現成公案凡有關涉之國未免仍懷疑慮應將全案原委請各國舉行公會議商為是為此照復須至照會者

照譯美外部致美國駐京署使電 西一千九百五年正月十四日 光緒三十年十二月初九日

因代辦知悉俄國政府謂中國屢次不守中立指明各節內有日本招募紅鬍子為兵日本教習訓練中國兵勇日本借用廟島在烟台運達禁貨物往大連灣漢陽鐵政局辦運生鐵往日本數端並稱中國現下整頓軍務以備助戰等情請勸外務部堅守中立不移是所厚望倘有變動於中國自必大有不便且前認劃限戰界各國亦有所不便也

日本外務省大臣小川男爵致駐美日使高平小五郎電 西一千九百五年正月二十八日即光緒三十年十二月二十二日日使面交美外部

茲特請貴大臣面達所駐在國之外部如下

近日俄國照會各國聲稱中國違犯中立一節實動我帝國政府之注意雖我政府無代中國辯護之義務然所指各節實與我日本對於要約之誠信頗有關係不得不逐條拒駁

一俄國以間接之詞謂來施帖尼雷艇被拘一案為日本犯中國中立之事不知拘艇之舉實以俄國首先蔑視中國中立之故我不過為此公平之舉出此自護必需之計當時我帝國政府已將此案實情全行表明現在可毋庸再為贅述

二俄國照會又稱屢次查得(甲)中立境所集紅鬍匪係歸

日官統帶(乙)該匪成隊投入日軍受日本政府糧餉(丙)日本陸軍教習恆在中國駐防直北軍中等語以上各節疊經查實全無根據是以我帝國政府一概不認並聲明俄國斷不能指出足為證佐之憑據

三又稱查得日本用廟島為海軍調遣之根本地等語向不聞有此說亦斷不能有此說足為指控真實之據惟確查該島一帶經俄國用為海軍根據地直至遼東半島聲告封禁及旅順陷落而後已俄國以該島為由山東載運軍儲闌入旅順運船轉接之所當旅順將陷之時我日本軍艦雖曾遊弋該島一帶防察此等運船之舉動至謂作海軍根本地我日本向無是議不能承認再查上年三月間有並非日本政府所有及行駛之日商輪船名哈尼伊丸者正在廟島海界内被俄國軍艦砲擊沉沒

四又稱日本由烟台及中國別口將多數戰禁貨品運入大連灣並無攔阻等語我國曾因平民得由烟台及中國別口運入用物供我軍在野之需我帝國政府不必諱飾此項物件有意載往該處顯係戰禁貨品亦不必不認若以此事為中國或日本破壞中國中立之舉則大非矣戰禁貨品互為貿易萬國公法固所不禁祇言有捕獲之權而已現在俄國實處不能復行此權之地故以此等貿易為不合法否則必視為合法矣使俄國佔踞旅順一日則與中國以戰禁貨品貿易不視為違犯中國之中立而且因以為利觀旅順被困之時俄人

會有多數軍需由中國運入是其明證統計船隻之圖
入封口而被獲者輪船六七艘民船十餘隻由此推之
則往來之多亦可想矣而俄國又非若日本之僅得供
給於平民也竟在中國口岸數處分派船隻裝運禁貨
顯犯中國之中立而不顧
五所稱中國漢陽官廠以鑄鐵供給日軍一節實與上款
事同一律實情如下約四年前日本商曾與漢陽鐵廠
訂立合同供收豕鐵若干中國政府並非與訂之一面
亦未曾干預其事可爲此款指摘之根據者僅商人實
行合同一事而已也
六俄國照會末稱中國不特僅以違犯中立爲事且極力
預備顯有干預軍事之意中國民情騷動近更加甚將

大不利於歐人皆因日本之非行及其壓力施於北京
政府所致等語似此等莫須有而無情理之誣誠不知
何以復加矣所謂中國戒備戎兵爲有意襄助日本一
節毫無實據所謂中國有仇洋舉動及仇洋之見益加
一節亦屬無根至謂日本欲牽引中國入於戰爭及煽
動中國仇洋之見尤於事實相悖我帝國政府深信爲
各國所共曉矣當戰事之初起也我帝國政府於劃限
戰界一說特表同情並允願尊視中國中立之權惟聲
明須俄能堅守成約方能照辦在案我帝國政府誠實
守約至今未改自開戰以來我於中國之事亦嚴密查
察遇有事端極力勸中國政府嚴守中立設法保護外
人之身命財産將來如仍遇有事故我國自必堅持宗

旨照前力辦試觀俄國照會結語足見其誣揑此等無據之款圖卸尊視中國中立之責實無疑義蓋就軍事上而論中立之守今已無益於彼也

並請貴大臣於面交上項節畧之時將下開節畧一併詳告

該將俄犯中國中立權之尤為顯著者列為節畧

一俄國常派軍隊前往蒙古以便其軍事之展布又常在該省搜購馬匹糧食以供軍用皆衆所共知之實事也

二上年十月（陽歷）俄國在天津包僱德國輪船名富平裝載砲械軍火糧食等物該輪歸俄國武員守備威且士卡路提管理專為闖入旅順禁口之用當駛赴該口時中途在北皇成島海面被我帝國海軍艦捕獲解送佐世保軍俘裁判所查出實情

三上年十二月（陽歷）俄國私將彈子三百六十萬顆分藏在二千三百五十包羊革之內欲由張家口運往旅順經中國官員在豊台地方查獲又有同上物件四千包在張家口等處及馬鞍四千副在宣化府被獲均查係俄國所運觀上文所開夾帶情形及其數目之多則所有各件為運赴戰場軍事需用無疑

四去年六月（陽歷）有無線電機設在烟台俄國領事館界內等處與旅順砲台電報通信雖屢經中國官員抗爭而電機仍復留存依然通電

五俄砲艦暑佐於宣戰時灣泊上海經中國官員逼令立刻駛出竟留數來復之久不肯離境又經會議多時該艦艦長始允拆卸砲械去年八月十日（陽歷）海戰之後俄

國亞士哥勒得及格魯蘇哇二艦逃入上海艦長等多
方推託不肯離境亦不卸械亦屢經爭辯始勉强將砲
械卸去
六去年十一月來施帖尼艦弁兵由烟台解往上海拘管
行抵吳淞該艦長託辭往俄領事館私離運船即日附
輪逃往歐洲此舉直蔑視中國政府拘管之權而俄皇
反獎以寶星不啻許其非行矣其後俄艦拉思託尼弁
兵亦經在上海拘管其艦長蒲連把總謝留潛登商輪
轟格列夏假裝轉運經紀欲逃往海參崴被日本海軍
捕獲送由佐世保軍停裁判所審訊供認
七去年十二月俄戰艦波路他哇副艦長米先努扶及俄
人七名內一人係海軍官由旅順駕小帆船抵烟台中

國地方官員與該口俄領事議將該副艦長等由中國
拘管該領事假稱皆是商人縱令逃往天津等處
八我帝國政府為限定現在戰域至極小界地起見於遼
河以西中國中立之權極為重視而俄國則屢屢侵犯
現竟在彼處屯駐大隊軍兵
今我帝國政府為此處辦固欲將節畧所載實情明告各
國冀邀鑒察尤願表明我國堅守中國中立之約實與
誠信固結之意相悖並希
貴大臣向駐在國聲明可也

收卅 二月十三日

照譯駐美俄使喀希尼致美外部說帖 西一千九百五年正月十三日 光緒三十年十二月初八日

溯查俄日宣戰之始

美國政府垂意於戰事布置之地界及中國境土之中立將所定辦法於上年西二月五六日(俄歷)(西歷)通電各大國知照辦理我帝國政府承其指導和平為念曾於所議表示同情我國以上開中立一節關繫甚大所有中國應守中立之職務及日本重視中立之誠意均經按理嚴密伺察開戰至今十一閱月矣我所經歷已有確據顯見中國既無此能力復無此願念以勉盡其中立之責任凡不虞之事如來施帖尼雷艇(在烟台被日軍拖去)等案即不具論而中國破壞中立職務以便日本之事連類枚舉固甚易易姑舉數端為證如紅鬍子匪隊在中立境地歸日本兵官統帶而紅鬍子之投充日本陸軍受東京政府糧餉者甚多直隸省北界所駐華軍恆有日本教習在內又自開戰之初日本即用廟島為水師經畫之根本地又有大幫禁貨由烟台及中國濱海別口運入大連灣並無攔阻又漢陽官局將鑄鐵供給日軍疊經我帝國政府陳說聲詰而中國各大臣總以虛言允諾或以遁詞見復近又探得中國不特違犯中立

三七

敬啟者，本月十五日肅布美字第二十五號函，度邀
貴鑒。日俄事已决裂，日本海軍得利，聞陸路布置尤頗
周備，俄人雖横暴，未必能制彼島國也。連日各國政
府多已頒布局外中立諭文，我
政府辦法若何，未見明文，西人報章頗多臆度之議。
二十二日誠往謁海外部約翰，談及此事，海以俄人居心
叵測，中俄接壤數千里，若一防護未周，被其闌
入，中國之局外固不能守，東南之民心且恐揺動，內而
京師戒嚴，外而洋兵登岸，種種禍患，不可不預為防
備。誠查所稱各節，於我國情形尚不隔膜，且觀其詞
誼頗有願為我助之意，因説以中立要危，擬仿遜淺
庚子之役，曾承美國照會各邦，不許侵佔我國疆
土。雖俄獨食言，然其在東三省舉動尚不能無所顧
忌。此次美國必將又有妙策，使得彼此相安，有裨大
局。誠遂陳辦法，擬聯請各國同告日俄，認遵中國
局外中立之地位，以及行政現存之權。已分電駐英
德法等使，及時達告該政府，候得復音，誠即電
請日俄照行矣。聞駐美德使已表同情，英政府欲

限明戰事地方，法政府則視俄意為從違。大約日
俄必將決第一次復也。誠查遼瀋地方現有俄兵，斷
非我國勢力所能約束，若不及早聲明，將來必至合
混。且不論何國勝負，我亦須預為籌畫，以為他日收
復之計。今得美廷仗義執言，倘能善為操闔，
可以不煩一兵收回三省，未始非計。至於京師暨
各省平靖，尤可上紓
宵旰之勞，下奠商民之業。我
部堂碩畫經化，及人所不能，措施而要宜之，其亦不可易
常計也。當將美外部所議辦法，於議電肅陳
貴鑒。續有聞再當電達。

三八

庶務司

呈爲照復事本年二月初二日接准

來照並轉送

貴國外部大臣所寄原文均已閱悉

貴國政府向各國聲明不欲侵佔中國地土並

不願爲租借何地之地主惟於東方已開門戶

俾各國同享通商之利等因本爵大臣具紉

公誼惟願各國永遠守此宗旨不侵中國土地

不碍中國主權實於大局有益相應照復

貴署大臣查照即希轉達

貴國外部爲荷須至照復者

美固署使

光緒三十一年二月　日

三九

敬啟者本月初八日肅布美字第七十號函計荷
堂鑒日俄海戰之後美總統有意調和各節經於四月二
十日六十九號函陳報在案上月之杪總統連次接
見日俄兩使又與德使面談數次至本月初六日電
飭駐日駐俄美使轉達兩國政府備言美國願為調
停息戰其議和條款應由俄日自訂美國亦可為之
介紹擇地會議等語電文殷殷以兩國自議不須第
三國干涉為詞蓋恐別有牽制致碍和局尤不願與

聞其事致啟猜嫌此美總統之用心亦慮美人議其
多事也旋接日俄復電均允言和連日日俄兩使頻
往白宮請見動移晷刻所談之事均甚秘密議和地
方仍未擇定俄國欲在巴黎而日本以俄法同盟必
有暗助日本欲在烟臺而俄國以國體所關不肯俯
就兩國有借地華盛頓之意而美總統又慮爲所牽
涉堅請另擇且以天氣炎熱議事不便爲辭俄人又
欲就荷蘭之海牙或瑞士之真奈瓦指定一處刻仍

未決大約事關重大固非朝夕可以成議也以上各節計馨吾星垣兩星使必已次第電聞矣美總統不顧别國干預和議實係德皇所授意德皇以為開集公會調議和款日俄兩國未必受益而東方大局已先受害不如聽由兩國自行商議如其有礙他國再當出而理論較為得計論者謂德於山東正擴利權頗慮公會加以限制殊覺近理美總統則慮列强集議或不能相尚必及瓜分問題於中國

殊有窒碍故亦以德皇所持為有裨大局也總之今日之事東三省歸還為第一要義其如何歸還之法尤為要義中之要義我能索還管轄全權祇由日本管現有之鐵路上也除現有鐵路外酌給商礦等利以酬日本之勞次也若僅得地主之虛名而授人以治理之實事則下矣應請

密電楊使就近要求日本政府務將管轄全權一概歸還毋食宣戰之言毋蹈俄人之覆轍誠一面密託

美總統外部如可為力從中主持以全大局至東三
省歸還之後應如何廣開利益萬國同沾似宜及早
議定頒布各國俾得為我助力東三省全權既已收
還則此外各地更不虞狡焉之逞矣是否有當務乞
代回
邸堂列憲主持採擇施行大局幸甚附呈美總統調和電
文譯稿即希一併
代呈備核不勝叩禱之至正繕函間探聞日俄已定在

華盛頓議和日間即可各派全權約西八九月可以
會議一切和款仍由兩國自議美國亦不允干預除
電達外合併馳陳專肅敬請
均安
梁誠頓首
光緒三十一年五月十三日
美字第七十一號

附譯件

附件

卅十二月卅日

譯件

照譯美總統調和日俄戰事電文

本總統審度時勢以爲日俄兩國宜及時息戰故體好生之德欲爲兩國調停也敝國與貴國友誼久敦實願兩國享和平之實益兩貴國干戈實阻碍萬國文明之進步故力勸大日本大俄國言和非獨爲兩國之利且爲天下萬國之利計也本總統意欲兩貴國自行開議自擇全權大臣不用第三國干涉設善法罷干戈永遠和好望兩貴國立即定意不可再延若兩貴國未便遽行開議本總統亦願爲之介紹爲之發端爲之擇地使彼此得以面訂倘兩貴國不欲別國幫助尤本總統所切禱也本總統實無他意不過欲早罷干戈保全生靈免碍萬國文明之進步云爾

四〇

逕啓者，茲奉本國政府訓條云，美國兵部定準各國軍艦進口於波多里各口海島之散歡與加里福尼亞之門得類地方，礮台為回答他國軍艦敬礮之所，囑達

貴國政府相應函轉知照，並乘機提醒

貴親王前於西八月二十四號所請將中國鳴礮答禮處所開單送館，迄未接有復函，即希轉飭該管之員作速開送，以便

轉報本國是荷特此沥布即頌

爵祺 附送洋文

名另具 八月十九日

柔克義

附件

AMERICAN LEGATION,
PEKING, CHINA.

To F.O. No.
W.

October 6, 1906.

Your Imperial Highness:-

I have the honor to inform Your Imperial Highness that I am in receipt of instructions from my Government to the effect that San Juan, Porto Rico, and the Presidio of Monterey, California, have been designated as saluting stations to return salutes of foreign men-of-war, and directing me to so advise Your Imperial Highness.

In communicating this information to Your Highness, I have the further honor to remind Your Highness that on Aug.24, last I wrote asking for a correct list of the saluting stations in China and of the batteries which will return salutes, but up to the present have received no reply.

I trust that Your Highness will at once direct that the list be sent without delay.

I avail myself of the occasion to renew to Your Imperial Highness the assurance of my highest consideration.

Envoy Extraordinary and
Minister Plenipotentiary
of the United States.

To His Imperial Highness, Prince of Ch'ing,
President of the Board of Foreign Affairs,
etc. etc. etc.

四一

逕啟者茲有本館武隨員都司連那得擬赴山東濟南府
第五鎮常備軍所駐營所地方看視演操並在濟南一帶
查考軍情事務等因相應函達
貴親王查照望即行囑該省管理軍政官員於連都司往
閱時照常接待俾其易於查考一切是荷此泐即頌
爵祺附洋文　名另具八月二十三日

柔克義

附件

AMERICAN LEGATION,
PEKING, CHINA.

To F.O. No.
W.

October 10, 1906.

Your Imperial Highness:-

I have the honor to request that Your Imperial Highness will kindly obtain permission for Captain Leonard, Military Attaché of this Legation, to visit the Fifth Division of the Chinese Army whose headquarters are at Chinan Fu in Shantung, to inspect the troops of said division and to acquaint himself with other matters of military interest in the vicinity of Chinan.

Trusting that Your Imperial Highness will instruct the authorities concerned to extend the usual courtesies and facilities to Captain Leonard, I avail myself of the occasion to renew to Your Highness the assurance of my highest consideration.

Envoy Extraordinary, and
Minister Plenipotentiary
of the United States.

To His Imperial Highness, Prince of Ch'ing,
President of the Board of Foreign Affairs,
etc. etc. etc.

四二

咨練兵處美國武隨員那連得擬赴山東第五鎮看視演操并考查軍情希查核見復由

行 行

左侍郎聯 八月廿六日

右侍郎唐 八月廿日

和會司

呈爲咨行事准美國柔使函稱本館武隨員都司那連得擬赴山東濟南府第五鎮常備軍所駐營所地方看視演操並在濟南一帶查考軍情事務望囑該省管理軍政官員於連都司往閱時照常接待俾其易於查考等因相應咨行

貴處查核見復以便轉復該使可也須至咨者

練兵處

光緒三十二年八月　日

欽命總理練兵處王大臣 爲

咨覆事。案准

貴部咨開：准美柔使函稱，請將中國各海口遇有外洋兵艦進口時應在何處點放敬礮，及中國應於何處礮臺鳴礮答禮開單送館，轉送美國海軍備查，俾可照單施行。因美國海軍所存之單年月甚遠，恐有不符，故請轉囑練兵處開一清單送館，轉達本國政府，定當感謝等因，咨行查明見覆，以便轉覆該使等因。到處，查向來章程，外洋兵艦進口施放敬礮，長江一帶應於江蘇之吳淞、金陵之下關，閩省應於福州及厦門兩口岸，粤省應於虎門口外，若鳴礮答禮

吴淞應於二石塘礮臺下關應於儀鳳門内獅子山礮臺
福州應於長門礮臺厦門應於磐石礮臺虎門應於沙角旗
山礮臺如兵艦由粤省内河駛出者則以口内長洲博兎岡
爲施放敬礮答礮之處相應咨覆
貴部查照轉覆該使可也須至咨者
右　　咨
外務部
光緒　　年九月　　初七　日
應　之件

欽命總理練兵處王大臣　爲

咨復事准

貴部咨開准美國柔使函稱本館武隨員都司那連得擬赴

山東濟南府第五鎮常備軍所駐營所地方看視演操並在

濟南一帶查考軍情事務望囑該省管理軍政官員於連都

司往閱時照常接待俾其易於查考等因咨行查核見復以

便轉復該使等因前來查陸軍第五鎮調赴河南會操計該

鎮軍隊操竣回營須俟十月初旬屆時應即札飭該統制預

備接待相應咨復

貴部查照希即轉復該公使飭於十月初五日以後前往可也須至咨者

右咨

外務部

光緒三十三年九月廿八日

四五

函復美柔使美議院所定禁止逼令充作水手條例均已閱悉由

行 行

左侍郎聯

郵傳部左侍郎兼署外務部右侍郎唐

十月 十月

廿六日 日

行

逕復者：前准

函稱：兹將美國議院會所定條例轉達，特為中國政府明晰此條，係一千九百六年六月二十八號批准條内大意，係無論美國及何國之船在美國境内，禁其設法逼

及誘騙或用言恐嚇致人登船勉作水手

本大臣接本國所囑將此條附送查照等

因前來本爵大臣等均已閱悉相應函復

貴大臣查照可也此佈順頌

日祉

全堂銜

光緒三十二年十月　日

四六

逕啓者：茲接本國外部文，囑將本國海軍衙門來函之意轉達
貴國政府，請將中國水師兵艦各等旗幟繪成圖式，註明顏色
大小尺寸，附送本國海軍衙門，庶可轉知美國亞西亞艦隊
昭（照）會（當）用之旗，先行預備，本大臣甚望
貴親王按照所請
見復爲荷。此頌
爵祺。附送洋文

名另具 十一月十八日

附件

LEGATION OF THE UNITED STATES OF AMERICA,
PEKIN, CHINA.

To F.O. No.200.
W. January 2, 1907.

Your Imperial Highness:-

I have the honor to communicate to Your Imperial Highness a request from the Navy Department of the United States, transmitted to me through the Department of State, that Your Imperial Highness' Government will kindly supply the said Department with plates representing the flags of the Chinese navy, showing the standard dimensions and colors, so that the ships of the Asiatic Fleet of the United States may be supplied with proper flag outfits.

Trusting that Your Imperial Highness may be able to comply with this request, I avail myself of the occasion to renew to Your Imperial Highness the assurance of my highest consideration.

Envoy Extraordinary and
Minister Plenipotentiary
of the United States.

To His Imperial Highness, Prince of Ch'ing,
President of the Board of Foreign Affairs,
etc. etc. etc.

四七

榷算司

呈爲咨行事。先緒三十二年十一月十八日准美國柔使函稱：接本國外部文，囑将本國海軍衙門來函之意轉達貴國政府，請將中國水師兵艦各等旗幟繪成圖式，註明顔色大小尺寸，附送本國海軍衙門，庶可轉知美國亞西亞艦隊照當用之旗先行預備，甚望見復等因前來。除咨南北洋大臣外，相應咨行貴大臣查照，轉飭水師將領，即將兵船各等旗幟繪成圖式，註明顔色大小尺寸，咨送到部，以憑轉送美使可也。須至咨者。

南北洋大臣

光緒三十二年十一月　日

四八

逕啟者西本年正月二號本大臣曾奉外部囑請
貴國將水師兵艦各旗幟繪圖註明尺寸顏色送由本館轉
送本國海軍衙門等因茲復接本國外部文請詢中國若
能將各兵艦旗幟繪有全圖即希
貴親王允照所請見復為荷特布順頌
爵祺 附洋文
名正具 正月二十四日

附件

AMERICAN LEGATION,
PEKING, CHINA.

To F. O. No. 219.
LW.

March 7, 1907.

Your Imperial Highness:-

I have the honor to call the attention of Your Imperial Highness to my request of January 2, 1907, for plates representing the flags of the Chinese Navy, for the use of the Navy Department at Washington.

As I am again in receipt of instructions from the Department of State, directing me to procure such plates if possible, a reply to my previous request will be much appreciated.

I avail myself of the occasion to renew to Your Imperial Highness the assurance of my highest consideration.

Envoy Extraordinary and
Minister Plenipotentiary
of the United States

To His Imperial Highness Prince of Ch'ing,
President of the Board of Foreign Affairs,
etc. etc. etc.

四九

復美柔使函

逕復者：光緒三十三年正月二十八日准

函稱，前奉外部囑請將水師兵艦各旂

幟繪圖註明尺寸顏色，送由本館轉送本

國海軍衙門。茲復接本國外部文，請詢中

國若繪有全圖，即希允照所請見復等因。

查此事前經本部於光緒三十二年十一月

二十一日咨行南北洋大臣轉飭水師將領

將兵船旗幟繪圖送部在案。茲准前因，

除再咨催南北洋大臣從速繪送，一俟

到日即行函送外，相應函復

貴大臣查照為荷。此復，順頌

日祉。

全堂銜

光緒三十三年二月　日

五〇

咨北南大臣兵船旗幟全圖從速送部由

行 行

右侍郎聯

郵傳部左侍郎兼署外務部右侍郎唐

二月 初二日 行

二月 日 畫

榷算司

呈爲咨行事。光緒三十三年正月二十八日准美柔使函稱：前奉外部囑請將水師兵艦各旗幟繪圖註明尺寸顔色送由本館轉送本國海軍衙門。兹復接本國外部文，請詢中國若繪有全圖，即希允照所請見復等

因查此事前經本部於光緒三十二年十一月
二十一日分咨轉飭水師將領將兵船旗幟
繪圖送部在案茲准前因除咨南北洋大臣
外相應咨行
貴大臣查照轉飭水師將領將前項全圖
從速繪送到部以憑轉送美使可也須至咨者
南北洋大臣
光緒三十三年二月　日

五一

欽差大臣太子少保陸軍部尚書都察院都御史辦理北洋通商事務直隸總督部堂袁　為

咨呈事據總理南北洋海軍事務廣東水師薩提督呈稱

竊於光緒三十二年十二月初五日奉宫保咨開十一月

二十三日准

外務部咨開光緒三十二年十一月十八日准美國柔使

函稱接本國外部文囑將本國海軍衙門來函之意轉達

貴國政府請將中國水師兵艦各等旗幟繪成圖式註明

顏色大小尺寸附送本國海軍衙門庶可轉知美國亞西

亞艦隊照當用之旗先行預備甚望見復等因前來除咨

南洋大臣外相應咨行貴大臣查照轉飭水師將領即將
兵船各等旗幟繪成圖式註明顏色大小尺寸咨送到部
以憑轉送美使可也等因准此咨請查照辦理見復以憑
咨送等因奉此查中國海軍旗幟前經英國外部繪畫稿
本附錄說帖問題請爲照答曾奉宫保咨行考核見復當
經提督詳核具復在案嗣因各項旗幟尚多未備復經提
督恭擬
皇上專旗暨京外大員各旗式呈請宫保並
前署南洋大臣周　核定頒行俾資遵守均尚未蒙核示
兹奉前因謹將已經頒行海軍各旗式照繪一份註明顏

色尺寸備文呈請察核等情到本大臣據此相應咨呈

貴部謹請查照施行須至咨呈者

計咨呈 旗圖一紙

右 咨 呈

外 務 部

光緒三十二年三月 日

附件

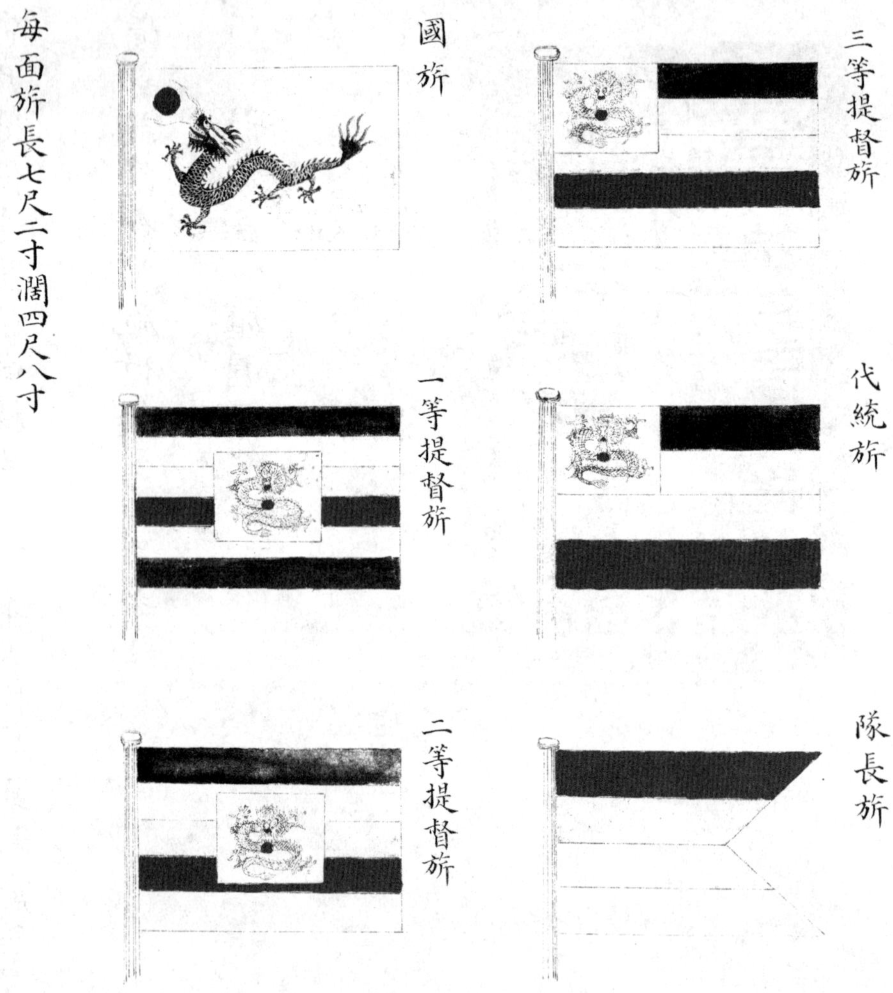

五二

函復美柔使中國海軍旗式准北洋大臣繪送一分請轉送由

行　行

左侍郎聯

郵傳部左侍郎兼署外務部右侍郎唐

三月　日

三月　日

行

初七

復美柔使信

逕復者：上年十二月十八日准

函稱接本國外部文囑將本國海軍衙門之意轉達

請將中國水師兵艦各等旂幟繪成圖式，註明顏

色大小尺寸，附送本國海軍衙門，庶可轉知西亞西亞

艦隊，照常用之旂先行預備，甚望見復等因。當

經本部分咨南北洋大臣去後，兹准北洋大臣將

頒行海軍各旗式照繪一分，註明顏色尺寸，咨

送前來，相應將原送海軍旂圖一分，函送

貴大臣查收轉送

貴國海軍衙門可也。此復，順頌

日祉。附旂圖一張

光緒三十三年三月　日

五三

敬密啟者：上月二十二日肅呈美字第一百三十七號公函，計荷
堂鑒。近來各省會匪煽惑游民，滋擾地面，事發捕急，輒以外洋為逋逃藪，句結餘黨，接濟軍火，時有所聞。誠經密飭各口領事嚴密稽查，隨時具報。美國出口鎗械為數本不甚多，大都運赴日本、東俄等處，皆係洋行交易，未得實在主名，又在別國境内，不便遽加盤詰。初十日奉
鈞部午密電咨，以近來各省匪徒句串洋商私運鎗

械有害治安迭經各關查扣飭向外部據約聲明
轉飭嚴禁洋商私運　誠遵向外部聲告請其按約
辦理外部路提素以東亞和平為宗旨立即允為
轉行嚴禁並有奸徒貪圖小利不顧大局實堪痛
恨之語　誠諷以如能轉商戶部於美國出口處嚴
密稽查更有把握路提亦欣然允諾經於十四日
馳電復陳計達
冰案竊維美國憲法素號自由私家貿易更難干涉
今向外部一言竟爾慨然允禁體念邦交顧全大

局實堪嘉許然歐美鎗廠極多奸人影射最易尤
應於我國各關卡嚴切偵查務使有案必破無私
不獲始足以杜外人之口而塞匪黨之心聞向來
各關監督皆有准運鎗械執照預印空白聽人請
領其鎗械數目往往任意填寫甚至有填鎗一枝
繳銀一兩之事冒濫走私由此而起及至偶爾發
覺僅將鎗件充公而執照之濫給仍復不已實非
慎重認真之道誠聞之稅務中人確非浮游無據
應請

部通咨各督撫嚴飭各關監督稅務司等不論華
常關卡務須將此項准運鎗械准照編列字號填
寫數目面交承運員弁領用仍於進口時按數點
驗不得仍前濫發亦可稍杜私運之路即希
回
邸堂列憲核奪施行專肅敬請
均安

制梁誠頓首

光緒三十三年四月十五日
美字第一百三十八號

五四

逕啓者兹准美國衛隊統領固都司理克函稱有美兵船運來駐京衛隊應用軍火擬在烟台卸岸請本大臣轉請
貴部允其起運前來查該軍火數目約計一百零四箱均係轉運駐京衛隊自用應請
貴親王查照行知該處及沿途該管官員查驗放行

可也特泐即頌

爵祺附送洋文

名另具六月十四日

柔克義

附件

AMERICAN LEGATION,
PEKING, CHINA.

To F.O. No.

H.

July 23, 1907.

Your Imperial Highness:

I have the honor to inform Your Imperial Highness that I am in receipt of a communication from Captain L.M.Gulick, Cammanding the American Legation Guard, requesting that permission be obtained to land some ammunition from the American ships at Chefoo for transportation to his detachment here.

I have the honor, therefore, to request Your Imperial Highness to issue the necessary orders that the ammunition referred to may be landed. There are approximately one hundred and four cases, all of which are to be forwarded to the American Legation Guard here.

I avail myself of the opportunity to renew to Your Imperial Highness the assurance of my highest consideration.

To His Imperial Highness, Prince of Ch'ing,
President of the Board of Foreign Affairs.
etc. etc. etc.

五五

榷算司

呈爲咨行事光緒三十三年六月初七日准駐美梁大臣函
稱禁運軍火一事歐美鎗廠極多奸人影射最易尤應
於我國各關卡嚴切偵查務使無私不獲始足寒匪党
之心聞向來各關監督皆有准運鎗械執照預印空
白聽人請領其槍械數目往往任意填寫甚至有
填鎗一枝繳銀一兩之事冒濫走私由此而起偶爾發
覺僅將鎗件充公而執照之濫給仍復不已此事關
之税務中人確非浮游無據應請通咨各督撫嚴飭
各關監督并税務司等不論洋常關卡務須將此
項准運鎗械准照編列字號填寫實在數目仍於進
口時按數點驗不得仍前濫發亦可稍杜私運之路

等因本部查禁運軍火原經
貴處定有章程兹准前因相應咨行
貴大臣查照核辦并將如何辦理之處聲復本部可
也須至咨者

税務處

光緒三十三年六月　日

五六

庶務司

呈爲照復事光緒三十三年八月二十一日准

照稱本館衛隊統領稱本營有三寸徑口戰

礮兩尊并備配用輪螺等零件由京運至

漢口交美國運煤南山軍艦查收再將該

艦與此二礮同式之礮二尊調換運京請

行該管海關繕發運礮出入口單照務於

西十月一號送來以便派一武員往返押解

等語本部查該武員起程在即海關單照

赶辦不及除已電達南北洋大臣湖廣總督

轉飭該管關道查照放行外相應照復

貴大臣查照飭知可也須至照會者

美柔使

光緒三十三年八月　日

五七

敬肅者頃奉
鈞電美柔使来照美館衛隊有礮二尊由秦王
島運至漢口調換美艦同式之礮二尊仍由
漢口至秦王島運京等因業已遵
示電飭津海關道查驗放行耑肅祇請
鈞安
楊士驤謹肅

五八

敬復者奉到九月初八日

鈞函内開接准來函以此次北洋大臣袁宫保奏奬各

口隨辦中立出力洋員寶星祈將感謝之意代為轉

達惟山海關經辦中立内有四員頗費心力因彼時

該處地方官遷去以致保奬一節闕如可否奏請奬

敘等因前來查山海關經辦中立各員與江海東海

津海三關洋員事同一律即希將該四員銜名國籍
暨應請寶星等第開單見復以便轉達北洋大臣續
請奏奬等因奉此副總稅務司遵將山海關經辦中
立出力之四員開列銜名國籍並擬請寶星等第備
函附請
貴部鑒核希即轉咨

北洋大臣續行辦理可也專此佈復順頌

升祺

附單一件

名另具

光緒叁拾叁年玖月初拾日

裴式楷

附件

行北洋照鈔 附件

隨稅字第貳百伍拾玖號

册仅

署上海郵政司副稅務司克立基 美國人 於光緒三十〔三十一〕年署山海關稅務司 擬請
雙龍三等第一寶星

署總司署漢文稅務司赫美玲 德國人 於光緒三十〔三十一〕年充山海關三等幫辦 擬請
雙龍三等第一寶星

署總司署稽查帳目副稅務司安得士 奧國人 於光緒三十年充山海關三等幫辦 擬請
雙龍三等第一寶星

山海關理船廳總巡施得龍 丹國人 於光緒三十〔三十一〕年充該關總巡 擬請
雙龍三等第三寶星

五九

大亞美理駕合衆國欽命駐紮中華全權事務大臣費　為

照會事、茲有住奉天美商休根於西本年四月二十四號、曾函
達外洋公司、購運手槍十八支、計九種式樣、每種二支、並
連每槍應用什件、及子彈各二百粒、皆係為作式樣之用、彼
時係按中國海關軍械進口章程運來、迨該貨運至大連灣、已屆
西本年九月間、適在中國復定槍彈入口新章之後、是以該處
税務司、將該貨扣留、按新章不允放行辦理、茲該商休根擬具
保結、買主非有確切憑據、彼必不能賣給槍支、故本署大臣請

照會

貴親王查照希轉行該處稅務司速將所扣之槍彈等件

文還可也須至照會者 附洋文

右 照 會

大清欽命全權大臣便宜行事軍機大臣總理外務部事務和碩慶親王

一千九百柒年拾貳月貳拾捌日

光緒叁拾叁年拾壹月貳拾肆日

附件一

AMERICAN LEGATION,
PEKING, CHINA.

To F.O.
No.

December 26, 1907.

Your Imperial Highness:

I have the honor to inform Your Highness that Hugh Gunn, an American Merchant residing at Mukden, purchased on April 24th last and ordered sent to him 18 revolvers, two of each kind, with accessories and two hundred rounds of ammunition for each, which he intended to use solely as samples and which were to be imported in strict accordance with the regulations governing the importation of arms in force on that date. They arrived at Dalny after the new regulations governing the importation of arms of September last circular 1456, had been put into force, and are now held by the Commissioner of Customs at that place who refuses to release them in view of the new regulations.

As the arms were purchased five months before the promulgation of the new regulations for the importation of arms; as they were imported in good faith and in conformity with the rules then in force; and as Mr. Gunn engages not to sell any of them except upon presentation by the purchaser of a properly issued

permit

His Imperial Highness, Prince of Ch'ing,
President of the Board of Foreign Affairs,
Etc., etc., etc.

permit; I have the honor to request that Your Highness will cause the necessary orders to be issued to secure the prompt release of the goods in question by the customs authorities at Dalny.

I avail myself of this opportunity to renew to Your Highness the assurances of my highest consideration.

[signature]

American Chargé d'Affaires

附件二

AMERICAN LEGATION,
PEKING, CHINA.

To F.O., No.

December 26, 1907.

Your Imperial Highness:

I have the honor to acknowledge the receipt of Your Highness' note of November 20th last, in reply to my note of November 6, 1907, with regard to the collection of a contribution or tax on American kerosene oil by the central likin office at Nanking.

In my note of November 6th last, to which I have the honor to refer , I called Your Highness' attention to the case of two native dealers in American Kerosene oil who had been arrested for non-payment of this contribution, and compelled to pay it, as well as to give security that they would pay it in the future.

In reply Your Highness quoted the reply of the Superintendent of Southern Trade to the following effect:

> "The central likin station reports that this contribution was voluntarily levied on themselves by the merchants; that recently one or two dealers, selfishing seeking their own private gain, and having no regard for the public wellfare, had refused to pay their contributions; that after urgent exhortations, however, these men had paid the money as before, and the affair had been closed; that the likin station had arrested no one and taken no compulsory measures; and finall, that this contribution was levied after the cancellation of the duty certificates and the delivery of the goods to the Chinese firms, and therefore was no concern of any foreign merchant.

"Since

To His Imperial Highness, Prince of Ch'ing,

President of the Board of Foreign Affairs,

Etc., etc., etc.

"Since the case had thus been settled, then the collection of the contribution should go on as formerly. And as the money is used for charitable purposes of assisting the Chinese-foreign hospital the American Minister will doubtless be glad to give us his hearty cooperation at all times.
"Please transmit to him this reply".

Your Highness stated in conclusion that it appeared that no arrests had been made and no compulsion brought to bear and that as the case in question had been settled the collection of the contribution will be continued as formerly.

Upon receipt of Your Hgihness' reply, the American Consul at Nanking was again instructed to investigate the case and to make a full report, and his attention was called to the fact that it had been reported to Your Highness that no arrets had been made. I am now in receipt of his reply informing me that two native dealers (Ma Ting Liang and Wang Lien-chên) were on the 22nd of the 8th moon of this year, arrested by the Kiang Ling Magistrate at the request of the likin office and incarcerated in the Magistrate's jail because of their refusal to pay this oil contribution. The former was detained fourteen and the latter nine days and were only released upon signing a written statement that they would in future pay this tax and were compelled to give security to that effect. They were then assessed $283.00 and $168.00 respectively, and informed that if in future they refused to pay this tax they would be severely punished and thei shops closed. Since then they have refused to deal in American kerosene oil

and

and American trade has thus suffered a severe injury.

The Superintendent of Southern Trade in his reply above quoted states that:-

"This contribution was levied after the cancellation of the duty certificate and delivery of the goods to Chinese firms, and therefore was no concern whatever of any foreign merchant".

Against this position the Legation feels bound to enter its protest, and as stated in my note of November 6th last, cannot agree to the imposition of any additional tax or charge whatsoever, in the form of a contribution or otherwise upon American goods which have paid the duties provided for by treaty, irrespective of whether the goods are in Chinese or foreign hands, and whether the duty certificates have been cancelled or not.

It becomes my duty therefore to again request Your Highness to instruct the local authorities to refrain from the collection of this socalled contribution.

I avail myself of this opportunity to renew to Your Highness the assurance of my highest consideration.

American Chargé d'Affaires.

六〇

榷算司

呈爲咨行事本年十一月二十四日接准美費署使

照稱茲有住奉天美商休根於西本年四月二十四號

曾函達外洋公司購運手槍十八支計九種式樣每種

二支並連每槍應用什件及子彈各二百粒皆係爲作

式樣之用彼時係按中國海關軍械進口章程運來

迨該貨運至大連灣已届西本年九月間適在中國復

定槍彈入口新章之後是以該處税務司將該貨扣留

按新章不允放行辦理茲該商休根擬具保結買主

非有確切憑據彼必不能責給槍支故本署大臣請貴

親王查照轉行該處税務司速將所扣之槍彈等件

交還等因相應咨行

貴大臣查照見復以便轉復該使可也須至咨者

税務處

光緒三十三年十一月 日

六一

欽命督理稅務大臣　為

咨呈事光緒三十三年十一月三十日准

咨稱准美貴署使照稱住奉天美商休根曾

函購外洋公司手槍十八枝計九種每種二

枝並子彈各二百粒皆係為作式樣之用迨

該貨運至大連灣適在中國復定槍彈入口

新章之後是以該處稅務司將該貨扣留按

新章辦理茲該商擬具保結買主非有確切

年　月　日

憑據彼必不能賣給槍枝故本署大臣請貴
親王轉行該處稅務司將所扣之槍彈交還
等因洛行查照見復等因前來查美商休根
訂購外洋槍彈運到大連灣被該關稅務司
緝獲擬辦詳由總稅務司申經本處覆准有
案嗣據東三省總督奉天巡撫查明美商訂購槍彈在新章
未頒之前且每種委係一枝願送交奉省軍
械局存儲作樣謂非有意私運等因電請轉

年　月　日

監印委員分省補用知縣白甯良

飭放行前來本處以斯案既經該督撫查明
原委據實電達所請轉飭放行運奉交局作
樣之處尚可通融照准當經電覆東三省總督奉天巡撫並
劄總稅務司轉飭大連關稅務司查照放行
送交該局等因各在案茲准前因相應將本
處與東督奉撫往來電稿並劄行總稅務司
文稿一併抄錄咨送
貴部查核備案並希即照復美使可也須至
到 月 呈
監印委員分省候補知縣勾宥炅

咨呈者附抄件

右咨呈

外務部

光緒三十二年十二月貳拾貳日

預用空白

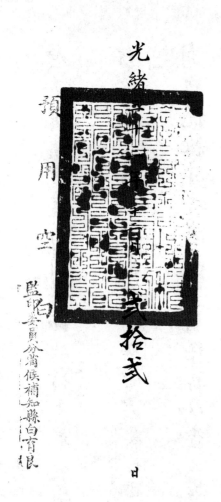

監印委員分省候補知縣白育良

附件

照錄本處與東三省總督奉天巡撫往來電文底稿 美商報運槍枝事

東三省總督奉天巡撫來電 光緒三十三年十一月初五日到

稅務大臣鈞鑒：美商根曉由大連運入手槍十八枝、槍彈三千八百顆，前准大咨轉據大連稅務司詳稱，因與新定槍彈進口章程不符，擬請扣留罰辦在案。茲准美總領事照稱：槍彈進口章程須行係西歷九月，該美商定購槍枝係西歷四月，實非有意違背。且該手槍委係每種兩枝到奉後，感送交軍械局存儲，作為樣式，請飭大連稅關放行等語。查該美商既愿將槍存儲軍械局，似非有意私運，且定購在新章未頒以前，應請轉飭大連稅務司將此項槍彈放行運送來奉，請酌核施行。電覆遵辦。世昌、紹儀。江

寄東三省總督奉天巡撫電文 光緒三十三年十二月十五日發

洪江電悉。美商根曉被大連稅司扣留之手槍子彈，既願送交軍械局存儲作樣，並經貴督撫查明定購日期在新章未頒以前，應即通融准其報運一次，已飭大連稅司放行。送交該局，其起貨辦法仍應照新章第二條辦理。嗣後東省營局如須購用槍枝子彈及外洋官商請運打獵防身或為營中作樣之各項槍彈，務當按照新章辦理，免致槍商藉端影射，實為至要。稅務處。咸

劉總税務司文 光緒三十三年十二月十五日

為札行事光緒三十三年十一月初五日准東三省總督奉天巡撫電開美商根曉由大連運入手槍十八枝槍彈三千八百顆前准大咨轉據大連税務司詳擬扣留罰辦在案茲准美總領事照稱槍彈進口章程須行係西歷九月該美商定購槍枝係西歷四月實非有意違背且該手槍委係每種兩枝到奉後願送交軍械局存儲作為樣式請飭大連税關放行等語查該美商既願將槍存儲軍械局似非有意私運且定購在新章未頒以前應請轉飭大連税務司將此項槍彈放行運送來奉請酌核施行等因本處查美商根曉之手槍槍彈係九月初二日由天草丸船運到大連被該關税務司派員緝獲後復為日本巡捕扣留未允交關該税務司擬俟日本巡捕放行時立行緝獲照案辦理詳由總税務司申經本處覆准有案茲准東三省總督奉天巡撫查明該美商訂購前項槍彈日期係在新章未頒以前現願送交軍械局存儲作樣尚可通融照准即由該關放行送交該局其起貨辦法仍令照新章第二條辦理除電覆東三省總督奉天巡撫查照並飭東省各營局嗣後如須購用槍彈及外洋官商請運打獵防身或為營中作樣之槍彈務當按照新章辦理免致槍商藉端影射外相應札行總税務司查照即飭該税務司遵辦可也須至札者

照復美費署使美商休根購運槍彈被大連關稅司扣留已經稅務處轉飭放行由

行　行

左侍郎聯　十二月

右侍郎汪
署右侍郎梁　十二月

榷算司

呈為照復事前准

來照以美商休根由外洋購運槍彈等件皆係為作式樣之用經大連灣稅司扣留請即交還等因當經本部咨行稅務處查辦去後茲准復稱查美商休根訂購外洋槍彈運到大連灣被該關稅務司緝獲擬辦詳由總稅務司申經本處覆准有案嗣據東三省總督奉天巡撫查明美商訂購槍彈在新章未頒以前且每種委係二枝願送交奉省軍械局存儲作樣謂非

有意私運等因電請轉飭放行本處以斯案既經該督撫查明原委據實電達所請轉飭放行運奉交局作樣之處尚可通融照准業經電復東三省總督奉天巡撫并劄總税務司轉飭大連關税務司查照放行送交該局各在案兹准前因應咨請轉復等因前來相應照復

貴署大臣查照可也須至照復者

美費署使

光緒三十三年十二月

六三

逕啓者，茲接本國外部來文，據兵部咨稱，前擬定美國口岸鳴炮致賀國旗各處炮台名目，印成版函內，列有美國西北方華盛頓省之福來勒耳炮台，茲已擬改在該省之瓦耳頓炮台鳴炮致賀國旗矣，請為轉達各國云云。本署大臣按照外部所囑，函達

貴親王，希即查照轉知是荷。此泐，順頌

爵祺。附送洋文

費勒器啓 三月初一日

附件

AMERICAN LEGATION,
PEKING, CHINA.

To F.O. No. 377.
P.

April 1, 1908.

Your Highness:

I have the honor to inform Your Highness that I am in receipt of instructions from the Department of State saying that the War Department has made an alteration in the list of saluting stations which this Legation had the honor to forward to Your Highness in its despatch of August 3, 1905, said alteration being the substitution of Fort Worden for Fort Flagler as a saluting station in the state of Washington.

In transmitting the above information I avail myself of the opportunity to renew to Your Highness the assurance of my highest consideration.

Charge d'Affaires.

To His Highness
Prince of Ch'ing,
President of the
Board of Foreign Affairs.

六四

和會司

呈為咨行事准美費署使函稱本國外部來文據兵部咨稱前擬定美國口岸鳴炮致賀國旗各處砲台名目印成版函內列有美國西北方華盛頓省之福來勒耳炮台茲已擬改在該省之瓦耳頓炮台鳴炮致賀國旗請為轉達等語函請轉知等因前來相應咨行

貴督撫查照可也須至咨者

南北洋大臣 閩浙兩廣總督

光緒三十四年三月　日

六五

照會

大亞美理駕合衆國欽命駐劄中華便宜行事全權大臣柔　為

照會事西本月三十號係為美國致祭已故海陸軍兵士之期駐京本館衛隊已統領聶特擬率兵五十名赴阜城門外洋塋地葬美國故兵墳所致祭已故之兵並施放排槍三次以致誠意此係按照營規相應照會

貴親王查照轉知該處免致驚疑並望以允照施行見復可也須至照會者　附送洋文

右照會

大清欽命全權大臣便宜行事軍機大臣總理外務部事務和碩慶親王

一千九百捌年伍月貳拾陸日

光緒叁拾肆年肆月貳拾柒日

六六

照復美參使衛兵出阜城門致祭已轉行知照由

行　行

左侍郎聯　四月　日

右侍郎汪　四月　日
署右侍郎梁

和會司

呈爲照復事接准

照稱西本月三十號係爲美國致祭已故海陸軍兵士之期駐京本館衛隊巴統領聶特擬率兵五十名赴阜城門外洋塋地葬美國故兵墳所致祭已故之兵並施放排槍三次以致誠意此係按照營規相應照請轉

知該處免致驚疑並望見復等因前來除由本部行
知步軍統領衙門轉知外相應照復
貴大臣查照可也須至照復者
美柔使
光緒三十四年四月　日

六七

交際鳴礮致賀

和會司李寅齡呈

閱

美國口岸鳴礮致賀國旗礮台遷移案

交際門

交際類

美國口岸鳴砲致賀國旗砲台遷移案

美署使費勒器致外務部函 光緒三十四年三月初一日

接本國外部文據兵部咨稱前擬定美國口岸鳴砲致賀國旗各處砲台名目印成版函內列有美國西北方華盛頓省之福來勒耳砲台茲已擬改在該省之瓦耳頓砲台鳴砲致賀國旗等語囑為轉達等因為此函請查照轉知是荷

外務部咨南北洋大臣兩廣閩浙總督文 三月初六日

准美費署使函稱等因相應咨行查照

美公使柔克義致外務部函 五月十四日

接本國外部文據兵部咨稱前擬定美國口岸鳴砲致賀國旗砲台印就版函內所列之奧克特里滋地方改在畢里西地之砲台鳴砲致賀等語囑為轉達等因相應函請查照轉知為荷

外務部咨陸軍部文 五月二十九日

准美柔使函稱等因相應咨行查照轉行南北洋大臣遵照、

六八

員外郎謙豫
分省補用道麥信堅謹
稟
宫保王中堂大人鈞鑒敬稟者竊司員等猥以菲材謬膺
委任自維譾陋深懼弗勝六月間道出滬江謁見薩提督先與籌商
一切抵廈後迭與劉道慶汾及
閩督憲所派委員駐廈美領事會商接洽以求事臻妥善所有組織接待場建造碼頭開闢馬路訂裝電燈定造運送淡水輪船建築宴會廳搭蓋棚廠購辦各國旗幟及花木陳設煙酒餐饌記念品等項均已部署周妥此次接待之事固為我國所創見而以上數大端似亦必不可少之舉此司員等之辦理大概情形也竊謂用財之多寡無定亦以局面之大小各殊儻對於此事處處悉從簡畧原擬之數詎有不敷之理司員等亦無時不以撙節公帑為心但事關國體又未敢因陋就簡貽人訕笑現在應辦各事雖已粗具規模惟於濱海寥廓之區頓闢為樽俎雍容之地憑空結構事倍功半無論巨細皆須置備齊全本埠百物俱無應用各物均從他處購運又因承辦者來自遠方動必居奇抬價職道並於月內親赴滬粤就近訂購總期於可省者不敢稍有虛糜於當用者亦不敢過存吝惜現計大宗用項共需銀四十三萬餘兩此外零星雜費積累頓成巨款為預計所不及者尚不在內約畧計之總須在五十萬兩左右此司員等之辦理為難情形也用特據實披

陳並將預算用款開具清摺呈請
鑒核除先蒙
憲部咨請
度支部飭津海關道撥給庫平銀八萬兩及
閩督憲飭發江海關道撥款庫平銀二十萬兩外其餘不敷之款
伏祈
迅賜籌撥以濟要需愚昧之見是否有當祗候
訓示遵行再此次所呈預算清摺均係約計之數或稍有增減尚在
臨時酌定俟事竣後得有實用數目再行詳細造報合併陳明專
肅禀陳恭叩
崇安伏乞
垂鑒司員豫職道信堅謹禀
計呈清摺二扣接待場圖一紙分日讌樂總目一紙菜單一紙
光緒三十四年九月　初七　日

六九

大亞美理駕合衆國欽命駐劄中華便宜行事全權大臣柔　為

照會

照會事、茲奉本國外部大臣文囑、據本國陸軍部

大臣文稱、本部茲將陸軍武員往來酬答所乘船

面懸掛之旂幟、定有新章、請照會

中政府等因、本大臣相應按照、將美國陸軍部新

定陸軍武員、於由水路答拜時、船面所懸之旂式、

洋文章程照錄一分、附送

貴親王查照、希為轉達陸軍部知照可也、須至照、

會者、附送洋文及章程一分

右　照　　會

大清欽命全權大臣便宜行事軍機大臣總理外務部事務和碩慶親王

一千九百捌年拾月拾伍日
光緒叁拾肆年玖月貳拾壹日

附件一

AMERICAN LEGATION,
PEKING, CHINA.

To FO No. 455.

October 15, 1908.

Your Excellency:

I have the honor to inform Your Imperial Highness that I have received from the Department of State a copy of a new regulation of the War Department in reference to the flags and pennants to be used by certain officers of the American army when making official visits by water, with the request that I would communicate the same to the Chinese Government.

I have the honor to enclose copies of the new regulation and request Your Imperial Highness to forward the same to the Board of War.

I avail myself of this opportunity to renew to Your Imperial Highness the assurance of my highest consideration.

Enclosures:

Five copies of the regulation referred to above.

To His Imperial Highness
Prince of Ch'ing,
President of the
Board of Foreign Affairs.

附件二

COPY

EXTRACT FROM GENERAL ORDERS, No. 128,
WAR DEPARTMENT, 1908, AMENDING PARAGRAPH 236,
ARMY REGULATIONS, 1908.

236. Boat flags and pennants for the use of officers of the Army when making official visits by water are authorized as follows:

For General Officers: A flag of scarlet bunting, rectangular in shape, 3-foot hoist and 4-foot 9-inch fly; the rank to be indicated by white stars of suitable size placed in the center line of the length of the flag; for a brigadier-general, one star; for a major-general, two stars and for the Lieutenant-General, three stars.

The Chief of Coast Artillery and the chiefs of bureaus of the War Department will use the general officer's flag with the appropriate number of stars.

For Artillery District Commanders: A flag of scarlet bunting, rectangular in shape, 1-foot 6-inch hoist and 2-foot fly for small boats and launches, and 2-foot 3-inch hoist and 3-foot fly for larger boats. In the center, on both sides, crossed cannon in yellow, with a medallion at their intersection, in scarlet, having an oblong projectile in yellow.

For Post Commanders: A pennant of bunting, triangular in shape, 1-foot hoist and 3foot fly; the third nearest the staff to be a blue field bearing thirteen white stars and the remaining two-thirds to be scarlet.

The truck of the staff for general officers, artillery district commanders, and post commanders above the rank of captain to be a gilt ball, and for post commanders of lower grade to be flat.

使已译

七〇

咨陸軍部咨送美國陸軍旗幟章程由

行　行

外務部左侍郎聯　九月廿五日　行

外務部右侍郎梁　九月　日

和會司

呈為咨行事准美柔使照稱奉本國外部大臣文囑據陸軍部將陸軍武員往来酬答所乘船面懸挂旗幟定有新章請照會中政府等因將洋文章程照錄附送希為轉達前来相應將原送洋文章程一分咨送

貴部查收見復可也須至咨者 附洋文章程三分

陸軍部

光緒三十四年九月　日

七一

照復美柔使來照致謝接待艦隊司
深欽佩由

行
外務部左侍郎聯 十月 十七日

行
外務部右侍郎梁 十月 日

和會司
呈為照復事接准
照稱本大臣代表赴廈之黎都司旋館備述中
國厚待艦隊之舉且
朗貝勒梁大臣特設盛筵接待
總統聞之尤為心感是以本大臣再代本國政府與伊
提督厦領及本國臣民特為致謝本大臣亦深
為鳴謝等因此次

旨前
貴國艦隊抵厦
朗貝勒、梁侍郎奉
往勞問，樽俎聯歡，主賓款洽，備徵兩國邦交
日臻親密。所有各接待官員，本應勉盡地主
之誼，迺承
貴大臣來照殷殷致謝，情詞周至。本爵大臣
接閱之餘，同深欽佩。相應照復
貴大臣查照可也。須至照復者。
美柔使
光緒三十四年十一月　日

七二

List of Those to Attend the Audience

Granted to General Miles.

****

H.E. E.H.Conger, U.S.Minister. 康格

Lieutenant General Nelson A. Miles, Commanding U.S.Armies. 麥勤思

Colonel Whitney, Adjutant. 懷璮尼 翼長隨員副將

Colonel Moss, 瑪斯 副將

~~Commodore~~ Mr Rouse, 饒司 水師總統

Mr. Friborg, 腓步格 隨員

Mr. Hoyt, 何愛特 隨員

Mr. John G. Coolidge, First Secretary of Legation. 固立之

Captain Brewster, Military Attaché, 布魯司

Dr. Hartsock, Surgeon. 哈特撒 醫官

Mr. E.T.Williams, Chinese Secretary of Legation. 衛理

List of those to Attend the Audience

Granted to Mrs. Miles and others.

****

Mrs. Conger, 康夫人

Mrs. Miles, 麥夫人

Mrs. Moss, 瑪夫人

Mrs. Williams, 衛夫人

Miss Campbell, 剛姑娘 Daughter of prominent Citizen, + guest of Mrs Conger for the winter

Miss West, 魏姑娘 Daughter of prominent Banker + Capitalist guest of Mrs Conger for the winter

士得 Mrs. Ragsdale, 若夫人 Wife of U. S. Consul Tientsin

~~Miss Porter and~~ Mrs. Gatrell (Lady Interpreters).

葛煥章 翰 ~~傅姑~~娘 葛太太 女繙譯

Mr. E. T. Williams, Chinese Secretary of Legation. 漢文參贊衛理

七三

欽命督理稅務大臣　為

咨呈事本年五月初八日准

貴部咨稱准美使照稱據住山東省美國教士費

里體稟稱現由美國來華携帶打獵小來復槍一

枝藥彈五十七枚行至青島地方被中國新關將該

槍彈扣留並諭以須領有執照方能交還等語本

大臣以此係為小槍一枝抑且子彈無多可請轉飭

給發該教士執照或行知青島關將該教士之槍彈

發還等因本部查貴處設訂槍彈進口新章第四
款甲節内載洋人來華行李内准携帶獵槍三枝
獵彈共不得逾三千顆進口時報關查驗完税放行
又乙節内載在中國居住之洋人欲買獵槍獵彈須
於進口之前先請監督發准運護照各等語茲美教
士費里體由美携帶獵槍獵彈來華是否按照新章
甲節令其報關完税放行無庸發給護照應咨行查
核電飭膠州關税務司遵辦並聲復本部以憑轉復

該使等因前來查該教士由美帶來打獵槍彈等
件核與本處改訂槍彈進口新章第四款甲節所限
數目並未逾額若查明確係散子獵槍獵彈應准照
章完税放行除劄行署總税務司電飭膠海關税務
司遵辦外相應咨呈
貴部查照轉復美使可也須至咨呈者
右　咨　呈
外　務　部
宣統元年正月　拾陸　日
預用空白
監印委員候選布理問唐佑衡

七四

照復美柔使美教士費里体来華所帶獵槍被膠海關扣留税務處已電飭放行由

外務部左侍郎聯
行
正月十九日
行

外務部右侍郎鄒
行
正月十九日
行

榷算司

呈為照復事本年正月初五日接准

照稱美國教士費里体由美来華攜帶打獵小来復槍一枝、葯彈五十七枚行至青島地方被中國新関將該槍彈扣留請轉飭發還等語當經本部咨行税務處核辦去後兹准咨復該教士由美帶来打獵槍彈等

件核與改訂槍彈進口新章第四款甲節所限數目並
未逾額若查明確係散子獵槍獵彈應准照章完稅
放行已由稅務處劄行署總稅務司電飭膠海關稅務
司遵辦相應照復
貴大臣查照可也須至照復者
美國柔使
宣統元年正月　日

七五

欽差出使美墨秘古國大臣伍　為

咨呈事案准美外部照稱頃准兵部大臣咨開美國小汽船祖盧在水東港外擱淺並遭盜刼附錄飛律賓督署行政官暨兩美國人信函三件均稱中國官員竭力援助被刼物主緝拏盜匪足見友誼克敦無任銘佩等因貴國官員之盛意本部至為感激為此照會貴大臣據情轉達貴國政府代達謝忱為荷等因准此本大臣查我國官員救災恤鄰不分畛域洵能盡義務而篤邦交相應據情轉咨為此咨呈

大部謹請察照須至咨呈者

右咨呈

外務部

宣統元年二月初貳日

七六

咨駐美伍大臣奏給上年美艦來華各武官寶星請轉達美外部由

行 行

外務部左侍郎聯

外務部右侍郎鄒

二月 日

二月初三日

行

和會司

呈爲咨行事准軍機處鈔交貝勒毓 尚書梁

具奏美艦來華懇

恩賞

給寶星一摺宣統元年二月初一日奉

旨著

照所請外務部知道單併發欽此欽遵到部除已

將寶星暨執照照送駐京美使轉給各該武官祇

領外相應抄錄原奏咨行
貴大臣查照即轉達美外部可也須至咨者 附抄奏
駐美大臣伍
宣統元年二月 日

七七

照會美柔使上年艦隊来華各武官奏　賞寶星希轉交祇領由

外務部左侍郎聯　行

外務部右侍郎鄒　行

二月　日

二月初四日　行

和會司

呈為照會事前以

貴國艦隊游歷来華於上年十月初間行抵厦門

曾奏

諭旨派貝勒毓　本部尚書梁　前往勞問所有

統領艦隊海軍副提督伊摩利施羅達等率同

各艦長暨各武官遠道来游具徵中美邦交從此

各艦長暨各武官遠道來游具徵中美邦交從此
日加親厚茲經貝勒毓　尚書梁　等繕單從
優分别酌擬請
賞副提督伊摩利等十六員寶星於宣統元年二月
初一日奉
旨允准除由本部咨行出使伍大臣轉達
貴國政府外茲照章製造頭等第三寶星二座二
等第二寶星九座二等第三寶星一座三等第
一寶星四座並各繕給執照一張相應開列清單
照送
貴大臣查照轉交各該員祇領可也須至照會者

附清单外寶星十六座執照十六張

計開

美國前任統領艦隊海軍副提督伊摩利

美國統領艦隊海軍副提督施羅達

以上二員

頭等第三寶星

賞給

美國戰艦艦長鼐爾思

侯獲

冠爾思

褒若

沙菩

赫勤士

畢立

戴義

美國駐京使館海軍隨員統帶官鄧格地

以上九員

賞給

二等第二寶星

美國駐厦門領事官阿訥爾

以上一員

賞給

二等第三寶星

美國艦隊中軍旗官韓德孫

克烈文

美國駐京使館衛隊統帶官都司黎富思

美國陸軍體操員守備威劳

以上四員

賞給

三等第一寶星

美柔使

宣統元年二月　　日

七八

逕啟者，接准本國外部大臣函，以牛約克呼得桑河開會，請中國派員赴會。緣一千六百零九年，有名和迪森之人，初尋得呼得桑河。嗣於一千八百零七年，間又有弗勒屯者，始在該河試行輪船。是以牛約總督選派該處著名紳董四百人，由西本年九月二十五號至十月九號，在該河適當處所開辦記念會。其中首事之董二十一人，備有請帖，由本國政府轉請中政府派員乘艦前往與會等因。本署大臣按照所囑，將寄到請帖附送。現在本國政府深望中政府允如所請，特派人員及兵艦前往。無須轉行駐美大臣，就近派員，緣本國政府已另請伍欽使屆時派員一同與會。該會現由牛約省籌有金洋四十萬圓，牛約城亦備有金洋二十萬，均作為開會經費。所有各國派來與會人員，均係該會來賓，從九月二十五號至十月九號，此十數日內，會中首事等即盡東道之禮，以款接來賓。兹將開會逐日應辦事務單，隨同請帖一併附送，即希

貴親王查照，特派人員為荷。特此泐頌

爵祺。附送洋文並請帖及單

費勒器啟　五月初七日

美國使署

附件

AMERICAN LEGATION,
PEKING.

To F. O. No. 540.

June 23, 1909.

Your Imperial Highness:

From Saturday, September 25, to Saturday, October 9, 1909, there will be celebrated at the City of New York and along the Hudson River the three hundredth anniversary of the discovery of the river by Henry Hudson in 1609, and the one hundredth anniversary of the first application of steam to the navigation of the river by Robert Fulton in 1807.

The celebration will be in charge of a commission consisting of four hundred prominent citizens appointed by the Governor of New York. The officers of this commission, comprising twenty-one of the leading citizens of New York City, have sent to my Government, with a request that it be delivered through the diplomatic channel, an invitation addressed to the Government of China to be represented at the celebration 'by its official representative and vessels of its navy.'

Under the instructions of my Government I have the honor to transmit the invitation to you with the expression

pression

To His Imperial Highness
Prince of Ch'ing,
President of the Board
of Foreign Affairs.

pression of my Government's hope that the Government of China may find it convenient to accept it. I am to explain to Your Imperial Highness that by the expression 'its official representative' is meant the sending of an official representative from China and not the designation of its diplomatic representative at Washington, to whom a separate invitation has been extended.

Accompanying the invitation Your Imperial Highness will find a printed program containing full information regarding the celebration and the exercises set apart for each day.

I am to say also that the State of New York has appropriated $400,000 and the City of New York $200,000 to defray the expenses of this celebration, and that the diplomatic, naval, and other official representatives of foreign nations will be guests of honor of the commission and will be accorded hospitality, both of a public and private character, from the time of their formal reception on Saturday, September 25, until the close of the celebration.

I avail myself of this opportunity to renew to Your Imperial Highness the assurance of my highest consideration.

Charge d'Affaires.

Enclosure:

Invitation as stated.

七九

和會司

呈為咨行事。准出使美國伍大臣電稱：美外部照稱，嘉里科尼省金山開埠距今百四十年，定期西十月十九至二十三號止為紀念節，擬請各國派一二兵艦來助慶會，請轉達政府。查日本各國已允派艦，可否照允，順道撫慰華僑等語。又准美國費署使函稱：接本國外部大臣來函，以紐約克呼得桑河開辦記念會，紐約總督選派著名紳董四百人，由西本年九月二十五號至十月九號在該河適當處所開辦，本國政府轉請中政府派員乘兵艦前往與會，附送請帖，希查照等因。查美國

金山紐約兩處開會能否派兵船前往相應將
美使送來請帖一併咨行
貴部轉行海軍提督查核見復以便分別
轉復可也須至咨者 附請帖
陸軍部
宣統元年五月 日

八〇

已抄

不入檔

行船

外務部收

舊金山華商總會鄧廣英等電一件 外人金山大會各國均派艦來我國是否能派乞示由

外務部左侍郎聯 月

太子少保署東閣大學士軍機大臣外務部會辦大臣那 月

太子少保文淵閣大學士軍機大臣署外務部會辦大臣世 月

軍機大臣總理外務部事務和碩慶親王 月 日

外務部尚書會辦大臣梁 月 日

外務部右侍郎鄒 月 日

宣統元年六月初十日鳳字三百二十二號

行船

宣統元
光緒卅四
年

八一

逕啟者頃接本國陸軍部來文飭本館武隨員黎富思與中國陸軍部互換帶槍刺之新式軍槍及槍彈十粒並佩帶槍刺槍彈之各式皮具因欲將此項物件陳列於本國陸軍學堂之所設博物院若中國肯為允准本國陸軍部即將本國之新式槍枝及一切各物均照數由黎隨員送交中國陸軍部等情本署大臣查互換新式軍器乃各國常情況本國陸軍學堂現有貴國留學肄業生本署大臣於此節甚望貴國陸軍部應允相應函達貴部即希轉達陸軍部查照可也此頌

日祉 附洋文

美國使署

費勒器啟 六月十七日

附件

AMERICAN LEGATION,
PEKING.

To F. O. No. 559.

August 2, 1909.

Your Imperial Highness:

Captain James H. Reeves, Military Attache of this Legation, has been directed by the Adjutant General of the United States Army to propose an exchange of arms with the Chinese Board of War. He asks that China may furnish one of the latest small arm rifles, complete with bayonet and ten rounds of ammunition with carrying device for the same (cartridge belt and boxes). This is desired for the purpose of placing in the ordnance museum of the United States Military Academy at West Point, New York.

In return the Ordnance Department of the War Department will forward to the Chinese Board of War the latest corresponding equipment of the American Army.

As exchanges of this sort are common courtesies between governments and especially in view of the fact that Chinese students have been admitted to the American Military Academy for training there, I trust that China will accede to this request, which I ask Your Highness' Board to transmit to the Board of War.

I avail myself of this opportunity to renew to Your Imperial Highness the assurance of my highest consideration.

Charge d'Affaires.

To His Imperial Highness, Prince of Ch'ing,
President of the Board of Foreign Affairs.

八二

欽命籌辦海軍大臣郡王銜多羅貝勒載
廣東水師提督軍門薩 為

咨覆事查本處接管卷內准陸軍部移交
貴部來咨內開准出使美國伍大臣電稱美外部照稱
嘉里科尼省金山開埠距今百四十年定期西十月十九
至二十三號止為紀念節擬請各國派一二兵艦來助慶會
請轉達政府等語又准美國貴署使函稱接本國外部大臣
來函以紐約克呼得桑河開辦紀念會由西本年九月二十五號
至十月九號在該河適當處所開辦本國政府轉請中政

府派員乘兵艦前往與會附送請帖希查照等因查美
國金山紐約兩處開會能否派兵船前往相應將美使送來
請帖一併咨行陸軍部轉行海軍提督查核見覆以便分别轉覆
可也等因准此當經本處照飭海軍提督查核去後兹據該
提督稟覆前來據稱海圻等艦日前奉差駛赴南洋東
洋現適回國正須修理器機屆時未能前赴金山紐約兩
處與會等語此係實在情形相應咨覆
貴部希即分别轉覆出使美國伍大臣暨美國署使并

代達歎忱可也須至咨者

右 咨

外務部

宣統元年六月拾捌日

監印官孫慶連

八三

考工司

呈為咨行事准美貴署使函稱接本國陸軍部來文飭本館武隨員黎富思與中國陸軍部互換帶槍刺之新式軍槍及槍彈十粒並佩帶槍刺槍彈之各式皮具因欲將此項物件陳列於本國陸軍學堂所設之博物院若中國肯為允准本國陸軍部即將本國之新式槍枝及一切各物均照數由黎隨員送交中國陸軍部等情本署大臣查互換新式軍器乃各國常情況本國陸軍學堂現有貴國留學肄業生本署大臣於此節甚望陸軍部應允等因前來相應咨行

貴部查照核復以便轉復美貴署使可也須至咨者

陸軍部

宣統元年六月　日

八四

外務部收

卅

欽命籌辦海軍大臣郡王銜多羅貝勒載、廣東水師提督軍門薩　為

片復事。准

貴部來片內開：案查美國金山開辦紀念會一事，前准復文，業經電達駐美吳代辦去後，茲准電復稱：金山紀念會各國多允派艦，該省瀕太平洋，中國口岸相對，華僑旅此最眾，久盼

國家兵輪巡視，該省官紳揣中國必允所請，擬格外優待華兵，可否再商海軍處勉派一艦，以睦邦交而慰眾望等語。片行酌核見復等因前來。查各艦中其能遠涉重洋者業已拆卸器機，正在修理，屆時

斷難畢工前往相應片復
貴部希即照復駐美吳代辦分別轉達
該省官紳華僑并代申歉忱可也須至
片者

右片行

外務部

宣統元年陸月二十八日

監印官陳 瑚

應 之件

八五

陸軍部爲咨呈事准外務部咨稱准美貴署使函稱接本國陸軍部來文飭本館武隨員黎富思與中國陸軍部互換帶槍刺之新式軍槍及槍彈十粒並佩帶槍刺槍彈之各式皮具因欲將此項物件陳列於本國陸軍學堂所設之博物院若中國肯爲允准本國陸軍部即將本國之新式槍枝及一切各物均照數由黎隨員送交中國陸軍部等情本署大臣查互換新式軍

器乃各國常情况本國陸軍學堂現有貴
國留學肄業生本署大臣於此節甚望陸
軍部應允等因前來相應行貴部查照核
復以便轉復美費署使等因前來查本國
所製之六米里八口徑槍枝子彈等項係
近年試造一切機件尚待逐細研究漸次
修改茲准前因應先將此項試造槍枝等
件與美槍互換以資參考除飭該管人員
趕將各件全分備送外相應咨呈

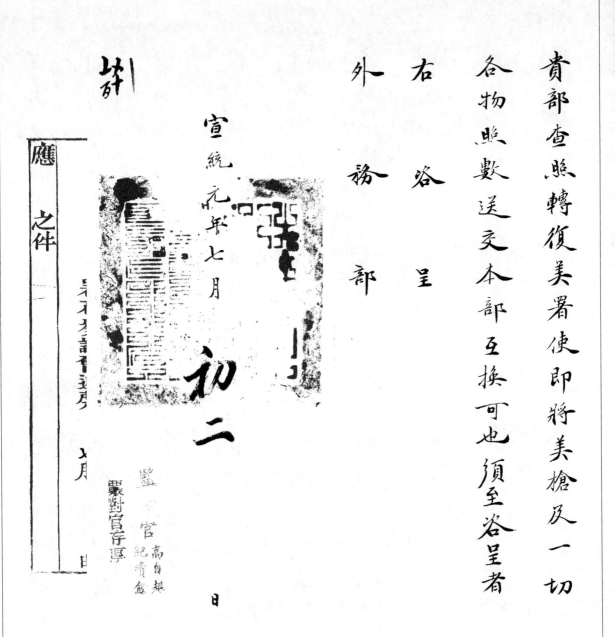

貴部查照轉復美署使即將美槍及一切
各物照數送交本部互換可也須至咨呈者

右　咨　呈

外務部

宣統元年七月初二日

監　官　高自棨　紀清愈

覆對官存厚

應　之件

月　日

八六

函復美費署使互换槍枝希轉知送交陸軍部互换由

外務部左侍郎聯 七月初五日 行
外務部右侍郎鄒 七月初五日 行

復美費署使

逕復者，前准
函稱接本國陸軍部來文，飭本館武隨員黎富思與中國陸軍部互换帶槍刺之新式軍槍等項，若爲允准，即將本國之新式槍枝等項送交等因，當經本部咨行陸軍部去後茲准復稱查所製之六米里八口徑槍枝子彈等項係近年試造應將此項試造槍枝等件與美槍互換以資參考應請照知美國駐京大臣即將美槍及一切各物照數送交本部互換等因前來相應函復貴署大臣查照轉飭該武隨員送交陸軍部互換可也此復順頌

日祉

堂銜

宣統元年七月　日

八七

逕復者，前准

函稱，以豫親王府

園寢三處，不知何國兵丁不時進内騷擾，恐日久不無

衝突，爲此函請查照，傳知衛隊人等不得率行游玩等

因。本署大臣當即函知巴統領去後，兹據查明美國兵

丁並無在豫親王府

園寢騷擾情事，現已飭知兵丁以後不得前往游玩，以

昭肅静。爲此函復

美國使署

貴王大臣查照可也。此候

日祉。附洋文

費勒器啟 十二月初一日

附件

AMERICAN LEGATION,
PEKING.

To F.O. No.604.

January II, 1910.

Your Imperial Highness:

I have the honor to acknowledge the receipt of Your Highness's note of January 5th., complaining of the tresspassing upon the cemeteries of Prince Yü on the part of some of the foreign soldiers stationed at Peking.

I have referred the matter to the Commandant of the American Legation Guard, who now reports that a careful investigation fails to show that any of the American soldiers have been implicated in the tresspass complained of, but that he has issued strict orders on the subject, prohibiting the soldiers of the Legation Guard from ever entering the enclosures referred to in Your Highness's note.

I avail myself of the opportunity to renew to Your Imperial Highness the assurance of my highest consideration.

[signature]

Charge d'affaires.

To His Imperial Highness
Prince of Ch'ing/ President of the
Board of Foreign Affairs.

八八

逕啟者，據本國克羅特軍器製造廠經理人巴樂德文稟稱：茲有克羅特機器砲一尊，擬欲運往杭州、福州、廣州、南京、武昌、天津、北京呈請中國各武員閲看，希代請中國政府頒發執照一紙，准將此項砲位運往各該處云云。查該經理人此舉實與貴國有益，相應函達貴王大臣查照，即希轉達陸軍部繕就執照一紙，送交本署大臣發給該經理人收執可也。此頌日祉。附洋文。

費勒器啟　十二月初二日

美國使署

附件

AMERICAN LEGATION,
PEKING.

To F.O. No.605.

January II,I9I0.

Your Imperial Highness:

I have the honor to report that I have received a communication from Mr. A.M.Baldwin, the Agent of the Colt's Patent Fire Arms Manufacturing Company stating that he wishes to take a Machine Gun to exhibit to the Chinese Military Authorities at Hangchou, Fuchow, Canton, Nanking, Wuchang, Peking, Tientsin, and asking that a permit may be issued by the Imperial Chinese Government, allowing him to transport the Machine Gun to the above mentioned places for the purpose specified. I have the honor to request Your Highness's Board to refer the matter to the proper Authorities and obtain the necessary Permit, which I ask may be sent to me for transmission to Mr. Baldwin.

I avail myself of the opportunity to renew to Your Highness the assurance of my highest consideration

[signature]

Charge d'affaires.

To His Imperial Highness,
Prince of Ch'ing,
President of the
Board of Foreign Affairs.

八九

咨陸軍部美巴樂德文運礮赴杭州等處請發執照希查核見復由

行　行

外務部左侍郎聯

外務部右侍郎鄒

十二月初五日　行

十二月初五日　行

考工司

呈爲咨行事。准美費使函稱：據本國克羅特軍器製造廠經理人巴羅德文稟稱，茲有克羅特機器礮一尊，擬欲運往杭州、福州、廣州、南京、武昌、天津、北京，請中國武員閱看，希代請中國政府頒發執照一紙，准將此項礮位運往各該處云云。查該

經理人此舉實與貴國有益函請轉達陸軍部
繕就執照送交轉給等因前來相應咨行
貴部查核見復以憑轉復可也須至咨者
陸軍部

宣統元年十二月　日

九〇

陸軍部爲片覆事軍實司案呈准外務部咨稱准美費使函據本國克羅特軍器製造廠經理人巴羅德文禀稱茲有克羅特機器礮一尊擬欲運往杭州福州廣州南京武昌天津北京請中國武員閲看希代請中國政府頒發執照一紙准將此項礮位運往各該處函請轉達陸軍部繕就執照送交轉給等因咨行本部查核見覆前來查軍械進口事宜前經税務處改訂槍彈進口新章第二款内載洋商欲運營中作様槍枝子彈須由各該領事向監督請領准運護照自貨到口憑照報關後方能起貨等語歷經辦理有案茲美使請將克羅特機器礮一尊運往各省閲看自應比照税務處改訂槍枝進口新章辦理本部未便繕發執照相應片覆

貴部查照轉覆可也須至片者

右　片　覆

盍字叁合弍佰

外　務　部

宣統元年十二月拾貳日

承辦官一等科員□□

覆對官額外科員頤慶

九一

函復美費署使巴樂德文運砲赴各省一事准陸軍部稱未便發給執照由

行　行

外務部左侍郎聯
外務部右侍郎鄒

十二月十五日　行
十二月十五日　行

復美費署使函

逕復者，前准

函稱本國克羅特軍器製造廠經理人巴樂德文稟兹有克羅特機器礮一尊擬欲運往杭州等處請中國武員閱看希轉達陸軍部須發執照一紙准將此項礮位運往各處等因，當經本部咨行陸軍部去後

兹准復稱查軍械進口事宜前經税務處改訂槍彈
進口新章第二款内載洋商欲運營中作樣槍枝子
彈須由各該領事向監督請領准運護照自貨到口
憑照報関後方能起貨等語歴經辦理有案今美國
駐京大臣請將克羅特機器礮一尊運往各省閲看
自應比照税務處改訂槍枝進口新章辦理本部未
便繕發執照等因前來相應函復
貴署大臣查照轉達可也此佈順頌
日祉

宣統元年十一月　　日

九二

逕啟者十二月十五日接准
函復准陸軍部咨稱火藥軍械軍裝砲台等局向來各
國參觀人員均未允准看視歷經辦理在案該武員黎
富思此次詢訪恐係傳聞之誤等語又
貴部於十二月十九日以陸軍部咨文見復並附送護
照一紙等因本館黎武員已稟明本國陸軍部轉咨外
部查照去後茲接外部來文囑令函達
貴親王以從前
美國使署
貴國官員遊美本國陸軍部曾允於各該處隨意閱看
因兩國友誼素敦辦理各事皆當互相有益是以本署
大臣函請
貴親王轉咨陸軍部於此事再為酌商如果黎隨員不
獲看
貴國之各該處本國政府恐欲另定章程不准游美
之中國官員閱看美國砲台等處此等辦法最為可
惜不如彼此商酌妥定和平辦法藉全睦誼現該隨
員於數日內即欲起行前往南省遊歷相應函請
貴親王查照速為
見復可也此泐順頌
日祉並賀
年禧 附洋文
費勒器啟 新正月初七日
美國使署

逕啟者，前准本國統帶太平洋海軍第三艦隊何提督函稱，現擬於西四月初一日前後，假浙江象山附近之海灣，操演打靶，希代達中國外務部轉咨該管官員知照等因，相應函達

貴王大臣查照，請轉咨海軍處、閩浙督撫札行該處官員，妥爲照料，即希見復是荷，此頌

日祉。附洋文

費勒器啟　正月十六日

美國使署

附件

AMERICAN LEGATION,
PEKING.

To F.O. No. 624.

February 25, 1910.

Your Imperial Highness:

I have the honor to inform Your Imperial Highness that I am in receipt of a communication from Rear Admiral John Hubbard, Commanding the Third Squadron of the United States Pacific Fleet, asking that I request permission from the Chinese Government for the vessels under his command to engage in target practice in the vicinity of Nimrod Sound on or about April 1, 1910.

In transmitting the above request I avail myself of the opportunity to renew to Your Imperial Highness the assurance of my highest consideration.

Charge d'Affaires.

To His Imperial Highness
Prince of Ch'ing,
President of the Board
of Foreign Affairs.

九四

欽命籌辦海軍大臣郡王銜多羅貝勒載海軍提督軍門薩　爲

咨覆事。准

貴部咨稱：准美費署使函稱本國統帶太平洋海軍第三艦隊何提督擬於西四月初一日前後假浙江象山附近之海灣操演打靶，請轉咨海軍處、閩浙總督劄行該處官員妥爲照料等情前來。查象山爲吾國新開軍港，似未便准外人借用。事關海軍，應如何拒駁之處，相應咨行酌核見復。

以便轉復該使等因到處查象山業經闢建軍港附近一帶海灣亦須詳加測勘佈置所有美國何提督擬請之處未便照准相應咨覆

貴部希即婉達該使轉知何提督另覓合宜之處可也須至咨者

右　咨

外務部

宣統二年正月廿三日

九五

陸軍部為

咨行事准

貴部咨開宣統二年正月初七日准美費署使函稱本國武員

黎富思擬參觀軍隊砲台一事准函復准陸軍部咨稱火

藥軍械軍裝砲台等向來各國參觀人員均未之准看視等

語又准函復附送護照一紙等因黎武員業經稟明本國茲接

外部來文以貴國官員遊美曾允各處隨意閱看應請轉咨陸

軍部酌商如果不准黎隨員看貴國各處本國政府恐欲另

定章程不准遊美之中國官員閱看美國砲台等處此等

辦法最為可惜不如彼此和平辦理藉全睦誼該員於日內

起行請速見復等因此事應如何酌量辦理之處除咨軍諮
處籌辦海軍處外相應咨行貴部查核見復以便轉復該使
等因到部查陸軍砲台等處不令外國人員參觀各國所有
此項辦法固於國際睦誼毫無損傷茲准美使函開前因自
係爲兩國交情日益親密起見惟查美外部所稱曾允我國游
美官員各處隨意閱看等語查本部前派赴美人員並未令其
參觀砲台等處據該員等回部報告亦無曾在美國參觀砲
台等處之件且所稱如果不准黎隨員閱看恐欲另定章程
等語是美政府必有此項原定章程惟原章各條本部未經
閱看無憑查核擬議布由

貴部照會美使即將此項原定章程錄送

貴部轉行本部查閱再行核辦現經本部咨商軍諮處意

見相同相應咨呈

貴部查照辦理可也須至咨呈者

右咨呈

外務部

宣統二年五月廿三日

監印官劉光瀅

九六

函復美費署使准海軍處咨稱何提督擬在象山附近操演未便照允由

行　　行

外務部左侍郎聯

外務部右侍郎鄒

正月　廿五日

正月　廿五日

行

行

復美費署使函

逕覆者：前准

函稱本國統帶太平洋海軍第三艦隊何提督擬假浙江象山附近之海灣操演打靶，請咨海軍處。閩浙總督等語。當經本部咨行海軍處去後，兹准覆稱：象山業經闢建軍港附近一

帶海灣現正在測勘佈置未便於該處操演
打靶應請函知美國駐京大臣轉達何提督
另覓合宜之地等因相應函復
貴署大臣查照轉達可也順頌
日祉

堂銜

宣統二年正月　日

九七

復美費署使黎富思參觀砲台等處事准陸軍部咨稱各節希查照見復由

行 行

外務部左侍郎聯
正月廿五日 行

外務部右侍郎鄒
正月廿五日 行

覆美費署使函

逕覆者美武員黎富思擬參觀軍隊砲台等處一事
本月初七日接准
函稱各節當即咨行軍諮處陸軍部核復去後兹准
陸軍部覆稱陸軍砲台等處不令外國人員參觀各
國原有此項辦法固於國際睦誼毫無損傷美國駐

京大臣函開前因自係為兩國交情日益親密起見
惟查美外部所稱曾允我國游美官員各處隨意閱
看等語查本部前派赴美人員並未令其參觀砲台
等處據該員等回部報告亦無曾在美國參觀砲台
等處之件且所稱如果不准黎隨員閱看恐欲另定章
程等語是美政府必有此項原定章程惟原章各條本
部未經閲看無憑核議希轉復美國駐京大臣即將
此項原定章程録送再行核辦等因相應函復
貴署大臣查照見復可也順頌
日祉

堂銜

美費署使

宣統貳年正月　日

九八

逕啟者，接

來函盡悉。查陸軍部復函，於美武員看視炮台等處一事，甚不樂從，因該部函意尚無定見，須將酌定何處可以看視再為聲明。現在本署大臣甚為詫異者，以陸軍部意見於美陸軍部所談允准游美華員各處隨意閱看之語，疑為不實。雖

貴國官員未報告看視砲台各處，而美陸軍部從前已准華員看視。況近年曾有留美

美國使署

貴國學生二名在本國陸軍大學堂肄業，均照章看視砲台、軍械所、製造廠等處，即演砲處所亦無不閱看。其所參觀之各要地，雖美國人民亦未嘗盡行任便閱看。茲聚武員請看之處，即美陸軍部准華員看視之處。本署大臣以此等事件辦理當互有益，如

貴國核定專准美武員看視軍隊、學堂，斷不准看視他處，請即

函復，以便達知本國政府。現在聚武員已至南省，相應

函達

貴親王查照，即希轉行陸軍部速為核定見復可也。此頌

日祉。附洋文

費勒器啟 二月初一日

美國使署

附件

AMERICAN LEGATION,
PEKING.

To F.O. No.629.

March 11,1910.

Your Imperial Highness:

I have the honor to acknowledge the receipt of Your Highness' note of March 7,1910 in regard to the request of the Legation that permission be granted to Captain Reeves, the Military Attaché of this Legation, to visit the forts, arsenals, and military factories of China, in which Your Highness' Board quotes the substance of the reply of the Board of War, from which I gather that the last named Board is unwilling to accord Captain Reeves this privilege.

But, as this request is rather evaded than refused in the answer of the Board of War and as it is extremely important that the matter be clearly understood, I permit myself to ask for a definite reply to this request. And, in this connection, I must express great surprise that the Board of War should doubt for a moment the statement of the American War Department that the Chinese officials visiting America have been allowed to inspect freely the corresponding places in the United States.

It should not be necessary for me to reiterate that such permission is always accorded to Chinese officials in the United States, and the fact that no reports of such inspections have been made does not in any

way affect

His Imperial Highness,
Prince of Ch'ing,
President of the Board
of Foreign Affairs.

(2)

the accuracy of the statement of this Legation. The E Board of War cannot fail to remember that two young Chinese have but recently completed a four years' course of study at the United States Military Academy at West Point which course included visits not only to the American forts,arsenals,and gun factories,but also to the ordnance proving ground where but few Americans even are allowed to go.

I would repeat that,as reciprocity usually governs in cases of this kind,I must report to Washington whether Your Highness' Government adheres to the decision formerly communicated to me that our Military Attache will be allowed to inspect military schools and camps only,and no other of the places of military interest which Chinese officials visiting America have heretofore been permitted to inspect. Captain Reeves is now in South China on a visit of inspection and I have the honor to request an early reply.

I avail myself of this opportunity to renew to Your Imperial Highness the assurance of my highest consideration.

Charge d'Affaires.

九九

逕啓者上年六月十七日本館費前署大臣曾以恭
武員欲與
貴國陸軍部互換槍枝一切各物函請查照當經
貴部於七月初五日復稱陸軍部准其互換等因茲
該武員已將美國槍枝一切各物如數接收相應
函請
貴王大臣查照希即咨行陸軍部請其擇定地址時
日並派何員互換先行
美國使署
見復以便該武員遵照可也此泐順頌
日祉 附洋文
嘉樂恆啓五月初四日

附件

AMERICAN LEGATION,
PEKING.

To F.O. NoI2. June IO, I9IO.

Your Imperial Highness:

On the 2nd. of August, I909, Mr. Fletcher, the Charge d'affaires of this Legation, addressed a note to Your Highness, informing you that Captain Reeves, the Military Attaché, had been directed by the Adjutant General to propose an exchange of arms with the Chinese Board of War.

On the 20th. of August, Your Highness replied saying that the proposal had been accepted by the Board of War.

Captain Reeves now informs me that he has received the American rifle and accessories. Will Your Highness be so kind as to inform the Board of War, asking them to designate a date and place and to appoint a person to whom Captain Reeves may transmit the articles received by him from the American War Department, and from whom he may receive in return the equivalent articles from the Chinese Board of War.

I avail myself of this opportunity to renew to Your Highness the assurance of my highest consideration.

American Minister.

To His Imperial Highness, Prince of Ch'ing,
President of the Board of Foreign Affairs.

一〇〇

咨陸軍部美使稱黎武員現將美國槍枝接收請咨互换等語希查照辦理見復由

行 行

外務部左侍郎鄒
署外務部左侍郎曹
外務部右侍郎胡

五月 日
五月 日
行
發八

考工司

呈爲咨行事。美國請互换新式槍枝一事，上年七月初二日准

貴部來咨，准其互换等語。當經本部函復美使去後。兹准復稱：美黎武員已將美國槍枝一切各物如數接收，請咨陸軍部擇定地址

時日並派何員互换先行見復以便該武員
遵照等因前來相應咨行
貴部查照辦理並聲復本部以憑轉復該
使可也須至咨者
陸軍部
宣統二年五月　日

復美嘉使信

逕復者前准

來函以黎武員已將美國槍枝一切各物如數接收

請咨陸軍部擇定地址時日并派何員互换見復

等因當經本部咨行陸軍部去後茲准復稱本部

現將槍枝子彈暨附屬各品檢齊并派科員文斌

定於六月初五日午前十鐘在本部督練公所與美

武員接洽請轉復

美國駐京大臣屆時互换並希先行見復以憑辦

理等因前來相應函復

貴大臣查照轉達黎武員仍希先行見復以便知

照陸軍部可也順頌

日祉

堂銜

宣統貳年陸月　日

一〇二

美國使署

逕復者：前准

函稱，槍枝互换一事，業經陸軍部定於六月初五日

午前十點鐘，派文科員在督練公所與黎武員互换，

等因。現該武員因公外出，不克如期互换，俟該武員

函禀到時，再行荅復，以便改訂時日，相應函復

貴王大臣查照，希即轉達陸軍部可也。此泐，順頌

日祉。

嘉樂恒啟　六月初五日

忙

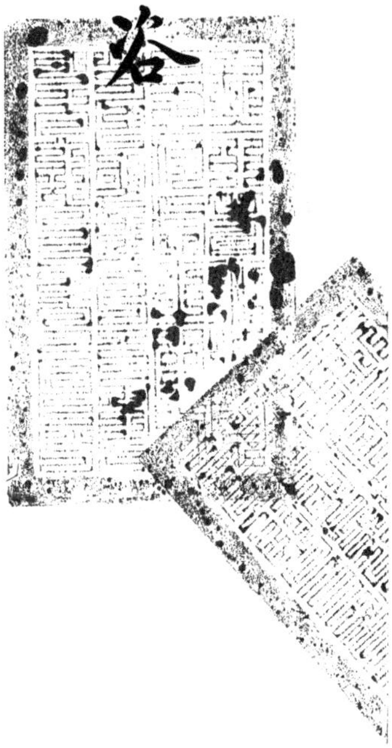

咨

欽命籌辦海軍大臣郡王銜多羅貝勒載
海軍提督軍門薩 為

恭錄咨行事。本處於六月十四日具奏擬
酌帶隨員前赴美日二國考察海軍
一摺並單，同日奉

硃批依議欽此相應恭錄

硃批印刷原奏原單咨行

貴部欽遵並希飭令周左丞自齊

馮道國勳遵照可也須至咨者

右

咨 印刷原奏原單各一件

外務部

宣統二年六月　日

監印官榮 壽

附件

橫字四千五號

附

外務部收

海軍處文一件

具奏酌帶隨員赴美日二國考察海軍一摺錄

批知照并

飭周丞馮道遵照由

陳按

奏為臣等擬於本年七月前赴美日二國考察海軍並酌

帶隨員以供任使恭摺仰祈

聖鑒事竊上年臣等奏赴歐美各國考察海軍事宜業經

俞允飭下外務部知照英法德奧義俄美日八國駐京使臣

通告各該國政府在案上年臣等出洋係先赴歐洲

周歷英法德義奧俄六國道經俄國考察東事已屆歲

闌即取道西比利亞鐵路先行回京清理臣處業牘現

計臣等回京已逾數月一切業牘清理完竣美日二國既

經通告在前自應及早首途前往考察庶不失信於外人現在公同商酌擬於本年七月放洋先赴美國次赴日本所有途中一切事務亟須酌帶隨員以資佐理查上年所帶各員其任謀贊海軍事宜者係就臣等各國員中遴選奏派其任晉接酬酢之事者係就熟悉外交人員中奏明咨調此次出洋擬援案辦理仍就臣等遴選相當人員令其隨同考察惟所選者宜新舊參半不必盡是上年奏派之員蓋藉此參錯調換則臣等可多培植數員使其經歷外洋參觀一切庶將來籌軍備多收群助之益至外交人員一項上年所調者係通曉英法文字之員本年前赴美日酬酢之間無需法語自應調取嫻習英語日語人員藉通情款而資肆應惟臣等先赴美國通曉日語者不必同行擬令其先行留京俟臣等在美國考察完竣前赴日本有期乃電飭各該員由京赴日以期節省經費茲謹將臣等前赴美日擬帶各員繕單恭呈

御覽如蒙

俞允即由臣等分咨京外各該衙門飭令遵照所有本年

七月臣等擬赴美日二國酌帶隨員繕單謹恭摺具陳伏乞
皇上聖鑒訓示謹
奏
謹將宣統二年臣等前赴美日二國擬帶各隨員繕單
恭呈
御覽

計開

外務部丞參上行走前署左丞周自齊
軍學司司長曹汝英
軍法司司長鄭汝成
軍制司司長徐振鵬
駐滬參謀官鄭祖彝
軍防隊司長林葆綸
軍儲司司長趙鶴齡
軍樞定司長張怒
軍法司司法官李景鉌
廣西試用道張步青

袁海

以上十員擬帶赴美日二國張步青一員係自備資斧不支領薪水上年業經奏咨

俞允在案合併陳明

民政部右丞延鴻

江蘇補用道馮國勳

以上二員擬俟臣壽在美國[illegible]發電飭由京起程前赴日本

G.
To F. O. No. 21.

AMERICAN LEGATION,
PEKING.

August 3, 1910.

Your Imperial Highness:

I had the honor to receive Your Highness' despatch dated July 8, 1910, in which Captain Reeves was invited to be present at the Board of War on Monday, July 11, at 10 o'clock in the morning, in order to effect an exchange of arms, on behalf of the American War Department, with a specially deputed officer of the Board of War. But at that time, inasmuch as Captain Reeves was not at the Capital, I had the honor to request Your Highness to await Captain Reeves' return when another date might be set.

Captain Reeves has now returned to Peking and I have the honor to beg Your Highness to request the Board of War once more to set a date and depute an official to effect the said exchange of arms, and to acquaint me accordingly in order that I may inform Captain Reeves.

I avail myself of this opportunity to renew to Your Imperial Highness the assurance of my highest consideration.

For Mr. Calhoun
W. W. Peck.

To His Imperial Highness,
Prince of Ch'ing,
President of the Board of
Foreign Affairs.

附件

逕啟者，六月初二日接准

函稱，互換槍枝一節，經陸軍部派科員文斌，定於六月初五日午前十鐘，在督練公所與黎武員接洽，以便屆時互換，仍希先行見復等因。當經本大臣復以該武員因公外出，不克如期互換，俟其旋館，再行改定時日答復等語。兹該武員現已回京，仍請

貴王大臣轉致陸軍部，請其再定時日，並派何員接待，先行函復，以便飭令該武員遵照可也。此泐，順候

日祉

美國使署

嘉樂恒啟 六月二十八日

一〇五

復美嘉使函互換槍枝事陸軍部定於八月初六日在督練公所仍派科員文誠接洽由

行 行

外務部左侍郎胡

外務部右侍郎曹

七月 日

七月 日

復美嘉使信

逕復者：互換槍枝一事，前准

來函以黎武員現經回京，請轉致陸軍部再定時日，并派何員接待，先行函復，以便飭令該武員遵照等因，當經本部咨行陸軍部去後，茲准復稱：所有互換槍枝一節，定於八月

初六日下午二點半鐘仍派科員文斌在近
畿督練公所與該武員接洽請轉復
美國駐京大臣先行見復以便辦理等因
前來相應函復
貴大臣查照轉飭該武員遵照并希見復以
憑轉行陸軍部可也順頌
日祉
堂銜
宣統二年七月　日

逕復者前准
函稱互換槍枝一節准陸軍部函復定於八月初六日下午二點半鐘仍派科員文斌在近畿督練公所與該武員接洽請即見復等因查八月初六日本大臣偕同黎武員因公外出屆期不克回館恐難踐約爲此函達
貴部查照即希轉行陸軍部請於初九初十十一三日内擇訂一日并於何時接待先行
見復以便飭令該武員即行遵照前往可也此復
順候
日祉 附洋文
嘉樂恒啟 八月初三日

美國使署

附件

AMERICAN LEGATION,
PEKING, CHINA.

To F. O. No.31.

September 6, 1910.

Your Imperial Highness:

I have the honor to acknowledge the receipt of Your Highness' despatch dated September 2nd, 1910, informing me that the Board of War had determined upon Friday, September 9th, at 2:30 in the afternoon, as the time and had designated Wen Pin, Head of a Bureau, to meet Captain Reeves at the offices having in charge the troops attached to the Capital in order to effect the proposed exchange of arms. I have now the honor to inform Your Highness that Captain Reeves will be absent from the city in company with the American Minister on that date. I accordingly request that the Board of War be asked to arrange for either Monday or Tuesday or Wednesday, the 12th or 13th or 14th of September, for the exchange of arms and that the Legation may receive a reply as to the date determined upon in order to inform Captain Reeves thereof.

I avail myself of this opportunity to renew to Your Highness the assurance of my highest esteem.

W. J. Calhoun
American Minister

To His Imperial Highness,
Prince of Ch'ing,
President of the WaiWu Pu.

一〇七

復美嘉使函互換槍枝事陸軍部訂於八月初十日在督練公所派科員接洽由

行　外務部左侍郎胡　八月初九日

行　外務部右侍郎曹　八月　日

復美嘉使函

逕復者前准

來函以互換槍枝一事初六日恐難踐約請轉行

陸軍部於初九初十十一三日內擇訂一日并與

何時接待先行見復等因當經本部片行陸軍

部去後茲准復稱現訂於初十日下午三點鐘派

科員文斌仍在近畿督練公所與該武員接洽等因相應函達
貴大臣查照轉飭該武員屆時前往可也順頌
日祉
堂銜
宣統二年八月　日

一〇八

今有貴署派武便到敝使館言明日黎武員赴陸軍部至操槍技能台前住現今黎武員斐參贊具莫在京署副參贊盡樂亦未能定若黎武員斐參贊回京速為貴衙行文

署副參贊盡樂

一〇九

現世列國侵畧。重在海軍。茲特首先調查其與吾國最有關係之英德法俄美日六國所有艦隊。余兹合數。依列於下。並各附以本年度之海軍預算額。則其原有之武裝。及其擴張之勢力。不難一覽而得也。

英國海軍總數

艦種	隻數	排水量
戰鬥艦	四二	七三六八五〇噸
舊式戰艦	二三	三二五〇〇〇
裝甲巡洋艦	五五	七三三八五〇
二等巡洋艦	三九	二二七、三一〇
三等巡洋艦	三四	一〇九、四八五
驅逐艦	二、〇九	、、、
水雷艇	一、一六	、、、
潛水艇	八四	、、、

本年度預算額約合華銀四億六百零三萬兩

德國海軍總數

戰鬥艦	二八	四五九、二〇〇
老齡同上	九	九四、三六六
裝甲巡洋	一三	一五二、八四五
二等巡洋	六	三四、二四五
三等同上	三四	一〇七、〇五九
驅逐艦	一、四〇	、、、
水雷艇	七〇	、、、
潛水艇	一四	、、、

本年度預算額約合二億一千二百四十七萬

法國海軍總數

戰鬥艦	一五	二五三、五三一
老齡同上	一〇	一一二、三二六
裝甲巡洋	一五	一六九、〇二七
二等巡洋	一二	七八、五四一
三等同上	二一	六六、七七三
驅逐艦	八三	、、、
水雷艇	一、五〇	、、、
潛水艇	九〇	、、、

本年度預算額約合一億三千六百五十九萬兩

俄國海軍總數

戰鬥艦	一一	一九〇、七二二
老齡同上	九	四三、〇五八
裝甲巡洋	六	六三、〇五八
二等巡洋	八	五二、六一〇
三等同上	二	六、三九八
驅逐艦	八七	、、、
水雷艇	四七	、、、
潛水艇	三七	、、、

本年度預算額約合、、、、、

美國海軍總數

戰鬥艦	二六	四五五、四三〇
老齡同上	九	一〇〇、〇六七
裝甲巡洋	一五	一八六、八九五
二等巡洋	一三	二〇、六二〇

三等同上	一四	四八、七九九
驅逐艦	四〇	〃
水雷艇	二八	〃
潛水艇	三九	〃

本年度預算額約合二億六千五百十五萬兩

日本海軍總數

戰鬥艦	一四	二二二、二三四
老齡同上	一一	一〇九、六〇〇
裝甲巡洋	一三	一三八、〇五二
二等巡洋	七	三八、〇五六
三等同上	一三	四三、七一三
驅逐艦	六一	〃
水雷艇	五九	〃
潛水艇	一〇	〃

本年度預算額約合七千六百八萬

按論列國海軍者。自以戰鬥艦及鐵甲巡洋艦為艦隊之主力。然欲考究其實際。則須就進水後之年限計算之。按戰鬥艦可運用十五年。鐵甲巡洋艦可運用十三年。過是即陳腐無用。不能認為主力艦隊。茲特據此原則。調查列強主力艦隊。列表如左。

計本年內列國艦隊之主力

國名	戰鬥艦	裝甲巡洋艦
英國	五二	四五
德國	三三	一二

法國	一九	一五
美國	三二	一五
日本	一四	一三

計七年後列強艦隊之主力

國名	戰鬥艦	裝甲巡洋艦
英國	四七	三一
德國	三一	一四
法國	二六	四
美國	三七	六
日本	七	七

按右兩表所示。計七年後。英之主力戰艦。由五十二減至四十七。日本之主力戰艦。由十四減至七。德國之主力戰艦。由三十三減至三十一。法國之主力戰艦。由十九增至二十六。美國之主力戰艦。由三十二增至三十七。此其相差之數。皆就新舊艦之多少。為之乘除。就中尤以裝甲巡洋艦之變動為最大。觀此可以覘七年後國力之消長矣。雖然。以現時論。列強派遣東洋之艦隊。勢力甚為薄弱。暫時仍不能不推日本為太平洋之主人。至七年後之變遷。則非所敢預知。姑舉列強將來可派遣東洋之艦隊。列表如左

計本年內列強在太平洋之艦隊

國名	戰鬥艦	裝甲巡洋艦
英國	二六	二三
美國	三二	一五
德國	三三	一二

法國	十九	一五
日本	一四	一三

計七年後列強在太平洋之艦隊

國名	戰鬥艦	裝甲
英國	二四	一六
美國	三七	六
德國	三一	一四
法國	二六	四
日本	七	七

據右列兩表觀之。以列強海軍主力艦隊。與日本海軍主力艦隊。相爲比較。其在戰鬥艦類。計英比日本多十七艘。美比日本多三十艘。德比日本多二十四艘。法比日本多十九艘。其在裝甲巡洋艦類。計英比日本多九艘。德比日本多七艘。惟美則比日本減其一。而法則比日本減其三。蓋以二國近皆多造戰鬥艦。少造裝甲巡洋艦也。

致海軍部函

敬啟者接准駐美張大臣電稱美外部稱中國
在美定造練船合同內載機器礮位由英配造
一款有失美國體面應由美配造云祈核復等語
本部正在核辦間復准該大臣電稱美屢催覆希電復等因
特此函達
冰案即希
查照從速核復以憑轉復可也此佈順頌
勛綏

外務部啟

宣統叁年叁月　日

一一一

敬覆者，准
貴部函開，接駐美張大臣電稱，美外部稱中國在美定造練船合同內載機器礮位由英配造一款，有失美國體面，應由美配造一節。日前本京美使署韓參贊到部面談，本部業將各種理由明白答覆，當由該參贊轉達美公使在案。昨日韓參贊又來部面談，據稱美公使於前項理由極爲滿意，業經照達美外部等語，相應函覆
貴部即希查照可也。此佈，并頌
公安。

海軍部啓

逕覆者：准
貴部函開：美韓使面詢海圻抵美日期，貴
部如得有碻信，即希示知，以便轉覆等因。
前來。查海圻現入英廠修理汽鼓等件，前
據巡洋艦隊統領程璧光禀稱，本月下旬工
竣等語，業由本部電飭工竣後啟行赴美
在案。相應函覆，希先照達美使，并告以
俟有確期，再行知照
貴部，以便轉達可也。專覆，即頌
公安

海軍部啟

一一三

函美衛署使海圻兵艦遊歷到美希加意照料由

外務部左侍郎胡 七月 行 日 署
外務部右侍郎曹 七月 行 日 堂

函美衛署使

逕啟者，海圻兵艦前經海軍部奏准，於英加冕禮成後就近開往美洲遊歷，藉聯交誼，經本部函達
嘉大臣在案。茲准海軍部函稱，接巡洋艦隊統領程璧光由英電禀，海圻約中歷七

月十八日可到紐約等語即希

貴署大臣查照前函轉達

貴國政府爲荷此佈順頌

日祉

全堂銜

宣統三年七月　　日

一一四

十二月初二日京奉局來電

本日有美國兵五百名由秦皇島登岸，内撥一百八十名保護鐵路，餘三百廿名駐紮天津，特禀。同全到叩。

鐵路總局譯員趙相齡校

一一五

十一月初三日京奉局來電

據唐山洋稽查電稱：昨到之美國兵現已分派各站駐紮，計雷莊駐官一員兵四十名，古冶駐官二員兵七十名，窪里駐官一員兵廿名，開平駐官一員兵三十名，唐山駐官一員兵四十二名。所有以上各站前駐之英國兵一律撤退等情稟報前來，理合稟聞。全列叩

鐵路總[illegible]員趙[illegible]

一一六

IX

廿一 六 初十

照會

大亞美理駕合衆國欽命駐劄中華便宜行事全權大臣田　為

照會事、案查一千八百六十年、北洋大臣在天津紫竹林地方、指撥英法美租界各一段、所撥給美國租界由美國領事管理多年、嗣於一千八百八十年十月十二日美國領事官照會津海關道、擬將所撥之租界、仍交中國管理並經聲明嗣後如欲定立工部局章程、亦可歸領事官復行辦理、是年十月十四日、經津海關鄭道照復、云嗣後美領事如欲復管租界、

須先與閣道妥商，如何辦法，如所定之章無礙，可以照租界原章歸美領事管理，均有存案可查，又從一千八百八十年，本國駐京大臣與本國外部大臣迭辦此事，本國政府未云嗣後決不管理本國之租界，以棄此權，此時本大臣不必於此租界本國應復行管理，詳加辯論，俟有辯論為不應復行管理，再為詳細辯明，現聞有一二國或數別國，欲請中國將原撥歸美國租界之地讓與管理，茲不過先達知

貴署備案中國如允與彼抑或有意與之本大臣決不能照允除已詳報本國聽候如何辦理再行照會外相應照會

貴王大臣查照請即咨行北洋大臣無論現欲將原撥美國租界讓與何國立即停止可也須至照會者

右　照　會　附送洋文

大清欽命總理各國事務王大臣

乙未年陸月初拾日

附件

Copy.

Mr Denby to the Tsungli Yamên

No 19.

Peking July 31st 1895

Your Imperial Highness and Your Excellencies

I have the honor to inform Your Imperial Highness and Your Excellencies that in the year 1860 the Superintendent of Northern Trade set out at Tientsin three tracts of land for English, French, and American residents.

The American Consul exercised jurisdiction over the land so allotted to Americans for many years. The 12th day of October 1880, the American Consul wrote to the Customs Taotai that he proposed to relegate the concession back to its "former status" with the understanding that if, at some

future

future time it should be desirable to establish suitable municipal regulations therein, it shall be competent for the Consular Authorities to do so"

Under date of 14th October 1880, the Taotai Cheng acknowledged receipt of the Consul's despatch and stated that if any American Consul, in future, should "desire to have the settlement resort to the present system of administration he must first arrange with the Customs Taotai as to the mode of administration and if there be nothing objectionable in same then there should be nothing to prevent the settlement from reverting to the original government"

All this appears of record, and it also appears since 1880

throughout

through repeated action of the United States Minister here and the Honorable Secretary of State that the Government of the United States has never relinquished its rights over the American Concession.

I do not propose at this time to present a full argument on the question of the right of my government to retake jurisdiction over the ceded territory. It will be time enough to do this when this right is disputed.

All that I desire to do now is to give Your Imperial Highness and Your Excellencies notice that I have understood that proceedings are pending having for their object to cede the territory mentioned to one or more other powers.

Against such cession or attempt

at

at cession I enter my solemn protest.

I have referred this matter to my Government and will address Your Imperial Highness and Your Excellencies when I shall have received instructions.

What I now ask is that Your Imperial Highness and Your Excellencies immediately instruct the Viceroy at Tientsin to cease all action looking to the cession of any portion of the American Concession to any power whatever.

I avail myself of this opportunity to renew to Your Imperial Highness and Your Excellencies the assurance of my most distinguished consideration.

(sig) C. Denby

一一七

咨北洋大臣美國所退租界勿得讓與他國由

行

戶部左堂張

六月十六日

美國股

呈爲咨行事光緒二十一年六月初十日准美國田使照稱一千八百六十年北洋大臣在天津紫竹林地方指撥英法美租界各一段嗣於一千八百八十年十月十二日美國領事官照會津海關道擬將所撥之租界仍交中國管理是年十月十四日經鄭關道照復嗣後美領事如欲

復管租界須先與關道妥商如何辦法均有存案可查現聞有一二國欲請中國將原撥美國租界讓與管理中國如允與彼本大臣決不能允除已詳達本國請即咨行北洋大臣無論欲將租界讓與何國立即停止等因前來查該使所稱各節雖未指明某國惟此項地段既與美國立有案據自不能讓與他國以昭公平兹將田使來照鈔錄咨行貴大臣查照務即轉飭關道妥核辦理仍復本衙門可也須至咨者 附抄件

北洋大臣

光緒二十一年六月 日

照復美國田使紫竹林原撥美國租界已行查北洋大臣由

行

戶部左堂張

六月十三日

美國股

呈爲照覆事。光緒二十一年六月初十日准

貴大臣照稱：一千八百六十年北洋大臣在天津紫竹林地方指撥英法美租界各一段，所撥給美國租界由美國領事管理多年。嗣於一千八百八十年十月十二日美領事官照會津海關道，擬將所撥之租界仍交中國管理並聲明嗣後如欲定立工部局章程亦可歸領事官復行辦理是年十月十四日經津海關鄭道照復云嗣後美領事如欲復管理租界須先與關道妥商如何辦法如所定之章程無礙可以照租界原章歸美領事管理均有存案可查現聞有一二國或數别國欲請中國將原撥歸美國租界之地讓與管理相應照會請即咨行北洋大臣無論現欲將原撥美國租界讓與何國立即停止等因查此事本衙門並未聞有此等情形且未據北洋大臣咨行有案恐係傳聞之誤除已咨行北洋大臣查復外相應照復

貴大臣查照可也須至照會者

美國田使

光緒二十一年六月　日

一一九

美國股

呈為咨行事光緒二十一年六月十四日准

咨開據美國駐津領事官李德函稱奉到駐京田大臣來文內稱天津紫竹林英法美租界自西歷一千八百六十年租定後即責令駐津領事常年管理嗣於一千八百八十年經前孟領事照會津海關鄭前道以美國租界設有公所一處目下光景有不方便之處擬欲將公所全行裁撤其地方應仍照舊章辦理如將來美國官員擬再設立之時自應仍准設立以昭允當於光緒六年九月初十日准鄭前道照復以此事應即照辦各在案茲聞中國官員欲將美國租界有轉租之議特飭李領事陳請緩商等情除分飭津海關道天津道會同候選伍道招商局黃道查案妥商辦理相應咨會等

因前來查此事昨於光緒二十一年六月初十日准美國田使照會前因當經本衙門鈔録來照咨行署北洋大臣轉飭關道妥核辦理在案惟此項租界既與美國立有案據自不能另給他國以昭公平相應再行咨行
貴大臣即希轉飭各該道等務將英法美租界妥勘繪具畝數方向圖説并現在擬給德國租界在於何處及畝數方向一併繪圖咨送本衙門以便查核辦理可也須至咨者
李中堂
光緒二十一年六月　日

一二〇

頭品頂戴兵部尚書兼都察院右都御史總督兩廣等處地方軍務兼理糧餉陶　為

密咨事。美法兩國領事擬請於粤省河南地方開設租界一事，節經電咨

貴部密商辦理，迭次承准

貴部電復，以闢作公共租界，英使意見相同，囑即察勘明悉，轉商各領事妥定

具奏等因。正在籌勘辦理間，適英國薩使、德國穆使先後來粤，本部堂及

廣東巡撫部院德與之接晤，談及此事，薩使深以設立公共租界為然，並謂在京

時謁見

慶親王亦以為正辦。美領事請闢租界，康使先並不知。穆使則謂各國如不阻

攔，德國亦無異議，惟他國如在河南自立租界，德國在廣州生意極盛，商人亦

多，應請於河南對岸之花埭地方開一租界各等語。當以此事關繫重要，必

須先事熟籌各國領事意見設有參差終恐議辦無成轉多窒礙是以復經派
員密探各國之意除英領事外餘皆不甚允洽揆其隱衷大率因粵省商務
以英國為巨擘倘設公共租界恐英偏享其利各國領事意見既不相同猝與
議辦一時斷難就範又探據法領事密稱沙面法租界餘地尚可敷三四年之用
推廣租界原不亟亟如他國不提法不催辦前有駐京使署參贊來云美請
租界並非美使之意等語是法請租界意既不甚亟亟美領事所請僅係一己
私見且美商在廣州者甚屬寥寥自以婉却美請從緩置議為宜現接美領
事文稱河南租界一事康使來文催理縱非設詞亦係出自該領事所請除
婉復外相應抄錄來文復稿咨呈倘美使向
貴部提及務請堅持設法推宕是為至禱相應密咨

貴部謹請察照施行

計鈔呈來文復稿各一件

右 咨 呈

外 務 部

附件一

鈔録美國點領事來照會

為照會事，纔接本國

駐京欽差康大臣來文，飭即催理前請將河南地段讓為美國租界之事，並知會本領事官，以此事係先由

貴部堂一人准許後乃再請

皇上批行等因。奉此，本領事官當即會同

貴國

貴部堂商辦讓地一事，然後呈報

北京，敬悉

貴體仍稍違和，倘非奉有

康大臣命，兹斷不以此事親詣煩擾。現

康大臣專候本領事官電復相應，照請

貴部堂賜晤，須刻晤期，最宜即在本禮拜内，並喜於靜室候會，概免官場套文，因彼此和好，均著急力為中美兩國敦崇睦誼也。為此照會，順頌

貴體安好，須至照會者。

光緒二十七年十二月十三日到

復美國點領事照會

為照復事。接

貴領事官十二月十三日照會，以接

貴國駐京欽差康大臣來文，飭即催理前請將河南地段讓為美國租界之事，並以此事須先由本部堂一人准許後再請

附件二

康大臣專候本領事官電復相應照請
貴部堂賜晤頃刻晤期最宜即在本禮拜内並喜
於静室候會概免官場套文因彼此和好均著急
力為中美兩國敦崇睦誼也為此照會順頌
貴體安好須至照會者
光緒二十七年十二月十三日到

復美國默領事照會
為照復事接
貴領事官十二月十三日照會以接
貴國駐京欽差康大臣來文飭即催理前請將河
南地段讓為美國租界之事並以此事須先由本
部堂一人准許後再請

皇上
批行等因照請訂期晤商等由前來查議闢租界
一事前准
來文節經轉咨
外務部核辦嗣接
外務部來電以粤省商務日增各國均有請拓租
界之意若立一國專界他國必請援照辦理諸多
窒礙是以議將該處闢作公共租界而
駐京各國欽差大臣意見不一有欲設立專界有
欲設立公界以致驟難商辦
貴國商人在廣州口者現亦無多尚非亟需租界
居住若從緩商議於彼此均有裨益
貴國於中國之事愛助有素此事當能

格外體諒即希
貴領事官代將此意轉達
康大臣爲荷至
台駕欲惠顧面談並以本部堂抱恙未愈囑請勿
拘煩文具見
關愛情殷曷勝感紉惟本部堂患病日久困憊殊
甚平日偶見僚屬言語稍多即覺喘促且步履維
艱日卧床褥接談諸多不便幸勿有勞
玉趾至爲感荷爲此照復並佈謝忱順頌
日祺須至照會者
光緒二十七年十二月十五日發

[illegible]為

密咨事案照美法兩國領事擬請於粵省河南地方開設租界

一事前接美領事照稱康使來文催理等語業經婉復並鈔錄

來文復稿於本年十二月十七日密咨

貴部察照並以美使倘向

貴部提及務請堅持設法推宕在案茲於光緒二十七年十二月

二十三日接美領事照會仍以請設專界為言除照復外合再鈔

錄來文復稿咨呈為此密咨

貴部謹請察照須至咨呈者

計鈔呈清摺一扣

右　咨　呈

外　務　部

光緒二十八年正月十一日

附件一

鈔錄美國默領事來照會

為照會事案接

貴部堂十二月十五日照會以美國租界一事本領事

官均已閱悉業經電達美國

駐京欽差康大臣知照即奉電復諭開

駐京各國欽差於租界事均同一心並無互異等因

而此事情形

貴部堂自已洞悉一切其德國人已蒙

駐京德國欽差准在花埭地段請劃為德國專界其

法國人已蒙

駐京法國欽差准在河南即與美國請作租界處連

近之地段請劃為法國專界而美國

駐京欽差亦欲在河南地段另劃為美國專界何

貴部堂於此事仍遲疑不決如合國混同公界勢必易

為相觸滋事無論何人一遇有事其咎責難決歸何

國是與各一專界者顯然相反蓋租界各專則各界居

人自必和好相安且中國地方有此各專界商務定益

振興於地方大有裨益現聞有人於美國請為租界

之河南地段起鋪並急買地伊等用意顯為

貴部堂知悉想美國欲照公值之價承之乃近日河南所經

回祿之地現紛紛建造鋪屋並買曠地意欲居奇以逼美

國改用厚價是其意念與美國之意必不相合租界之事

因此延緩辦理則

貴部堂與本領事官均屬無益倘美國當受中國好

處綏辦則領之非甚厚恩現有美商二十五人之多欲
於美國所請租界地段建貨倉住屋等美商中如火
水公司係天下最大最旺之生意也本署時常接美商
稟請於該處覓租界地段而中國無論何處有美國
人到該處即旺此亦久矣成為古語現美商務在中
國南方日益振興敬詢如此綏辦租界之法果合宜否
況美國常以好朋情待中國人用特照請
貴部堂細想公當如何待美國為荷再
貴體現尚違和於心殊多不安惟禱丹誠望秉目下
天氣改常因而全愈也為此照會順頌
日祉須至照會者

光緒二十七年十二月二十四日到

附件二

復美國默領事照會

為照復事接
貴領事官十二月二十三日來文言河南租界一事本部
堂均經閱悉查擬設租界本為振興商務起見必須中
外官民詢謀僉同庶臻妥洽若彼此意見參差徒多
窒礙殊無裨益
駐京各國欽差大臣中如
英國欽差大臣即欲設立公共租界早經照會
外務部而本省紳民亦皆以設立公共租界為然
貴領事官意見既不相同自應從緩商議以免扞格
此事關繫重大無論或設專界或設公界均應由
外務部體察情形核示辦理本部堂不能作主至
河南花棣地方早准洋商承租地基建置棧房屯儲貨
物目下如有
貴國商人欲在該處設棧屯貨儘可自向業主議租田
地呈請地方官援案辦理也賤恙日前似覺漸有起
色近因天氣驟冷喘咳復增屢承
注問感謝無既為此照復順頌
日祺須至照會者

光緒二十七年十二月二十八日發

榷算司

呈爲咨復事光緒二十八年正月初八日接准

函稱美法兩國領事請於粵省河南地方開設租界一事昨

接美領事照稱康使來文催理等語業經婉復相應抄録

來文復稿函送貴部詧照倘美使向貴部提及務請堅持設

法推宕等因前來兹又准

咨稱前因查粵省河南地方各國均未設立專界勢難允美

此事美康使刻下並未來言未便先向提及倘該使向本部商

論自當力爲堅持相應咨復

貴督查照可也須至咨者

兩廣總督

光緒二十八年二月　　日

一二三

具奏閩省鼓浪嶼租界未便兼護厦門擬將該督原訂第十五款章程删除由

署左侍郎那

署右侍郎聯

奏

十月十四日

奏

奏

謹

奏

為閩省鼓浪嶼地方議作各國公共租界未便兼護厦門擬將該督原訂第十五款漢文章程删除恭摺仰祈

聖鑒事竊准光緒二十八年正月間閩浙總督許應騤奏稱閩省厦門為各國通商要埠鼓浪嶼係距厦西南

小島四面環海商賈素稱繁盛自臺灣外屬之後厦門地當衝要民心浮動鎮撫維艱美國巴領事請將鼓浪嶼開作公地藉可保護厦門當由興泉永道延年與各國領事會商再三磋磨時閲數月始克就範現議各款揆以公地之義尚屬相符且厦門均歸一體保護實於地方有裨當將章程草約會同簽字咨送外務部查覈等語臣等細繹該督原奏所稱於兼護厦門一節極為注重乃檢閲原約漢文第十五款載有鼓浪嶼既作公地各國官商均在界内居住厦門為華洋行棧所在商務尤重應由中外各國一體互相保護而檢查洋文於此條則空留未填不特漢洋文原約不符且究竟各國領事於此條曾否議定甚有關繫當即咨行該督查明聲覆去後旋准領銜美國使臣康格照稱鼓浪嶼

公界章程各國兼護廈門一事各使臣以為僅於
鼓浪嶼立租界合同不能言及兼護中國地土
各國領事實無此權即各使臣非奉本國之囑亦
復無此權力合同内立此條款係屬無用請按前
定章程辦理等情復經臣部電令許應騤奏明辦
理茲於九月十七日復准許應騤奏稱鼓浪嶼草
約合同第十五條兼護廈門一節各領事以此條
洋文須候駐京各國公使覈填現在各使既稱領事
無權則外間無從商辦惟華洋合同未便兩歧請
飭外
務部與各國公使仍照華文填寫或即以華文為憑
此項草約本已聲明必須候
朝廷
批准方能遵行倘各使不允儘可將前約作廢等因

臣等伏查厦門地當衝要，實為閩省屏藩。該督議訂鼓浪嶼租界章程，擬令各國一體兼護，意在預防他國專行窺伺，不為無見。惟厦門係中國地方，本非外人所能干預，若明定約章，强令各國互相保護，轉失自主之權。於義無取，若因各國不允保護，遽議將前約作廢，無論各使未必允從，即令就我範圍，竊恐名既不正，言又不順，亦將重貽列邦訕笑。現在領銜使臣康格既稱非奉本國之囑，無此權力，又謂合同内立此條款係屬無用，原訂洋文章程又未載明。臣等公同商酌，不如將原訂漢文章程第十五款保護厦門一節，逕行删除，較為簡淨。查該督咨送鼓浪嶼漢文地界章程第十七款除删去第十五款外，其餘十六款於公地之義尚屬相符，自應請

旨准行以符原約而敦輯睦如蒙

俞允即由臣部咨行該督並照復領銜使臣康格知會各使臣一體遵照辦理所有鼓浪嶼租界未便兼護廈門情形理合恭摺具陳伏乞

皇太后

皇上聖鑒謹

奏

光緒二十八年十月二十一日具奏奉

旨依議欽此

一二四

咨閩浙總督本部具奏鼓浪嶼租界章程删除第十五款一摺録旨鈔奏知照由

行　行

署左侍郎那　十月廿五日
署右侍郎聯　十月廿五日

榷算司

呈爲咨行事。光緒二十八年十月二十二日本部具奏鼓浪嶼租界未便兼護厦門，請將原訂章程第十五款删除一摺，奉
旨：依議。欽此。除照會美國駐京大臣外，相應恭録
諭旨，鈔録原奏，咨行
貴督查照欽遵可也。須至咨者。粘鈔

閩浙總督

一二五

権算司

呈為照會事按查閩省鼓浪嶼公共租界章程第十

五款前准

貴大臣照稱

各國駐京大臣以為僅於鼓浪嶼立租界合同不能言

及兼護中國地土各國領事實無此權即

各國大臣亦復無此權力合同内立此條款係屬無用

等語當經本部電達閩浙總督奏明辦理並由本部

按照

貴大臣照會語意詳晰具摺奏請將此漢文章程第

十五款即行删除期與洋文一律其餘各款於公地

之義均尚符合請

旨依
議欽此除欽遵咨行閩浙總督遵照外相應照會

旨批
准等因本年十月二十二日奉

貴大臣查照並轉達

各國駐京大臣查照可也須至照會者

美康使

光緒二十八年十月　日

一二六

逕啟者昨接本國駐漢口領事官函稱現於該處所商閣日本漢口租界彼所欲展界内有美國人之地該數美國人以將其地歸入日本界内多有不便未能情願等因本大臣茲按所應有本分應行達知貴親王查照如美國人決不願將其地歸入他國界内美國政府亦斷不能應允甚望貴親王迅速設法按所應行辦法以成此事可也特此奉布即頌爵祺附洋文

名另具十二月初四日

附件

F.O.No. 1152

LEGATION OF THE UNITED STATES OF AMERICA,
PEKIN, CHINA.

January 2nd, 1903.

Highness:

The United States Consul at Hankow reports that negotiations are now in progress at that place, contemplating the extension of the Japanese concession, which will include the property of certain citizens of the United States who believe that their interest will be jeopardized by such inclusion.

It is my duty, therefore, to notify Your Highness that the United States Government cannot agree to the inclusion of any property owned by its citizens in any foreign concession without their consent.

Trusting that Your Highness will take such prompt and effective measures as may be necessary in this matter, I improve the opportunity to reiterate the assurance of my highest consideration.

Envoy Extraordinary and
Minister Plenipotentiary
of the United States.

His Highness Prince of Ch'ing,
President of the Board of Foreign Affairs.

一二七

[illegible]九月廿日

詳咨事據署湖北漢黄德道江漢關監督陳兆葵詳稱竊照上年十一月間准職關稅務司斌爾欽照稱據美商美孚洋行稟擬在議展日本租界内萬家廟地方建設火油池並蓋造火油棧房遵照德商瑞記咪吔章程辦理一案前經岑升道以查勘美孚擬建油池棧房基地與中國鐵路車站相近未便准行照復令其另行擇地建造並因駐漢美領事魏禮格照會不願將美孚洋油行之地任別國圈作租界復經援引前定日本初次租界條款分[illegible]美兩領事[illegible]並因續准美領事照稱美孚洋油堆棧費銀二十五萬兩是本不任美孚作事則大受虧折[illegible]錄送駐京大臣[illegible]當將辦理情形詳報

憲台咨明

外務部備查旋奉行准

外務部歌電内開美康使函稱漢口商展日本租界彼所欲展界内有美國人之地多有不便美國人不願將其地歸入他國界内美政府亦斷不允請迅速設法等語希詳查妥籌辦理等因又經查案呈請咨覆在案嗣美國魏總領事迭赴憲轅暨職關饒舌以美孚油池所化費用甚鉅必欲准予設立而後已查該油池[illegible]營造在先其勢難以中止亦係實情不能不予通融辦理以敦睦誼惟萬家廟地方現在雖未劃給日本展拓租界

將來如果定議必須該總領事將他日此地如歸日界當遵租
界章程與日本領事自行商辦不與中國相涉並聲明遵照瑞
記咪吔章程合同凡進口火油每一加倫繳報効捐款錢七分
半即此地日後劃歸日本租界亦須議歸中國收捐照復立案
方能照辦由岑升道暨職道先後照請明晰示復去後茲准魏
總領事照復紐約美孚公司在萬家廟自置地基建造洋油池
棧並另建房舍貿易請貴監督給一允准字樣一案該公司願
遵照二公司章程辦理每十加倫繳捐銅錢七個半文該地方
將來如歸別國租界該總領事自當與該國領事自行商辦不
與中國相涉所有油池捐款前有照復與咪吔瑞記一律辦理
倘日後地歸租界彼時相干此事之人妥議和平抽捐辦法
復查照等因並送華洋文合同一紙前來職道伏查此案既准

美總領事照復美孚油池地基將來如歸別國租界當與彼國
領事自行商辦不與中國相涉[illegible]捐項彼時[illegible]
書立華洋文合同由該總領事簽字蓋戳照送前來[illegible]
建造除照會該總領事查照飭知並札行地方印委各員查照外
理合具文詳報查核咨明
外務部查照等情到本兼署部堂據此相應咨呈為此咨呈
貴部謹請查照施行須至咨呈者
右　咨　呈
外　務　部
光緒二十九年八月　日

一二八

逕啟者本大臣茲有一事達知
貴親王查附近前門東邊城上現在建造小房一處該房地址係稍有佔使館租界請查閱一千九百零一年九月初七日所立和約附件十四款並是年六月三十日領銜大臣所致中國全權大臣之照會即可曉然按此附件照會所言在城墻上使館西界丿字處在城墻上正陽門樓東一百英尺自此處界綫往北稍偏二百十六英尺至乙字即係大清門前周基盤街白石欄東南角云云本大臣茲非願刻即拆去此房惟須向
貴親王聲明寔係有佔租界地址並欲
貴國政府明晰本國政府必不能照允若將來本國政府索此佔用地址
貴國政府即須將所建之房往西拆移也特此泐布即頌
爵祺 附送洋文

名另具 十月初五日

附件

F.O. No.

Legation of the United States of America,
Pekin, China.

Nov. 23d. 1903.

Your Imperial Highness:-

I have the honor to call Your Imperial Highness' attention to the fact that there has recently been built upon the city wall just east of the Ch'ien Men a guard house, which encroaches to some extent upon the boundary of the Legation Quarter, as may be seen by a reference to the Final Protocol of Sept.7th. 1901, Annex No. 14 and the letter of the Dean of the Diplomatic Corps of June 30th. 1901 to the Chinese Plenipotentiaries. From these documents it appears that the limit of the Legation Quarter at the point mentioned is fixed at a distance of 100 feet from the East side of the superstructure of the Ch'ien Men, and is further determined by the statement that from this point the boundary runs almost due North to the South-east corner of the white stone balustrade which incloses the open paved space before the principal entrance of the Imperial City.

I have no disposition at present to insist upon the removal at once of the guard house, but call Your Imperial Highness' attention to the encroachment that has been made, that Your Government may understand that the United States does not acquiesce in it and that, should occasion require, my Government may demand the removal of the guard house to a point outside the lim-

its

2

(F.O. No.)

its of the Legation Quarter.

I have the honor to seize this opportunity to renew to Your Imperial Highness the assurance of my highest consideration

Envoy Extraordinary and
Minister Plenipotentiary of
the United States.

To His Imperial Highness, Prince of Ch'ing,
President of the Board of Foreign Affairs.

一二九

敬肅者日昨奉
鈞函敬悉正陽門東堆撥房有佔美使館租界各節查敝處此次承修正陽門城上堆撥小房係照舊基丈尺建蓋監修委員不知堆撥房基已於二十八年劃歸美國新租界之内致有此誤殊深抱歉惟門樓工程限期促迫各項應用料物均在該房堆存無處遷徙美國公使來函亦謂非願刻即拆去足見其誼敦友睦辦事和衷無任感佩現仍擬暫時借用此項地段俟工程完竣再酌量遷移應請
大部函復美國公使可也肅復恭請
鈞安

袁世凱
陳璧謹肅

十月十六日

再啟者：肅覆正函係按照美使函稱租界丈尺轉飭監修委員將新建之東堆撥房詳加丈量，實屬有佔租界地址，特聲明現擬借用工竣遷移等語，庶可兩全。至美使所稱附件照會及乙字、丙字兩處界址是否相符，

來函未經敘及，應請

飭查明確，再據徼處所肅正函轉覆美使，以昭慎重。再肅，恭請

鈞安

袁世凱
陳　璧　又肅

十月十六日

一三〇

春卿
康民 仁兄大人閣下：昨會同袁慰公為復陳一函，當達
鈞署矣。十九日派正陽門工程總辦王、尹兩道詣商康使，議有辦法，
可否將會銜復件暫緩照復美使，容弟再行會袁制軍銜復呈
鈞署，准據二次復函照會，尤為公便。蓋康使允我不住人、不置物，此
堆撥始終不折也。耑泐馳商，即敂
均安

弟璧頓首 十月二十日

一三一

敬肅者日前接准

鈞函敬悉正陽門東堆撥房有佔美使館租界各節查敝處承修正陽門樓東堆撥房係照舊基丈尺建蓋不知該房地基已於光緒二十八年載入美使館租界之内致有此誤殊深抱歉惟現在各項物料均在該房堆存無處遷移美國公使來函亦謂非願刻即拆去足見其誼切邦交和衷辦事無任感佩現仍擬借用以後搭架豎柱所需地段尤寬擬請一併借用以便工作至堆撥小房東西各有一所將來工竣所有東堆撥房現用租界地址如美國

政府暫不需用擬請美國公使派員會同敝處勘明即將該房門窗用磚砌閉非特不准住人並不存放物件不過留此東邊房座以配西邊房座俾備觀瞻尤爲感洽當飭天津道王仁寶候補道尹家楣於十月十九日已刻前往美國使館將以上酌擬辦法詳細面達均經美國公使一一允准由該道等禀覆前來相應函達大部查核辦理可也肅此恭請

鈞安

袁世凱
陳璧 謹肅

十一月初九日

一三二

逕復者昨接

貴親王函復承修正陽門東邊城上建造堆撥小房一事、本

大臣茲已閱悉工程處袁陳二大臣、囑天津王道仁寶候補尹

道家楣來館面談、誠有此事、惟謂於該二道所言、本大臣一

一允准、則微有錯處、即係所言將來工竣仍留此東邊房座、

以配西邊房座之一語、本大臣所言固有並非願刻即拆去之

語，並有言將來若各國欽使公會以爲應行拆去所佔租界之房，

貴國必須照拆辦理，是以應再備函聲明，即請

貴親王將昨函内所敘與該二道面談之言即行改正，免致將來有所誤會，所應重申之言係該東邊城上之房，有佔租界之址，嗣後各欽使公會以爲應行拆去，

貴國即應照辦可也，特此泐復，即頌

爵祉。附送洋文

名另具　十一月十三日

F.O. No.

Legation of the United States of America,
Pekin, China.

Dec. 31, 1903.

Your Imperial Highness:-

I have the honor to acknowledge the receipt of Your Imperial Highness' note of yesterday concerning the guard house at the east side of the Ch'ien Men on the city wall.

It is true, as reported by their Excellencies, Yüan and Ch'en of the Bureau of Public Improvements, that the Tientsin Taot'ai, Wang Jen-pao, and the Expectant Taot'ai, Yin Chia-mei, called to see me regarding the matter, but the statement made by them is slightly inaccurate. I said that I did not demand that the house should at once be torn down, but I also said distinctly that if at any time the Diplomatic Corps should decide that it ought to be removed, it would be necessary to have that portion which encroaches upon the boundary of the Legation Quarter taken away. It therefore becomes necessary for me to write again to Your Imperial Highness to correct the statement made by the Taot'ais Wang and Yin, as quoted in your note of yesterday, that I consented that the guard house on the east side of the gate might remain in order to preserve the symmetrical appearance of the gate. It must be clearly understood that the building encroaches upon the Legation Quarter and must be removed whenever the Diplomatic Corps may so request.

I

2

(F.O. No.   )

I avail myself of the opportunity to renew to Your Imperial Highness the assurance of my highest consideration.

E. H. Conger

Envoy Extraordinary and

Minister Plenipotentiary

of the United States.

To His Imperial Highness, Prince of Ch'ing,

President of the Board of Foreign Affairs.

一三三

敬肅者前奉
鈞函具悉美國康使覆稱正陽門東邊城上建造堆撥房一事前
經天津王道仁寶等來館面談誠有此事惟謂於該道等所言
本大臣一一允准則微有錯處即係將來工竣仍留此東邊房屋
以配西邊房屋之一語本大臣固非願刻即拆去惟將來若各國
欽使公會以為應行拆去此房貴國必須照辦應再備函聲明
請即更正免致誤會等因又查前次
貴部轉到十月初五日美國康使函内亦有本大臣兹非願刻即

拆去此房若將來本國政府索此地址即須將所建之房往西拆
移等語敝處前覆之函所稱將來工竣如美國政府暫不需用此
項地址擬請留此東邊房屋以配西邊房屋藉備觀瞻等語係
僅承茲非願刻即拆去此房一語而言自應再行聲明以免誤會
所有東堆撥房現用地段若將來美國政府索此地址即將所建
之房往西拆移准可照辦應請
大部函覆美使可也肅此恭請
鈞安
陳璧謹肅
十一月二十一日

再肅者敝處前次覆函所稱暫不需用擬請留此房座以備觀瞻等語固已暗含有如果需用仍可拆移之意兹美使恐將來誤會函請聲明自應添出此層仍乞飭查和約附件並照會一切是否相符再行具覆以昭慎重而免歧誤是為至要再肅恭請

鈞安

陳璧又肅

一三四

逕啟者：茲有甚關營口商務一事函達
貴親王，美國駐營口總領事官來函云：該處有數美商欲於營口對面遼河地方置買地段，該地係坐落平常行用地界之内，原係河塘葦地，經沙淤嗣複填土成岸，有數華人欲將此地賣與洋人。該美商以此地未悉彼是否果有執業確據，不無疑慮，是以請本大臣代爲轉詢。一此項地段是否

係中國官地二如係官地是否可租抑可買用三如
可租與買應向何官員相商並有何租與買之章等因
相應函達
貴親王查照希即轉行查明望早
見復是荷此泐即頌
爵祺附送洋文
名另具九月二十七日

柔克義

附件

LEGATION OF THE UNITED STATES OF AMERICA,
PEKIN, CHINA.

To F.O. No. October 25th.1905 .
W.

Your Imperial Highness:- I have the honor to ask the attention of Your Imperial Highness to a matter which deeply concerns the commercial interests of the port of Newchwang (Ying-k'ou).

I am in receipt of a despatch from the American Consul General at that port, stating that certain American citizens , doing business in the port, want to purchase lands on the opposite bank of the Liao River, but within what are regarded as the limits of the port. These lands consist of reed lands and certain fore-shore accretions adjoining them, and have been offered for sale by certain Chinese, but, as there appears to be some doubt as to their title to the lands, the American Consul General requests me to ask Your Highness

1° Whether or not the lands in question belong to the Chinese Government; and, if they do,

2° Whether or not they can be purchased or leased of the Chinese Government; and

3° If open to lease or purchase, to what authorities application should be made to learn the price and other conditions of sale or lease.

Trusting that Your Imperial Highness will favor me with an early reply, I avail myself of the occasion to renew to Your Highness the assurance of my highest consideration.

E.E. & M.P. of the United States.

To H.I.H. Prince of Ch'ing,
President of the Board of Foreign Affairs,
etc. etc. etc.

一三五

榷算司

呈為咨行事光緒三十一年九月二十七日准美柔使函稱茲有美國駐營口總領事官來函云該處有數美商欲於營口對面遼河地方置買地段該地係坐落平常行用地界之內原係河塘葦地經沙淤嗣復填土成岸有數華人欲將此地賣與洋人該美商以此地未悉彼是否果有執業確據不無疑慮是以請本大臣代為轉詢一此項地段是否係中國官地二如係官地是否可租抑買用三如可租與買應向何官員相商並有何租與買之章等語將此函達查照希即轉行查明望早見復等因前來相應咨行貴將軍大臣查照迅速查明此項地畝是否官荒有無民人盜賣情事迅速聲復以便轉復美柔使可也須至咨者

盛京將軍

北洋大臣

光緒三十一年十月　日

一三六

欽差大臣盛京將軍兵部尚書都察院右都御史總督奉天旗民地方軍務兼理糧餉趙　為

咨呈事。承准

大部咨開：光緒三十一年九月二十七日准美柔使函稱：茲有美國駐營口總領事官來函云：該處有數美商欲於營口對面遼河地方置買地段。該地係坐落平常行用地界之内，原係河塘葦地，經沙淤嗣復填土成岸。有數華人欲將此地買與洋人。該美商以此地未悉彼是否果有執業確據，不無疑慮。是以請本大臣代為轉詢一此項地段是否係中國

官地二如係官地是否可租抑可買用三如可租與買應向
何官員相商並有何租與買之章等語特此函達查照希
即轉行查明望早見復等因前來相應咨行貴將軍查照
迅速查明此項地畝是否官荒有無民人盜賣情事迅速
聲復以便轉復美柔使可也等因承准此查該處地畝原
係葦塘向歸
盛京工部管理確係官地且地在遼河之北並未開為通商口岸
亦未定有租買章程至民間有無盜賣情事自應飭查

嚴禁相應咨覆為此咨呈

大部謹請查照轉覆施行須至咨呈者

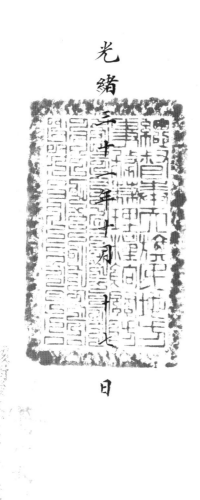

右咨呈

外務部

光緒三十一年十月十七日

一三七

欽差大臣太子少保全權大臣參預政務大臣會辦練兵大臣督辦電政大臣鐵路大臣兵部尚書都察院右都御史辦理北洋通商事宜直隸總督部堂袁　為

咨呈事據山海關道文韞申稱光緒三十一年十月初十日
蒙憲台札開十月初三日准
外務部咨開九月二十七日准美柔使函稱茲有美國駐營
口總領事官來函云該處有數美商欲於營口對面遼河地
方置買地段該地原係河塘葦地經沙淤嗣復填土成岸有
數華人欲將此地賣與洋人等語轉行迅速查明此項地畝
是否官荒有無民人盜賣情事具復核咨等因蒙此查營口
河北一帶葦塘係屬官地早年有民人王姓等五家由

盛京户部領有執照按年認納葦税所産蘆葦歸該五家出售
歷有年所嗣於光緒二十五年間有駐營口英國領事及日
本領事先後函請將河北葦塘劃作英日租界當經明前故
道保分稟前憲台暨
奉天軍督憲
總理各國事務衙門核准旋經明道會同英日領事在於河
北中國鐵路界限之外留有餘地一百丈以為將來辦公局
所之地此地迤東劃有日本租界一段計東西寬三百丈南北
長一百四十丈又東劃有英國租界一段丈尺與日本相同
此外所餘之地仍歸葦商經理將來開辦之時所佔地段准

其銷去葦課繪圖存案尚未辦理茲事營口遠遭兵燹案卷
燬失無存本年九月初二日接有營口英國領事祿福禮來
函以河北葦塘現在該票商王姓五人擬將餘地出賣據
云係奉
旨允准之事查光緒二十五六年本國領事曾與貴前道商劃租
界皆以該塘係官地並無華商私產現在該地有英商價買
本領事竊有所疑用特專函奉詢查明復知等因當即函復
英領事聲明該塘實係官地未便令英商價買以免葛藤正
擬札飭海城縣查禁間據署海城縣知縣管鳳龢呈稱本年

九月初二日接准美國撒總領事照會內開據本國商行美孚
商人麥克司林聲稱今憑中價租到河北葦塘之地二段共
計一百八十三畝三分三厘三毫共合洋六萬四千一百六
十六圓五角五分經該商挽中立永遠出租地契二紙前來
存案并請稅契等因本總領事查葦塘本係五大票商已產
永遠出租應由地方官稅契合行備文照會并將該契二紙
送照貴縣請煩飭差丈量蓋用印信貼粘契尾是否之處即
祈貴縣查覆施行須至照會者計照送營口河北葦塘永遠
租契二張等因准此正在飭差往查旋准英國祿領事函開
本口河北葦塘現在該票商王姓五人擬將餘地出賣據云

條奉

旨允准之事查光緒二十五六年本國領事曾在河北劃商租界

皆以該塘係官地並無華商私產現該地有英商價買本領

事竊有所疑用特函詢貴縣查明復知是荷等因卑職查英

領事所稱光緒二十五六年商劃租界卑署、無案可稽現在

應如何核辦理合呈請迅賜查案酌核示遵等情職道當據

前劃英日租界並葦塘原屬官地各等情批飭照覆美英兩

國領事請其查禁洋商並由該縣設法查禁私售各在案茲

奉前因除再飭海城縣查覆外理合先將辦理情形申覆查

核轉咨

外務部實爲公便等情到本大臣據此相應咨呈

貴部謹請查照須至咨呈者

右 咨 呈

外 務 部

光緒三十一年 月 日

一三八

上 四月十九日

照會

大亞美理駕合衆國欽命駐劄中華便宜行事全權大臣康　為

照會事西四月二十七號准

貴親王照會以勘估奉天安東兩處新開商埠劃界定章之事當於二十八號照復在案茲應達知

貴親王美政府已派有駐劄營口總領事撤門司為代美政府會同華員勘定安東租界並商定一切章程請將中政府所派辦理此事人員能在何時何處與本國所派撤總領事會同商辦早為示悉俾該員

等得以按約商酌合宜辦法以期不致遲延勘定

為要為此照會

貴親王查照須至照會者附送洋文

右 照 會

大清欽命全權便宜行事軍機大臣總理外務部事務和碩慶親王

一千九百六年五月拾貳日

光緒叁拾貳年肆月拾玖日

附件

AMERICAN LEGATION,
PEKING, CHINA.

To F.O. No. 125

W. May 12, 1906.

Your Imperial Highness:-

Referring to Your Imperial Highness' despatch of April 27, concerning the selection of sites for the foreign settlements and the adoption of regulations for the control of the same at the newly opened ports of Mukden and Antung, and to my reply of April 28, last, I now have the honor to inform Your Highness that the American Consul General at Newchwang, Mr. Thomas Sammons, has been appointed to represent the American Government in the matter of determining a suitable locality for the proposed settlement at Antung and arranging regulations for the same, and I have the further honor to request that Your Imperial Highness will at as early a date as possible inform me when and where Mr. Sammons may meet the officer deputed by the Chinese Government to act in this matter, so that they may consult together, as required by the Treaty, and that all questions involved may be satisfactorily disposed of without delay.

I avail myself of the occasion to renew to Your Imperial Highness the assurance of my highest consideration.

W. W. R.

American Minister.

To His Imperial Highness, Prince of Ch'ing,
President of the Board of Foreign Affairs.

一三九

榷算司

呈爲照復事。接准

照稱：美政府已派駐紮營口總領事撤門司代美政

府會同華員勘定安東租界，並商定一切章程，請

將中政府所派辦理此事人員能在何時何處與撤

總領事會同商辦，早爲示悉等因。當經本部電詢

盛京將軍、北洋大臣去後，茲准復電稱：已電約美國

撤總領事於本月二十四日來奉，在省會同開埠局員

商辦等語。相應照復

貴大臣查照可也。須至照復者。

美國柔使

光緒三十二年四月 日

一四〇

川二　五月初八日

大亞美理駕合眾國欽命駐劄中華便宜行事全權大臣柔　為
照會事據本國駐營口總領事文稱該處有不愜
意之事即係奉天大吏阻碍在該處租地人稅契
一事該處美孚行租地一段將所立之契呈送蓋平
縣請蓋用印信該令云若願照納新章所定之稅可
允稅契該行當即允遵照納嗣奉省洋務局奉軍
憲諭阻此辦法內云一照通商口岸章程洋人租地
應由關道衙門稅契若由縣逕行稅印殊屬荒謬

二今營口租界尚未劃定在未經劃界以前永租地畝

顯背約章云云本大臣想

貴親王應不俟明言業知該口係按一千八百五十八

年中英兩國立約開作通商口岸該約係於一千八

百六十年批准互换於六十一年即准洋人在營口租地

通商由彼時迄今均准洋人租地建房租界雖未劃定

按照此約洋人寔有租地權利茲已閲四十五年忽

云未劃定租界不允税契此言係不合理人所盡悉

似屬顯然

貴親王並應知此未經劃界口岸不獨營口在他處

口開辦多年尚亦有未經劃定之處該未劃之處

已有洋人費用鉅款建立行棧生意興隆若忽改此辦

法必俟劃定界址始准税契係待洋商實爲不公

至洋行請縣税契弗請關道緣近二三年中有戰

事該處並無關道是以無法只可在縣税契按中

例縣令係有征收中國人税契之責該任營口洋人

於未有關道之時按近年辦法請縣印契亦係理所宜

然相應照會

貴親王查照希即咨行該省轉飭該地方官不再延緩

即按美孚行所請准其稅契可也須至照會者 附送洋文

右 照 會

大清欽命全權大臣便宜行事軍機大臣總理外務部事務和碩慶親王

一千九百陸年陸月貳拾玖日

光緒叁拾貳年伍月初捌日

AMERICAN LEGATION,
PEKING, CHINA.

To F.O. No. 141

W. June 28, 1906.

Your Imperial Highness:-

I have the honor to call the attention of Your Imperial Highness to a complaint submitted to me by the American Consul General at Newchwang that the Chinese authorities at Moukden have interfered to prevent the registration of land titles at the port of Newchwang.

It appears that the Standard Oil Company, having purchased a tract of land at the port of Newchwang, sent the deeds to the Magistrate of K'ai-p'ing District, who agreed to register them, provided the fees required by the new Regulations should be paid. The Company agreed to this, but the Bureau of Foreign Affairs at Moukden, acting under instructions from the Viceroy, wrote to the Consul General objevting to this procedure on the grounds, (1) that the Regulations regarding treaty ports require deeds to land leased by foreigners to be registered by the Customs Taot'ai, wherefore their registration by the District Magistrate would be irregular; and (2) that the boundaries of the foreign

To His Imperial Highness, Prince of Ch'ing,
President of the Board of Foreign Affairs,
etc. etc. etc.

eign settlement at the said port have not yet been defined, so that the leasing of land to foreigners is not in accordance with Treaty provisions.

I need hardly remind Your Imperial Highness that the port of Newchwang was opened to foreign residence and trade by the British-Chinese Treaty of 1858, ratified in October 1860, and that the foreign settlement was established at Ying-k'ou in 1861, since which time foreigners have been permitted by the Chinese authorities to lease ground and build houses. It seems quite plain that, if the limits of the settlement have never been clearly defined, that can not now be adduced, after 45 years, as a reasonable objection to the continued enjoyment of a right granted by the Treaty mentioned. It is well known to Your Imperial Highness that the settlement at the port of Newchwang is not peculiar in this respect; there are several ports open now for many years to foreign residence and trade, the limits of whose settlements have never been clearly defined. It would be manifestly unjust to those who have invested their capital at these ports and developed important business interests if now by a sudden change of policy the registration of land titles were to be stopped until at some indefinite date in the future the limits of the settlements could be accurately determined.

As to the registration of deeds by the District Magistrate instead of the Customs Taot'ai, this seems to have been made necessary by the withdrawal of the Taot'ai during the recent military occupation. Inasmuch as the

registration

registration of deeds for Chinese subjects is one of the duties of the District Magistrate, it seems but right that so long as the functions of the Customs Taot'ai are suspended foreign residents of Newchwang should register their deeds also in the District yamen, as they appear to have been doing for some time past.

In view of these facts, I have the honor, therefore, to request that instructions be issued to the authorities concerned to allow the deeds of the Standard Oil Company to be registered without unnecessary delay, as requested.

I avail myself of the occasion to renew to Your Imperial Highness the assurance of my highest consideration.

Envoy Extraordinary and
Minister Plenipotentiary
of the United States.

一四一

咨盛京將軍美孚洋行在營口租地應由該縣報明閱道稅契由

左侍郎聯 行 五月十一日

右侍郎唐 行 五月 日

榷算司

呈為咨行事光緒三十二年五月初八日准美國柔使照稱據本國駐營口總領事文稱該處有不愜意之事即係美孚行租地一段將所立之契呈送蓋平縣請蓋用印信該令云若照納新章所定之稅可允稅契該行當即允遵照納餉奉省洋務局奉軍憲諭阻此辦法內云

一照通商口岸章程洋人租地應由關道衙門稅契若由縣經行稅印殊屬荒謬二今營口租界尚未劃定在未經劃界以前永租地畝顯背約章云云本大臣按一千八百五十八年中英立約該口開作通商口岸洋人實有租地權利茲已閱四十五年忽云未劃定租界不允稅契此言係不合理似屬顯然至該行請縣稅契并請關道緣近二三年中有戰事該處並無關道只可在縣稅契該住營口洋人按近年辦法請縣印契亦係理所應然請咨行該省轉飭該地方官不再延緩等因前來本部查營口係通商口岸美孚洋行在該處租地投稅係按約辦理勢難禁阻該行既已援照近年辦法報縣請印應由該縣將原契轉呈奉錦山海關道

驗明蓋印以符定章除照復英使外相應咨行
貴將軍查照轉飭遵照辦理並聲復本部以便
轉復可也須至咨者
盛京將軍

光緒三十二年五月　日

一四二

欽命鎮守盛京等處將軍兵部尚書都察院右都御史總督奉天旗民地方軍務兼理糧餉趙　爲

咨呈事。光緒三十二年五月十六日承准

貴部咨開：光緒三十二年五月初八日准美國柔使照稱：

據本國駐營口總領事文稱：該處有不愜意之事，即係美

孚行租地一段，將所立之契呈送蓋平縣請蓋用印信，該

令云若照納新章所定之税，可允税契。該行當即允遵照

納嗣奉省洋務局奉軍憲諭阻此辦法，内云一照通商口

岸章程，洋人租地應由關道衙門税契，若由縣徑行税印

殊屬荒謬二今營口租界尚未劃定在未經劃界以前永租地畝顯背約章云云本大臣按一千八百五十八年中英立約該口開作通商口岸洋人𡨋有租地權利兹已閱四十五年忽云未劃定租界不允税契此言係不合理似屬顯然至該行請縣税契弗請關道緣近二三年中有戰事該處並無關道只可在縣税契該住營口洋人按近年辦法請縣印契亦係理所應然請咨行該省轉飭該地方官不再延緩等因前來本部查營口係通商口岸美孚洋行

在該處租地投稅係按約辦理勢難禁阻該行既已援照近年辦法報縣請印應由該縣將原契轉呈奉錦山海關道驗明蓋印以符定章相應咨行貴將軍查照轉飭遵照辦理並聲復本部以便轉覆等因承准此查營口洋商租賃房地稅契一事現在各國領事皆照會有案不獨美孚洋行一處爲然迭經本軍督部堂照覆須俟該口交還租界劃定後方能照章辦理等因各在案良以該口通商雖已歷四十五年之久惟從前劃定之租界早已被水冲失

其時該口洋商不過數家租賃房地亦不過零星數處故未續議另劃界限所有洋商租賃房地契據均由海蓋兩縣就近印税現在該口商務漸臻繁盛且中日條約有劃定該口租界明文自未便仍照向來辦法致與將來劃界一事轉多窒礙是以前次英德瑞奥各領事轉行呈請税契之時當即查得該商等所租房地或距該口有十餘里之遥將來萬難劃入且關道現亦不駐該口礙難照舊辦理即未便遽予税契此近來該口洋商税契均未遽即照

准之原因也今美領事既據美孚洋行呈請照會

貴部轉咨應由關道飭縣税契等因查該地距洋人現在所

居不遠將來當能劃入界内自可通融先行照准惟他國相

距過遠者不得援以爲例除分札飭遵外相應咨呈

貴部謹請查照施行須至咨呈者

右　咨　呈

外　務　部

光緒　　　　　　　日

監印官候選知縣啟綱

校對發文官藍翎補用防禦繼恩

一四三

逕啓者兹將崇文門内孝順胡同美以美女佈道會所買房地各産新舊契紙二十七卷凡九十二張及該會地圖一紙一併附送

貴部查照緣該會産業多係庚子年以前所購均經納過稅項該契於庚子年間被匪燬搶無存現所送之二十七卷契據係圖内有四處黑綫闌内之契據是以本大臣即請

貴親王轉囑該管衙門將該會庚子年前後所買之産業按圖内四址立爲契據一張希送本館轉交收執是荷特此順頌

爵祺 附契紙二十七卷 圖式一張

並附洋文

名另具 六月十二日

附件

LEGATION OF THE UNITED STATES OF AMERICA,
PEKIN, CHINA.

To F.O. No.
W. August 1, 1906.

Your Imperial Highness:-

I have the honor to inclose in separate cover and forward herewith twenty-seven lots of deeds, numbering altogether 92 documents, new and old, and covering purchases of land made by the Women's Foreign Missionary Society of the Methodist Episcopal Church of the United States.

I send also in the parcel containing the deeds a plan of the property of the said Mission in Peking.

Most of this property was purchased before the troubles of 1900 and stamped deeds were granted for the same. These deeds were all destroyed during the Boxer Rising of that year. The deeds now sent cover the portions marked with a black line on the plan.

I have the honor to request that one official deed be issued for the whole lot of ground, both that portion purchased prior to the troubles of 1900 and the small pieces bought since that date.

I avail myself of the occasion to renew to Your Imperial Highness the assurance of my highest consideration.

W. W. Rockhill

American Minister.

To His Imperial Highness, Prince of Ch'ing
President of the Wai Wu Pu.

一四四

照復美參使美孚洋行在營口租地投縣税契因房地距洋人所居不遠自可通融先行照准由

行 行

左侍郎聯 六月十四日

右侍郎唐 六月十二日

榷算司

呈為照復事。前准照稱美孚洋行在營口租地税契一事，當經本部咨行奉天將軍轉飭洋務局援照近年辦法所有美孚洋行在營口租地投税，報縣請印。由該縣將原契轉呈奉錦山海關道驗明蓋印，以符

定章去後茲准復稱查中日條約有劃定營口租
界明文洋商租房稅契自未便仍照向來辦
法是以前次英德瑞典各領事轉行呈請稅契之
時當即查得該商等所租房地或距該口有十餘
里之遙未便遽予稅契今美孚洋行所租房地
距洋人現在所居不遠自可通融先行照准推
相距過遠者不得援以為例等因前來相應
照復
貴大臣查照可也須至照復者
美柔使
光緒三十一年六月

一四五

逕復者西本月初七日准
貴部函復以崇文門内女佈道會請立總契一事云所送之
二十七卷契據均係庚子年閏八月間所購未經納過税項
之契其庚子以前所購已經納税之契既被匪搶燬無存自應
補契該會請將前後所置之産總立契據一張應請轉囑該會
將庚子前所置之産共㡀起某年月納過税銀若干開具清單

補送等因當即轉知該會開單去後茲據稟稱庚子前所置
之產底册已經焚燬無從開送又未便由他處查考備具清單
云云至所送二十七卷契紙已經送部尚未稅契一節應請
貴部將該各契共須納稅若干開明該會自必按照交納也特復
即頌
時祉 附洋文
名另具 六月二十一日

柔克義

附件

AMERICAN LEGATION,
PEKING, CHINA.

TO F.O. No.

W. August 10, 1906.

Your Imperial Highness:-

I have the honor to acknowledge the receipt on the 7th. inst. of a note from Your Imperial Highness' Board, in relation to the application of the Women's Missionary Society for an official deed to its property situated within the Ch'ung-wen Gate. Your Highness says that the property covered by the 27 lots of deeds sent was all purchased in the Intercalary Eighth Moon of the year 1900, and that the registration fees for these deeds have not yet been paid; that as to the property registered before 1900, deeds to which were destroyed by the Boxers, substitute deeds will of course be issued, but, that, as the Mission requests one official deed for the whole property, Your Highness' Board asks that the Mission be instructed to prepare and forward a list, stating how many pieces were bought, the dates on which the deeds were registered, and the amount of the fees paid.

In reply I have the honor to say that I have requested the Mission to prepare the list asked, and am now in receipt of a reply, saying that, as all the records of the Society

were

To His Imperial Highness, Prince of Ch'ing,
President of the Board of Foreign Affairs,
etc. etc. etc.

were destroyed in 1900, it has no data from which such a list can be prepared.

As to the new deeds sent, registration fees for which have not been paid, the Mission will of course pay the fees required by Regulation, when notified of the amount due.

I avail myself of the occasion to renew to Your Imperial Highness the assurance of my highest consideration.

Envoy Extraordinary and
Minister Plenipotentiary
of the United States.

榷算司

呈為劄行事接准美柔使函送崇文門內孝順胡同美以美女佈道會所買房地各產新舊契紙二十七卷凡九十二張及該會地圖一紙並稱該會產業多係庚子年以前所購均經納過稅項該契於庚子年間被匪燬搶無存現所送之二十七卷契據係圖內有四處黑線闌內之契據請轉囑該管衙門將該會庚子年前後所買之產業按圖內四址立為契據一張送本館轉交收執等因當經本部函復該使轉飭該會將庚子年以前所買產業共有幾起於某年月納過稅銀若干分晰開具清單補送本部以便併各契紙轉行查核辦理去後茲准復稱據該會稟稱庚子前所置之產底冊已經焚燬無存又未便由他處查考備具清單云云至所送之二十七卷契紙應請貴部將各該契共須納稅若干開明該會自必按照交納等因前來本部查美使送來契紙二十七卷均係庚子年閏八月間所購產業未經納過契稅之件其庚子年以前所購已經納過契稅之契紙既據稱於庚子年被匪燬搶無存自應查照向章准其補契至該教會請將庚子前後所購產業

歸總立爲契據一張應由順天府轉飭該管地
方官按照圖内四址詳查庚子年前所購産業
已經納税之案是否相符並庚子年後所購未經
納税之契紙二十七起共應納税若干分别查明繕
立總契以便轉交收執相應將原送契紙二十七
卷照譯圖式一張並鈔録本部與美使來往各函
劄行順天府酌核辦理迅即申復可也須至劄者

附原送契紙二十七卷 照譯圖式一張 抄録來往各函

右劄順天府府尹 准此

光緒三十二年六月 日

一四七

順天府爲咨呈事

案准

貴部文開接准美柔使函送崇文門内孝順胡同美以美女佈道會所買房地各産新舊契紙貳拾柒卷凡玖拾貳張及該會地理圖一紙並稱該業多係庚子年以前所購均經税過税項該契於庚子年間被匪燬搶無存現已送之貳拾柒卷契據係圖内有四處黑綫閩内之契據請轉囑該管衙門將該會庚子年前後所買之産業按圖内四址立爲契據送本館轉交收執等因當經本部函復該使轉飭該會將庚子年以前所買産業共有幾起於某年月日納過税銀若干分晰開具清單補送本部以便並各契紙轉行查核辦理去後兹准復稱據該會稟稱庚子年前所置之産冊底焚燬無存又未便由他處查考備具清單云云至所送貳拾柒卷契紙應請貴部將各該契共須納税若干開明該會自必按照交納等因前來本部查美使送來

契紙貳拾柒卷均係未經納稅之契其已經納稅之契紙據稱於庚子年被匪燬搶無存自應查照向章准其補契至該會請將庚子年前後所購產業歸總立爲契據一張應由順天府轉飭該管地方官按圖内四址詳查庚子年前所購產業已經納稅之案是否相符庚子年後所購未經納稅之契紙貳拾柒卷共應納稅若干分別查明繕立總契以便轉交收執等因到府准此業經本衙門將原送契紙貳拾柒卷照譯圖式壹張並抄錄來往各函札發大興縣遵照辦理去後茲據該縣詳稱當經飭差會同美國達牧師中華劉牧師執持地圖前往崇文門内孝順胡同按圖查明四隣並無轇轕妨礙情事惟查該會納稅之案卑縣自經庚子兵燹卷檔不全無憑查考茲查該會共房地二十七處其中共永租得房十三處價銀一千四百八十七兩又轉租房一處價銀四百兩又買得房地十一處價銀

八百零五兩又買得房一處價銀一百五十兩共
計房地二十六處合價銀二千八百四十二兩應納
稅捐庫平足銀一百四十兩零六錢七分九厘每
張契尾合銀三錢官紙銀一錢又內有第二
十七號孝順胡同路南房一所僅有紅白老契
各一張並無賣與該會字據其價銀稅銀
若干無憑核算等因具詳前來本衙門細加
查閱該會納稅之案自經庚子兵燹卷檔不
全無憑查考至所購二十七處契紙內有一處
並無賣與該會字樣其餘契紙多係永
租轉租字據均應分別確切查明方可
准予稅契除批示外相應將原送契紙二

十七卷一併咨覆
貴部請煩函詢查核明白酌定辦法知
行轉飭遵照辦理可也須至咨呈者
計咨送 原契紙二十七卷
右 咨 呈
外 務 部
光緒叁拾貳年[illegible]月 拾捌 日

一四八

榷算司

呈爲咨行事。所有本部照復美使辯論奉省通商居住地界一事，業於本月十七日鈔稿函達在案。兹准美使復稱，貴國政府恐商人雜居各處不爲方便，本國政府願讓此端權利，限美商居住租界以内，不過先須承認美商於約内所列權利，即係於奉天、安東二城内外附近地方貿易，有權在該各處設立棧房，用華人於該各處代辦生理，免納内地一切稅項等語。相應抄録來照，咨行貴將軍查照，酌核商辦，並聲復本部可也。須至咨者。

奉天將軍 粘抄

光緒三十二年十二月　日

一四九

逕啓者、前以美國美以美女佈道會、於崇文門內、孝順胡同、所
買數處地段契據一事、於一千九百六年、九月十二號、接到
貴部來函、內云、查該會納稅之案、自經庚子兵燹、卷檔不全、無
憑查考、該會租買房地二十六處、合價銀二千八百四十二兩、應
納稅捐、庫平足銀一百四十兩零六錢七分九厘、每張契尾合銀三
錢、官紙銀一錢、又內有第二十七號一所、僅有老紅契白契各一張、

並無賣與該會字樣等因，當經本大臣據情轉達該會，茲復收
到第二十七號賣與美以美會契紙一張，轉送
貴親王查閱，至以税契之税單，因庚子兵變，檔卷不全，無憑查
考，未悉付過税價與否，是以該會現按照
來函所列之數，交與本大臣滙豐銀行支票，庫平銀一百五十六
兩四錢八分，特爲交納二十七張契税，及契尾官紙等全費之

用此票即轉送

貴親王查照，甚盼足數所用，即請轉飭該管官員，如能將契紙、上塡

統歸列成一契，或書永租，或寫賣契，均可。若果碍難辦理，亦可

仍按二十七張税契，即請税畢送還，以便轉給收執可也。特此函

達，順頌

爵祺。附洋文及契紙一張、

銀票一張。

名另具 二月十二日

柔克義

附件

AMERICAN LEGATION,
PEKING, CHINA.

To F.O. No.228.
W.

March 25 1907.

Your Imperial Highness:-

On September 12 1906 I had the honor to receive from Your Imperial Highness' Board a reply in reference to the registration of deeds to certain property in the Hsiao Shun Hu T'ung, purchased by the Women's Foreign Missionary Society of the Methodist Episcopal Church of the United States, in which I was informed that, as the records had been destroyed in 1900, there were no data to show that the fees had been paid for any of the deeds; that there were twenty-six pieces which had been either bought or leased for sums aggregating Tls 2,842, the fees upon which would amount to K'u-p'ing Taels 140.679; that the fee for the certificate attached to each deed would be Tls 0.30 and for the official paper Tls 0.10; and that there was one other piece for which one old red deed and one white one were produced, but no deed of transfer to the Mission.

I at once communicated the substance of the above note

To His Imperial Highness, Prince of Ch'ing,
President of the Board of Foreign Affairs,
etc. etc. etc.

note to the Mission, and am now in receipt of the missing deed to the twenty-seventh lot, which I forward inclosed to Your Imperial Highness.

Inasmuch as it is impossible to produce evidence of the payment heretofore of any of the fees due upon the deeds, the Mission has also sent me a check for K'u-p'ing Taels 156.48 in payment of fees due upon all the deeds.

I send this check inclosed to Your Imperial Highness, and trust that it will be found sufficient to cover the expenses, as reported in the note above-quoted. I have the further honor to request that, if it be possible, the authorities concerned will issue one deed for the whole property, either of sale or of perpetual lease, as this will be more convenient. If, however, this should prove to be impossible, I have to request that the deeds may be registered in the usual manner.

I avail myself of the occasion to renew to Your Imperial Highness the assurance of my highest consideration.

Envoy Extraordinary and
Minister Plenipotentiary
of the United States.

卅

照會

大亞美理駕合衆國欽命駐劄中華便宜行事全權大臣柔　為

照會事茲接駐漢口美總領事來函云日本官員與中國地方官議商展闢日租界一事該處有美國美孚洋行所置之地一段坐落於所擬展界之內日領事擬定欲將該行之地歸入該管轄下美總領事已於地方官未允此辦法之先辯駁不允華官將美商地產劃入日本展界內歸其管轄等因查此事本大臣無庸長言致辯不過應行聲明定不允湖廣總督議商何約將美商在未定該約之先所置地產歸於他國轄下管理無論所定展界約內已聲明此地段歸何國管轄或未聲明此節日後謂該地既在何國所展界址之內即應歸何國管轄本大臣均不能照允並不允

貴政府將如是劃展租界之約批允也特此照會

貴親王查照須至照會者　附送洋文

右

大清欽命全權大臣便宜行事軍機大臣總理外務部事務和碩慶親王

一千九百柒年叁月貳拾伍

光緒叁拾叁年貳月拾貳日

附件

AMERICAN LEGATION,
PEKING, CHINA.

To F.O. No.
H.

March 25, 1907.

Your Imperial Highness:

I have the honor to inform Your Imperial Highness that I have received a communication from the American Consul General at Hankow with regard to the Japanese Concession Extension Agreement at that place. In this communication he says,

(1) that the property of the Standard Oil Company of New York is situated within the limits of this extension.

(2) that the Japanese Consul has stated that according to the Agreement the property of the Standard Oil Company must be included with that which is under their authority and control.

(3) that before the Agreement was ratified, he had protested emphatically to the Viceroy, stating that the Company could not be forced to enter the Japanese Concession, and that he could not acknowledge the right of the Chinese to turn them over in that way.

I think it is unnecessary to do more than point out to Your Imperial Highness the fact that the property in question was purchased by the Standard Oil Company from the Chinese some time before the Japanese Concession extension Agreement was drawn up, and that therefore I cannot but strongly object to the making of any agreement by the Viceroy of Hu Kuang, or the ratifying

thereof

thereof by the Chinese Government, when such agreement carries with it either the stipulation or the understanding that authority over any property previously purchased by American citizens or American firms is thereby transferred to any other nationality.

I avail myself of the opportunity to renew to Your Imperial Highness the assurance of my highest consideration.

W. W. Rockhill

Envoy Extraordinary and
Minister Plenipotentiary
of the United States/

To His Imperial Highness, Prince of Ch'ing,
President of the Board of Foreign Affairs?
etc etc etc

榷算司

呈爲劄行事前准

咨覆以美以美女佈道會所買孝順胡同房地稅契一事當經本部函詢美使查明見復去後茲准函稱接到貴部來函内云查該會納稅之案自經庚子兵燹卷檔不全無憑查考該會租買房地二十六處合價銀二千八百四十二兩應納稅捐庫平足銀一百四十兩零六錢七分九厘每張契尾合銀三錢官紙銀一錢又内有第二十七號一所僅有老紅契白契各一張並無賣與該會字樣等因經本大臣據情轉達該會茲復收到第二十七號賣與美以美會契紙一張轉

送查閲至以稅契之稅单因庚子兵燹檔卷
不全無凭查考未悉付過稅價與否是以該
會現按照來函所列之數交與本大臣匯豐
銀行支票庫平銀一百五十六兩四錢八分特
為交納二十七張契稅及契尾官紙等全費之
用即轉送查照並請轉飭該管官員如能
將上項契紙統歸列成一契或書永租或寫
賣契均可若果碍難辦理亦可仍按二十七
張稅契即請稅畢送還以便轉給收執等
因前來相應將美使原送來契紙二十七卷
並補送契據一張劄行順天府尹酌核辦
理可也須至劄者 附契紙二十七卷又契據一張並銀票一張

右劄順天府府尹 准此

光緒三十三年十月 日

咨呈

順天府爲

咨覆事前准

貴部文開據美使函稱美以美女佈道會所買孝順胡

同房地二十六處應納稅捐銀兩並二十七號契紙壹張洋文

銀票壹紙如數交到請轉送酌核辦理等因到府准此

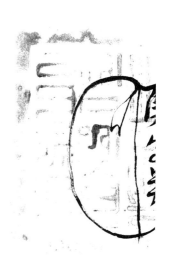

當經本衙門札發大興縣遵照查明分别粘尾蓋印去
後茲據該縣詳稱該會租買二十七處房地共價銀貳千
玖百肆拾貳兩應納税庫平銀壹百肆拾伍兩陸錢貳
分玖釐又契尾官紙銀肆錢共庫平足銀壹百肆拾陸兩
零貳分玖釐擬合將税妥紅契並原發契紙合併詳送
再所發匯豐銀行支票據該行言稱票内未經農工商部
加蓋印信不准支取茲將原票附呈轉請一併咨明等情
具詳前來本衙門復核無異除批示外相應咨呈

貴部查照轉行支給見覆可也須至咨呈者

計送税契紅契壹套　原發契紙壹張

銀票壹紙　紅白契貳拾陸卷

右　咨　呈

外　務　部

光緒叁拾叁年貳月　貳拾玖　日

一五三

止

大美國欽命駐劄中華便宜行事全權大臣柔

公文灋章

一千九百柒年 貳拾壹

光緒叁拾叁年伍月拾壹日

收 三十三年五月十一日

照會

大亞美理駕合衆國欽命駐劄中華便宜行事全權大臣柔 為

照會事。本年西三月二十五號，本大臣照會

貴親王以漢口美孚行所置之地產，不允歸於日本

租界一事，該照會所論因美孚所置中國民產，係置

於日本展界合同之前，不過達知

貴親王設地方官訂立合同，或

貴政府批准之合同內，有將美商地主之權，議讓

與他國，本大臣不能不行辯駁等因，迄今未准照，

復查此案頗易明晰、本大臣所論亦甚合理、且未
復行照會、茲復接有論及此事之函、是以復申前
說、再行照會
貴親王查照、並望見復可也、須至照會者、附洋文

右　照　會

大清欽命全權大臣便宜行事軍機大臣總理外務部事務和碩慶親王

一千九百柒年陸月貳拾壹日
光緒叁拾叁年伍月拾壹日

LEGATION OF THE UNITED STATES OF AMERICA

附件

AMERICAN LEGATION,
PEKING, CHINA.

To F.O. No.

M.

June 21, 1907.

Your Imperial Highness:

On March 25th of this year I had the honor to address a communication to Your Imperial Highness with regard to the effort being made at Hankow to include some property belonging to the Standard Oil Company within the limits of the new Japanese Extension Concession at that place.

In that letter I stated that I thought it would only be necessary to point out to Your Imperial Highness the fact that the property in question had been purchased by the Standard Oil Company from the Chinese before the Japanese Extension Agreement was drawn up, and that I could not but object, therefore, to the making of any agreement by the local officials, or to the ratifying thereof by the Chinese Government, if any authority over property belonging to American citizens or American firms is thereby transferred to another nationality.

Up to the present time no reply to my note has been received, but the case is such a simple one, and the objection on my part so reasonable, that I have not referred to the matter a second time. Now, however, the case has been called to my attention again, and it becomes my duty, therefore, to communicate with Your Imperial Highness once more reiterating my former objection and requesting that you will give the matter your early attention.

I avail myself of the occasion to renew to Your Highness the assurance of my highest consideration.

W.W. Rockhill

To His Imperial Highness, Prince of Ch'ing.
President of the Board of Foreign Affairs.

一五四

榷算司

呈為照復事光緒三十三年二月十三日接准

來照所有漢口美孚行所置地産不允歸日本展

界管轄一事當經本部於二月十五日電達湖廣總

督查明電復去後迄今未據查復兹復准

照稱前因除再行電達湖廣總督從速查明電

復外相應先行照復

貴大臣查照可也須至照會者

美柔使

光緒三十三年五月　日

一五五

大亞美理駕合衆國欽命駐劄中華便宜行事全權大臣柔　為

照會事西本年三月二十五號本大臣以漢口地方官擬將美

孚行所置地產歸於日本租界轄下一事照會

貴親王延至西六月二十一號三月之久未准照復故於是日

本大臣復行照會提議此事至六月二十六號准復稱當經本部

於二月十五日電達湖廣總督查復去後迄未查復茲准前因已再

行該督速復等語查此事自本大臣初次照會

貴部至電催該督速復時已六月之久現又延至數禮拜之期

貴部仍未將該督如何查覆知照是以本大臣不能不再達

貴親王本館係以此事為緊要甚望早得照復以免焦急可也須

至照會者 附送洋文

右 照 會

大清欽命全權大臣便宜行事軍機大臣總理外務部事務和碩慶親王

一千九百柒年玖月初拾日

光緒叁拾叁年捌月初叁日

附件

AMERICAN LEGATION,
PEKING, CHINA.

To F.O. No. 302

H. September 10, 1907.

Your Imperial Highness:

On March 25th of this year I had the honor to address a note to Your Imperial Highness with regard to the attempt being made at Hankow to include some property belonging to the Standard Oil Company within the limits of the new Japanese Extension Concession at that place.

Nearly three months later, on June 21st, no reply having been received to my former letter, I again communicated with Your Highness reiterating my former most reasonable objections to such action.

On June 26th I received Your Highness' acknowledgement of the receipt of these letters. You informed me therein that upon receipt of my first ~~letter~~ telegraphic instructions had been sent to the Viceroy of Hu Kuang directing him to report upon the matter by telegraph, and that upon receipt of my second a further telegram had been despatched urging him to send this reply at once.

It is now many months since my first letter, and many weeks since these last urgent instructions were sent to the Viceroy, but no reply from him has been communicated to me as yet. It becomes my duty therefore to call Your Highness' attention once more to this important matter, and to state that this Legation anxiously awaits a reply from Your Imperial Highness.

I avail myself of this opportunity to renew to Your Imperial Highness the assurance of my highest consideration.

W. W. Rockhill

To His Imperial Highness, Prince of Ch'ing,
President of the Board of Foreign Affairs.

一五六

照復美su使美孚地產不願劃入日本租界希向日本自行商議由

行　行

左侍郎聯　八月十七日　行

右侍郎汪　八月十七日

署右侍郎梁

權算司

呈為照復事漢口美孚行所置地產歸于日本租界

轄下一事前准

照會當經電催護鄂督速復去後兹准復稱此事

張前督曾面告美領事並委員與之辯論華外國租

界內多有他境商人行棧惟有照本國商人一律看待

便是公平如必不願在日本界内可往下游自行覓
地遷移中國地方官只能幫同尋覓如有無礙之地
可勸導地主賣給倘因此攔阻中國與他國所給租
界則萬不能等因前來本部查外國租界内他境商
人行棧既照本國商人一律看待實係公平辦法自無
因此攔阻中國劃展租界之理如該美商必不願將
所置地産劃入日本租界希由
貴大臣飭美領事向日本領事自行商議相應照復
貴大臣查照可也須至照復者

美柔使

光緒三十三年八月

一五七

卅

照會

大亞美理駕合衆國欽命駐劄中華便宜行事全權大臣柔　爲

照復事。西本月二十四日接准

來照，以美孚行在漢口所買地産歸日本租界轄下一事。

貴親王云此事不能攔阻中國與他國開展租界，請飭美

國總領事與日本領事官議結等因。查此事現又生有

繁雜，即係漢口道又不肯將地契蓋印。該行末次所買

之地，係於西去年十二月間立契，惟因待至本年二月間

方送道蓋印，該道謂該地所置之時，無憑係在展

交日本租界之前、總領事有足可憑之據、亦可送道
查閱、此次地契實係按照上開年月買定、並悉去年
十二月間該行曾將所買之契、呈交本領事、係在未展
日本租界以前、其延日未即送道蓋印之故、係因尋
覓糧卷所致、迨至尋獲、即於二月初八號照送關道
云云、查
貴親王已請本大臣行飭美領事與日本領事官
議結此事、相應即請

貴親王查照，速飭該道即以美領事所云憑據為準，
並即刻蓋印，不得因該道延誤，俾本大臣與
貴親王經手之案不得先行了結也。須至照復者。附洋文

右　照　會

大清欽命全權大臣便宜行事軍機大臣總理外務部事務和碩慶親王

一千九百柒年玖月貳拾捌日

光緒叁拾叁年捌月貳拾壹日

AMERICAN LEGATION,
PEKING, CHINA.

To F. O. No.

H. September 26, 1907.

Your Imperial Highness:

I have the honor to acknowledge the receipt of Your Highness' note of September 24, 1907, on the subject of the inclusion of the property of the Standard Oil Company at Hankow within the limits of the Japanese Concession Extension, in which Your Highness states that the ownership of this property by these American merchants cannot be permitted to stand in the way of China's granting the concession extension and asking me to instruct the American Consul to consult with the Japanese Consul with regard to a settlement of the question.

The settlement of this question is delayed and complicated by the refusal of the Taot'ai at Hankow to stamp the deeds of sale of this property to the Standard Oil Company. The last of these deeds was made in December of last year (November 16th, December 15th, 1906) but as it was not presented for stamping until February, 1907, the Taot'ai states that district officials cannot recognize it as evidence that the sale was made prior to the granting of the Japanese Concession Extension, because said deed was not presented to the officials for stamping at the time it was made out.

The

To His Imperial Highness, Prince of Ch'ing,
President of the Board of Foreign Affairs,

The American Consul at Hankow is prepared to furnish proof to the Taot'ai that these deeds were made on the date which they bear, and were delivered to the Consul in December, 1906, a long time before granting the Japanese Concession Extension, and that his delay in presenting them for stamping was due to the absence of certain tax receipts which he afterwards obtained and forwarded to the Taot'ai along with the deeds on February 8th last.

Inasmuch as Your Imperial Highness has requested me to deal with the Japanese authorities with regard to the inclusion of this land in their concession, I have the honor to request that the Taot'ai be instructed to accept the proof of the American Consul as to the truth of the date of these deeds and to stamp the same without delay, so that the settlement of this question may not be delayed by him.

I avail myself of this opportunity to renew to Your Imperial Highness the assurance of my highest consideration.

一五八

照復美費署使漢口美孚地產一事准護鄂督電稱美領未送印之先已劃入租界未便印給契據由

行 行

左侍郎聯 九月 日

右侍郎汪 九月初二日

署右侍郎梁

榷算司

呈爲照復事。美孚行地產歸日本租界轄下一事，

前准

貴大臣照稱：漢口道不肯將地契蓋印，該行末次所買之地，係於西去年十二月間立契，惟因待至本年二月間方送道蓋印，該道謂置地之時無憑係在

展交日本租界以前總領事有足可憑之據可送道
查閱請速飭該道即以美領事所云憑據為準即
刻蓋印等語當經本部電達護湖廣總督查明
情形辦理去後茲准復稱飭據關道查復美孚
買華商史普生基地係於三十三年正月初六准美
領補送契卷請飭蓋印　日本展拓租界係於三十
二年十二月內訂定條款是前項基地美領未經送
印之先業已劃入日本拓界內自未便再聽華民
賣與他國商人致起轇轕雖史普生所立新契
書有三十二年十月立字樣然當時並不即行送
請印稅地方官無從得知即不能認為先買之據
是以未便印稅等情查業已劃入租界之地不便

再聽華人轉賣印給契據致起糾轕該道係
屬照章辦理希照復美駐京大臣等因前來相
應照復
貴署大臣查照可也須至照復者
美費署使
光緒三十三年九月　日

一五九

仁

大亞美理駕合衆國欽命駐劄中華管理全權事務大臣貴　爲

照復事西本月八號接准

照復本館柔大臣上月二十六號照會請漢口關道將美孚行地

契蓋印一事

貴親王惟將兩湖護督所復稱飭據關道查復美孚買華商

史晉生基地係於三十三年正月初六日准美總領事補送契卷

請飭蓋印日本展拓租界係於三十二年十二月內訂定條款是前

項基地美領未經送印之先業已劃入日本拓界內自未便再聽

華民賣與他國商人致起轇轕雖史普生所立新契書有三十二年
十月立字樣然當時並不即行送請印税地方官無從得知即不能
認爲先買之據是以未便印税等情查業已劃入租界之地不便再聽
華人轉買印給契據致起轇轕該道係屬無章辦理希照復美駐京大
臣等因查此事内只有該地契是否係在華歷去歲十二月間展拓
租界定議以前所立按向常辦法總以立契之日爲憑如有謂契内
所書年月不寔者必應有該人出爲左證此事美總領事轉願爲之
作証以明該地契寔係立於西上年十二月之時足見係於中歷十二

月之先已經立契不必將該關道未便聽華民賣與他國商人之一
語爲憑總應以總領事所言爲確證設視此猶爲不足該領事尚有
他據送閱相應按柔大臣西上月二十六號所請再請
貴親王轉飭漢口關道將該契速行蓋印並望早日允准見復
可也須至照會者 附送洋文

右　照　會

大清欽命全權大臣便宜行事軍機大臣總理外務部事務和碩慶親王

一千九百柒年拾月拾壹日
光緒叁拾叁年玖月初伍日

附件

Fa

AMERICAN LEGATION,
PEKING, CHINA.

To F.O.
No.

October 10, 1907.

Your Imperial Highness:

I have the honor to acknowledge the receipt of Your Imperial Highness's Note of the 8th instant, in reply to Mr. Rockhill's note of September 26th last requesting the stamping of the deeds for the land purchased by the Standard Oil Company at Hankow

Your Imperial Highness quotes the reply of the Temporary Acting Viceroy of Hu Kuang, to whom this matter was referred, as follows:

> "The Customs Taot'ai, whom I directed to look into the matter, reports that the deeds and tax receipts for the land purchased by the Standard Oil Company from Shih P'u-sheng were received from the American Consulate-General for stamping on February 13, 1907; that the Japanese extension agreement was made in the twelfth moon of the last Chinese year (January 14th to February 12th), or before the deeds to the property were received from the American Consul; that since the property is situated within the limits of the Japanese Concession extension as marked out, it is not possible to take the word of a Chinese subject who says that he previously

sold

To His Imperial Highness, Prince of Ch'ing,

President of the Board of Foreign Affairs,

Etc., etc., etc.

sold the property to a merchant of another nationality; that as regards complicating matter, although the new deed made out by Shih P'u-sheng, bore the date of the 10th Moon of the 32nd year of Kuang Hsu (November 16th to December 15th, 1906) still, inasmuch as it was not sent at that time to be stamped, the local officials had no means of knowing that the property was purchased on the date mentioned; they could not, therefore, recognize the date on the deed as evidence that the property was previously purchased, and had to refuse consequently to stamp the deed.

"It appears to me that, inasmuch as the Concession has already been granted, we cannot afterwards take the word of the Chinese subject who sold the property as evidence upon which to stamp the deed. As to the complications, there are no regulations under which the Taot'ai can act otherwise than as he did. Will you kindly reply to the American Minister to this effect?"

The only point at issue in this case is whether the deed in question was executed before January 14-February 12, 1907, (the Twelfth Moon of the last Chinese year), in which month the Japanese Concession extension was granted.

Ordinarily a deed is presumed to have been executed on the day it bears date, and the burden of proof is on him who asserts the contrary, but in this case the Consul is prepared to go farther and to certify,- to prove if necessary,-

that

that the deed in question was presented to him in December, 1906, and that it must, therefore, have been executed before January-February, 1907. The Taot'ai is, therefore, not obliged to take, as he says, "the word of the Chinese subject who sold the property", but can have absolute proof of the facts.

It is my duty to repeat the request contained in Mr. Rockhill's note dated September 26, 1907, and I trust that Your Imperial Highness may see Your way clear to give such instructions as will secure the prompt stamping of these deeds, the facts being as above-stated.

I avail myself of this opportunity to renew to Your Imperial Highness the assurance of my highest consideration.

Henry P. Fletcher

Chargé d'Affaires.

一六〇

榷算司

呈爲照復事。漢口美孚洋行地契請蓋印一事，本年九月初六日接准

照稱：該地契實係於華歷去歲十二月間展拓租界定議以前所立，美領願爲作証，請飭漢口關道速行蓋印等因。經本部電達湖廣總督，轉飭商辦去後。茲准電復稱：美孚地契已飭關道印稅，美領既願作証，如有糾葛，美領應擔責任，祈轉告等語。相應照復

貴署大臣查照可也。須至照會者。

美費署使

光緒三十三年九月　日

美國商船在台遭風略　無年月日　同治六年三月間

同治六年三月間，有美國商船一隻，名羅妹，在台灣琅𤩝洋次
紅頭嶼冲礁擊碎，船主水手共十四人坐杉板逃至琅𤩝尾龜仔
鼻山登岸，被生番將十三人殺害，逃出中華水手一名至台灣港口
向英國領事報明，僱水手坐兵船一隻往該地方查驗，尚未登岸，
忽見叢林中放鎗及鳥槍，致傷一人。經美國駐京大臣照會總理
衙門，請行知閩省地方官會同美國兵官查辦，總理衙門
以該處雖係生番，究係中國地面，必須設法妥辦，行由
閩省督撫辦理。此中國地方由中國官辦理，總理衙門行
文催辦，並無他義也。生事處美國駐廈領事李讓理
暨美國帶兵官在台灣照知鎮道，請兵會辦，台
灣道吳大廷有台地生番穴處猱居，不隸版圖
之説，而其係生番回台地生番仍告以其意祇謂生番爲中國地方不隸版圖係中國之人
辦理，並未推諉不認，彼時李領事即謂台
灣統地，歷今二百餘年，爲中國管轄，即
生番亦歸轄地人，非華民，地屬華土云云，是
李讓禮即確知台灣生番歸中國管轄，地屬

華土也。迨後經閩省督撫以事關重大，斥台灣道
前文言爲非，以事關重大派前任台灣鎮曾元福、同知王文棨、
前往會同現任台灣鎮道等，帶領兵勇，迋至枋
藔伐山開路，直抵琅𤩝，設法招令番目卓杞篤
綑送兇番，務期盡法懲辦，而李讓禮堅爲生番
乞恩，據稱十八番社互約，嗣後遇有遭風中外
船隻，必加保護，請免深究，如再有前項情事，閩
粵頭人當立保結，幫拿兇番，旋有閩粵頭人暨
番目卓杞篤等，亦到營出具甘結，如前説，然後
撤兵回國。此李讓理躬親之事，設其地非中國
地土，閩省督撫何以如此辦法乎？即以此案而
論，總理衙門文書如此，閩省督撫辦理如此，其
爲中國土地無疑矣。大廷所言已經駁斥，且該
道亦有候中國辦理之説，何得據以爲言？且況彼
此案件，無庸牽涉，兩國辦事，應以條約爲憑，以
章程爲憑，即引證案件，亦應以結案辦法爲憑，
豈總理衙門文件、閩省督撫辦法，皆不足憑，而指
一曾經斥駁議論偶及之言爲憑乎。

一六二

頭品頂戴兵部尚書兩江總督部堂劉 為

知照事光緒十八年閏六月二十日准

吏部咨内閣抄出劉坤一片再光緒十四年間江蘇安徽兩省水旱為災經前督臣

曾國荃奏准部議開辦蘇皖賑捐咨行各省廣為勸募推及外洋凡華人之

出洋貿易者仰懷

聖朝德澤普徧遐荒莫不慷慨好施輸捐助賑節經曾國荃分別奏咨給予獎敘

嗣經前出使美日秘等國使臣張蔭桓經勸在美之華商捐洋二萬九千四百八十五元

有奇滙由上海交前蘇松太道龔照瑗分解江蘇安徽河南山東等四省賑濟當

以此項捐款張蔭桓來咨已在部限截止獎案之後照章不能給獎即經曾國荃

撰擬匾額致送以昭激勸迄今時閱四年固不得為重請獎勵而該商等在山陬

荒僻之區猶能捐集鉅款救災卹隣其急公好義之忱亦不可沒臣 清理案

牘如有此等善舉不敢壅於

上聞理合附片陳明伏乞

聖鑒謹

奏光緒十八年五月二十二日奉

硃批着劉坤一傳旨嘉獎欽此欽遵抄出到部相應知照可也等因到本部堂准此

相應咨會為此合咨

貴大臣請煩查照施行須至咨者

右

咨

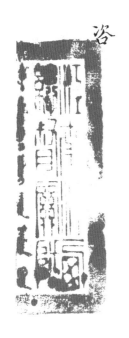

總理各國事務衙門大臣張

光緒十年閏五月初九日

伍大人鈞鑒敬啟者紅十字會已在牛莊設立分局俾
得醫治因此戰受傷之人其有危難者亦可代為
保護本局共派辦事人十員代理俄美華丹德
英六國襄辦一切局事以美領事米勒爾為
總辦渥布司特爾為司事達勒為支應官現
已速議詳細章程過有應為之事即可作速
辦理茲特早日奉
聞俾
大人得知牛莊地方已立此會一切局事均歸以上各
員管理本局將特行設法考查滿洲内地居民之
情形該處居民如有危難時本局即可仰懇
大人助成本局之舉凡關保護華民應為之事
大人如有所見即請
示知則合力辦理成功更易矣專泐順頌
日祉
駐營口美國領事總辦米勒爾
司事渥布司特爾
全啟
一千九百零四年三月二十五日由牛莊具

一六四

三月廿日

咨呈

欽差出使美秘古墨國大臣梁　為

咨呈事竊照本大臣於光緒三十年二月初十日在美都華盛頓使署拜發具

奏擬請聯約各國仿設紅十字會摺一件單一件相應鈔稿咨呈

貴部謹請察照須至咨呈者　附鈔件

右咨呈

外務部

光緒三十年二月初拾日

附件

奏為擬請聯約各國仿設紅十字會以廣
皇仁而裨軍政恭摺仰祈
聖鑒事竊臣伏讀
諭旨設練兵處參用各國章程期成勁旅仰見
皇太后
皇上整軍經武發奮圖强實深欽佩臣維我武維揚
聖人原不得已之舉民命至重王者有不忍人
之心近今各國行陣救疾扶傷不分畛域其法
良意美尤推紅十字會為最該會命意畧如內
地善堂以拯灾卹難為義務而於國政宗教不
相關涉與會之人出入行間各國皆公認為局
奏稿　清秘閣
外同治三年始於瑞士國之真奈瓦地方創設
公會議定條約十款鐵押者十二國嗣後推行
日廣各國次第入會歷年兵事無役不從甚至
后妃命婦之尊亦能不避艱危親調醫藥論者
謂於兵凶戰危之中行仁至義盡之道文明進
化已信有徵而將士恃此志氣益揚忠勇百倍

尤為兵家制勝之長策環球各國日孳孳然討
論而利用之中國尚未聯約入會似非
聖朝恩周庶類整飭戎行之本意惟會體宏大經費
浩繁基礎未堅勢難集事臣查各省善堂成效
昭著董其事者富而好善若令兼辦可毋庸另
設會所至於籌集經費自以勸募為正義儻蒙
奏稿　清秘閣
天恩酌撥內帑為臣民倡明定賍格按捐資之多寡
別勳章之高下捐款鉅者准佩帶該會金銀銅
寶星次者准用該會徽章再次者亦得列名會
籍用紅十字為衣飾以京師善堂為總會復於
行省商埠酌設分會平時施醫贈藥兼辦軍醫
學堂戰時防病療傷責令隨營照料遇有他國

兵事亦一視同仁派人前往經歷愈多收效愈
廣軍醫可資補助將士恃以無虞竊以為我
皇太后
皇上如天之仁超越隆古必有以慰薄海喁喁之慕
也臣體察近情覺紅十字會為練兵不可少之
舉謹將貞奈氏公會聯約條款各國入會年分

奏稿　清秘閣

暨美國紅十字會章程譯成漢文照錄清摺恭呈
御覽並就管見所及畧陳辦法擬請
飭下外務部照會瑞士國政府聲明願入紅十字會
聯約緣由俟覆文到日專派大員簽約一面查
取東西洋各國紅十字會章程按照現在情形
參訂會章頒發總會剋期舉辦庶幾上張

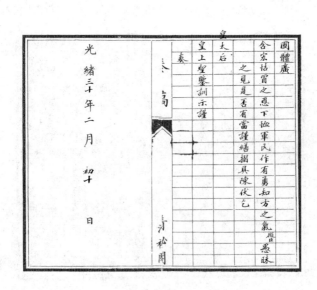

國體廣
含宏括冒之恩下恤軍民作有勇知方之氣臣愚昧
之見是否有當謹繕摺具陳伏乞
皇太后
皇上聖鑒訓示謹
奏

奏稿　清秘閣

光緒三十年二月初十日

一六五

王爺殿下
大人閣下三月十六日沈道敦和任道錫汾施道則敬送
閱津電轉奉
商部飭催上海萬國紅十字會捐册當經商酌備具
公函檢同捐册一百本寄交
大部司務廳轉送當蒙
鈞鑒緣自客臘上海中國紳商聯合英法德美在滬紳商會議至今春二月特設上海萬國紅十字會公舉中國記名海關道沈敦和前四川川東道任錫汾直隸候補道施則敬為中國辦事總董英按察威金生副總稅司裴式楷英工部局董安德生高易律師麥尼而教士李提摩太法工部局董勃魯那德國寶隆醫生美國豐裕洋東葛羆為西國辦事總董麥尼而將會章詳細譯明中西分別募捐酌設分會醫院救護戰地無關戰事人民出險應商請兩戰國政府承認先由中國與商沈道等因與海寰等熟商以上海絲業會館為中總董辦事處凡與西董會議及交涉各事由沈道等三人合辦一面邀集眾紳商刊擬捐啟聯名公寄各省各埠懇為勸募一面籌擬商請兩戰國承認之法適奉
商部電囑勸辦因據情電復並電請
大部與日俄駐使電駐日俄使商請兩戰國政府承認又准北洋往來電商南北合辦乃兩戰國政府均以已設有紅十字會足敷分布為詞而戰地情形日亟勢難延待迭經中西總董會議以營口最為衝要先行設立分會由美領事密勒教士魏伯詩德等遴舉中西董事酌設醫院並救護無關戰事人民出險該處向無法人據稱已舉丹國人俄國人與會就近商明該處俄官允准照辦海道業已梗塞難民出險祇可取道鐵路以距山海關天津較遠深恐照料不及又由滬遴舉蘇紳候選通判張慶桂同知周傳誠帶同俄法英文繙譯人等附輪至津商請
袁慰帥示飭與賑撫局毛道慶蕃會辦張紳等函商

營口於該分會已展設奉天遼陽分會外再添設新
民屯溝邦子山海關塘沽四處分會電滬請添派人
往辦事又由滬遴舉歷辦義賑同辦庚子東南濟急
會之蘇紳直隸候補知縣劉芬指分直隸候補知州
任錫琪雲騎尉世職徐信謨前安徽候補通判左楨
並令酌帶向曾共事可靠之員友俾可分投辦事以
資得力現正部署啟行滬又添設煙台分會以聯津
滬旅青之氣查此會宗旨重在醫療其救護難民出
險一層本係條議中之緒餘實為今日之要著蒙
大部一再據情轉商並已奏請
頒給駐英張星使全權補畫瑞士總會原約尚有應行聲明
之處擬另備函電商請張星使酌辦俄政府久無復
音似已無暇及此日政府於救護難民出險一層據
總領事面稱必可商辦惟戰地情形迭據各分會電
函及迭次來人籲訴自去秋以來農氓失業商賈裹
足日用昂貴耕畜餘糧概被搜括俄兵每退於可攜

帶之物外必焚燬無遺轉瞬飢荒自在意中向來飢
荒之後必有大疫將來分局施診施藥亦須籌及現
在分會傳單所到僑民均陸續内徙而土著之人則
以出走亦無以為生仍祇株守待斃東三省雖向為
産糧之區農氓久已失耕秋收無望亟應接濟惟幅
員遼濶無論禁令如何糧食從何購運隨後甚煩計
議目前山海關外俄兵將退日兵未到鬍匪横行人
有戒心各分會均依傍鐵路車站與北洋官紳聯絡
一氣據報截至三月底止合營口奉天遼陽新民屯
溝邦子山海關六處救護出險難民二千餘人均有
名册來電據稱即當錄寄又據烟台分會電由沙河
東溝等處民船冒險渡到第一次一百餘人二次三
百餘人工匠居多酌量撫恤資遣隨後造册函報除
總分會往來電報商懇免費外所有輪船火車又
懇蒙
袁慰帥飭由毛道慶蕃印摯免票在事南北官紳一

體領用其有已給免票而尚難啟行者按口量與津貼俾回原籍或另謀生尚無出險而致失所之人其未領用免票以前各該分會商明車站於各人手心衣襟鈐印圖記分起派人護送至火車站驗明免費運送醫院現祇設營口一處購運藥物兩次現又擬購寄各該分會治暑防疫諸藥品所費均尚無多至在事中西官紳士商中西總董因皆不支薪水夫馬西總董公延書記月薪由英法工部局捐給中總董公延繙譯書記月薪及油燭筆墨紙張由滬道等另行設法籌給各分會中西董事暨由滬前往之張周劉任徐左諸紳亦不支薪水其沿途來往川費所用繙譯書記人等均萬不可少斷無再令捐給之情理均令量給薪水據實樽節開支就目前而論捐啟分寄各省荷蒙籌募陸續撥寄滬市則下至優伶亦集資相助具見好善人有同心經費尚無虞不給惟將來分會推廣兼辦賑濟其地方廣潤難限其時日久暫難知所費浩繁設竟見絀點金何術將何以仰體

聖慈如傷之隱慰災黎待命之情此尤旰夕旁皇難安寢饋而不能不遍呼將伯也前

倫貝子過滬經在會紳商面陳辦理情形蒙諭捐啟刋印告成可寄交帶至沿途各埠酌量勸募遵經並寄三百本並分別並寄各國駐使暨張弼士張榕軒兩京卿懇為廣募現接日本楊星使陸續並滙捐款此外尚無復音除未盡事宜隨時並電馳陳外專肅

恭請

鈞安

盛宣懷 呂海寰 吳重憙 謹肅 四月初九日

一六六

艮

照會

大亞美理駕合衆國欽命駐劄中華便宜行事全權大臣康 爲

照會事，於壹千玖百三年七月壹號有美商之帆船名曰喀里耳得甫者，即繙爲傳書鴿之意，在洋面忽遭風暴，水滿將沉，幸有招商局輪船二艘，一名愛仁，譯音，一名海安，譯音，將美商船主及水手等救護，經

大伯理璽天德聞此，即以金表二枚，一爲獎給愛仁船主約翰斯，一爲獎給愛仁輪船之二副馬拉肯，又將雙筒千里鏡，送獎海安船主瓦拉思，等情，飭屬轉送前來

合就將金表及千里鏡備函附送

貴親王轉飭招商局交該船主等祇領可也併附收條

三張即希囑領受者將收去物件及姓名簽列用便

徵銷爲此照會須至照會者 附洋文 並收條三紙

外附包封一件

右 照 會

大清欽命全權大臣便宜行事軍機大臣總理外務部事務和碩慶親王

一千玖百肆年捌月 初十日

光緒叁拾年陸月 貳拾玖日

一六七

敬啟者本月二十一日馳上美字第一百零五號公
函度荷
堂鑒美國舊金山爲太平洋極大商埠市廛駢接人物
喧闐屋宇之瑰麗財產之富豐舍紐約外莫與倫
比華人流寓是邦皆以爲根據之地商店數百僑
民數萬安土樂居數十年矣廿五日忽聞該埠有
地震之事初以爲海濱地氣使然不至大礙不適
時又聞市場一帶房肆坍塌所值以千兆計傷人

無算翌日又聞地震甫定又有火災華人聚居之所亦已殃及電局車路均已斷塞該口鎮將調兵彈壓施行軍令情形危急已可想見先經屢電該處領事迄未得復當即肅電上陳

冰案二十七日又聞火勢益加蔓延全埠將成灰燼該埠地勢三面臨海一面阻火數十萬居民欲出不得感以災祲餘生流連奔走無貴無賤凍餒待斃華民處此劫厄其困苦情形當必有百倍於土

著者自應急籌救濟之法徐圖善後之方業經電飭各埠商民迅速集款並電廣東香港各善堂協力助募誠亦率同僚佐湊捐廉俸以爲倡導伏念海外華僑久在深宫廑念際此非常災變未便壅於上聞故敢瀝陳實情籲乞恩旨今晨探聞美國政府已於前日撥給美金一百五十萬元交紅十字會經理由兵部轉運局購備糧食

特撥專車前往災區散放現在尚擬續百萬其餘
各省商民解囊捐助亦有數百萬元之譜各國國
主均有專電慰問西報議論頗有美辭獨我國
國電尚未頒到當係海綫梗阻不能不稍遲數日也現計
事起至今已經四日領事等固無消息華商會館
亦無稟報正不知情形何若而目前散放賑食安
置難民將來清理財產規復商務均須專派人員
及早籌畫查有美館二等參贊周道自齊情形熟

悉物望素孚委令辦理可無貽誤當經飭令即日馳往金山查訪領事下落招集會館紳董會同地方官員紅十字會人等將應辦一切賑撫善後事宜妥為經理隨時電稟備核約計下月初三四日可抵該埠應俟稟報到日再行馳布所有往返盤川及旅居費用均應請准作正另銷金山領事署自經此次奇災案卷鋪陳公私蕩然已在意中亦應責成該參贊察看情事或在金山附近要埠暫

設領署以資辦公所需經費亦應請准援案列銷所有以上各節統乞

代回

邸堂列憲俯賜訓示俾得遵行無任感盼專肅敬請

均安

梁誠頓首

光緒三十二年三月二十八日

美字第一百零六號

敬再啟者，正繕函間，聞美總統以本國財力贍富，足資賑濟，外國助款一概璧退。誠即晤詢紅十字會長，據云確有此說，惟各國款項專為接濟該國僑民者，仍可自行散放等語。所有各處捐款，擬即交周參贊會同領事督飭會館收放，仍刊報章，用徵信實。合併附陳。再請

均安

梁誠再頓首

光緒三十二年三月二十八日

美字又第一百零六號

賑捐

外務部收

駐美梁大臣電一件

沁電計達災重待款已率屬捐銀派周參贊赴金山查明領事下落并辦善後事宜各國均電慰總統乞請旨辦理由

形六十三

左侍郎聯　月　日

會辦大臣那　月　日

軍機大臣總理外務部事務和碩慶親王　月　日

協辦大學士軍機大臣外務部尚書會辦大臣瞿　月　日

右侍郎唐　月　日

光緒三十二年三月二十九日　海字一千六號

521

THE CHINESE TELEGRAPH COMPANY.

Telegrams accepted for all Telegraph Stations in the World

STATION

TELEGRAM Nr. 113 Class Words.

Given in at Washington the 190 H. M. /m.

Waiwupu Pk 22276 91167

62670 13845 64221 45027 82468 2955 18712 07062

57400 30072 22200 05814 21068 65111 63915 13572

21305 34397 71460 03500 26569 82017 0362 85526

75684 11424 67511 71917 54698 13675 48215 28757

96606 36859 53856 7544 50685 20584

一六九

奉

旨朕欽奉

慈禧端佑康頤昭豫莊誠壽恭欽獻崇熙皇太后懿旨

美國舊金山地震災情甚重朝廷深為憫惻著須發

帑銀十萬兩由外務部交美國駐京使臣迅速匯寄

災區以資拯濟而篤邦交欽此

一七〇

奉
旨朕欽奉
慈禧端佑康頤昭豫莊誠壽恭欽獻崇熙皇太后懿旨
舊金山地震被災華民甚衆朝廷深為軫念著發給
帑銀四萬兩由外務部迅速匯往並傳知梁誠妥為
振濟毋任失所欽此

一七一

戶部爲片呈事三月三十日准軍機處

交出奉

旨朕欽奉

慈禧端佑康頤昭豫莊誠壽恭欽獻崇熙皇太后

懿旨舊金山地震災情甚重朝廷深爲憫惻

著發帑銀拾萬兩由外務部交美國駐京使

臣迅速匯寄災區以資拯濟而篤邦交欽此欽奉

旨朕欽奉

慈禧端佑康頤昭豫莊誠壽恭欽獻崇熙皇太后
懿旨：舊金山地震被災華民甚衆，朝廷深爲
軫念，著發給帑銀肆萬兩，由外務部迅速匯
往，並傳知梁誠妥爲賑濟，毋任失所。欽此。欽遵
鈔交前來。除劄知銀庫司員在於
庫存項下提庫平銀拾肆萬兩，驗明
印領平單照數開放，並咨呈外務部
出具印領派員赴部關支可也。須

至片者

右片呈

外務部

光緒叁　　叁拾　　日

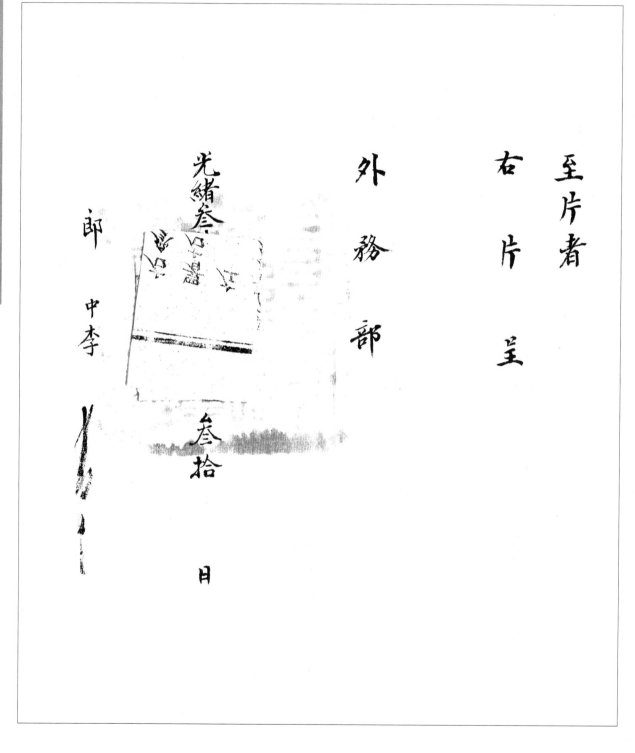

郎中李

一七二

逕復者，接准三月三十日

来函内云奉

皇太后

大皇帝

諭旨爲美國舊金山災情甚重，著頒發帑銀十萬兩拯濟，欽此。本

部由户部領到庫平銀十萬兩，請迅滙寄，並請電知美國政

府等因。本大臣當將

皇太后優待之厚惠電達敝國政府，兹據電復本國

大伯里璽天德深謝

皇太后

大皇帝頒賜拯濟之情，現有數别國欲賑捐此災，本國人民均深心

感惟

大伯里璽天德意定不需他國之款，是以本大臣將
貴親王送來户部銀行十萬兩銀票奉還
貴親王查收，并請將
大伯里璽天德與美國民庶感激
皇太后
大皇帝憫惻之忱代爲奏謝，是盼。特此恭頌
爵祺。附送洋文。

名另具 四月初二日

AMERICAN LEGATION,
PEKING, CHINA.

To F.O. No. 119
W.

April 25, 1906.

Your Imperial Highness:-

I have the honor to acknowledge the receipt of Your Imperial Highness' note of the 23 inst. in which you communicate to me the substance of an Imperial Decree by which Their Imperial Majesties have ordered the contribution of One Hundred Thousand Taels to the relief of the great distress occasioned by the earthquake at San Francisco, and in which Your Highness transmitted to me a bill of the Board of Revenue Bank for Tls.100,000.

In compliance with Your Imperial Highness' request I at once telegraphed to my Government notifying of this most generous action of Their Imperial Majesties, and I am just in receipt of a reply, saying that, the President expresses his sincere thanks for the aid offered; that many similar offers are being received from other foreign countries, all of which are most gratefully appreciated, but that the President has decided that it will not be necessary to receive contributions from abroad. In accordance with my instructions, therefore, I have the honor to hand you inclosed the bill of the Board Of Revenue Bank for One Hundred Thousand Taels, and

To His Imperial Highness, Prince of Ch'ing,
President of the Board of Foreign Affairs,
etc. etc. etc.

and, in returning the same, I have the honor to request Your Imperial Highness to convey to Their Imperial Majesties the sincere gratitude of the President and people of the United States for this manifestation of sympathy.

I avail myself of the occasion to renew to Your Imperial Highness the assurance of my highest consideration.

Envoy Extraordinary and
Minister Plenipotentiary
of the United States.

一七三

片

戶部為片呈事准外務部咨稱所有領到賑濟美國舊
金山災區帑銀十四萬兩當將銀四萬兩匯寄出使梁
大臣查收賑濟華民其餘十萬兩經本部送交美國
柔使去後茲准該使函稱當經電達本政府茲據覆
電本國恤款業已備齊別國賑款亦均未收受茲將
銀票十萬兩親來送還等因應將庫平銀十萬兩原
票一張派員送交戶部查收前來　查前項送還庫
平銀十萬兩本部銀庫於四月初三日照數收訖相

應片呈

貴部查照可也須至片者

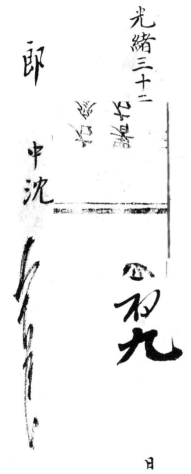

右片呈

外務部

光緒三十二 四 初九日

郎中沈

一七四

江南海關一件呈報奉撥

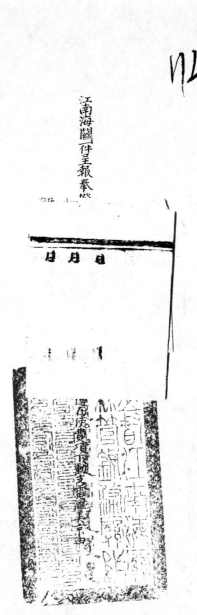

二品銜監督江南海關分巡蘇松太道爲呈報事光緒三十二年三月三十日奉

憲部卅電内開本日奉

旨朕欽奉

慈禧端佑康頤昭豫莊誠壽恭欽獻崇熙皇太后懿旨舊金山地震被災華民甚衆朝廷深爲軫念著發

給帑銀四萬兩由外務部迅速滙往並傳知梁誠妥爲賑慰毋任失所欽此即撥庫平銀四萬兩電滙駐美

梁大臣該款由應解部墊出使經費項下扣還等因到關奉此遵在提存出使經費項下照數動支

庫平銀四萬兩於四月初二日向花旂銀行購兑美幣三萬六百八十八金元即令該行妥速電滙美都中國

使署交納一面由道備具文批呈請

梁大臣飭收印發批迴備案並呈報

南洋大臣外理合具文呈報仰祈

憲臺鑒核為此備由呈乞

照驗施行須至呈者

欽命總理外務部事務衙門

光緒叁拾年四月初十日

署關巡道瑞澂

敬啟者前月二十八日肅具壹百零陸號公函諒邀
堂鑒舊金山地震為灾仰荷
聖慈撥發美賑拾萬兩華僑賑款肆萬兩經誠電請
代奏叩謝
恩施並將飭派周參贊自齊馳赴辦理賑撫事宜電達
鈞部各在案周參贊於二十九日起程後迭據鍾領事
函電陳報遷徙屋崙埠情形茲將旬日以來迭據稟
報各節撮要為
鈞部陳之查該埠於三月二十五早起地震四五次屋
宇先後倒塌煤氣管斷裂火光四起自來水管亦被
震斷無從施救金山三面濱臨大海其餘陸路一面
皆為火勢所蔓延路電梗斷中外男女由是早至翌
晨流離道路露坐於公園曠地之中衆口嗷嗷不得
食息其時省政府以灾況過巨深慮莠民搶掠即日
改行軍政二十六日由美兵官發出帳棚俾衆棲止
食品亦陸續運到散給灾民領事暨華僑奔走倉皇
無策施救至二十六傍晚晤商美提督撥船陸續渡

過對海之屋崙地方由紅十字會散放賑品領事派定紳商五十人為值理領得火食帳棚分散華僑該處尚有留學生章宗元等幫同照料旋定安輯辦理尚屬得宜約計商民之逃在屋崙者五千餘人卜忌利者千餘人附近各小埠二千餘人留在金山兵房者千餘人住金門園者四千餘人痕特斯盤者千餘人總共一萬五千餘人美賑與各國人一律平均統計此次之災沿燒三晝夜該處大市場幾於一洗淨盡領署華店同罹浩刼惟兵官衙署鑄幣局郵局戶部分局等工程堅固者尚巋然獨存各國死傷人數不能確指華僑死傷約二十餘人此被災最先之情形也先是誠慮華旅被災美人歧視然苦無自賑之法故於二十七日將卒屬捐助之七千兩攜交美外部請其轉發代賑美雖未收此款次日總統即有華民與各國人一律賑濟不應參差之諭及蒙

恩頒帑款尤足以動美人之感情且自奉

上賞之後海內外善士靡然風從半月之間集款多至美金

拾柒萬圓而美屬各埠華民之捐交地方官者尚不
在此數之内此則非 誠始願所及者也周參贊馳抵
屋崙晤商領事即在該處賃屋辦公並召集中華會
館董事及留學生等籌辦賑撫之法查紅十字會計
口授食每人日需美金七角華旅日需萬圓以外若
自行辦賑非特無此財力而且轉運施放各事必不
能如善會經理之得宜惟是辦賑日長須由該省政
府自籌經費 誠知該省正值財力支絀已飭周參贊
先撥美金伍萬圓助賑用是頗荷該處之歡遇為目
前計賑救之外籌撫為先華旅性質不齊但能坐食
即不奮志營業竟有數百人先允充捕魚工者及至
放賑遂不應募且羣居無業必至為非 誠已飭周參
贊等設法陸續遣散其有親友可投者甯給予車費
俾免生活但使少壯者得以餬口四方其餘老弱婦
孺即不難賑濟惟目前散往之數尚屬寥寥此則亟
應設法籌辦者也金山華旅向為該處美人所嫉惡
華埠居全城之中心點平時報館著論頗以迫遷為

宜今值蕩析離居又將重申此議初時畫出亨得士砵一地即華人向稱猪欄者擬令徙居嗣以華人抗拒者多遂又改圖由府尹派出董事五人籌議此事日前邀同周參贊鍾領事等會議以為亨得士砵既不合宜可由華人另覓一地總以交通利便衛生相宜為主周參贊等覆以是否可遷係箇人自有之權華人在美居住自由恐難施以官力等語誠竊以為遷埠一事現時或無大恐荅經此奇變勞來安集非一日可以為功尤非擴張商務不能如前興威東方商利實該埠所利賴假使辦理不善則太平洋勢力將遷移於舍路砵崙如其顧慮及此當不致淵魚叢雀再擾華埠動我感情至於開寬街道封堵隘巷高閎屋宇整頓衛生等事是為地方應盡之義務非惟華埠不能違其政令即他人亦不能違也華民所有地址若干刻間固未及清釐所慮即有地基亦無力興建至於賃居之屋原因過於汙穢不能轉租他人故久為華人盤踞今若重新興築租值過昂亦非華

商力所能賃通例如經焚燬合同即廢房主不能令租客再出租錢租客亦不能逼房主重造接租是交易已斷恐地主重建亦不願賃與華人由此推之將來華埠是否仍在原地亦祇還於天然之事勢而非還於美國之勢力也誠自本月初間即擬馳赴災區詧看一切誠恐禁例事或有消息遲遲吾行逾日音信全杳決計二十一日登程馳往查看以便布置一切

上賞美賑一款經美外部飭令柔使婉謝計此次外國助賑者坎拿大十萬圓墨西哥三萬圓瓜里哇打一萬圓日本二十萬圓咸威崙二萬五千圓均經總統外部婉詞卻謝經飭議院撰文為全國團體敬伸謝悃矣餘容續布以上各情統乞

代回

邸堂列憲為叩專此敬請

台安惟希

賜照

梁誠頓首

光緒三十二年四月十七日
美字第壹百零柒號

撫卹 金山

外務部收

四六九

駐美梁大臣電一件

本日親赴金山查看賑撫由

左侍郎聯

會辦大臣那

會辦大臣瞿

右侍郎唐

協辦大學士軍機大臣外務部尚書會辦大臣瞿

光緒三十二年四月二十三日

鹹字八百十三號

662

THE CHINESE TELEGRAPH COMPANY.

Telegrams accepted for all Telegraph Stations in the World

STATION

TELEGRAM No. .... Class .... Words.

Given in at .... the .... 190 .... H. .... M. .... /m.

Washington

[illegible]	5208	[illegible]	[illegible]
1483	05340	[illegible]	43191
[illegible]	85276	[illegible]	

一七七

外務部收

駐美梁大臣電一件 詳陳舊金山美政府協濟安置華民情形乞代奏由

電八十五

左侍郎聯 月 日

體仁閣大學士外務部會辦大臣那 月 日

軍機大臣總理外務部事務和碩慶親王 月 日

協辦大學士軍機大臣外務部尚書會辦大臣瞿 月 日

右侍郎唐 月 日

光緒三十二年閏四月初一日河字四十二號

699

THE CHINESE TELEGRAPH COMPANY.

Telegrams accepted for all Telegraph Stations in the World. Ch. great Northern

M
6 10 a
Chang

STATION.

TELEGRAM Nr. 4/1307 Class 65 Words.

Given in at Oaklandcal the 190 H. M. /m.

waiwupu JK 5492 試 4 能

53577 報 31445 金山 13543 察 7311 8 看 精 47169 形 57410 美 22921 踈 50708 府

48347 差 會 60650 協 31544 辦 78903 筆 61028 僑 備 12681 極 07781 周 18001 安

64203 往 商 86427 處 08544 品 63644 與 10286 美 民 50001 一 17210 律 91800 並

08279 不 55857 設 視 54960 現 96750 在 賞 1583 還 74451 老 36080 病 93609 回

55131 國 113552 安 真 置 12331 婦 29914 需 19499 居 處 62035 添 23055 散 14041 衣

49406 米 等 33933 物 57453 辦 44015 理 17248 有 26382 頭 42890 緒 30846 不

53297 致 流 46249 離 11302 失 02810 所 55190 堪 11912 慮 06950 屋

05201 乞 18114 代 奏 05249 誠 46870 懇

一七八

敬啟者上月二十一日肅布美字第一百零八號
公函計荷
堂譽舊金山鉅災華僑罹難情形及派員賑撫親往察
看各節經於前函陳明文於 誠抵金後將所定辦
法詳細電達並請
鈞部代奏各在案 誠於四月二十四行抵金山對岸
之屋崙地方暫居旅館接見派辦賑撫之美館參
贊周道自齊駐金山領事鍾守寶僖各會館董事
紳商及辦賑値理人等詳詢救濟辦法難民情形
備悉美國地方官及諸善會待遇華僑尚無歧視
心爲稍慰次日晤見嘉省總督屋崙金山兩府尹
太平洋濱防兵統帥等首先宣布
朝廷德意次則謝其待遇難民無不同深欣服維時救濟
等事均歸軍人料理該統帥特派專員陪觀華民
營帳計金山屋崙各有數百人男女分棚衛生得
法衣服飲食均無缺乏其散居華人洗衣舖菜園

教會書館及賃居民房者兩埠共四千人老弱婦
稚居其小半均按日分給口糧得以度活熙來攘
往頗不知災難之苦矣前以少壯遊手太多聚處
易於生事曾飭該參贊等設立薦工會並助車費
俾得他往工作去者以千數計又以難民分往鄰
近小埠施賑恐未普及特在檀香山砵崙紐阿連
等處採購食米數千包專派董事值理確查人數
計口授食又添購衣服被褥分給婦稚統計各埠
不下數千人皆得飽煖安居矣惟是麕聚待賑究
非長策而時交夏令野處固有霪雨之虞室居又
有湫穢之苦若不及時設法將來必多不便　誠因
與屋崙府尹面商擇租曠地一區託美兵官代築
板屋百所招集布帳衣舖菜園等處婦孺入居其
中以十所為一排排設廚廁各一處以供十家之
用選派兵目常川監察時遣醫生檢視潔淨並由
領署派員與會館董事等認真料理限居六箇月

之久令其男子出外謀生另圖養贍逾六箇月勒
令遷移他往以示限制其年老貧苦流落多年者
先經該參贊等商准輪船公司減收水腳四期背
遣回國約五百人然恩惠未周尚多無告誠特議
展限一月准老弱自陳由領事代購船票酌助資
斧並函香港東華醫院俟船抵港派人照料轉送
回籍俾得生入玉門同沾
天澤一時報名願去者幾及千人以上二事均關緊要已
諄囑領事與地方兵官妥速辦理矣此籌辦賑撫
之情形也金山華埠為華人始初抵美聚居之所
數十年來有舖戶千五百餘間會館八所戲院二
座居民約一萬八千餘衆婦女數百土生子女二
千有奇儼然成一都市近年金山日見繁盛華埠
四周或闤市通衢或高門廣第圍繞其間以致地
價日昂租值日漲美人覬覦厚利久思壟斷每藉
口於華僑不脫惡俗不講衛生輒倡為移徙華埠

之議而政黨之欲得官者亦附和此議以為要結工黨之媒今年天災同成焦土益復重申前說昌言逼遷竟派有紳士五人專議此事有欲以痕特斯盤為華人居留地者又有以電報山為華人商業地者先與該參贊等商酌復邀識往履勘痕特斯盤地勢低窪距市太遠斷非華人所宜電報山則與華埠相隔僅一小山以為民居尚屬合式以為商廛實失地利均不及華埠之居中便利也該紳等堅請指定一處願為經營興築務合華僑之用識以自由居住人各有權不能舉萬數之生人置之一隅之地願遷與否願往何處應聽華僑自便復之彼亦無詞再辯竊謂華埠舖產為華人所有者幾五十家其餘業主願租華人者又居大半茍華人願回原處金山政府斷不能强行干預且金山收入稅餉華商居三之一諒不欲驅之他往自損利權況復中美商務日有增加太平洋商埠

金山實居其首尤不至過為已甚傷我感情雖有政黨工黨之喧呶料難成遷埠之謬舉也惟是華人實業地契多已焚燬各項保險情事亦復紛歧非得精於法律聲望素隆之人為之認真清理吃虧勢必不輕業經代中華會館延訂律師俾資謀畫當可無虞華人會館商店均有揭借會項數及千萬平時賴以周轉市面得以流通其交易之法一按內地規約非美國法律所能範圍旣經此次奇災必有狡黠之徒藉口無力相率捲逃將銅山西崩洛鐘東應不特金山華埠無復興起之機即全美華僑亦有影響之及所關實非淺鮮經　諭飭令領事督同會館妥定規條認明債欠設法分還如有訛詞詐騙者准會館稟由領事查明情節詳請洛籍查抄拘押勒追用警貪頑而維大局此籌辦善後之情形也誠初擬駐金旬餘遍為慰問嗣以美館公事叢積議院尚未散會未便久離因於

本月十二日率同周參贊自齊等巡返美都清釐
一切所有應辦事宜亦經逐款列明札發領事妥
為遵辦矣此次鉅灾上荷
聖慈眷念之隆下得官紳將伯之助前後收款將及美金
二十二萬圓合華銀四十餘萬圓得以廣為施濟
幸無一夫不獲足以仰答
朝廷痌瘝在抱之懷遠慰
邸堂列憲子惠羈僑之意而美國總統推誠相待一視
同仁地方文武官員紅十字會救濟善會皆能仰
體此意畛域不分使萬數華民得安衽席此情此
誼實堪嘉許不料內地報章粵廣輿論猶有訾議
詆毀以美人虐待華僑為言者殊非公道待人適
以阻其向上經誠將救濟實情詳電各善堂商會
俾知真相而免誤會所有查看賑事情形理合專
函馳報即乞
代回
邸堂列憲鑒核訓示是荷專肅敬請
均安　梁誠頓首 光緒三十二年閏四月十四日 美字第一百零九號

一七九

欽差出使美秘古墨國大臣梁 為

咨呈事竊照本大臣於光緒三十二年閏四月十四日在美京使館拜發具

奏遵

籌辦金山賑恤摺一件又改調人員片一件相應鈔稿咨呈

貴部謹請察照須至咨呈者 計粘鈔奏稿

右咨呈

外務部

光緒三十二年閏四月拾肆日

一八〇

欽差出使美秘古墨國大臣梁 為

咨呈事竊照本年三月下旬金山地震繼以大火全埠幾成灰燼華僑數萬財產蕩然饑困流離情殊可憫當經本大臣倡率捐廉遴派駐美二等參贊官廣東補用道周自齊攜往會同總領事及美國官商善會救濟華民一面電請

貴部代奏荷蒙

恩旨賞撥帑金四萬兩又承中外官紳商會善堂撥款協濟旬日之間得美金二十餘萬疊據周道稟報施賑辦法及美國官民待遇華民情形均經隨時電達

貴部轉行查照本大臣旋於四月中旬馳往察看晤商美國官紳督飭各員暨

會館各董籌辦一切畧有頭緒始行遄返美都所有一切情形經於閏四月十四

日恭摺奏報理合鈔錄原奏咨呈

貴部謹請察照備案須至咨呈者 附鈔件

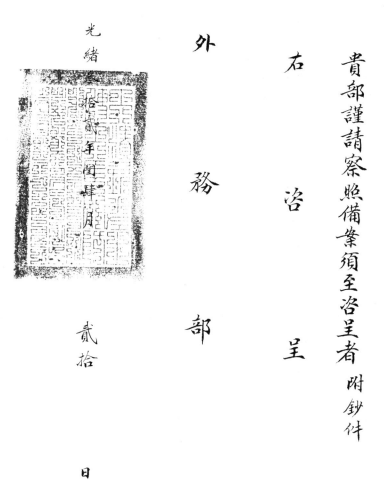

右 咨 呈

外 務 部

光緒叁拾貳年閏肆月貳拾日

附件

謹
奏為美埠地震華僑災重荷蒙
發帑賑恤謹將遵
旨前往籌辦情形恭摺具陳仰祈
聖鑒事竊臣於光緒三十二年三月二十六二十七等日以美
國舊金山地震成災華埠全燬派員查勘救濟各情
電咨外務部代奏旋於三月三十日承准軍機處電寄奉
旨朕欽奉
慈禧端佑康頤昭豫莊誠壽恭欽獻崇熙皇太后懿旨舊金山
地震被災華民甚衆朝廷深為軫念著發給帑銀四萬兩
由外務部迅速匯往並傳知梁誠妥為賑慰毋任失所欽此
仰見我

皇太后
皇上子惠黎元不遺在遠不獨海外華民沐霑
闓澤歡呼歌頌感激涕零即美國上下亦以
皇仁廣被奔走相告歆慕於無極經臣於四月初一日率領
華民專電叩謝
天恩並於四月二十二二十八等日疊將臣馳赴災區查看賑

撫暨擬定辦法電請外務部代奏在案伏查舊金山
素以繁富著名人物喧闐市廛駢接實為太平洋第
一商埠華人自道咸閒航海來美擇地僦居垂數十
年計有商店千五百餘家居民男女二萬有奇實業貲
財值數千萬儼然成一都聚三月二十六日晨閒該埠忽
覺地震迴復不絕者數時房屋倒坍無算午後火起

勢頗燎原，嚮夜風力尤猛，無法施救，經三晝夜火始熄，
滅華人居留之地及領事衙署皆在刼中，全埠存者僅
三之一，實百年未有之奇災也。維時中外人等奔走流
離，饑餓不得食，露宿於公園曠野間者數十萬衆。至
二十八日，美政府撥款辦賑，紅十字會及他善會亦次
第開辦，張設布幕，轉運糧食，被災華民皆與美民一
律相待。統計傷斃華人僅二十餘名口，此外無一失所
者，美總統不分畛域之功實
朝廷懷柔有素所致也。臣於災起之先，經已馳電海内外募
款助賑，並率屬捐俸以為之倡，特派美館二等參贊官
周自齊飛速前往，會同總領事妥商地方官吏暨紅十
字會員協同救濟，先將災民分散各埠，俾便就食，所

有老病婦孺或躉居棚帳或賃住民房計口給糧分
施衣被使無凍餒其少壯力强者則設薦工會代覓
工作量助川貲使得外出謀食亦免滋生事端迭據
稟報所辦尚稱妥協四月二十二日臣以美館公事稍
閑馳往金山晤商嘉釐福尼亞省總督金山屋崙府尹
太平洋鎮將等隨往查看一切以為目前救濟要旨業
經猶有規模則安插之方善後之計實有萬不容緩者
遂分別辦法約為兩端一關於難民之事金山華僑貧
老無依者以千數計平日傳食親朋得以全活經此灾
難奚能自給與其流落異邦徒損一國之譽何如遣回
本籍使享垂老之年經飭各會館董事查明人數代購
船票運送歸國夏令已交婦孺所居非苦卑濕即虞湫

穢特租曠地權建木屋百椽勸令遷入仍由領事及美國兵官等監察照料務期秩序井然衛生有益一關於商務之事華人實業保險所值不貲經理苟不如法權利必將盡失特飭會館延請著名律師為之照料當可無虞華埠揭借各項市面藉以流通事定之後必有奸徒託詞倒騙於大局不無摇動經臣出示誥誡並札

總領事商同會館妥定規約切實施行庶幾華埠可復舊觀殷商不至牽累此則臣所為竭力圖維不敢稍存忽視者也其餘應辦事宜亦經分別條畧發交總領事參酌照行遇有緊要事件隨時稟陳俟臣核奪臣即於本月十二日率同參贊等回抵美館清理積牘一俟賑務完竣即行詳細縷陳藉以仰慰

宸廑。再此次賑款，除外洋各埠商民交由地方官逕解災區外，其京外官商匯交使署者，旬日之間，得美金二十餘萬圓，踴躍慷慨，實所僅見。經臣先後發交領事及會館董事等公同收放，刊發布告，昭示大衆，以廣
慈恩而宏善念。所有金山地震華僑被災，微臣遵
旨籌辦賑恤緣由，理合恭摺具陳，伏乞
皇太后
皇上聖鑒訓示。謹
奏。
再，舊金山地方華僑聚處，工黨鬬爭繁劇，疲難甲於各埠。總領事官非得精幹廉敏之才，不足以資撫馭。臣抵任後，爲地擇人，再三遴選，以原駐古巴總領事周自齊

調補旋因美署二等參贊官陳昭常未能到差改令留
充美署參贊其金山底缺委隨員鍾寶禧代理旋復改
為署任均經奏報在案現在鍾寶僖三年期滿銷差回
華而周自齊已補駐美二等參贊官正資得力金山總
領事既屬要缺目前賬務未畢不便久聽虛懸亟應選
員充補查有留美差遣派駐祕魯二等參贊官孫士頤
才具開展年力富强堪以調補業經照案飭令先行赴
任又署小呂宋總領事官蘇銳釗抵任一年諸臻妥協
應請改為實授以重職守除咨呈外務部外理合附片
陳明伏乞
聖鑒謹
奏

一八一

東 梁誠

〇至外務部

六月十三日

內閣侍讀學士出使美墨秘古國大臣臣梁誠跪

奏為美埠地震華僑災重籲懇

發帑賑恤謹將遵

旨前往籌辦情形恭摺具陳仰祈

聖鑒事竊臣於光緒三十二年三月二十六二十七等日以美國

舊金山地震成災華埠全燬派員查勘救濟各

情電達外務部代奏旋於三月三十日承准軍

機處電寄奉

旨朕欽奉

慈禧端佑康頤昭豫莊誠壽恭欽獻崇熙皇太后懿旨

舊金山地震被災華民甚衆朝廷深為軫念著發給

帑銀四萬兩由外務部迅速匯往並傳知梁誠妥為賑

慰毋任夫所欽此仰見我
皇太后
皇上子惠黎元不遺在遠不獨海外華民沐霑
闓澤歡呼歌頌感激涕零即美國上下亦以
皇仁廣被奔走相告歆慕於無極矣臣於四月初一日
率領華民專電叩謝
天恩並於四月二十二二十八等日疊將臣馳赴災區查
看賑撫暨擬定辦法電請外務部代奏在案
伏查舊金山素以繁富著名人物喧闐市廛
駢接實為太平洋第一商埠華人自道咸間航
海來美擇地僦居垂數十年計有商店千五百
餘家流民男女二萬有奇實業貨財值數千萬

儼然成一都聚三月二十六日晨間該埠忽覺地震迴復不絕者數時房屋倒坍無算午後火起勢頗燎原竟夜風力尤猛無法施救經三晝夜火始熄滅華人所留之地及領事衙署皆在劫中全埠存者僅三之一實百年未有之奇災也維時中外人等奔走流離饑餓不得食露宿於公園曠野間者數十萬衆至二十八日美政府撥款辦賑紅十字會及地善會亦次第開辦張設布幕轉運糧食被災華民皆與美民一律相待統計傷斃華人僅二十餘名以此外無一失所者美總統不分畛域之功實

朝廷懷柔有素所致也臣於災起之先經已馳電海

内務府籌款助賑，並辟房捐，俾以爲之倡。特派美館二等參贊官周自齊馳速前往，會同總領事及華商、地方官吏暨紅十字會員協同救濟。先將災民分散各埠，俾便就食。所有老弱病婦孺或暫居棚帳，或僦住民房，計口給糧，分施布衣被，使無凍餒。其壯力强者，則設勞工會代覓工作，量助川資，俾得分出謀食，亦免滋生事端。迭據報所稱，尚係妥協。四月二十二日復以美館公使稍閑，馳往金山，晤商嘉利福尼亞省總督、金山區府尹、太平洋艦將等，隨往查看一切，以爲日後救濟要旨。業

經猶有規模制度補苴之方善後之計實有
萬不容緩者茲遂分别擬法約爲兩端一關
於難民之可以出洋僑貿營業依者以千
數計平日倚食親朋均以全活經此災難
實能自給與居住外邦待擬一國之譽
何如造回華籍使享垂老之年經紀和
會館董事查明人數代購船票運送歸
國及今已交婦孺所居雖甚卑濕即實
漸織特租賃地權建木屋以棲之寄令還
入仍由領事及美國兵官等監察照料務期
秩序井然衛生有益一關於商務之可
華人實業保險所值不貲經理尚不如
法權利必將盡失特飭會館延請著名律

師為之照料，當可望冀美埠擴俾各項市
面藉以流通。至定之後，必有奸徒託詞偽
騙，於大局不無搖動。經出示誥誡，並札飭
領事商同會館，嚴定規約，切實稽查，庶幾
美埠可復舊觀，就商不致虧累，否則以
為謠言固結不散，移存忽視者也。至館應
辦事宜，亦經分別條累，發交擬領事參酌
照行。遇有緊要事件，隨時稟陳，報以核
奪。日即於本年月十二日偕同參贊等回抵美
館，清理積牘，一俟館務完竣，即行詳細繕
陳，藉以仰慰

宸廑再由次賑款項分詳各埠商民並由地方官
通行災區分送京外官商匯交使署者旬日
之間約美金二十餘萬圓踴躍慷慨實所
僅見經日先後發交領事及會館董事出
國收放刊發布告昭示大衆以廣
慈恩而宸慕念許有金山地震華僑被災欽遵
旨籌撥賑恤緣由理合恭摺具陳伏乞
皇太后
皇上聖鑒訓示謹
奏。
光緒三十二年六月十三日奉
硃批知道了欽此
閏四月十四日

一八二

收南京發來一等電報錄

兩江總督

外務部

美國人李佳白在上海開設中外義賑公会尚賢堂籌款出力各國公使提及此事誌謝

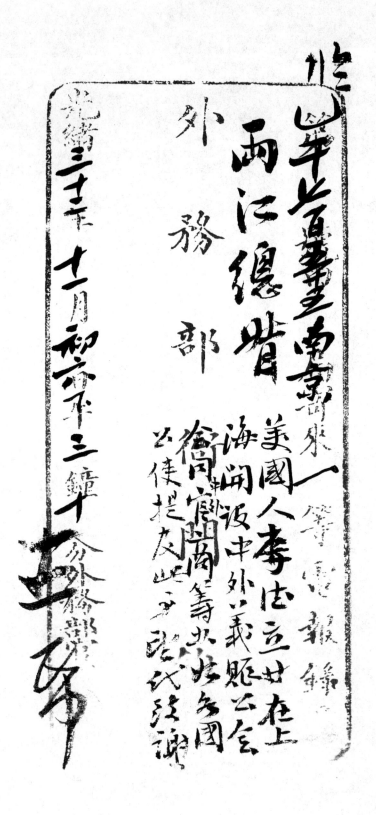

光緒三十三年十一月初六日下午三鐘十分外務部收

1755

THE CHINESE TELEGRAPH COMPANY.

Telegrams accepted for all Telegraph Stations in the World

STATION

TELEGRAM Nr. 76 Class 124 Words. 294

Given in Nanking the 9 11 H. 7 /m.

Peking

1120 0152 6752 6874
7003 3162 1425 2485
2447 3885 3601 3173 6122 3190 5718 6490
3565 4014 1609 0017 3173 0601 2088 1825
2893 2877 2191 5702 0181 4402 0005 2447
4842 5164 5967 6756 4842 6398 2941 2782
1682 0009 0006 0003 0211 0691 5710 4801
3885 2283 4055 1674 0456 3281 2941 7021
6982 2782 1395 7050 1932 2842 4853 1704
0371 2994 1441 4271 5878 1725 0005 2447
7086 6784 0075 1672 4862 2961 0225 3493
3493 6784 0075 1672 1332 0839 0581 5764
5767 6756 4862 6394 1171 2172 1770 5767 7046
1672 0181

1755 ~~459~~

THE CHINESE TELEGRAPH COMPANY.

Telegrams accepted for all Telegraph Stations in the World

STATION

TELEGRAM Nr. .... Class .... Words.

Given in at .... the .... 190 ...... H. ...... M. ...... /m.

6602 0751 1709 7466

0033 6981 0219 2876 1272 0641 0606 7050

2777 1682 4402 0783 6595 5796 4703 0452

6499 5007 0044 5496 5189 5967 0839 2994

1441 4271 0456 1362 6886 6611 2941 5007

7531 6762 6756 2377 1211 5472 0592 0092

1730 7501 2914 2974 7086 2782 7056 7046

5111 1672 2397 0219 3053 2877 0001 0274

3502 7454 0075 1709 5764 5690 5205 1971

2941 5396 4030 1325 2397 0812 1074 7486

2015 3053 7454 0230 1730 2941 3253 0754

0305 1415 0676 0556 5396 1705 1741 1606

0001 3053 0059 0470 0606 6522 3533 5472

429

THE CHINESE TELEGRAPH COMPANY.

Telegrams accepted for all Telegraph Stations in the World

9

STATION

TELEGRAM Nr. .... Class .... Words.

Given in at .... the .... 190 ...... H. ...... M. ...... /m.

7901. 2233. 0017. 0092.
2492. 2311. 0001. 0404. 2822. 2063. 2490. 0055.
6853. 0217. 0148. 1058. 1464. 2492. 2311. 6786.
4154. 1074. 2582. 6328. 2783. 0364. 5571. 2092.
1312. 2942. 0385. 4747. 0392. 0470. 2576. 2962.
2994. 1734. 6887. 3861. 4152. 1680. 2420. 2959.
0456. 1756. 6394. 3902. 1771. 5662. 5764. 2943.
0302. 2894. 6783. 8071. 6993. 2493. 0754. 5209.
4154. 0001. 0481. 2782. 0296. 0347. 4431. 4068.
2620. 1089. 6756. 2823. 2433. 1255. 6701. 0871.
1709. 0213. 0452. 1074. 1948. 2221. 0180. 2933.
2850. 0148. 0358. 5742. 6901. 2965. 0786. 2941.
2787.

[illegible]

一八三

上
著○西號由美國寄來一等電報錄呈

駐美梁大臣

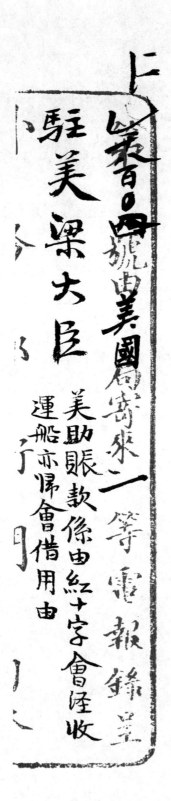

美助賑款係由紅十字會經收
運船亦歸會借用由

1801

THE CHINESE TELEGRAPH COMPANY.

Telegrams accepted for all Telegraph Stations in the World

STATION

TELEGRAM Nr. 1377 Class Words.

Given in at Washington the 190 H. M m.

Waiwupu Peking

48320	61062	49277	20469
41025	13466	91099	72498
52092	67208	39228	53222
06105	28951	94447	60298
04416	57329	74348	92117
27825	14318	91054	50029
38607	12417	09720	86299
50410	67629	40481	12493
05146	94168	32136	[illegible]

一八四

廿一

第四十二號收美國商務來電等電報錄呈

駐美梁大臣電

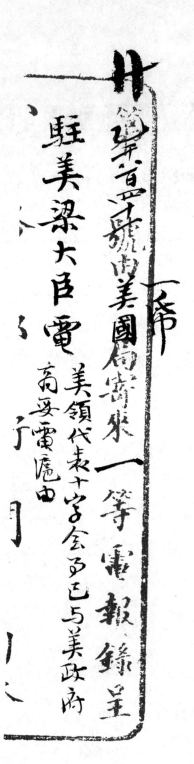

美領代表十字会面已與美政府商妥。電應由

1841

THE CHINESE TELEGRAPH COMPANY.

To Prince Ching
Foreign Office
Peking

Telegrams accepted for all Telegraph Stations in the World

STATION

TELEGRAM Nr. 1479 Class 5 33 Words.

Given in at Washington the 1st 190 H. M

Wanonpu
Peking

17095	00748	32264	61542
05591	08969	84454	[illegible]
74460	38548	55069	10997
58904	70643	[illegible]	60382
00192	94460	94064	40003
10284	41536	62569	05198
05560	69316	21204	44471
67564	15468	02262	

一八五

兩江總督

第壹千八百叁拾號由南京寄收 一字電報錄呈

美廷賑款已由華董散放，所賑麵包亦經起運，祈晤美使稱謝。由

1852

THE CHINESE TELEGRAPH COMPANY.

Telegrams accepted for all Telegraph Stations in the World

STATION

TELEGRAM Nr. 1 **Class** **Words.**

Given in at the 190 H. M. m.

Peking 1120. [illegible]. [illegible].

6874. 7003. 3162. 1344. 6491. 2894. [illegible]. [illegible].
1472. 6394. 2782. 5209. 3100. 0476. 5007. [illegible].
2876. 1272. 0889. 1089. 4400. 5666. 5690. 2898.
2877. 0691. 0997. 3498. 4706. 1374. 5471. 2965.
1089. 3656. 2941. 4431. 6814. 7600. 1322. 5764.
1089. 2965. 3876. 3362. 3406. 2994. 1441. 4271.
0456. 6981. 6394. 7772. 0711. 5710. 0714. 0692.
0256. 1682. 6134. 6699. 7160. 5492. 3100. 4023.
0456. 6853. 6702. 6901. 3571. 2941. 3661.

一八六

始州

光緒三十三年三月十六日收兩江總督電稱

各國兩次電稱華洋義賑收款多美國助運面粉乞移謝梁使由

一八七

逕啓者：接准南洋大臣電稱，准呂盛兩大臣電：
江北災荒，近美國善會助賑麪粉八萬四千担，專運
來華，直送鎮江乞轉謝美國駐京大臣等語。查此次
江北水災極重，飢民衆多，承
貴國善會拯濟情殷，助賑麪粉爲數甚多，災民
受惠不少，本爵大臣極爲欣感，即希
貴大臣代爲致謝。專此，順頌
日祉。

致美桑使

全堂銜

光緒三十三年三月　日

一八八

逕復者接

貴親王本月二十二日函稱接准南洋大臣來電云美國善會將麪粉八萬四千擔運來中國賑濟江北災民請將

貴親王欣謝之意轉達該善會等因查此麪粉係美國紅十字會運來江北以為助賑之舉本大臣甚願按照所請將

貴親王感謝之情轉知該會也特此泐復即頌

爵祉 附送洋文

名另具 三月二十四日

一八九

逕啓者，茲據本國醫生唐嘉利繕有戒烟函稟一紙，擬呈明
恭親王查核，特囑本署使代遞云云。查唐醫生戒烟之法，實屬有益無損。想
貴國政府早已知之，有素相應，將原稟函送
貴部，希爲轉達可也。此候
日祉。附洋文并原函

費勒器啓 七月十一日

美國使署

附件

AMERICAN LEGATION,
PEKING, CHINA.

To FO No. 565

August 24, 1909.

Your Imperial Highness:

I have the honor to request Your Highness to transmit the enclosed communication by the representative of Mr. Charles B. Towns on the subject of a cure for the opium habit, to His Highness Prince Kung.

The character of Mr. Towns' treatment is well known to several officials of Your Highness' Government and I would commend the enclosed letter to His Highness'attention. I avail myself of this opportunity to renew to Your Highness the assurance of my highest consideration.

Henry P. Fletcher

To His Imperial Highness
Prince of Ch'ing,
President of the Board
of Foreign Affairs.

一九〇

交外務部

十二

再，上年廣東水災，經臣電飭各參贊領事倡捐賑款，各埠華僑踴躍慨捐，均能集成鉅款，以資拯濟，足見海外僑民尤能樂善好施，殊堪嘉尚。惟查前兩廣督臣袁請傳
旨嘉獎案內，美洲止有舊金山、紐約兩埠，自餘各埠未及聲敘，不免向隅。茲查美國砵崙埠華僑共捐華銀八千餘元，沙加免度埠華僑共捐華銀二千元，檀香山華僑共捐華銀一萬四千三百餘元，秘魯華僑共捐英金一千鎊，古巴華僑共捐華銀一萬二千元，均係由各該處自行電匯交善堂会所接收散賑，迭據各參贊領事詳請奏獎前來，合無仰懇
天恩，俯准援照兩廣督臣袁請傳
旨嘉獎，以昭激勸。伏乞
聖鑒訓示。謹
奏。

宣統元年十二月十六日奉
硃批：著照所請，該部知道。欽此。

一九一

致盛尚書函

逕啟者，本部現接駐美張星使電稱，美紅十字會擬日内派船載糧食赴江皖賑濟等因。除已電達江督皖撫外，相應函請查照，並希轉達馮大臣接洽。專此，順頌

勛綏

堂銜

宣統三年正月　日

一九二

敬肅者頃奉

台函接駐美張星使電稱美紅十字會擬日内派船載糧食赴江皖振濟希轉達馮大臣接洽等因查美紅十字會載糧赴振一節昨接上海華洋義振會電達敝處已據電轉告馮大臣矣肅復敬請

鈞安伏祈

藎詧盛宣懷謹肅

一九三

敬肅者頃據上海華洋義振會洋員福開森華董沈敦和電稱准美國善會捐助本會振粉五千噸約市值五十六萬元美政府已派運艦運華約中歷三月初到滬謹先稟聞等語查江皖豫三省災區甚廣現值春振需糧孔亟茲承美國善會捐助振粉五千噸並由美政府派船專運救災郵隣情實可感應請

大部先行致函
駐京美嘉使道達謝悃至歉值較鉅施當
其時尤徵中美邦交愈形敦厚應否據情
面奏之處並祈
鈞裁肅此敬請
台安伏乞
藎詧

盛宣懷謹肅
正月十七日

一九四

復盛大臣函

逕復者，接准

函稱，據上海華洋義振會電稱，准美國善會捐助本

會麪粉五千噸，美政府已派運艦運華，約中歷

三月初到滬，應請致函駐京美嘉使道達謝悃，暨

應否據情面奏等因。此事業經奏明，並由本部函

謝美使矣。爲此函復

查照。順頌

勛綏

堂銜

宣統三年正月　日

一九五

上意

致美嘉使函

逕啟者頃准查賑盛大臣函稱據上海華洋義振會電稱准美國善會捐助本會麪粉五千噸美政府已派運艦運華約中歷三月初到滬情實可感應請據情面奏等因查江皖豫灾區甚廣承貴國善會捐助麪粉五千噸並由貴政府派船專運實紉厚誼本部業已奏明

深為嘉悦為此函請

貴大臣查照希將感謝之忱轉達

貴國政府暨善會為荷此泐順頌

日祉

全堂銜

宣統三年正月　日

一九六

逕啟者茲有一事擬向
貴親王聲明緣駐滬總領事官前曾來電本大臣查其大意所有安徽賑災運送米糧一節該領事云及本處有比必羅炳生二教士購買六萬圓上下米糧運至被災處所該二教士曾聞南京地方官接上憲札飭所有運到賑米惟美國方可免稅云云據本大臣愚見擬請札飭南京該管官員不但於美國所運賑米免稅凡由蕪湖上海及一切內地賑米經過南京運至被災處所均當免稅並須由地方官照料運送乃據懷遠正陽及各處稅卞遇有貿易米糧雖運至被災地方亦照常納稅在本大臣愚意因美民意中於照料賑災各事其重視之情已顯然有據故特為聲明凡有貿易米糧稅欵暫可豁免庶令被災處所能獲迅捷美滿照料之益是為至要相應函達
貴親王即希

美國使署

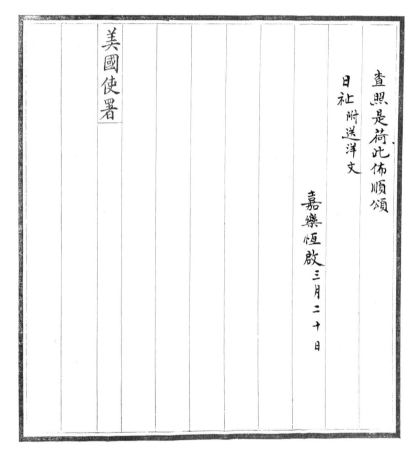

查照是荷此佈順頌
日祉附送洋文
嘉樂恒啟 三月二十日
美國使署

附件

附八号

AMERICAN LEGATION,
PEKING.

To F.O. No. 84.

April 17, 1911.

Your Imperial Highness:

I have the honor to bring to Your Highness' attention the substance of a telegram received by me from the American Consul General at Shanghai relative to the transpertation of supplies destined for the regions in Anhui now suffering from famine. He states that two American missionaries, Messrs. Beebe and Lobenstine, are purchasing locally some sixty thousand dollars worth of grain for shipment to the above regions and that they are informed that the Nanking officials have received instructions to pass only supplies from America. I have, the honor to suggest, therefore, and to request, that instructions be sent to the proper officials at Nanking freely to pass not only all supplies emanating from America, but also such as are shipped from Shanghai, Wuhu, and other interior cities, through Nanking to the famine-stricken regions.

I have the honor to state, also, that customs duties are still being levied at Huai-yuen, Cheng-yang, and other interior customs barriers on grain shipped commercially to the affected localities. In view of the interest now being manifested by the American people in the relief of the present distressing conditions I venture to suggest that these charges temporarily be done away with, to the end that the relief of the sufferers may be more speedily and effectively accomplished.

I

To His Imperial Highness
Prince of Ch'ing,
President of the Board
of Foreign Affairs.

I avail myself of this opportunity to renew to Your Imperial Highness the assurance of my highest consideration.

American Minister.

一九七

復美嘉使函

逕復者，本月二十日接准

函稱，駐滬總領事來電，有比必羅炳生二教士購買六萬

圓上下米糧運安徽被災處所，曾聞南京地方，所有

運到賑米，惟美國方可免税，擬請飭該管官員，凡由

蕪湖、上海及一切内地賑米經過南京運至被災處所，

均當免税，並由地方官照料運送懷遠、正陽及各處

税卡，遇有貿易米糧雖運被災地方，亦照常納税，在

本大臣意凡有貿易米糧税款暫可豁免等因。當經

本部電達兩江總督暨安徽巡撫去後，准該督撫復

電稱，無論何處運賑糧前往災區，概免税釐云云。兹本

部已電復，以比必羅炳生二教士所購米糧係爲放賑

之用應飭沿途關卡概免稅厘並由地方官照料運
送等語至貿易米糧能否暫免稅厘或減輕之處
亦經電囑該督撫妥籌酌辦相應函復
貴大臣查照可也專此順頌
日祉
全堂銜
宣統三年三月　日

一九八

照會和比英朱美嘉法斐代使呂大臣派吳桐林前往海外勸捐護照簽字蓋印送還並布電知保護由

行

外務部副大臣胡
署外務部副大臣曹

九月　日

考工司
呈為照會事准呂大臣咨稱奉
旨派充中國紅十字會會長兼辦慈善救濟事宜現甫
開辦經費支絀不得不廣為勸募茲委農工商部郎
中吳桐林前往和英美法國之爪哇巴達維亞蘇門答臘日里、星加坡吉礲坡大霹靂檳榔嶼仰光、非律賓、西貢暹羅地方勸募捐
款請照會駐京大臣電知保護並請發給護照等因前

來相應繕就護照一紙蓋用印信照送
貴大臣查照發字送還本部以便轉交孟布雷知各
處照章妥為保護可也須至照會者　附照一

和貝
英朱　使
美嘉
法裴代

宣統三年九月　日

一九九

逕復者七月二十四日准

貴部來函以據五城察院文稱有德國洋人及日本國洋人黑夜在前門外向鋪戶敲門情事請轉致各大臣查禁等因

本領銜大臣當已轉達各大臣知照據各大臣意見以為各國洋人如有不善行為請不必函送各國領銜公會應即逕達該洋人所管之

駐京大臣辦理相應函復

貴王大臣查照可也特此即頌

日祉附送洋文

名另具八月初三日

附件

LEGATION OF THE UNITED STATES OF AMERICA,
PEKIN, CHINA.

Le 4 Septembre, 1902.

Altesse:

J'ai l'honneur d'accuser reception de la dépêche datee le 27 Aout, 1902, dans laquelle Votre Altesse se plaint des méfaits de certaines personnes de nationalité allemande et japonaise.

Sur la presentation de cette question à l'attention de mes honorables collègues, ils m'ont chargé de suggerer à Votre Altesse que les plaintes au sujet de la mauvaise conduite des individus d'une nationalité spéciale soient portées à la Légation intéressée plutot qu'au Corps Diplomatique.

Veuillez agreer, Altesse, l'assurance de ma tres haute considération.

E. H. Conger

Ministre des Etats Unis, et
Doyen du Corps Diplomatique.

A Son Altesse, le Prince K'ing,
Président du Ministère des Affaires Etrangères.

二〇〇

逕啟者，茲因川省亂党滋擾一事，可惜尚須提醒
貴親王數日內接由成都來電云，亂党情形日愈猖獗，並未壓伏，
稍平，似係又與一千九百年拳匪變亂情形無異，地方官所行之法，
亦與從前辦法如出一轍。
貴國政府所用壓伏之力，仍未能勝於從前，難期得力，由此觀
之，將來結果，自必與前事從同也。查一千九百年所經變亂，頗

可為川省此事之殷鑒彼時
貴國政府若能致力剪除拳匪何致以後多傷生命現在川省
之事亦何不然今若能趕緊設法竭力壓伏必可免成大害現
在歐羅巴與亞美理駕兩洲人均拭目以觀川省拳匪復興之
亂深以中國此際必不可使他國視為不能或為不肯用力制
伏辦理係為最要該省一帶滋擾之處住有美國數人是以按

照本分本大臣應再行切詢
貴國政府現用如何即可成功辦法以免美國人或遭患害望速
示悉可也特此奉布即頌
爵祺附送洋文
名另具八月十八日

附件

F.O.No.

LEGATION OF THE UNITED STATES OF AMERICA,
PEKIN, CHINA.

September 18th, 1902.

Highness:

I regret to again be compelled to call the attention of Your Highness to the very serious troubles in the Province of Szechuen; but recent telegraphic information from Chentu reports increasing disturbance and danger there, instead of a suppression thereof.

The movement seems to be a veritable repetition of the Boxer uprising of 1900, the action of local officials the same, the efforts of the Government no more successful, and the ultimate result must be the same.

The experience of 1900 proves that the terrible massacre of that year might have been prevented by prompt, energetic and repressive action by the Government. I believe the same might be accomplished in this case.

All Europe and America are watching the progress of this revival of Boxerism in Szechuen; and China can illy afford to let the impression go forth that she either cannot or will not immediately suppress it.

There are several Americans in the disturbed Province, and it is my duty to again demand that such prompt

and

and effective measures be taken as will ensure their safety and protection.

I improve the opportunity to assure Your Highness of my highest consideration.

Envoy Extraordinary and
Minister Plenipotentiary of
the United States.

To His Highness, Prince of Ch'ing,
President of the Board of Foreign Affairs.

二〇一

逕啟者、本日早間、據美國人窪而任稟稱、日前來京作演馬戲、早數日由魏力邁、而未悉其屬何國所轄、買得洋產白小馬一匹、價洋七十五元、有肅府通曉洋語之中貴官員、喜愛此馬數次前來欲買、窪而任不願出賣、數日前、魏力邁而向窪而任云、汝買我之馬、寔在便宜、現有肅府中貴官員、願出洋二百元、欲買此馬、窪而任仍不願賣、昨晚已至演戲完畢之期、人所盡悉、於晚間魏力邁而同肅府中貴官員，並未知會馬主人，暗往馬棚去看馬，想必得知此馬拴在棚内何處。魏力邁而寓居北京飯店，窪而任亦寓此店中，故於昨日見魏力邁而與肅府中貴官員同在飯店用飯，昨晚因馬戲完畢，拆卸棚帳，收什行李之際，忽進馬棚，不見此馬，驗係被人割開棚後之席，將馬竊去。看切近沙土地方，有洋人與華人足跡之痕，而馬蹄之跡，則係牽往北去，此馬

北京有數洋人均行認識云云相應請
貴大臣查照希即特派地面官員並加人員遍爲踹訪惟望踹獲
此馬無須懲辦盜馬之人可也特此奉布即頌
日祉

名另具 九月二十一日

再者聞魏力邁而原係華人阮姓向住新嘉坡洋名呼作魏力邁而附及

二〇二

收九月廿三

照會

大亞美理駕合衆國欽命駐劄中華便宜行事全權大臣康　為

照會事、現奉本國、
政府來文、囑將華爾眷屬所索華爾遺留之款照會
貴親王、望即詳查此案細情、按其所應得者、公平商
辦、茲將寄到華爾之遺案説洋文一册、按照譯就繕
録一本一併送閲、若加詳閲、自應記憶此甚著名之
美國人、為中國出力捐軀、迄今未得如何酬報本大
臣深信

貴親王、披閱此遺案之説、自能提醒、明認彼時中國勢甚危迫、幸得此大有智勇之人、得以保全要地、將必設一妥善辦法、使此年久未了之遺款、畀與華爾後人、

貴國果能如此辦理、方顯明兩國睦誼最敦、按照現時情形、所應互相公平辦事之理也、為此照會

貴親王查照、須至照會者、附送洋文並譯册 洋文册前已函送

右　照　會

大清欽命全權大臣便宜行事總理外務部事務和碩慶親王

一千九百二年拾月貳拾肆日

光緒貳拾捌年玖月貳拾叁日

附件

F.O. No. 435

LEGATION OF THE UNITED STATES OF AMERICA,
PEKIN, CHINA.

Oct. 24th. I902.

Your Highness:-

By direction of my Government, I have the honor to present to Your Highness a claim of the heirs of General Frederick T.Ward, with the hope that it may be carefully examined and given such equitable consideration as it justly merits.

I inclose a concise history of the claim, and a carefully prepared Chinese translation thereof, a perusal of which will recall to Your Highness the unrequited services of the distinguished American, who gave his life in defense of the Chinese Empire; and I feel sure will prompt Your Highness to recognize China's immeasurable obligation to this great man, and to take such measures as will result in the payment of this long delayed claim to his legal representatives.

This would be a fitting expression on the part of China of the good will and spirit of fair dealing which under present conditions should be mutually entertained by both our countries.

E.H. Conger

Minister of the United States.

To His Highness Prince of Ch'ing,

President of the Board of Foreign Affairs.

二〇三

逕啟者適接美國駐漢口領事官函稱按一千九百零一年
所定之約有數道
上諭應於各省府廳州縣遍行張貼兹查有甘肅洮州岷州河南息
縣新蔡縣均未張貼等因據想
貴國應詳按和約所列各節遵守照辦現在和睦交涉方可久
而不渝諒必
貴親王亦有同心是以函達
查照請即於所指未曾張貼之處一律補貼可也特布即頌
爵祺 附送洋文
名另具 十月初七日

附件

F.O. No. 1341

LEGATION OF THE UNITED STATES OF AMERICA,
PEKIN, CHINA.

Nov. 6th. 1902.

Your Highness:-

I have the honor to inform Your Highness that I have just received a report from the United States' Consul at Hankow, stating that the Imperial Proclamations required by the Peace Protocol of 1901 to be posted in all district cities of the Empire have not been so posted in the following places:-

T'ao Chou in Kansu,
Min Chou in Kansu,
Hsi Hsien in Honan, and
Hsin-ts'ai Hsien in Honan.

I am sure Your Highness will agree with me that it is necessary to carefully observe the provisions of the Treaty in order to preserve the friendly relations which at present exist between China and the Powers, and I have to request therefore, that Your Highness will issue such orders as may secure the posting of these Edicts in the places mentioned.

I avail myself of the opportunity to renew to Your Highness the assurance of my highest consideration.

E. H. Conger

U.S.Minister.

To Prince Ch'ing, President of
the Board of Foreign Affairs.

二〇四

作

二月初一日收

欽派代辦出使美日秘古國大臣事宜三品頂戴分省補用道沈桐爲申呈事竊查接管卷内光緒二十八年七

月二十三日承准

養電開檀香山領事楊蔚彬屢被參控不洽商情應先撤差餘詳咨又本年八月二十四日承准

咨開本年七月初九日准軍機處片交軍機大臣面奉

諭旨有人奏檀香山正領事楊蔚彬古今輝同惡相濟魚肉華民有售煙販人聚賭各款請飭查辦等

語着外務部查核辦理欽此欽遵並鈔原奏知照前來本部查中國在各國設立領事原爲出洋華民

妥籌保護若如原奏檀香山領事楊蔚彬古今輝不法各款不惟貽笑外人轉使該處工商人等受其凌

虐何以宣

德意而慰輿情現經欽奉

諭旨交本部查核相應照録原奏咨行按照所參該領事等各款秉公確查勿稍瞻徇迅即據實聲復

本部以憑核辦可也附鈔件各等因當經前出使大臣伍　札派護理金山總領事刑部主事周汝鈞就近赴
檀香山查辦而前領事楊蔚彬以迭被商民來轅控告業經委小呂宋繙譯官李光亨調赴檀島就近密查
旋據稟復是保皇會黨挾洽辦之嫌列款上控多有不實之處適楊蔚彬上稟力辯並自請引退告假
回籍伍大臣以會黨誣控固多虛辭詆毀究屬不洽輿情當經批飭回籍聽候查辦由伍大臣電陳
鈞署九月十二日又奉
文開准美使康格照稱有住檀香山賀挪魯地方入美籍華人藍山在美國政府具控中國領事官楊
為賓曾函達廣東一道台將彼住華之祖母與母監禁彼母自盡祖母亦亡檀香山華人至領事者請領
執照納費過重華人均與之離心離德稟控查辦又據王亮另稟該領事文報粵東撫院謂王亮亦非善
類囑縣派兵圍彼之村向王亮合族祠堂屢屢勒索銀兩累及親眷傷財各等因由美政府囑該處副總
督查復詳核所供尚屬確實接奉本國所囑速將此重要之事照請中國政府查照甚望確按公平仁

愛之理以辦此事等因前來本部查本月初九日准軍機處鈔交軍機大臣面奉

諭旨有人奏檀香山正領事楊蔚彬古今輝同惡相濟魚肉華民有售煙販人聚賭各款請飭查辦等語著外務部查核辦理欽此當經咨行貴大臣秉公確查據實聲復在案茲復據美使照稱前因溯查光緒二十七年正月十九日欽奉

諭旨各處華民出洋謀生者甚多無不眷懷故土傾心內嚮乃孫汶康梁諸逆託為保國之說設立富有票會煽惑出洋華民斂資鉅萬若不詳切開導破其詭謀使知該逆等藉詞保國實圖謀逆乘機作亂誠恐華民受其蠱惑仍紛紛傾助款項蔓延日甚為患實深著呂海寰李盛鐸羅豐祿伍廷芳選派妥員前往各商埠詳察情形剴切曉諭務令各華民曉然於該逆等並非真心保國勿再聽其搖惑輕棄資財以定人心而弭隱患欽此恭譯

諭旨惟在開導出洋華民俾知去逆効順益堅其內嚮之忱若如美使所稱檀香山領事楊為賓藉端苛虐

各節殊不足以奉宣
德意楊為賓目即楊蔚彬屢遺物議不洽商情亟應按款查究相應鈔錄來照咨行貴大臣即將該領事先
行撤差歸入前案一併查明切實聲復勿稍徇隱
國家設立領事原期撫輯僑氓嗣後務於安分工商人等加意愛護即有曾經被惑之徒亦當遵
旨剴切勸導予以自新俾得各安生業是為至要等因當經伍大臣札發周領事歸入前案一併查辦旋據
護理領事周汝鈞稟稱查檀香山領事楊蔚彬前被商民鍾宇張良等稟控三月時經憲台委李緒譯
光亨查辦曾查明係因保皇會逆黨挾怨辦之嫌砌詞誣控稟復在案楊領事已於六月底告假卸任
副領事古今輝現兼理正領事卑職到檀香山即傳正埠商董趙蔭棠前副領事王殿璋等施濟局
董理余蘭芬嚴壬成等老成殷實商家劉球鄭金等辦理賠款單值理鄭善昭潘李良等嚴密查
究博訪周咨並調查案卷參諸輿論已盡悉其原委謹為憲台切實陳之原參謂檀香山正領事

楊蔚彬古今輝同惡相濟魚肉華民查楊蔚彬任正領事古今輝任副領事署中各事俱歸正領事主持前鍾宇等誣控及美康使照會亦止言楊蔚彬並無牽及古今輝今謂古今輝同惡相濟實非確論光緒二十五年冬洋人防疫燒埠華民流離失所楊領事倡議創設施濟局捐廉銀一千圓並捐米及買衣物施濟值銀數百圓古領事亦捐銀二百圓共集款鉅萬親自巡行放濟實惠及民並無魚肉華民之事原參謂私售煙土販賣人口查洋關於煙土收稅甚重盤查甚嚴最難走漏據各商民所言僉謂不聞楊領事有煙土出售且會黨曾控楊領事於美政府經美政府委員到稅關查究並無實據將案註銷稅關有案可稽似屬可信至販賣人口查無其事楊領事前在憲署當隨員時曾有使婢一口出嫁紐約埠李姓商人為繼室或怨家因此附會遂至傳聞之誤又原參謂開場聚賭擅取陋規各節查楊領事在署並無開賭華工回華如在洋稅關出入項紙者限一年返美若因病逾期須將情由稟明領事發一展限憑紙方能回美此項紙費向歸領署外銷以為辦公津貼楊領

事初收五圓一年以後以領事署事務殷繁自行延用通洋話人員幫辦發照事務所發之照每張加收五
圓二毫五仙過往華人妻孥登岸執照亦收銀五圓二毫五仙未有收至十二圓者此項執照現已停止又楊領
事設立保護執照凡會黨悔過自新退出逆會者准其領一護照以免回華時被人誣指每照一張收銀
三圓二毫五仙而商民未入會黨者亦多到領照以資保護此項護照意在誘勵商民勿入亂黨然未
免予人以口實又原參謂侵蝕會館公項一節查燒埠時楊領事創設施濟局各埠華洋商俱有捐助
共得銀二萬餘元除施濟支用尚餘銀九千五百圓存貯洋商畢淑銀行保皇會逆黨舉其黨鍾木賢鍾
宇為中華會館商董鍾宇欲將施濟局餘款提歸中華會館支銷楊領事謂此係施濟局款須留備不
虞之需不肯任其支取該會黨遂四播流言誣楊領事盤踞此款志在侵蝕其實此銀尚存在銀行前奉
憲批有不准官商借端侵挪留為地方善舉公費之諭自應遵照辦理至華民被焚燬財產議向美
廷索賠經集衆公舉值理十餘人在中華會館開辦華民索償單由會館先行代支估價及繙譯中

西文諸人工食並紙張等費俟賠款後抽還共支用銀二千四百餘圓此銀係公議支用由董值實支實銷
非經楊領事之手簿領可稽無從侵蝕現美廷已允賠償此款自歸有著又原參謂楊領事奸淫有
夫婦女未據指出何人無從查究亦未聞有人控楊領事淫其婦女者當是訛言此查明原參各款
之實在情形也美康使照會謂檀香山美籍華人藍山在美國政府具控中國領事楊為賓將彼住
華之祖母與母監禁彼母自盡祖母亦亡又據王亮另稟該領事文報粵東撫院謂王亮亦非善類
廣東官員因囑縣派兵圍彼之村向王亮合族祠堂屢屢勒索銀兩每次數百兩累及親眷各節查光
緒二十六年逆犯梁啟超到檀香山倡立保皇會意圖煽惑人心梁蔭南窩藏梁啟超在家黃亮充逆會
總理奉憲札飭查將為首逆黨詳請咨辦楊領事即稟請將梁蔭南黃亮二名咨廣東原籍押辦
家屬王亮即黃亮藍山即梁蔭南買得別人入美籍冊紙姓林名西者遂自稱梁林西實則林西本
人已故冒充顯然梁蔭南之母畏罪自盡其祖母亦因年老病亡非關逼勒縣役下鄉收受茶錢容

或有之斷不至每次索銀數百兩楊領事遠在外洋此皆非楊領事初意所及料案由出使大臣咨
前兩廣總督李 行縣查辦並非楊領事函達廣東道台亦非楊領事文報粵東巡撫此查明美使照
會各款之實在情形也至古領事在檀香山最久人甚誠樸前充中華會館副商董十年正商董六
年前任崔楊兩使憲皆倚用之加正領事銜委辦正領事事務光緒二十三年憲台飭留原差仍加正
領事銜辦領事事務商民向皆悅服光緒二十四年憲台奏派楊蔚彬為正領事古今輝為副領事數
年以來民皆愛戴自光緒二十六年亂黨倡立保皇會楊領事初則出示[illegible]繼則函請檀島總督阻止
發給准照又將亂黨為首之人稟請咨籍嚴辦又不准該會黨動支施濟局存款該會黨遂大肆
攻擊布散謠言反噬以圖傾陷該會黨設立報館名新中國報自稱為保皇會喉舌毀謗
宮廷詆斥政府語多狂悖其誣毀楊領事者幾無日無之檀山華報館三家華夏報及隆記報於楊領事
俱無貶詞可見該會黨挾嫌攻訐楊領事遇事與該會黨為難激以相持似亦操之過蹙然為

國家禁遏亂萌，爲僑氓消除邪慝，實屬因公起見。卑職與古領事曾剴切勸導，惟該會黨與其衆未
易遽行解散，請札飭古領事隨時開導，以冀徐知悔悟，漸渙其羣。古領事接任後，護照費已減收
五毫，惟展限憑紙現收費五圓二毫五仙，可否飭照金山例限收二元，以惠商旅。謹將查明各款據實
稟復，並附呈新中國報紙五張、洋報紙一張，伏候察核辦理等情。前來查前檀香山正領事楊蔚彬
屢被商民鍾宇等上控，迭經伍大臣派員查辦，所控各款一經澈究，事多不實。據該委員李光亨
前後稟復及該員自行明白稟復各件，大致尚屬相符。伍大臣以列款上控雖屬虛誣，該領事究屬
不洽輿情，已因其上稟告假，批飭回籍聽勘，業於六月交卸。嗣奉
鈞署洽電撤差，亦經札知在案。茲據委員周汝鈞查復各情，是魚肉華民實無其事，出洋華民
習聞平權自由之說，又熟知領事在洋無權拘辦斷，無俯首降心聽其魚肉之理，惟職居領事，自應
於僑寓工商一體撫輯，自能所至民樂，所去民思。今該領事屢致參控，不洽輿情，予以撤差，咎有

應得至稟請洛辦會黨實因羣情洶洶之時非擇尤嚴辦一二人不足以示懲儆而昭順逆雖遇事

相持操之過蹙而當官執法心跡可原怨家挾洛辦之嫌持其短長肆為誣詆刊有說貼廣播風謠

流聞京師即由於此觀於該委員查出會黨新中國報語多指斥謗及

乘輿則會黨恃洋籍為護符其肆無忌憚之情形已可概見特將報紙六張一並封呈備核至古副領

事在檀十有餘年辦事誠樸商民信服異口同聲茲因同官弃累究有公論可憑自應曲予保全

以為任事者勸現已密函授以方畧務將被惑愚民剴切勸導予以自新其有悔罪來歸者務當加意

愛護至誠相孚則感通自易民聽不惑則邪慝自消庶無負

朝廷撫綏僑民之至意其展限照紙應仿照金山成案每張限收二圓護照每張限收五毫飭令以後著為

定例不准溢收絲毫以紓民力仍於每季將收支款目詳列清册隨銷册一併報銷俾有稽核而杜流

弊所有查明領事屢被參控各款據實陳明伏乞

鈞署裁奪核辦爲此備文申呈

鈞部謹請察覈施行須至申呈者 附呈報紙六張

右 申 呈

外 務 部

光緒二[illegible]月[illegible]九日

附件一

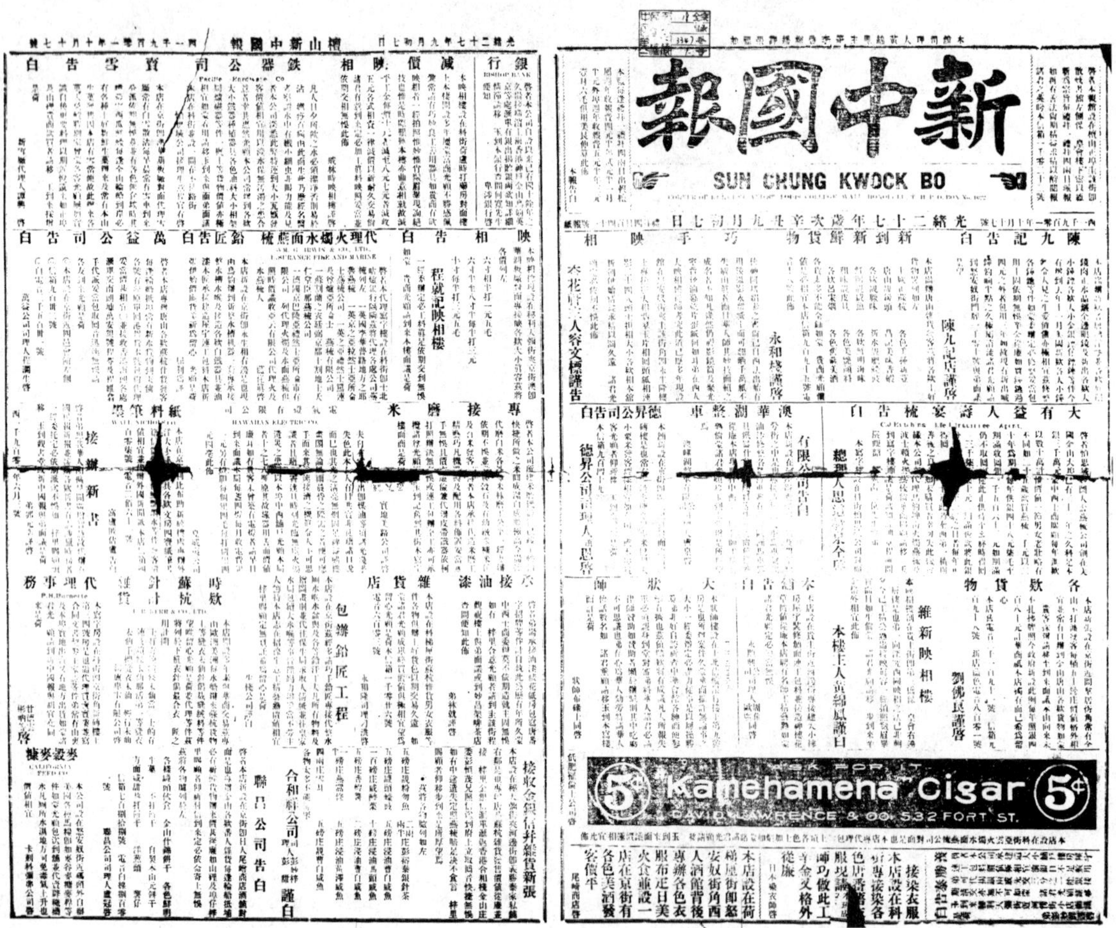

新中國報

SUN CHUNG KWOCK BO

光緒二十七年歲次辛丑九月初七日

Kamehameha Cigar

5¢

DAVID LAWRENCE & CO. 532 FORT ST.

詆斥宫廷並指中國大事爲分黨

木館設在檀香山正埠公會保衛壹號 ｜ 檀山新中國報 ｜ 木館新聞登件每期貳拾號

論說

本館新聞

擇錄各報

光緒叁拾柒年九月初七日 ｜ 檀山新中國報 ｜ 西一千九百零一年十月十七號

皇太后

本館司理人黄寬、主筆劉聘臣、翻譯鄺子熙、繙譯羅伯特……

新中國報

SUN CHUNG KWOCK BO

1016 SMITH STREET, HONOLULU, T. H. P. O. BOX No. 1022

光緒二十八年歲次壬寅元月初七日 禮拜四 第七百十二號報紙 一千九百零二年二月十三號

橫濱福生泰告白

李鴻章將到出賣

本館代派新民叢報

狀師告白

F. M. BROOKS

聯呂公司告白

淡那嚕爐鐵器有限公司

本公司啟

影相大減價

杏花軒映相樓開設在怒安奴街夾該主街角專接映大小相片今特大爲減價茲將價值錄下

本樓謹啟

雜貨店

永和隆司理刁洪啟

驢馬平沽

專接磨米

暫時代理廣告

道衙告示

代理人槎厘吉打刺啟

蘇杭雜貨藥材舖新張

廣德昌公司謹啟

廣智書局印行書目

最新萬國政鑑

政治學

中國文明小史

政治原論

廣智書局印行書目

埃及近世史

法學通論

東邦近世史

泰西史教科書

歐洲財政史

中國財政一班

中國疆域沿革說略

東亞口岸志

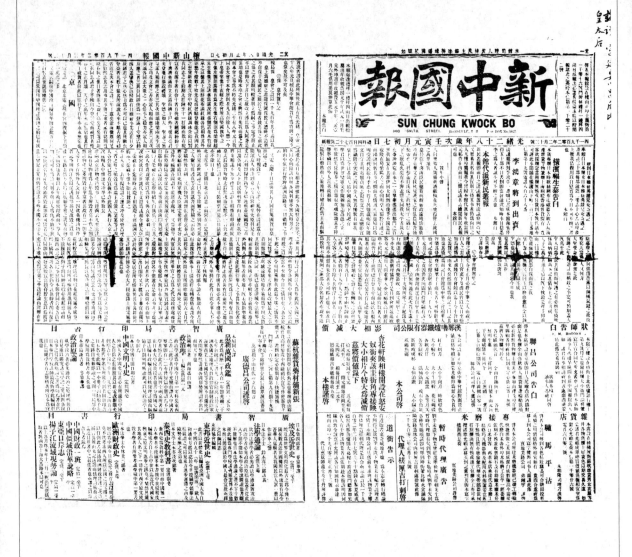

揚子江流域現勢論

檀山新中國報

各省

各國

續島

狀師告白

C. R. HEMENWAY

大狀師

GILL and FARLEY

賞格廣告

沐浴房

金時湯主人謹告

包辦鉛匠工程

代理稅紙事務

新張廣告

專醫雜症

櫻川本次郎啓

森口商店 帽子平沽

本店設在賀梯厘街近
怒安奴街角十四號門
牌巧手織造各款草帽
本店主人來埠將有十
年向操織帽之業現華
請有上手織工務要求
其精美且前者沽出各
款帽子均蒙中西人士
贊賞不已本店非好自
誇謂予不信請移玉到
來一顧爲幸再者華人
新年將近今特爲大減
價平沽以應華人賀年
佳節望各留意光顧小
店爲幸

發沽帽子店森口商店啓

檀山新中國報

鴻發公司新張告白

承頂生意廣告

謝□□君

鴻發公司遷舖告白

上海□□局收銀發票廣告

□蘭底文書館告白

安會館廣告

新式脚車

銀行

醫學士李啓輝診症廣告

李□□仝白

美酒發客

包辦鉛匠工程

大律師告白

新考狀師廣告

勁慎巡夜

上海廣智書局

編譯中學教科書

廣智書局小叢書

力詆楊領事并譏
使署文詆政府某中堂

新中國報

SUN CHUNG KWOCK BO

1016 SMITH STREET, HONOLULU, T. H. P. O. BOX No. 1022

每禮拜三期
五元 遠埠六元

一千零十六號 一千零二十二號 四六號

光緒二十八年歲次壬寅九月十四日

本館代派
橫濱新民叢報
金山文興日報
天津大公報
上海新世界報
上海選報

錄稿代論說

貴重地段出賃

催收股銀

信隆號信局廣告

來往信札

理人李瑞軒啓

包辦鉛匠工程 加意快捷

新到新鮮貨物

永和棧謹啓

劉商精畫油相炭精相

專接磨米

廣源興公司告白

Kwung Yuen Hing CO.

馬房生意出頂

頂退生意聲明

英文夜館復啓

各物俱全

代理聲明

竹勝記謹白

檀山新中國報

京國

以義堂告白

驄馬出賣

承受整車生意

接金收信

狀師廣告

旋唐託理

旋唐託理

醫學士李啓輝診症廣告

在新中國報

李啓輝 全白

代理火燭水險告白

遷舖廣告

思義合

義合接收金銀信滙單

啓者本店設在秘利天
彌街夾亞剌基街角專
接收香城隆艮兩鄱各
梓友金銀書信遞返香
港中環信來棧金山庄
轉滙石岐安九八行
委作派交並取回音交
回原人以慰急望如有
水陸不測致遭遺失照
燕梳例賠償若蒙見委
定當快捷無誤
本號並自辦金山各款
火食罐頭生蠔各樣生
菓當有煤油發客諸君
賜顧仰祈留心是禱
本號一在新魚市陳揚記代收

公司謹啓

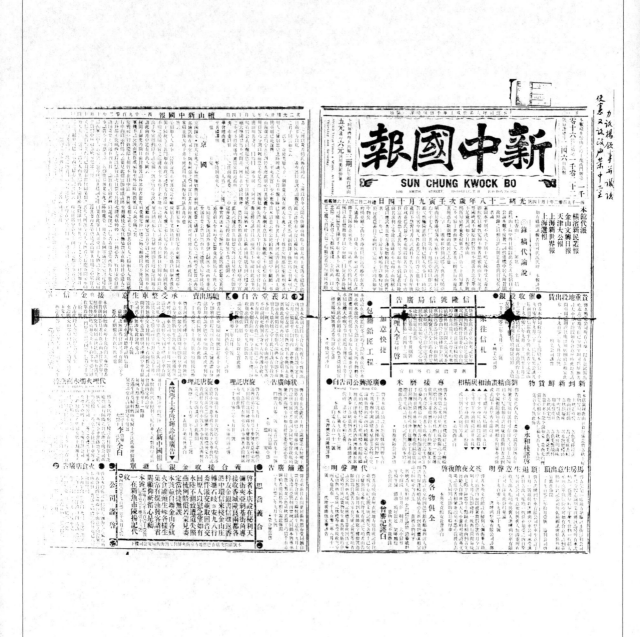

火倉店廣告

其三 在十 ... 街一千零十六號門牌　檀山新中國報　本館 ... 零貳拾貳號

◎本館譯錄新聞

●狀師廣告

華商會告白
本月十六號禮拜四晚議事
華商會同人公啓

旋唐託理
預先聲明

一千九百零二年十月十一號
拍思域有限公司管庫人
林顯暢古摩近預啓

QUON On SOCIETY
RIVER STREET BETWEEN BERETANIA AND KUKUI STR
HOnOLULU H. T.

●阜安閣當年董值告白●
啓者本閣十八月一號集議投筒公舉當年新舊董值人員辦理閣中事務茲將芳名列左
正總理 ... 副總理 ...
正管庫 郭裔勳 副管庫 古滿生
華紀錄 林杰朝 英紀錄 容 富
正查數 程緒棠 副查數 王 釗
管數 林敏繖
值理 陳 棠　譚渭山　程恭秉　程韶亭　楊日新　楊渭賓　古道生　周文煥　譚秉良　林 焯　黃紹卿　徐應麟　梁鳳亭　黃雲初　陳 齡　林乃光　盧仁山
一千九百零二年八月十八號
阜安閣紀錄事林杰朝譯啓

收盆貨物平沽
啓者本店生意現卽收盆卽將店中所存貨物由九月十三號卽禮拜六日起限四十五日內概將店中各樣貨物照成本價大減低盡賣無存欲買相宜貨物者祈勿失此好機緣也
一舖底什物架生厘時一概招人承受如意者請移玉到本店面議價甚相宜此佈
一千九百零二年九月九號
京街永來公司蘇杭舖啓

漢那嚕爐鐵器有限公司
減價平沽
●本公司啓

催收股銀

◎頂好煤炭發客◎

其四　光緒二十八年九月十四日　檀山新中國報　西一千九百零二年十月十四號

ORIENTAL BAZAAR
PHONG FAT CO

本號專辦
江西磁器　上海絲髮
廣東磁器　各式絲巾
日本磁器　頭綉物件
日本漆器　各式女鞋
頂好地蓆　各式拖鞋
籐枝椅梳　洋口網帶
樟木梳箱　欵禮名茶
籐床籐椅　古銅器具
紅毛綃邊　象牙器具
紅毛底彩　文銀器具
龍鬚草蓆　檀香器具
洋琴絃索　牙扇毛扇
…貨目太多未能盡錄
本信箱第九百四十七號
電話藍字第五百八十一號
鴻發公司謹啓

66-72 N.KING ST.COR.SMITH
P. O. BOX 947　HONOLULU, T. H.

除名告白
黃和興公司 ... 京街威地新 ... 張
黃和興公司啓

漢那嚕爐麻糖舖告白
Honolulu Candy Co.
漢那嚕爐麻糖舖告白

承股聲明

KALIHI FERTILIZER WORKS
啓者本公司有上好落田雀糞出賣此雀糞爲肥料中之第一美品凡華人之在夏威夷茂宜道威諸島者皆有購用至再用三用不已蓋落此肥則獲利勝于蝦糠麻屑等數倍也
又本公司有各種肥料出賣價極相宜
本公司在架厘希屯車站頭處
架厘希雀糞公司啓
架厘希雀糞公司

●董值告白●
茲將一千九百零二年十月一號公舉當年值理詳列
總理 劉長大　紀錄 周鼠安　管庫 黃 秋
查數 黃開邦　黃文煥
協理 陳利典　楊鼎全　林立禧　梁賢朱　劉顯華　林公有　鄧迪　趙根　張 知　俞 業　鄧 佑　黃阜喜　李 棣　陳 嫁

◎黃梁都公司謹啓

◎謹謝厚情

◎國安會館同人謝啓

●江夏堂捐欵新章●
W. W. Ahana
Nuuanu St.
Box 986 Honolulu, Oahu.

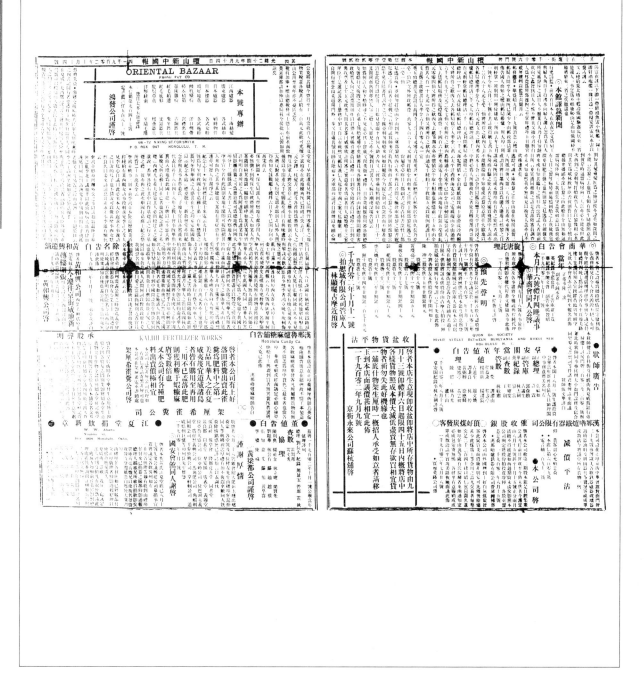

美委員到檀稅関查販烟事言無憑據实証不足准信

THE PACIFIC COMMERCIAL ADVERTISER, HONOLULU, AUGUST 30, 1903

EDITOR IS RELEASED

Y. Kimura Made an Acceptable Apology.

INDICTMENT IS THEN QUASHED

Court Wouldn't Sentence Chinese Boy for Criminal Assault. Court Notes.

Y. Kimura, the Japanese editor of the Honolulu News, who was indicted by the August grand jury for criminal libel, was discharged yesterday morning by Judge Gear, upon a nolle prosequi being entered by Mr. Cathcart.

Kimura was charged with having libelled a prominent Japanese merchant, one S. Kimura, in the News' issue of July 31st. In this article it was alleged that Kimura had not shown the proper respect for a deceased friend, and had danced naked in the room where his dead body lay. It was alleged further that he with others had been singing and otherwise enjoying themselves at the funeral.

In court yesterday morning Mr. Cathcart announced that he desired to enter a nolle prosequi. "It has been represented to me," said the deputy attorney general, "that the amende honorable has been made to the person who claimed to be libeled, and he is desirous of dropping the prosecution."

Judge Gear inquired if it wasn't a rather strange proceeding to drop the prosecution after an indictment had been returned, simply at the request of the prosecuting witness.

Mr. Cathcart replied that in his opinion the only reason libel had been made a criminal offense was because of the trouble a personal quarrel might cause. He thought it was but a personal matter and did not believe it worth while to take up the time of the court and jury with a trial when the offender had apologized and the prosecuting witness was satisfied.

The nolle prosequi was entered, Judge Gear stating that he didn't believe a grand jury indictment should be made the basis for an apology.

COURT NOTES.

Wo Chong, a Chinese boy 15 years of age, charged with a criminal assault upon a girl of 11, was released upon suspended sentence. Judge Gear stated that he did not feel justified in imposing even the minimum of three months, and the order was consequently entered.

Judge Gear yesterday appointed David Dayton as guardian of Richard N. Oliver. The boy has an estate of $[illegible].

Formal order was made yesterday for the continuation of the August term of court for 12 days from August 29.

Judge Robinson yesterday denied the motion for alimony in the Metcalf divorce case.

The accounts have been approved in the guardianship matter of Kate Kaahue and P. D. Kellett Jr. allowed a fee of $15 as master.

E. C. Ferreira has applied for license to practice in the district courts of the Territory.

David Dayton has filed his third annual account as guardian of Madeline C. K. Dowsett, showing receipts of $2180.85 and expenditures of $151[illegible], leaving a balance of $651.97 for the year. The inventory shows 275 shares of Dowsett Co. stock, par value $[illegible], and 50 $1000 Dowsett Co. bonds.

An inventory has been filed of the estate of the late David Center, showing property worth $23,890.92. The estate consists of 50 shares Honolulu Plantation Co. stock, 1950; 29 shares Waianae, $2900; 50 shares Waialua, $5000; 125 Hawaiian Sugar Co., $2500; 50 shares American Sugar Co., $500; 15 shares Honomu, $1500; cash, $840.92. The mother of the minor children has asked to be appointed guardian.

S. C. Allen has appealed from Judge Humphreys' order compelling him to pay $75 to E. M. Watson and $50 to J. J. Dunne for services as guardians of the Lucas minors.

Motion to dismiss the order vacating service in the case of Bishop & Co. vs. W. H. Pain et al. has been made.

Petition has been made for the appointment of George H. Huddy as guardian for Iokepa Kaie.

A divorce was granted yesterday to Kekula Kupihea from James Kupihea.

In the matter of the estate of Annie H. K. Dowsett, David Dayton as guardian reports receipts of $2198.16 and expenditures of $1593.22. The estate consists of 275 shares Dowsett stock and 50 $1000 Dowsett bonds.

Judge Robinson yesterday heard the case of Godfrey vs. Kidwell.

Motion to have the sale of the McCully tract confirmed will be presented to Judge Humphreys this morning.

Judge Humphreys yesterday granted a license to practice law in the district courts to Robert W. Shingle.

Divorce was granted by Judge Robinson to Alice A. Bryant from Edwin J. G. Bryant, on the ground of non-support.

Mrs. Kato Kiku has applied for letters of administration upon the estate of Kato Iwakichi.

A NEW FUR SEAL ROOKERY

WASHINGTON, August 19.—Lieutenant Ellsworth Berthoff of the revenue cutter service, who received a gold medal from Congress last spring for his part in the expedition in Alaska in the winter of 1897-98, has added to his exploits by discovering a new fur seal rookery in the Aleutian Islands. While cruising among the islands near the extreme western end of the chain early in July, as executive officer of the cutter Manning, Lieutenant Berthoff went ashore with a boat's crew on the island of Bouldyer. There he found a rookery of fur seals, similar to those found on the famous Pribyloff islands, which are situated 700 miles in a northeasterly direction from Bouldyer.

The scene of the newly discovered seal herd is a mere dot of land between Behring sea and the Pacific ocean, fully 3500 miles west of San Francisco, but still within American jurisdiction.

Lieutenant Berthoff approached the herd closely enough to learn that none of the seals had been branded and there was no sign that white men in search of fur seals had ever been near the island. Captain Shoemaker, chief of the revenue cutter service, heard through the Aleutian island natives that there was a seal herd near the western end of the long chain of islands and he issued instructions last spring that the report be investigated by the Manning. It is believed that further discoveries will be made which, in view of the gradually declining seal fisheries in the Pribyloff islands, will prove to be of great importance.

CIRCUIT COURT PLUM

(Continued from Page 1.)

ed practically the reorganization of my office to meet the conditions. I don't say yet that I shall not go to Honolulu but I think it very improbable. No other man is yet in [illegible] for the [illegible] but it is not likely that anyone will go out there before sometime late in the fall."

THE CASE OF CHINESE CONSUL.

It is probably already known in Honolulu that Territorial Senator Carter, who investigated the alleged cases of smuggling, in which the Chinese Consul at Honolulu was said to be implicated, found that there was not sufficient evidence to sustain those charges. Mr. Carter's report was forwarded here to the Treasury Department and thence referred to the State Department. There it was stated this afternoon that the charges had not been sustained against the Chinese Consul but for the good of the service it had been deemed expedient to transfer him to another post of duty. This, of course, was done through the Chinese government on the strength of representations from the State Department to the Chinese minister here.

HONOLULU CUSTOMS RECEIPTS.

The annual summary of receipts for customs at the port of Honolulu, covering the fiscal year ended June 30, last, has been received from Collector Stackable and is on file in the office of Mr. W. S. Chance, chief of the division of special agents. It will be printed as a part of the Secretary's annual report to be made public two or three months later. It shows that the receipts from customs in the Territory of Hawaii during the past fiscal year were $1,227,[illegible]. The amount of refunds and drawbacks was $16,[illegible]. The expenses of collecting this sum was $[illegible], of which $[illegible] was for salaries, $262 for rents, $[illegible] for miscellaneous expenses, and [illegible] for [illegible] paid directly at the Department.

Collector Stackable states that the number of vessels which entered Honolulu or Hawaiian ports from foreign ports was 216 that cleared there for foreign ports was [illegible], while the number of vessels which entered from domestic ports was 2[illegible] and that cleared for domestic ports [illegible]. The entries of merchandise for duty numbered 3,2[illegible] and the entries, which were free of duty, numbered 1[illegible]. The total number of entries of every character was 4,5[illegible].

BRAZILIAN SUGAR.

H. W. Furniss, the United States consul at Bahia, writes to the State Department the following account of a convention of sugar producers in Brazil:

"Pursuant to a call issued by the National Society of Agriculture at Rio de Janeiro, delegates assembled here on June 25, 1902 to take part in the first sugar producers' convention of Brazil.

"Delegates were present from all the sugar-producing States—Sao Paulo, Rio de Janeiro, Pernambuco, Bahia, Parahiba, Alagoas, Sergipe, Rio Grande do Norte, and Maranaao. They were not sent according to any basis of apportionment, but were designated by the various agricultural and commercial societies, municipalities, State governments, groups of cane raisers, and sugar producers.

"The national society had planned an elaborate programme, to include the discussion of such subjects as symptoms of the sugar crisis, its causes and remedy; condition and preparation of the soil and qualities of cane cultivated; methods of culture; methods of sugar making; production; foreign trade; internal trade and means of enlarging it; production and consumption of alcohol, its industrial application for light and heat, its use as fuel for large factories; use of sugar cane for feeding stock.

"The subjects were not assigned to delegates, but it was left to the individuals to take whatever part they might wish; and instead of discussing the points outlined on the programme, the convention virtually narrowed down to considering various plans which were proposed to better the condition of those engaged in sugar production. These plans included federal loans to planters; abolition of tax for foreign export and payment of bounty for sugar so sent; a consumption tax on all sugars, the revenue so derived to reimburse the States for the export taxes removed and the bounty established; the storing of sugar by the Government and the sale of same without the intervention of the middleman, etc.

"After a week of discussion, it became apparent that the interests of the delegates were so diverse that it would be impossible to come to any definite conclusion, and the convention adjourned on July 4, to meet in February, 1903, at Pernambuco. The only thing accomplished was the adoption of a motion to the effect that interstate duties should be abolished and protesting against the high rates of taxation in general."

ERNEST G. WALKER.

WILL GIVE A PLACE

Portuguese May Be Allowed a Man.

FOURTH DISTRICT REPUBLICANS ACT

Declare One Representative Candidate Will Be Selected From Names Submitted.

Republicans stand ready to place the name of a Portuguese upon the ticket for the Legislature if the members of the political club of that nationality will agree to support the nominees of the party. This was agreed to in the meeting of the Fourth district committee yesterday, although the members of the Fifth district committee decided that they could not agree to make such a nomination unless the Portuguese came into the party by the regular channels.

The meeting of the Fourth district committee was well attended, though the members did not get together until late. The motions of McClellan and Isenberg were set aside and finally after some discussion the following motion of Brooks was passed:

Resolved, That it is the purpose of the Fourth district committee to place at the meeting of the district committee, to be held next week, one Portuguese American on the legislative ticket this year, from the Fourth district, provided the Portuguese Political Club will select names from which such candidate is to be chosen, and will pledge themselves to unanimously support the entire Republican ticket in return for such nomination.

A letter was read from Major Camara, saying that he had been misrepresented, that he had said only that the Portuguese club would not affiliate with the Republican party, but would support the entire ticket if the club nominees were on it.

Members of the committee said that the statements of members of the club were that the Republicans must take the Portuguese as they found them, and that there would be no affiliation with any party.

The conference committee of the Fifth district committee reported the substance of the conference and the matter of representation was then taken up. McCandless offered the [illegible] proportional representation resolution. This was tabled after some discussion and the secretary was directed to notify the central committee that the Fifth district thought that Portuguese or other citizens should take the regular course of coming into the party, and should secure representation in the usual way.

The committee on rules reported and under this plan the following committees were appointed:

First precinct—Lot Lane and James Davis.

Second—Nahoa and Kekuku.

Third—Noukana and Goodale.

Fourth—Gilliland and Kekahuna.

Fifth—Douglass (only one member from the precinct).

Sixth—Nawnakoa and Woodward.

Seventh—Clark and Sherwood.

Eighth—Dwight and Kapena.

Ninth—Apio and Harris.

Tenth—Kwai Fong and Isaac.

Finance Committee—L. L. McCandless, George S. Harris and J. C. Lane.

On motion it was decided that a committee of three should be created for the purpose of conferring with a similar committee from the Fourth district and then deciding the date for the holding of the joint convention for the nomination of senators for the Third senatorial district.

Chairman Achi announced that he had made arrangements for the placing on file at the headquarters of the remarks of all the Home Rule orators, and that any member could see them so as to refute them.

WAS AN ORNERY SPANISH PARROT

Bird That Cursed Officers of the Chilian Customs Service.

There are nationalities among parrots as well as among men and when a parrot decides to stick to one nationality and to adopt but one language all the wiles of man will not prevent him from doing so. Captain Perry, of the barkentine Addenda has a parrot on his vessel which has been with him for some years but which declines to speak anything but the Spanish language. The bird has caused Perry some trouble.

This parrot is a large, bright, green colored bird. It was raised on the Isthmus of Panama. For months and months Captain Perry has been endeavoring to teach the parrot to speak English. The only reply he has received to his courtesy in this way toward the bird was a cursing in Spanish. The bird swears like a regular deep sea skipper but sticks to its Spanish.

The only friends that the parrot has aboard the ship are two Guam natives who speak Spanish and can thus understand the bird.

But the last time that Skipper Perry was in a Chilian port he came very near being in trouble and all because of the bird. When the Chilian customs officials boarded his vessel they inquired if he could speak Spanish. He replied that he could not but a moment later the officials heard a voice declaring in pure Spanish: "Captain is a d—— liar." Later the bird was shouting: "Get off the ship you thieving officers." This was too much for the officials. They looked high and low for the owner of the voice and finally learned that it was the bird. Captain Perry had considerable difficulty in explaining that the bird was an "old Spanish [illegible]" and that it had not been taught such bad and disrespectful language on his vessel.

CABLE COMING DEC. 1ST

(Continued from Page 1.)

by her. It may be of interest for your readers to have some of the measurements of this grand boat. A gross tonnage of 12,000, length 572 feet, beam 63 feet, and mean draft 27 feet. The writer had the pleasure of going over the vessel soon after reaching port. Her trimmings and furnishings are plain, but substantial and uniform. Her cabin staterooms are fitted up for 220 passengers and the dining saloon has seating for over 200 at first table. The beautiful bronze staircase is something unique in itself and exceedingly appropriate to the general finish of this magnificent boat. I find the staterooms to be quite roomy, high between decks, with air tube ventilators for the let out or take up of foul air. The suites, of which there are four sets, are complete in their furnishings and comfort, and suggest all the luxuries of travel that can be conceived. The social hall is unique in itself and entirely different from anything of the kind I have visited. The advent of this vessel in the Pacific will revolutionize ocean travel to the Orient, and we predict that this boat will bring about many progressive improvements for the comfort of passengers in other competing lines.

"COSMO."

BUSINESS LOCALS

Manufacturers' Shoe Co. advertise a swell football shoe at $3.50.

Call at Hawaiian News Co. and learn how to possess a beautiful Fischer piano on easy terms.

Three unfurnished rooms, rear of cottage, separate entrance, can be had at 539 Beretania street. Rent $8.

Supt. of Public Works Boyd will sell government land at Kaneohe, this island, at auction, on Sept. 30th next.

Read recommendation of prominent business men of Hawaiian Electric Co. new Adams-Bagnall enclosed arc lamp.

Party well acquainted with the city and island trade advertises today for position. Can give the best of references.

If you wish to pasture your horse close in to town, and have same well cared for, call at 601 Stangenwald building.

Order a dozen of Manilla Anchor lager from Lovejoy & Co. Nothing else to equal it in health building and tonic properties.

A man and wife advertise today for a furnished or unfurnished cottage of two rooms. For particulars see our classified ads.

William Keiki gives notice that he will not be responsible for any debts contracted in his name unless accompanied by a written order.

C. Sterling, the painter, is now ready to do paperhanging. An experienced wallpaper man is in charge of the new department. The latest patterns always on hand.

A window full of fox terrier puppies, demonstrating the value of Spratt's dog food, medicine and soaps, now on display at Pearson & Potter Co., Ltd., Union and Hotel streets.

A full supply of disinfectants of every description is carried in stock by the Hollister Drug Co. They wish to remind people not to forget to disinfect their outhouses occasionally. Disinfection is recommended by them for this purpose.

Good teeth, good health. Without good teeth you need not expect good health. For good, reliable information about your teeth, consult the up-to-date Expert Dentists, in the Arlington block, opposite Union. Work fully guaranteed. Prices very low.

SUNDAY'S CONCERT.

Program Which Will Be Rendered at the Capitol Grounds.

PART I.

The Old Hundred
Overture, Zampa ... Herold
Ballad, The Silver Path ... Beavan
Grand selection, I Martiri ... Donizetti
Vocal selections, Four Hawaiian songs and choruses

PART II.

New Vocal Selections—
(a) Ping Pong ... Penn
(b) The Rose of Killarney ... Johnson
Miss J. Kelliaa and Mrs. N. Alapai.
Suite, The Rose of Shiras ... Eilenberg
Song, Adieu, Marie ... Adams
Gavotte, Intermezzo ... Lewis
The Star Spangled Banner

Another Still Captured.

Internal Revenue Collector Roy H. Chamberlain made another raid yesterday with good results. Accompanied by Deputy Collector Cougens and Special Deputy Drake, he captured an okolehao still at Kalihi which had been in full operation just a few minutes prior to the capture.

Ah Fong, the Chinese distiller in charge, was arrested, and together with his still and a sample of manufactured spirits, was taken to the lockup. About 15 gallons of okolehao were destroyed. The still captured had a capacity of about [illegible] gallons per day, and the fire was still under it when the raid was made. Criminal information will be filed against the Chinese by United States Attorney Breckons today.

Cable Steamer on the Way.

NANAIMO, [illegible], August [illegible].—Superintendent Wilson of the Canadian Pacific Railway Telegraph Company has received advices that the steamer Colonia will be at Victoria September 15th. The [illegible] steamer which will lay the Pacific cable from Bamfield on Vancouver island to Fanning island. She [illegible] built by the Telegraph Construction and Maintenance Company of London, England. Both the [illegible] the necessary cable [illegible] ago in June and finished [illegible], are now on the way [illegible]. At Fanning island she will meet the Anglia, which is laying the other end of the cable.

Died of Rare Disease.

NEW YORK, August 22.—Rudolph Fliedner of New Brunswick, N. J., is dead after a lingering illness from a rare disease of the skin, known to scientists as pemphigus vulgarus. No other case of the disease has ever been known in the United States, it is asserted. Fliedner's skin became as if scalded and his nurses had to swathe his entire body in cotton. Mr. Fliedner was first taken ill in May. Specialists were called, who studied the case with great interest, but could no nothing to relieve him, and he died from exhaustion. He was 44 years of age, and starting as a factory laborer, had built up a large business.

Admiral Merry at Coast.

SAN FRANCISCO, Aug. 29.—Among the passengers who arrived from Honolulu yesterday was Rear Admiral J. F. Merry, U. S. N., retired. The admiral is returning from Hawaii after a service of three years in the islands. He was in command of the coaling station at Honolulu and superintended all the navy work in the Territory. He was succeeded by Captain Whiting. He is on his way to Washington.

A New Enterprise.

A cordial invitation is extended to the residents of the city to be present at the opening of the New Cafe Royal today. Mr. McTighe, the genial proprietor, has spared no expense in fitting up this new establishment. Cold lunches will be served at all hours, in fact, everything in the line of eatables that are to be found in the best of restaurants will be served. This new cafe is on King street, just Ewa of Maunakea.

To the Public

In order to accommodate children who wish to be admitted to the Kona Orphanage a new building should be erected. There are not sufficient funds to buy material. Five hundred dollars is needed. Those wishing to assist in raising this sum can leave the money [illegible]

LOCAL BREVITIES.

Horses bought, sold and exchanged by W. S. Withers.

The William McKinley Lodge meets tonight for work in the second rank.

Annie V. Napthaly and Mr. Edmund Johnson were married on Saturday, August 23.

Bishop Restarick preaches in St. Andrew's cathedral tomorrow evening at 7:30 o'clock.

The Grand Army will give up its quarters in San Antonio hall and start its campfires at Elks' hall soon.

Ernest Haas, a German from Honolulu, was swindled out of $100 by a San Francisco bunko man. He recovered the money.

Frank Romer, first mate of the Honolulu, was discharged by Commissioner Gill yesterday, the witnesses having disappeared.

The Woman's Guild of St. Andrew's cathedral will hold its regular meeting Monday, Sept. 1, with Mrs. Cathcart at College Hills.

The annual meeting of the stockholders of the Hawaiian Orphanage and Industrial Schools Association, Ltd., has been postponed till Nov. 15.

It is reported that G. R. Ewart has resigned his position as manager of Kilauea Plantation and will be succeeded by Andrew Moore, now on the coast.

On Monday next, Judge Luther Wilcox's commission as district magistrate for Honolulu will expire, but it is understood that it will be renewed at once.

The excavations for the storm sewer in Kapiolani street have been completed and the pipe put down. The street is now being restored to its proper condition.

Alexander W. Waters, formerly ticket agent of the Pacific Coast Steamship Company, has disappeared from San Francisco, and is thought to have gone either to Hawaii or Australia.

Assistant Superintendent J. W. Erwin of the free delivery system, who will make a stay in the city, will be asked to deliver his illustrated lecture on Our National Capital before the Y. M. C. A. during his stay.

J. W. Erwin, assistant superintendent of the free delivery for the Postoffice Department, who is to arrive on the Alameda, will probably give his first lecture in Honolulu next week under the auspices of the Y. M. C. A.

The semi-annual meeting of the Honolulu Engineering Association will be held in the Castle & Cooke assembly rooms the evening of Monday, September 1st. The reports of the secretary and treasurer will be received and the election of officers will be held.

Miss Ada Murcutt, one of two traveling agitators who were here a year or more ago and went on to Japan, is in San Francisco. She tells the Chronicle that she was the first English woman to land on the island of Saghalien, and the San Francisco paper apparently believes it.

Dr. C. B. Cooper, representative of the Honolulu lodge of Elks at the reunion held in Salt Lake, was met on the dock last night when the Alameda arrived by a number of Elks. He said he had had a jolly good time while away and would tell the herd about his trip later on.

A Porto Rican woman, making the plea that her husband was in jail and she had no home, applied to Jailor Henry for a resting place. She was given a room and some time after she gave birth to a girl baby. She was cared for, and will be kept until a home is provided for her.

J. F. Hackfeld yesterday brought suit against P. E. R. Strauch and Fannie Strauch, his wife, and J. P. Mendonca, to foreclose a mortgage for $[illegible] upon certain lands in Kalihi. The property is now in the possession of Mendonca, having been sold to him subject to the mortgage held by Hackfeld.

[illegible] was yesterday granted a license to practice law in the circuit courts of the Territory and before judges at chambers on appeals. [illegible] does not intend to practice law, but plans to continue the study of commercial law with a class of young business men now being formed.

The Board of Registration for Oahu will hold sittings in the old quarters next to the postoffice between [illegible] and 5 and 8 p. m., every day, beginning September 2, for the purpose of examining applicants for registration of voters in the coming election and determining their eligibility.

Members of the seventh precinct of the 5th district, Republican Club, are requested to meet tonight at [illegible] o'clock [illegible] corner of King and Maunakea streets, to consider some resolutions adopted by the district committee. After the meeting all will adjourn to the [illegible] to hear [illegible] Thursday [illegible].

Half-tone and zinco cuts made at the Gazette office. If you have a good photograph you may be sure of a good cut.

8 THE PACIFIC COMMERCIAL ADVERTISER, HONOLULU, AUGUST 30

Canadian-Australian Royal Mail Steamship Company

Steamers of the above line running in connection with the CANADIAN PACIFIC RAILWAY COMPANY between Vancouver, B. C., and Sydney, N. S. W., and calling at Victoria, B. C., Honolulu, and Brisbane, Q., are

Due at Honolulu

On or about the dates below stated, viz.:

FOR AUSTRALIA.		FOR VANCOUVER.	
MIOWERA	AUG. 30	AORANGI	AUG. 27
AORANGI	SEPT. 27	MOANA	SEPT. 24
MOANA	OCT. 25	MIOWERA	OCT. 22
MIOWERA	NOV. 22	AORANGI	NOV. 19
AORANGI	DEC. 20	MOANA	DEC. 17

Steamers now call at Suva, Fiji, on both up and down voyages.

The magnificent new service, the "Imperial Limited," is now running daily BETWEEN VANCOUVER AND MONTREAL, making the run in 100 hours, without change. The finest railway service in the world.

Through tickets issued from Honolulu to Canada, United States and Europe.

For freight and passage and all general information apply to

Theo. H. Davies & Company, Ltd.
GENERAL AGENTS.

Oceanic Steamship Co.

TIME TABLE

The fine passenger steamers of this line will arrive and leave this port as hereunder:

FOR SAN FRANCISCO.		FROM SAN FRANCISCO:	
*ALAMEDA	SEPT. 3	*ALAMEDA	AUG. 29
VENTURA	SEPT. 9	SONOMA	SEPT. 19
*ALAMEDA	SEPT. 24	*ALAMEDA	SEPT. 19
SIERRA	SEPT. 30	VENTURA	OCT. 1
*ALAMEDA	OCT. 15	*ALAMEDA	OCT. 10
SONOMA	OCT. 21	SIERRA	OCT. 22
*ALAMEDA	NOV. 5	*ALAMEDA	OCT. 31
VENTURA	NOV. 11	SONOMA	NOV. 12
*ALAMEDA	NOV. 26	*ALAMEDA	NOV. 21
SIERRA	DEC. 2	VENTURA	DEC. 3
*ALAMEDA	DEC. 17	*ALAMEDA	DEC. 12
SONOMA	DEC. 23	SIERRA	DEC. 24
*ALAMEDA	JAN. 7	*ALAMEDA	JAN. 2

*Local boat.

In connection with the sailing of the above steamers, the agents are prepared to issue, to intending passengers, Coupon Through Tickets by any railroad, from San Francisco to all points in the United States, and from New York by any steamship line to all European ports.

FOR FURTHER PARTICULARS APPLY TO

WM. G. IRWIN & CO.
LIMITED.
General Agents Oceanic S. S. Co.

Pacific Mail Steamship Co.
Occidental & Oriental S. S. Co.
and Toyo Kisen Kaisha.

Steamers of the above companies will call at Honolulu and leave this port on or about the dates below mentioned:

FROM SAN FRANCISCO.		FOR SAN FRANCISCO:	
KOREA	SEPT. 2	CHINA	SEPT. 5
GAELIC	SEPT. 10	DORIC	SEPT. 12
HONGKONG MARU	SEPT. 18	NIPPON MARU	SEPT. 20
CHINA	SEPT. 26	PERU	SEPT. 30
DORIC	OCT. 4	COPTIC	OCT. 7
NIPPON MARU	OCT. 14	AMERICA MARU	OCT. 15
PERU	OCT. 22	KOREA	OCT. 22
COPTIC	OCT. 29	GAELIC	NOV. 1
AMERICA MARU	NOV. 6	HONGKONG MARU	NOV. 8
KOREA	NOV. 14	CHINA	NOV. 18
GAELIC	NOV. 22	DORIC	NOV. 25
HONGKONG MARU	DEC. 2	NIPPON MARU	DEC. 5
CHINA	DEC. 10	PERU	DEC. 13
DORIC	DEC. 18	COPTIC	DEC. 19

For further information apply to

H. Hackfeld & Co., Ltd.
AGENTS

American-Hawaiian Steamship Company.

Direct Monthly Service Between New York to Honolulu via Pacific Coast.

THE SPLENDID NEW STEEL STEAMERS

S. S. "CALIFORNIAN," to sail about .... SEPT. 15TH
S. S. "AMERICAN," to sail about .... OCTOBER 15TH

Freight received at Company's wharf, Forty-second street, South Brooklyn, at all times.

FROM SAN FRANCISCO.

S. S. "NEVADAN," to sail .... AUGUST 27TH
S. S. "NEVADAN," to sail about .... OCTOBER 7TH
S. S. "NEBRASKAN," to sail about .... OCTOBER 20TH

Freight received at Company's wharf, Stewart street, Pier 20.

FROM HONOLULU TO SAN FRANCISCO.

S. S. "NEVADAN," to sail .... SEPTEMBER 20TH
S. S. "NEVADAN," to sail .... NOVEMBER 1ST

FROM SEATTLE AND TACOMA.

S. S. "HAWAIIAN," to sail .... AUGUST 10TH

For further particulars apply to

H. Hackfeld & Co., Ltd.
C. P. MORSE, General Freight Agent.

GLOBE NAVIGATION COMPANY, LTD.
PUGET SOUND-HONOLULU ROUTE

Connecting direct, without transfer, with the G. N. Ry., N. P. R. R. and C. P. R. R. Lowest rates of freight from all Eastern points; shortest possible time.

S. S. TAMPICO, from Seattle on or about .... SEPT. 10
S. S. METEOR, from Seattle, on or about .... DEC. —

For further information address **L. E. BEEBE,**
1 Brewer Building, Honolulu. AGENT HAWAIIAN ISLANDS.

Globe Navigation Company, Ltd., Seattle, Wash.; P. W. Rochester, 308 Market St., San Francisco, and agents of above railroads, will furnish information.

The Hawaiian Realty & Maturity Co., Ltd.
Real Estate and Investments for Sale

1—4 Lots at Kapiolani Park Addition, cheap.
2—Valuable leasehold and building (20 years to run) cor. Hotel and Kekaulike; sure income $50.00 per month; better than sugar stocks.
3—Valuable property on cor. of Fort and School; income $35 per month.
4—Valuable leasehold and buildings on Pauahi St.; income $115 per month.
5—Fine business property cor. Beretania and Kekaulike, area 4200 sq. feet.
6—House and lot Kewalo.
7—Lot on Chamberlain St., back of Kawaiahao church.

The Hawaiian Realty & Maturity Co., Ltd.
L. K. KENTWELL, General Manager.
Mcintyre Building, Honolulu.

THE PACIFIC
Commercial Advertiser

Entered at the Postoffice at Honolulu, H. T., Second-class Matter.

Issued Every Morning Except Sunday by the HAWAIIAN GAZETTE COMPANY, Von Holt Block, No. 65 South King St.

A. W. PEARSON .... Business Manager

SUBSCRIPTION RATES:

For the United States (including Hawaii Territory):

3 months	$2 00
6 months	4 00
1 year	8 00

Advertising rates on application.

OAHU RAILWAY & LAND CO.
TIME TABLE.

From and after Jan. 1, 1901.

OUTWARD.

Stations.	Daily ex. Sun.	Daily	Daily	Daily	Daily
	a.m.	a.m.	a.m.	p.m.	p.m.
Honolulu	7:10	9:15	11:05	3:15	5:10
Pearl City	8:03	9:48	11:40	3:45	5:30
Ewa Mill	8:33	10:08	12:00	4:05	6:10
Waianae	......	10:50	......	4:45	......
Waialua	......	11:55	......	5:40	......
Kahuku	......	12:32	......	6:15	......

INWARD.

Stations.	Daily ex. Sun.	Daily	Daily	Daily
			p.m.	p.m.
Kahuku	....	5:35	....	2:08
Waialua	....	6:10	....	2:50
Waianae	....	7:10	....	3:55
Ewa Mill	5:50	7:45	1:05	4:32
Pearl City	6:15	8:03	1:30	4:52
Honolulu	6:50	8:35	2:05	5:26

G. P. DENISON, Superintendent. F. C. SMITH, G. P. & T. A.

METEOROLOGICAL RECORD.

By the Government Survey, Published Every Monday.

[illegible]

Barometer corrected to 32 F. and sea level, and for standard gravity of Lat. 45. This correction is —.06 for Honolulu.

TIDES, SUN AND MOON.

Days	High Tide Large	Ht. of Tide	High Tide Small	Low Tide Large	Low Tide Small	Sun Rises	Sun Sets	Moon Rises and Sets
Mon 25	[illegible]							
Tues 26	[illegible]							
Wed. 27	[illegible]							
Thur 28	[illegible]							
Frid. 29	[illegible]							
Sat. 30	[illegible]							
Sun 31	[illegible]							
Mon. 1	[illegible]							

Last quarter of the moon on the 26th.

Times of the tide are taken from the United States Coast and Geodetic Survey tables.

The tides at Kahului and Hilo occur about one hour earlier than at Honolulu. Hawaiian standard time is 10 hours 30 minutes slower than Greenwich time, being that of the meridian of 157 degrees 30 minutes. [illegible] Sun and moon are for local time for the whole group.

WEATHER BUREAU.

Honolulu, Alexander St., Aug. 29.

Mean temperature—79.5.
Minimum temperature—76.
Maximum temperature—84.
Barometer at 9 p. m.—30.08, rising.
Rainfall, 24 hours up to 9 a. m.—0.
Mean dew point for the day—65.
Mean relative humidity—64.
Winds—Northeast, force 5.
Weather—Hazy to clear, slight showers in the evening.
Forecast for today—Strong trades; fair, with some showers.

CURTIS J. LYONS, Territorial Meteorologist.

ARRIVED.

Friday, August 29.

Tug Fearless, with schr. Honolulu in tow.
S. S. Alameda, Herriman, at 8 p. m., from San Francisco.
Schr. Malolo, from Hanalei, at 1:30 a. m., with 200 bags of paddy and 115 bags of rice.
Stmr. Helene, from Papaaloa, Kukaiau, Paauhau, Ookala and Hamakua ports, at 11:10 a. m.
Stmr. Waimanalo, from Kailua, at 3:15 a. m.
S. S. Hawaiian, Nichols, from Seattle, at 7 a. m.

DEPARTED.

Friday, August 29.

Stmr. W. G. Hall, at noon for Maui, Kona and Kau ports.
Stmr. J. A. Cummins, at 6 a. m., for Oahu ports.
Am. sp. J. F. Chapman, Kendall, for San Francisco, at 11 a. m.
Stmr. Ke Au Hou, for Ahukini and Anahola, at 5 p. m.
Schr. Lady, for Koolau ports, at 8 a. m.

NEXT MAIL FROM THE COAST.
Sept. 5.—Korea, from San Francisco.

NEXT MAIL TO THE COAST.
September 3—Per S. S. Alameda, to San Francisco.

NEXT MAIL FROM VICTORIA.
S. S. Miowera, due today.

PASSENGERS.

Arrived.

Per stmr. Niihau, August 29, from Kailua—Prince Kalanianaole, J. D. Paris, J. K. Nahale, A. S. Mahaulu.

Per stmr. Helene, August 29, from Papaaloa—Mr. and Mrs. Wilcott, son and two daughters.

Departed.

Per stmr. W. G. Hall, August 29, for Maui, Kona and Kau ports—Miss A. Beard, A. W. Carter, E. H. Carleton, Miss Stinson, Wm. Thompson, J. R. Rodgers, Mrs. F. L. Leslie, David Hallett, Miss Alice Kalaupa, C. C. Paxton and wife, Miss Wallpert, Geo. Huddy, Miss M. L. Lemsley, Miss Leslie, G. P. Kamauoha, Mary Pickard, Mrs. Minnie Sapley, Morris Keohakalole.

Negotiations are in progress toward transferring the army transport Hancock to the Navy Department.

MAY DELAY THE KOREA'S SAILING

Government May Refuse to Allow Transfer of Chinese Crew From Gaelic.

SAN FRANCISCO, August 23.—The Examiner says: The 23 Chinese sailors who were brought from the Orient under contract to work for the Pacific Mail Steamship Company as the crew of the Korea will not be permitted to land nor to go aboard the American steamship and they will be deported to China or Japan.

The original order allowing them to land in San Francisco, it is now learned, was based upon misrepresentations made to the department at Washington, presumably by the Pacific Mail Steamship Company. Assistant Secretary of the Treasury Taylor, upon learning the facts, countermanded the order and instructed Collector Stratton to hold the Chinese until the whole matter can be investigated.

"Our first information," said Assistant Secretary Taylor to a correspondent of "The Examiner" at Washington last night, "was that the Chinese aboard the Gaelic were [illegible] Treasury Department directed Collector Stratton to allow the Chinese sailors to land.

"We have a protest from the Sailors' Union at San Francisco that the Chinese aboard the Gaelic are to be used as a crew for the Korea. If that is the case it is clearly a violation of the laws. We will not permit it. I have countermanded the first order to allow them to land and today wired Mr. Stratton to investigate the matter fully and report to the department. When I have this report I will take action."

"The official investigation will show the facts to be exactly as the Coast Seamen's Union has represented them," said Secretary Andrew Furuseth last night. "These men are not sailors [illegible] law.

"We have heard of the misrepresentations [illegible] would have been shipped on the Korea as sailors and they would have remained there. We are confident that the Treasury Department will order their deportation, for we shall see that it is placed in possession of the facts."

It is understood here that the Chinese will be impounded on board the Gaelic until the matter is settled.

On August 22 Secretary Taylor of the Immigration Bureau in Washington said: "If they were simply Chinese trying to get back to Hongkong, we would let them go on the Korea or any other boat so as to get rid of them, but I doubt if a Chinese [illegible] permission to transfer has been rescinded."

VESSELS IN PORT.

ARMY AND NAVY.

U. S. S. S. Iroquois, Rodman, from a cruise, August 22.
U. S. A. T. Seward, Dowling, Seattle, August 27.

MERCHANTMEN.

(This list does not include coasters.)

Addenda, Am. bktn., Perry, Iquique, August 21.
C. D. Bryant, Am. bk., Colly, San Francisco, July 26.
Ottilie Fjord, Am. schr., Bosch, Eureka, July 21.
Gerda, Ger. bk., Stege, Bremerhaven, August 10.
Gertrud, Ger. sp., Henke, Hamburg, August 9.
Herman, Am. schr., Brown, San Francisco.
Rithet, Am. bk., McPhail, San Francisco, Aug. 15.
Erskine M. Phelps, Am. sp., Graham, Norfolk, August 19.
Mary E. Foster, Am. schr., Thompson, August 24.
S. N. Castle, Am. bktn., Nilson, San Francisco, August 25.
Mary Winkelman, Am. bktn., Guttomsen, Eureka, August 26.
Irmgard, Am. bktn., Schmidt, San Francisco, August 27.
W. H. Marston, Am. schr., Curtis, San Francisco, August 27.
Hawaiian, Am. S. S., Nichols, from Seattle, August 29.

Babcock Posted as Overdue.

The American ship W. F. Babcock, formerly commanded by Captain Graham, who is now in Honolulu as captain of the ship E. M. Phelps, has been posted as overdue, being 135 days out from Baltimore for San Francisco. The vessel is loaded with Cumberland coal, which is considered a dangerous cargo, owing to its liability to ignite easily.

Captain Mozzen of the Babcock was chief officer of the Roanoke last year when that big Sewall ship caught fire in her cargo of coal from Baltimore, while bound for San Francisco. The Roanoke ran for Honolulu, a leak adding to the vessel's danger, but this port was reached in safety. Mozzen, on account of his experience on that terrifying occasion, is believed to be taking every precaution against the ignition of the cargo of the Babcock.

The New Maine.

BOSTON, Aug. 23.—The new battleship Maine left her anchorage in the President Roads about 7:30 o'clock this morning for her trial trip over the Government course off Cape Ann.

Fire Insurance

THE B. F. DILLINGHAM COMPANY LTD.
General Agents for Hawaii.

Atlas Assurance Company of London.
Phoenix Assurance Company of London.
New York Underwriters Agency.
Providence Washington Insurance Company.
Phoenix Insurance Company of Brooklyn.

ALBERT RAAS, Manager
Insurance Department office Fourth Floor, Stangenwald building.

HONOLULU STOCK EXCHANGE.

Honolulu, August 29, 1902.

NAME OF STOCK	Capital	Val	Bid	Ask
MERCANTILE				
C. Brewer & Co.	1,000,000	100	.....	400
L. B. Kerr Co., Ltd.	200,000	50		
SUGAR				
Ewa	5,000,000	20		22
Haw. Agricultural Co.	1,000,000	100		[illegible]
Haw. Com. & Sug. Co.	2,312,750	100		[illegible]
Haw. Sugar Co.	2,000,000	20	19	
Honomu	750,000	100		
Honokaa	2,000,000	20		
Haiku	500,000	100		
Kahuku	500,000	20		12
Kihei Plan. Co., L'd	2,500,000	50		9
Kipahulu	160,000	100		70
Koloa	300,000	100		
McBryde Sug. Co. L'd	3,500,000	20		5
Oahu Sugar Co.	3,600,000	100		
Onomea	1,000,000	20		
Ookala	500,000	20		8
Olaa Sugar Co. Ass.	812,000	20		4
Olaa Paid Up	2,500,000	20		8
Olowalu	150,000	100		
Paauhau Sugar Plantation Co.	5,000,000	50		
Pacific	500,000	100		
Paia	750,000	100		
Pepeekeo	750,000	100		150
Pioneer	2,750,000	100		
Waialua Agr. Co.	4,500,000	100		45
Wailuku	700,000	100		270
Waimanalo	252,000	100		
STEAMSHIP CO'S				
Wilder S. S. Co	500,000	100		100
Inter Island S. S. Co.	500,000	100		110
MISCELLANEOUS				
Haw'n Electric Co.	250,000	100	80	90
Hon. R. T. & L. Co.	250,000	100		65
Mutual Tel. Co	30,000	10		10½
O. R. & L. Co.	2,000,000	100	80	90
BONDS				
Haw. Govt. 5 p. c.				
Hilo R. R. Co. 6 p. c.				
Hon. R. T. & L. Co. 6 p. c.			101	
Ewa Pl'n 6 p. c.			101	
O. R. & L. Co.			104	
Oahu Pl'n 6 p. c.				
Olaa Pl'n 6 p. c.				
Waialua Ag. Co. 6 p. c.				
Kahuku 6 p. c.				

Classified Advertisements.

WANTED.

BY man and wife, one or two room furnished or unfurnished cottage, vicinity of good board and Rapid Transit, no objection to rent. Address X., this office. 6260

WANTED—Unfurnished room, Punahou or the plains. Address D., P. O. Box 58. 6259

BY large wholesale house, an energetic young man to handle sewing machine agency. A good chance for the right man. Address S. M. Agency, Advertiser office. 6258

FOR RENT.

THREE unfurnished rooms, rear of cottage; price $8. Apply 539 Beretania avenue. 6260

HELEN'S Court—Nicely furnished, mosquito-proof rooms; central location. 6258

ONE or two ladies can get nicely furnished front room in private family, reasonable. Apply 38 School street, Ewa of Nuuanu. 6258

MODERN six-room cottage, with bath, electric lights. Apply 1460 Emma St. 6254

A DESIRABLE home with private family with or without board. Address Advertiser office, E. H. 6254

FURNISHED residence at 1071 Beretania street. Inquire W. L. Howard, room 7, McIntyre building; hours 8 to 12 a. m. 6246

COTTAGE in Palama, near Rapid Transit Line. Apply to C. F. Peterson, 15 Kaahumanu street. 6155

ROOM AND BOARD.

MAN acquainted with city and island trade; knows bookkeeping. Prefers city work. Best references. Address P. O. Box 65, City. 6260

NICELY furnished cottage of two rooms, with bath; also furnished room and board. Modern conveniences. At 1491 Emma street. 6217

FOR SALE OR LEASE.

THE well known Ridge House Hotel, South Kona, Hawaii, a three-story house; contains 14 rooms and large attic, servants' quarters, etc. Area 2 acres; more land if desired. Apply Mrs. J. A. Rodanet, 235 Hotel St. 6256

OFFICES FOR RENT.

IN BREWER building, Queen street, on reasonable terms. Apply to C. Brewer & Co., Ltd.

FOR SALE.

GENTLE, sound, small horse, ride or drive, between 4 and 5 years old. Also Toomey cart, single set of harness and English pigskin saddle and bridle. Inquire Hotel Stable. 6258

LOST.

A GENTLEMAN'S gold ring, solitaire diamond. Reward if returned to this office. 6257

FOUND.

A PURSE containing small amount of money and bunch of keys. Owner can have same by calling at this office and paying for ad. 6257

The Silent Barber Shop

OUR RAZORS are thoroughly disinfected before using.
JOSEPH FERNANDEZ, Prop.
Arlington Hotel. Hotel Street

Waverley Shaving Parlors

Corner Bethel and Hotel Streets.
MRS. D. W. ROACH.
CHAS. A. BIDINGER.
Proprietors

NOTICE

ANY WOMAN OR GIRL NEEDING help or advice, is invited to communicate, either in person or by letter, with Ensign Hattie E. Larrabee, matron of the Salvation Army Woman's Industrial Home, 468 King street, Honolulu. 6052

Halstead & Co., Ltd.
STOCK AND BOND BROKERS

Money Advanced on Sugar Securities.

921 Fort Street
Tel. Main 188.

THE ONLY DIRECT LINE

—TO—
DENVER,
KANSAS CITY,
ST. LOUIS
OMAHA,
ST. PAUL,
CHICAGO,
AND ALL
Principal Eastern Points

Three Trains Daily from SAN FRANCISCO.
Two Trains Daily from PORTLAND
THE QUICKEST TIME BY MANY HOURS.

UNION PACIFIC TRAINS ARE PALACES ON WHEELS.
New and Modern Equipment
Double Drawing Room Palace Sleepers.
Buffet Smoking and Library Cars.
Free Reclining Chair Cars.
Ordinary Sleeping Cars.
Dining Cars, Meals a la carte.

D. W. HITCHCOCK, G. A., 1 Montgomery St., San Francisco, Cal.
A. L. CRAIG, G. P. & T. A., O. R. & N. Co., Portland, Oregon.

FOR RENT

Green street, near Victoria street.

The two story house next to the residence of Mr. Reynolds; four bedrooms, best plumbing, high, healthful location, commanding good view of the sea. Lot 53x150. Within 250 feet of the Rapid Transit line.

Rent $50 Per Month

CASTLE & LANSDALE

Real Estate, Insurance, Investments.
Telephone 70 Main. 506 and 507 Stangenwald Bldg.

CHAS. BREWER & CO'S.
NEW YORK LINE
Bark Foohng Suey
Sailing from NEW YORK to HONOLULU
About July 1st
For freight rates apply to
CHAS. BREWER & CO. 27 Kilby St., Boston.
or C. BREWER & CO., LIMITED, HONOLULU.

HOUSES MOVED
HOUSES RAISED
HOUSES REPAIRED
NEW HOUSES BUILT
Stores and Offices Repaired.

W. T. Paty
Contractor and Builder
Office 1048 Alakea street, between King and Hotel.
Phone Blue 1801.

FANCY RIBBONS
Grass Linen and Silks for hat trimming on special sale this week at parlors of
Miss N. F. Hawley.
BOSTON BLOCK.

Honolulu French Laundry

MRS. LE BEUF, MANAGER.
1104 N. King St. All work turned out will be first-class and at reasonable prices. Lace curtains and laces a specialty. Also DYEING AND CLEANING. Work called for and delivered. Phone White 412.

COTTON BROS. & CO.
ENGINEERS AND GENERAL CONTRACTORS.
Plans and Estimates furnished for all classes of Contracting Work.
Boston Block, Honolulu.

16 PAGES. | PAGES 1 TO 8.

THE PACIFIC Commercial Advertiser.

ESTABLISHED JULY 2, 1856.

VOL. XXXV., NO. 6260 | HONOLULU, HAWAII TERRITORY, SATURDAY, AUGUST 30, 1902. | PRICE FIVE CENTS.

CABLE COMING DEC. 1ST

Approximate Date Has Been Fixed.

FRUIT SHIPMENTS FROM HILO PORT

Oil for Hawaii—The Knights in San Francisco—Islanders in the City.

SAN FRANCISCO, August 22.—Mr. S. S. Dickenson, representative of the Pacific Cable Co., is staying at the Palace hotel. He is booked to return to Honolulu on the Korea, leaving here the 30th. He will probably soon go on to Guam to arrange for the cable landing there upon the same lines that he has been doing at Honolulu. The cable has been finished and during the next few days the loading of it aboard the steamer will be completed. There have been some unexpected delays, however, and the probability is that the steamer will not get away from England until the first or second week in September, and the completion of the laying of the cable will accordingly be likewise postponed until approximately December 1. The terms proposed to the cable company by President Roosevelt upon which he will allow them the free use of the soundings between Honolulu and the Philippines, have not yet been accepted by the cable company, and it is not likely that they will be unless modified. The principal ground of objection is that the proposition requires the cable company to allow the government to take possession of the cable and operate it free of charge during war time. The cable company do not object to the government taking possession during war time, as the government has the right to take possession of any property under such circumstances, necessary for carrying on the war; but they do not see the justice of requiring them to surrender their property for an indefinite period without compensation. It would be cheaper for the company to make their own soundings.

Another minor point is the requirement that the operators shall all be American citizens. It is a fact that in the United States the Morse system is used exclusively, whereas all foreign telegraph and cable companies, as well as all of the American cable companies across the Atlantic, use the International system of signals, which is entirely different. Very few Americans have learned the International system, and in case an American operator of the cable on the Asiatic side should be disabled or unobtainable a foreign operator could readily be picked up, while the restriction to American citizens would endanger the whole operation of the cable. The company are still in hopes that a modification of the requirements by the government will be made. If not, there will probably be an additional delay in laying the cable beyond Honolulu, but this will not affect the laying of the San Francisco-Honolulu section.

PUNAHOU TEACHERS.

Mr. Griffiths, the new president of Oahu College, accompanied by his wife, is at the Occidental. They are booked to go to Honolulu by the Korea, which will land them in Honolulu on the 4th or 5th of September, in ample time for the opening of the institution on the 15th. Two other teachers newly engaged by Mr. Griffiths will follow him on the Sonoma, leaving September 4. Miss Hosforth, who has been spending the summer in and about San Francisco, also returns on the Sonoma.

THE FULLERTON.

The Fullerton, the Union Oil Company's first tank vessel, after a number of delays, finally sailed for Kihei on Tuesday last, carrying a load of a little less than 15,000 barrels of fuel oil. It is noteworthy that the Fullerton is the largest and most expensive wooden ship ever built on the Pacific coast; that she was built for a California company by a California shipbuilding company, almost exclusively of California materials; was christened with a California name, by a California Native Daughter, and will handle only California products; all of which goes to show that with all its modesty, California is getting there all the same.

FRUIT SHIPMENTS FROM HILO.

The steamer Enterprise arrived this week from Hilo with a shipment of several hundred bunches of bananas and quite a number of boxes of alligator pears. A few of the bananas were sewed up in gunny sacks and these were all in bad condition. Those wrapped in banana leaves were, almost without exception, in good condition. The pears were mostly packed in large boxes, which contained several hundred pears each, and the pears were not wrapped. The result was that as the pears ripened they were crushed by the weight of the others, so that scarce any were in good condition. A few of the packages were thin boxes containing only two or three layers of pears and the fruit was wrapped in paper. These as a rule, arrived in good shape, although quite a number were so green that they were worthless. It cannot be too strongly impressed upon the Hilo people that they will be wasting their money by sending alligator pears unwrapped and in large boxes. They should be packed so that if possible the pears will not come in contact with each other and will have no weight resting upon them. This can be accomplished by wrapping each pear in a double layer of paper or grass or leaves and having a partition of some kind between each layer of pears rigid enough to keep the next layer from resting upon the one beneath. Good pears bring a fancy price in the San Francisco market, as they retail all the way up to 75c apiece. Care in sending only fully matured fruit and in packing will secure these prices, while failure so to do will result in absolute loss. XXX.

(From Another Correspondent.)

SAN FRANCISCO, Aug. 23.—Thinking a few items from this busy mart might be of interest to your many readers, I send you the following.

The all absorbing topics in in this city for several days past have been the arrival and entertainment of the Knights of Pythias and the attack upon the administration of State Governor Gage. The conclave of the Knights of Pythias, 50,000 guests were expected, and although the actual number fell short, still there was no relaxation in the city's efforts to entertain the guests. I understand that $30,000 were raised and expended for that purpose. A notable feature of the display made for the entertainment were the electrical illuminations extending from the pier building to beyond Tenth street, exceeding anything ever attempted in the country outside of the display of the Pan-American at Buffalo. Conspicuous in the display was the ferry building, the Call building and the City Hall building. These buildings were equal in design and beauty of effect to many of the principal buildings of the Pan-American. In addition to these was the wonderful canopy design at the intersection of Third, Kearny and Main streets.

Honolulans are greatly in evidence throughout the city. Rear Admiral Merry, Dr. Howard and wife, left for the East by the flyer on the morning of the 21st. Rev. Mr Kincaid has taken private apartments on Sutter street. Mr. G. P. Castle and family are on the same street. A. F. Cooke and family are in Oakland. Franklin Austin is now connected with the Overland Monthly. Former Commissioner of Agriculture Joseph Marsden is hale and hearty, and Mr. James F. Morgan has greatly improved in health since his visit to the coast. The Wilcox brothers, B. F. Dillingham and family, Mr. Robert Lewers and family and many other kamaainas are at the Occidental. Mr. W. C. Weedon has been quite active with his lectures and has met with overcrowded houses.

THE KOREA.

This leviathan of the Pacific arrived in port and docked on the 11th. She is due to sail for the Orient via Honolulu on the 30th inst. and many of the Honolulu people have booked to sail

(Continued on Page 2.)

PREST. ROOSEVELT SPEAKS ON TRUSTS

Important Address Made to Republicans of Connecticut During His New England Tour.

The Executive Discriminates Between the Good and Bad Combines in Field of Business and Gives Sound Advice.

WILLIMANTIC, Conn., Aug. 23.—President Roosevelt, after spending the night at the house of John T. Robinson, at Hartford, today resumed his journey through New England. His train left that city promptly at 6 o'clock, but the early hour set for his departure did not deter the people from turning out in force and giving him a hearty send-off. As he drove up to the station in an open carriage accompanied by Senator Platt, the crowd cheered and the President responded by raising his hat. The floral horseshoe presented to the President by the workingmen of Hartford yesterday was by his request placed on the engine. All along the line the small towns turned out their entire population, each apparently anxious to share in the welcome which Connecticut is extending.

When Willimantic was reached the President was driven to the public square, where he delivered an address from his carriage. Following are the President's remarks:

THE PRESIDENT'S SPEECH.

"We are passing through a period of great material prosperity, and such a period is as sure as adversity itself to bring mutterings of discontent. At a time when most men prosper somewhat it always happens that a few men prosper greatly, and it is as true now as it was when the Tower of Siloam fell upon all alike that good fortune does not come only to the just nor bad fortune only to the unjust. When the weather is good for crops it is also good for weeds. Moreover, not only do the wicked flourish when the times are such that most men flourish, but what is worse, the spirit of envy and jealousy and hatred springs up in the breasts of those who, though they may be doing fairly well themselves, yet see others who are no more deserving doing far better.

"Wise laws and fearless and upright administration of the laws can give the opportunity for such prosperity as we see about us. But that is all that they can do. When the conditions have been created which make prosperity possible, then each individual man must achieve it for himself by his thrift, intelligence, energy, industry and resolute purpose. If when people wax fat they kick, as they have been prone to do since the days of Jeshurun, they will speedily destroy their own prosperity. If they go into wild speculation and lose their heads, they have lost that which no legislation can supply, and the business world will suffer in consequence. If in a spirit of sullen envy they insist upon pulling down those who have profited most by the years of fatness, they will bury themselves in the crash of common disaster. It is difficult to make our material condition better by the best laws, but it is easy enough by bad laws to throw the whole nation into an abyss of misery.

"Now, the upshot of all this is that it is peculiarly incumbent upon us in a time of such material well-being, both collectively as a nation and individually, each in his own account, to show that we possess the qualities of prudence, self-knowledge and self-restraint. In our government we need above all things stability, fixity of economic policy, while remembering that this fixity must not be inability to shape our course anew to meet the shifting needs of the people as these needs arise. There are real and great evils in our social and economic life. There is every need of striving in all possible ways, individually and collectively, by combinations among ourselves in private life, and through the recognized organs of government, for the cutting out of these evils. Only let us be sure that we do not use the knife of the ignorant zealot which would make it more dangerous to the patient than to the disease.

"One of the dangers of the tremendous industrial growth of the last generation has been the very great increase in large private, and especially in large corporate, fortunes. We may like this or not, just as we please, but this a fact, nevertheless, and as far as we can see it is an inevitable result of the working of various causes, prominent among which has been the immense importance steam and electricity have assumed in modern life.

"It is not true that the poor people have grown poorer, but some of the rich have grown so very much richer that where multitudes of men are herded together in a limited space the contrast strikes the onlooker as more violent than formerly. On the whole, our people earn more and live better than ever before, and the progress of which we are so proud could not have taken place had it not been for the great upbuilding of industrial centers, such as our commercial and manufacturing cities. But, together with the good, there has come a measure of evil. Life is not so simple as it was, and surely both for the individual and the community the simple life is morally the healthy life. There is not in the cities the same sense of common underlying brotherhood which there is still in country localities, and the lines of social cleavage are far more clearly marked.

"For some of the evils which have attended upon the changed conditions we can at present see no complete remedy. For others the remedy must come by the action of men themselves in their private capacity, whether merely as individuals or by combination one with another. For yet others, some remedy can be found in legislative and executive action, national, state or municipal. Much of the complaint against combinations is entirely unwarranted. Under present day conditions, it is as necessary to have corporations in the business world as it is to have organization among wage-workers. But we have a right to ask in each case that they shall do good and not harm. Exactly as labor organizations, when managed intelligently and in a spirit of justice and fair-play, are of very great service, not only to the wage-workers, but to the whole community, as the history of many labor organizations has conclusively shown, so wealth, not merely individual, but corporate, when used aright is not merely a benefit to the community as a whole, but indispensable to the upbuilding of the country, under the conditions which at present the country has grown not only to accept, but to demand, as normal. This is so obvious that it seems trite even to state it, and yet if we are to judge from some of the arguments advanced against, and attacks made upon, wealth as such, it is a fact worth keeping in mind.

"A great fortune, if not used aright, makes its possessor in a peculiar sense a menace to the community as a whole, just as a great intellect does if it is not accompanied by developed conscience, by character. But obviously this no more affords grounds for condemning wealth than it does for condemning intellect. Every man of power by the very fact of that power is capable of doing damage to his neighbors, but we cannot afford to discourage the development of such men merely because it is possible they may use their power to wrong ends. If we did so we should leave our history a blank, for we should have no great statesman, soldiers or merchants, no great men of arts, orators or of science. Doubtless on the average the most useful man to his fellow citizens is apt to be he to whom it has been given what the psalmist prayed for, neither poverty nor riches, but the great captain of industry, the man of wealth, who alone or in combination with his fellows, drives through our great business enterprises, is a factor without which this country could not possibly maintain its present industrial position in the world. Good, not harm, normally comes from the piling up of wealth through business enterprises. Probably the most serious harm resulting to us, the people of moderate means, is when we harm ourselves by letting the dark and evil vices of envy and hatred towards our fellows eat into our natures.

"Still there is other harm of a different kind and such harm it is our clear duty to try to eradicate if possible, and in any event to minimize. The corporations, and therefore those great corporations containing some tendency to monopoly, which we have grown to speak of rather loosely as trusts, are the creatures of the State, and the State not only has the right to control them, but

(Continued on page 3.)

Tom L.: "There's no harmony in that voice."
Bryan: "No, he never could sing, anyway."
From the Plain Dealer (Cleveland).

CIRCUIT COURT PLUM

Many Men Eager To Pull It Down.

CHINESE CONSUL CHARGE UNPROVED

Honolulu's Receipts for Customs, $1,327,518 23—Brazilian Sugar Statistics.

(Special to the Advertiser.)

WASHINGTON, D. C., Aug. 18.—The judicial aspirants out in Hawaii are not losing sight of the Circuit plum, which in the nature of things must fall within a few weeks. Bushels of letters and recommendations have been coming to the Department of Justice, particularly within a week or two. There are said to be a half dozen of candidates in the race, but the Department refuses to make public any of the names, in compliance with a long established rule and there seems to be no one else in the city aware of what the candidates are doing.

It was stated at the Department this afternoon that probably the President would not take the matter up for some weeks yet. He starts off in a few days from Oyster Bay for an extended tour, including a trip to New England, which would seem as though he did not intend to consider the Hawaiian judgeship at least before September, the date of Judge Humphreys resignation. As far as anybody here knows all the papers in the judgeship case are now on file in the Department of Justice. Attorney-General Knox is expected back here soon, however, and it is possible he may consider the applications, as is usual in such cases and make a recommendation to the President. Nevertheless, it is doubtful if the appointment is announced before the middle of September and, perhaps, not then, from all the information which can be gleaned here now.

HAYWOOD COMING HERE.

Hon. William Haywood telegraphed some of his friends in Hawaii by the last steamer that he intended to make a trip to Hawaii. He plans sailing on the Korea and may make quite a stay in the island. The small Hawaiian contingent in town are entertaining a view that Mr Haywood might prove an available candidate for delegate on the Republican ticket. He has been a very efficient man here in his place as representative of the Planters' Association, knows all the ropes, is familiar with the ways of securing legislation, and furthermore has the confidence of the people in authority in the legislative and executive departments of the government. His great familiarity with Hawaii is another factor to his credit mentioned here.

However, Mr. Haywood, so far as known, cherishes no such ambition for himself. He is making the trip to get in touch with the people in Hawaii and may have something to say during the campaign in behalf of his friends. "I believe Mr. W. O. Smith ought to run for Delegate," said Mr. Haywood here a few days ago. "He knows the interests of the islands and it would redound greatly to the benefit of the territory to send such a representative man to the Capitol."

POSTOFFICE BUILDING EXPERT.

Mr. Smith wrote here recently, requesting that the Supervising architect of the Treasury, Mr. James K. Taylor, come out to Honolulu to inspect the condition of the postoffice buildings at Honolulu and Hilo, as authorized by the recent act of Congress. Secretary Shaw would very much like to comply with Mr. Smith's request and send Mr. Taylor on that mission but at present it seems improbable.

"I mentioned the matter to the Secretary," said Mr. Taylor today, "and he told me it would be very difficult for me to get away for six or eight weeks this year. You see the omnibus public building law authorized the construction of some 150 public buildings over the country, which has necessitat-

(Continued on Page 2.)

二〇五

逕啟者：閏五月初十日接准工巡局來函，以查得西交民巷東頭剪子巷内路東門首懸挂洋轉盤賭幌，係美國人所設賭場，請飭禁止等因。本大臣兹已詳查，此賭場係在棋盤街西洋酒鋪内，有洋轉盤賭具，其後門則通剪子巷，確係美國人所設業經行飭禁止矣。相應函達貴親王查照，希即轉達工巡局知照是荷。特此。順頌爵祺。附送洋文

名另具 閏五月十三日

和會司

呈爲咨行事本月十三日接准美康使函稱准工巡局來函以查得西交民巷東頭翦子巷内路東門首懸挂洋轉盤賭幌係美國人所設賭場請飭禁止等因本大臣已詳查此賭場係在棋盤街西洋酒鋪内有洋轉盤賭具其後門通翦子巷確係美國人所設業經行飭禁止希轉行知照等因前來相應咨行

貴總局查照可也須至咨者

工巡總局

光緒二十九年閏五月　日

二〇七

頭品頂戴兵部尚書兼都察院右都御史署理兩廣總督岑　為
咨呈事案照光緒三十年八月十八日訪聞省城外
沙面地方有洋人溺斃華人情事正在飭查即據管
帶沙面勇營副將楊洪標稟據駐紮沙面西橋廠哨
弁譚慶稟報八月十七日定更時候有洋人四名由
西橋入沙面行至橋頂適與華人一名相遇該華人
當即閃避無如該洋人一齊上前將該華人扯住由
橋頂拋落新涌正在潮水漲滿追至撈獲施救業已
被溺斃命惟該洋人四名拋人落水後即行逃跑沙
面英租界巡差當即尾追不獲查該華人係太古洋
行甘肅輪船之幫買辦詢據甘肅輪船正買辦丁宗
禮聲稱伊伴何傑初又名采言廣東香山縣人現年
四十八歲是晚七點鐘左右由船上岸不料被洋人
四名拋落海面溺斃無辜被害現有寡婦張氏求望
伸冤並查得行兇之洋人四名均係美國兵輪水兵

其犯事地方係屬英租界內等情當經本署部堂飭
據南海縣傅汝梅前往相驗屬實並據洋務委員分
省補用道溫宗堯稟稱本案滋事兇犯有英國洋人
可以指証即經定期照會廣州口美國總領事哲士
並特派洋務處委員分省補用道溫宗堯奏調江蘇
候補知府高而謙廣州府沈傳義南海縣傅汝梅前
往美國總領事署會同查詢本案實情秉公核辦去
後旋據該印委會同美總領事傳集華洋証人詳加
研訊酌擬斷結均經先後電達
貴部察照在案茲復據該印委等稟稱本案於本年
八月二十五二十六二十七等日會同美國總領事
哲士在美領事署提訊駐守沙面橋之續備軍陳標
劉常張洪看守該橋巡兵林安等均供稱係美國水手兵
將何采言擲下河中淹斃屬實惟未能指認兇手為
誰並傳同附近華洋居住人等逐一審訊所供情形

大畧相同或當時未經目擊事後方知復將十七日
告假登岸美國兵輪水兵多名逐一傳訊堅不承認
將何采言淹斃情事飭令當時在塲之巡兵及華洋
人等指認均未能指出何人為本案兇手伏查此案
何采言係由美國兵輪水手將其拖擲河中淹斃身
死已屬無疑惟是日告假登岸之水手兵有四十二
名之多逐一提訊既未確指何人為兇手自應確切
查明再行核辦當經會同美總領事哲士酌議判斷
六條覆加查核祇得暫行照辦惟案關華民無故被
洋人棄水溺斃且何采言係充當英國甘肅輪船買
辦本有職役身家尤非尋常可比應請俯賜據情咨請
外務部照會美國駐京大臣切實酌議賠償卹款嚴
飭廣州口美總領事迅將美國兵輪水手內本案正
兇務獲交出確訊實情按照本國律例從嚴懲辦以
重人命而顧邦交等由到本署部堂據此查本案美
國水手無端逞兇不法已極兇手姓名面貌雖未能
確實指認而滋事者確為美兵業經華洋人証指供
確鑿衆口一詞實已毫無疑義閤省民心頗懷憤恨
若不迅將兇手查出嚴辦並將屍親優加撫卹誠恐
衆怒難平别釀事變現准
貴部電示美使已允切請該國政府籌款給卹並飭
廣州領事查兇按辦務請
貴部迅再照催美使速照原斷辦結以重人命而顧
邦交仍望賜覆望切施行須至咨呈者

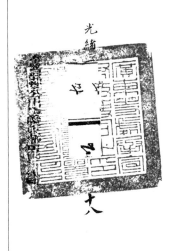

計抄清摺

右　咨　呈

外　務　部

光緒　　十八　日

附件

會審官洋務處總辦委員溫宗堯高而謙廣州府沈傳義南海縣傅汝梅
駐廣州口美國總領事哲士今將甘肅輪船買辦何采言於八月十七日被
溺斃命一案會訊供詞詳加研鞫判斷如左

一該副買辦何采言於八月十七日在沙面西橋溺斃之由確因被人擲入水中所
致毫無疑義

二本案會訊供詞其中有自相矛盾及所供情節僅得之傳聞者甚多
均不足為據可置勿論

三本案會訊各供詞以當日在沙面西橋面值班之中國續備營勇所
供最為切實可靠該巡勇等均係當日在場目擊此事並親見行
兇之人係穿美國號衣之水兵所供各詞均關緊要不能忽畧即參
以其餘証人供詞亦無與該巡勇等相反者

四本案真兇姓名面貌現尚未能確實指認

五此事在會審官之意尚應設法將真兇查出以後無論何時一經
將真兇查出及証明該兇手確有犯罪憑據應按其本國律例從
嚴懲辦

六因此次該副買辦何采言無辜斃命情形極為可憫並因各國洋
人在中國地方遇有被華民行兇致死情事屢經中國政府賠償有
案可稽應由駐廣州口美國領事詳報駐京美國大臣轉告美國政
府妥籌賠補以為該副買辦何采言家屬撫卹之資

欽差出使美秘古墨國大臣梁　　爲

咨呈事。光緒三十年十月初二日承准

貴部電開：八月十七美兵船水手在粤省沙面英租界將華民何呆言拋擲

落水溺斃，經督撫委員會同美領傳訊華洋證人，均指美水手爲真兇，與美

領議結約款六條，大致應由該領詳報駐使轉報美政府妥籌賠補，爲何呆

言家屬撫卹，仍設法將真兇查出，按例懲辦。本部已照美使據復，擬即轉

達，惟須聲明本國政府須查核各口供，恐各供未足證美水手爲真兇，因而

不肯議給撫卹等語。此案衆供確鑿，美領亦已承認，如有挑剔，恐人心不服，

希切告外部，務照原斷辦結，以重民命等因。承准此，當經本大臣面告美

外部認真究辦，並照會催促，旋准照復，轉咨海軍部核辦，所有疊次查

詢辯詰情形業經隨時函陳在案茲接美國署外部大臣盧密士照稱此案並無可以指證該船水手之據惟顧念貴國邦交以及貴大臣申論本部業已飭由駐上海總領事轉發銀一千五百圓交死者之妻親自收領等因前來本大臣查此案供證各件美國外部海軍部均指爲不足疊經再三駁論始照原議允給撫卹既稱飭由駐滬領事轉發願否承領應由該屍親自定至追兇一節來文並未提及理合照譯來文咨呈

貴部謹請察核須至咨呈者 計附譯文一件

右 咨 呈

外 務 部

光緒叁拾壹年伍月 拾叁 日

附件

附件

譯件

照譯美國署外部大臣盧密士來文 光緒三十一年五月十二日 西一千九百五年六月十四日

為照會事，案查本年西正月四日准

貴大臣第五十號來文，所指英公司甘肅輪船買辦何采言被寄泊廣州之美國希林拿兵船水手溺斃一案，經本部於正月二十日照復在案。查此案並無可以指證該船水手之據，惟顧念

貴國邦交，及

貴大臣來文申論，本部業已飭由駐上海美總領事轉發銀一千五百圓交死者之妻收領。理合備文照會

貴大臣，請煩查照須至照會者。

二〇九

收六百六十八

川仁 六月廿二日

七月二十四號接到本國駐厦門領事電稱西本月十八號夜間領事署懸旂之繩被人割去並於旂杆下出恭污穢未悉何人所為領事即行知照道台與提台均認此事有淩辱美國之意允必刑罰辦此事之人並聲敬礮以服禮使人知如此作為係不能允准之事嗣未照辦聲稱係恐畏海防廳之勢力領事又云該處地方官無有能力敵壓抵制美貨之事均係海防廳鼓動現已煽成極熱之勢有三十六家商人襄助内中大半係在呂宋滿尼拉之營商人其頭目首人巴蘭克前充駐小呂宋中國領事又云若海防廳官黄儔凱在此運動關係情形最為危險

收六月廿六日　光字七百六十號

照會

大亞美理駕合衆國欽命駐劄中華便宜行事全權大臣楊　爲

照會事。本大臣前日往

貴部面達　那大臣及聯大臣，爲西本月十八日廈門美國領事署有人行污穢之事，淩辱美國政府。本大臣業將此情告知二位大臣，即係該處道員及提台應許領事官必要服禮，嗣不照辦，云畏懼該處海防廳之勢力。故本大臣已告二位大臣，務使該處地方官刻即服禮。當二位大臣允必速辦，迄今已屆四日，並

未接有復函應再提醒

貴親王於此事切勿輕忽即希早日

見復爲此照會須至照會者　附送洋文

右　照　會

大清欽命全權便宜行事軍機大臣總理外務部事務和碩慶親王

一千九百伍年柒月貳拾捌日

光緒叁拾壹年陸月貳拾陸日

二一一

照復美柔使厦門領署被人汙穢一事茲將閩督來電照知由

左侍郎聯 七月初 日 行

右侍郎伍 七月 日 行

考工司

呈為照復事光緒三十一年六月二十六日接准

來照以前日面達那大臣及聯大臣為西本月十八日厦門美領事署有人行汙穢之事凌辱美國政府務使該地方官刻即服禮迄今四日並未接有復函應再提醒於此事切勿輕忽即希早日見復等因照會前來

查此事前
貴大臣來署面談當即電行閩浙總督迅速查辦電
復茲據復稱拒約一事前經出示勸諭且查鼓浪嶼係屬
公地按第十三款公地章程界內有肆横無忌擾亂地方皆
為工部局巡捕隨時拘究當飭洋務局會同工部局洋
董事確查並飭海防廳查復去後旋據美領事照會
細查此案詳情知此等行為實係有意汙衊敝國並國
章照請由道代該國剖白此意一面將本署所懸國章
照各國賀旂例升礮二十一聲等語當以公地設有工部
局洋巡捕究係何人折斷遭蹋應責成工部局查拏究
辦復催局廳查復念三日據洋務局張守禀稱公地章
程無論海濱道路均不准人便溺立法綦嚴仍時有違

犯罰辦之事今美署旂邊遺屎係在夜間且旂桿繩索有割斷痕跡現已會同工部局飭差查拏再美領事照稱該廳鼓動商人各節並無其事確查亦無證據至云提道均允聲礮服禮查在公地事犯應由洋巡捕查拏現尚未查明係何人所為並未應允鳴礮服禮等情電稟前來查中美兩國交際素稱親睦此次各商會議抵制美貨迭經通飭各該地方官曉諭商民嚴禁違禮滋擾在案厦門美領署旂桿有割索遺屎之事時在黑夜必係愚蠢之人無知妄為各處租界違禁便溺時有罰辦之事稍明理法之人斷不出此該領署係在鼓浪嶼公地應再嚴飭該地方官會同工部局訪查究辦併飭嗣後會同工

部局認真彈壓保護以免别生枝節等因相應照復

貴大臣查照可也須至照會者

美柔使

光緒三十一年七月　　日

二一二

頭品頂戴兵部尚書署理兩廣總督兼管廣東巡撫事岑　為
咨呈事光緒三十一年六月二十四日准
出使美秘古墨國大臣梁　咨開光緒三十年十月初二
日承准
外務部電開八月十七日美兵船水手在粵省沙面英租界
將華民何采言拋擲落水溺斃經督撫委員會同美領事
傳訊華洋證人均指美水手為真兇與美領議結約款六
條大致應由該領詳報駐使轉告美政府妥籌賠補為
何采言家屬撫卹仍設法將真兇查出照例懲辦本部已
照美使據復擬即轉達惟須聲明本國政府須查核各口供
恐各供未足證美水手為真兇因而不肯議給撫卹等語此
案衆供確鑿美領亦已承認如有挑剔恐人心不服希切告

美外部務照原斷辦結以重民命等因承准此當經本大臣面告美外部認真究辦並照會催促旋准照復轉咨海軍部核辦所有迭次查詢辯詰情形業經隨時函陳在案玆接美國署外部大臣盧密士照稱此案並無可以指證該船水手之據惟顧念貴國邦交以及貴大臣來文申論本部業已飭由駐上海總領事轉發銀一千五百元交死者之妻親自收領等因前來本大臣查此案供證各件美國外部海軍部均指爲不足迭經再三駁論始照原議允給撫卹既稱飭由駐滬領事轉發願否承領應由該處親自定至追兇一節來文並無提及相應照譯來文咨會謹請察核計附譯文一件等因到本部堂承准此查甘肅輪船副買辦何采言上年無端被美兵拋擲水中溺斃一案原議

緝辦正兇賠補卹銀兩節經與美總領事切寔議定並電達
撫卹既稱飭由駐滬領事轉發願否承領應由該處親自
定至追兇一節來文並無提及相應照譯來文咨會謹請察
核計附譯文一件等因到本部堂承准此查甘肅輪船副
買辦何采言上年無端被美兵拋擲水中溺斃一案原議
緝辦正兇賠補卹銀兩節經與美總領事切寔議定並電達
延辦不得因已賠補卹銀遂將此案作為完結並札行南
海縣查傳何采言家屬到案諭知此項卹銀飭赴美總領事
官署自行具領稟報察核在案現在何采言家屬已否自
行赴領前項卹款未據該縣稟報茲准前因除札南海縣
查明此案卹款何采言家屬曾否具領刻日稟復察核外
擬合咨呈為此合咨

貴部謹請察照施行須至咨呈者

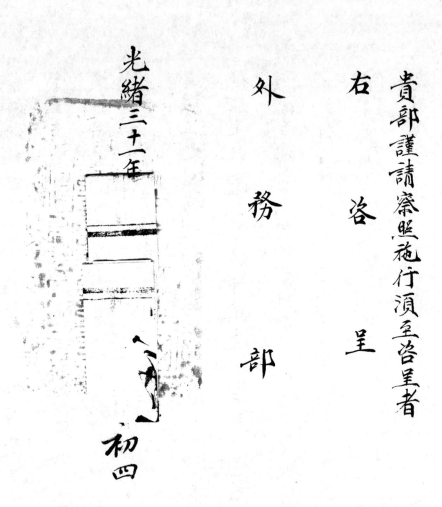

右 咨 呈

外 務 部

光緒三十一年 八月 初四 日

二一三

行

商部為咨呈事光緒三十一年九月初五
日接據上海復旦公學校董袁希濤等
電稱美兵搭坐淞滬火車驅出先乘華人
復旦教員三人被辱請照會美使約束並

定章程等情查鐵路行車自應妥訂詳細
章程以安行旅洋兵登岸乘車亦應照請
美國駐京大臣飭彼國管帶之員嚴定規
條以資循守庶不致有礙文明否則行車
搭客為鐵路利權所繫不特教員等體
面攸關且坐客視為畏途所損之利益匪
淺相應鈔錄原電咨呈
貴部查照希即酌核辦理可也須至咨者 附鈔件

右咨呈

外務部

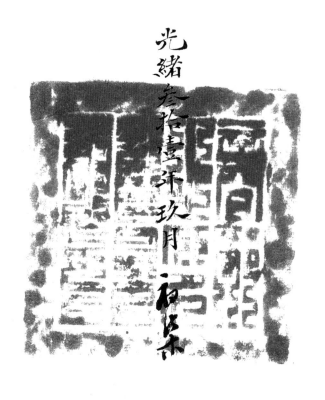

光緒叁拾壹年玖月初柒日

附件

復旦校董袁希濤等電

商部貝子爺大人鈞鑒：美兵搭淞滬火車驅出先來華復旦公學教員三人被辱，已告美領查究。請外部照美使約束，并定洋兵登岸乘車章程，整頓路政，保持主權。復旦校董袁希濤、上海各學校學會公叩。歌。

二一四

照會美柔使轉飭兵官妥定美兵搭坐火車章程由

行 左侍郎聯 九月 十一日

行 右侍郎伍 九月 日

考工司

呈為照會事。光緒三十一年九月初七日，准商部咨：據上海復旦公學校董袁希濤等初五電稱，美兵搭坐淞滬火車，驅出先乘華人，復旦教員三人被辱，請照會美國駐京大臣約束，並定章程等語。查洋兵登岸乘車，應請由駐京大臣轉飭管帶之員嚴定規條以資循守庶不致有碍文明否則不特教員等體面攸關且行旅視火車為畏途鐵路所損利益匪淺等因前來相應照會
貴大臣轉飭管帶之員妥定章程約束兵丁俾將來搭坐火車不至再有此等無理舉動須至照會者

美 柔 使

光緒三十一年九月 日

二一五

收

卅一年九月十三日樂字三百八十一号

照會

大亞美理駕合眾國欽命駐劄中華便宜行事全權大臣康　為

照復事本月十一日准
貴親王照會以准商部咨據上海復旦公學校董
袁希濤等電稱美兵搭坐淞滬火車驅出先乘華人
復旦教員三人被辱請轉飭管帶武員約束並妥定
規條以免再有此等情事等因本大臣當已咨行
上海美總領事官設法約束美國水陸兵丁一體
遵照矣相應照復

貴親王查照可也須至照會者 附送洋文

右　照　會

大清欽命全權大臣便宜行事軍機大臣總理外務部事務和碩慶親王

一千九百伍拾壹年拾月拾壹日

光緒叁拾壹年玖月拾叁日

二一六

咨商部美兵搭坐淞滬火車驅逐華人一案現准美使照復已咨滬美領設法約束由

行 行

左侍郎聯 九月 十六日 行

右侍郎伍 九月 日

考工司

呈為咨復事。光緒三十一年九月初七日，接准咨稱：據上海復旦公學董袁希濤等電稱，美兵搭坐淞滬火車，驅出先乘華人，復旦教員三人被辱，請照會美使約束，並定章程，以安行旅，希即酌核辦理等因。當經本部照會美使轉飭管

帶之員妥定章程約束兵丁俾將來搭坐火車不
至再有此等無理舉動去後茲准美使復稱本
大臣現已以咨行上海美總領事官設法約束美國
水陸兵丁一體遵照等語相應咨復
貴部查照轉復可也須至咨者
商部
光緒三十一年九月　日

二一七

為

咨復事案於光緒三十一年七月十二日承准

貴部咨開光緒三十一年六月二十六日准駐美梁大臣咨

稱美兵船水手在粵省沙面英租界拋擲華民何釆言落水

溺斃一案據美外部照稱此案並無可以指證該船水手之

據惟顧念邦交已飭由上海總領事轉發銀一千五百元交

死者之妻親自收領顧否應由該屍親自定至追究一節並

未提及等因相應抄錄來文並譯文照會咨行貴督查照酌

核辦理并聲復本部可也等因到本部堂承准此查甘肅輪

船副買辦何釆言上年無端被美兵拋擲落水溺斃一案原

議緝辦正兇賠補卹銀兩節經與廣州口美總領事切實議
定並電達
貴部照經美使覆允轉致美國政府照辦旋於本年五月間
接美總領事來函以接美政府來電允將美銀一千五百元
為何采言家屬撫卹之資惟緝兇一節來函並未提及當經
照復美總領事仍照原議設法訪查本案真兇以後無論何
時一經查出證明有犯罪憑据即按該國律例懲辦不得因
已賠補卹銀遂將此案作為完結並行縣查傳何采言家屬
到案諭知此項卹銀飭赴美總領事官署自行具領稟報察
核並咨呈

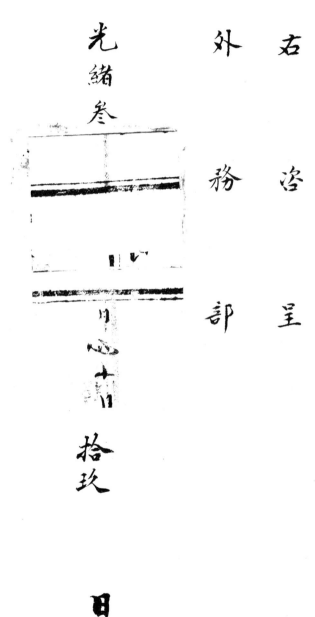

貴部察照各在案茲據署南海縣知縣陳伯侯稟稱此項郵
銀何采言家屬已於五月十二日自赴美領事署收領等由
前來除稟批發外擬合咨復為此咨呈
貴部謹請察照施行須至咨呈者
右　咨　呈
外　務　部
光緒叁　　月　　拾玖　日

二一八

照會

大亞美理駕合衆國欽命駐紮中華便宜行事全權大臣柔 為

照會事。西上月九號經
貴親王照會，以美國兵在淞滬火車之舉動一事，已於
是月十一號飭上海美總領事查核辦理，照復
貴親王在案。茲接准該領事覆函，現將該原函譯就
漢文附送
披閱，則可見駐滬美總領事不惟於此事實行盡力，且
其心中願免嗣有此舉，故格外設法禁止也。相應照會

貴親王查照可也須至照會者、附洋文及抄件

右照會

大清欽命全權大臣便宜行事軍機大臣總理外務部事務和碩慶親王

一千九百伍年拾壹月初捌日

光緒叁拾壹年拾月拾貳日

附件

譯就上海總領事原函

逕復者接奉 貴欽憲西十月十一號文囑內錄中國外務部照會以美國水兵在淞滬火車之事 查有數名美水師兵係乘本國兵輪得勒號而來在淞滬火車之上驅辱華人數名迨及總領事得聞此信特派人往該兵輪拘拿惜該兵輪係屬魚雷艦隊當已離吳淞開往加維德而去是以無法拿護

至美國水師兵在上海之行動一節本總領事已與本國依亥俄號兵艦水師都司要根及保勒的摩號兵艦水師都司薩振威商酌此外又奉函與本國水師提督特連爾議此事

本總領事因當時美國官員未能按中國所請得有機會拿辦水師兵丁實深抱憾也

二一九

咨商部抄送美使照送美兵搭坐淞滬火車驅出華人案美領來函由

行 行

左侍郎聯 十月十五日 行

右侍郎伍 十月 日 畫

考工司

呈為咨行事前准美國柔使照稱美兵搭坐淞滬火車驅出先乘華人復旦教員三人一案當已咨行上海美總領事官設法約束美國水陸兵丁一体遵照等語業經本部於九月十六日咨達在案茲復准該使照稱現接該領事復函現將該原函譯就漢文附送可見駐滬美總領事

不惟於此事實行盡力且其心中願免嗣有此舉故格外
設法禁止等因前來相應抄録原函咨送
貴部查照可也須至咨者　附抄件
商部
光緒三十一年十月　日

欽差出使美秘古墨國大臣梁　為

咨呈事。光緒三十二年九月二十六日，接美國署外部大臣愛地將美國按約派員赴華開辦駐華裁判所專理旅華美民詞訟等情，並開列銜名照會前來。理合將原文照録，譯漢備文咨送

貴部查核辦理。為此咨呈

貴部，謹請查照施行。須至咨呈者。附漢洋文鈔件各一分

右　咨　呈

外　務　部

光緒叁拾貳年玖月貳拾柒日

附件一

照錄美署外部大臣愛地來文

附件

DEPARTMENT OF STATE.

WASHINGTON.

No. 80. November 10, 1906.

Sir:

I have the honor to enclose herewith two copies of an Act approved on June 30 last "creating a United States Court for China and prescribing the jurisdiction therefor," and to advise you that in accordance with this Act a United States Court for China has been created, consisting of the following officials:

Lebbeus R. Wilfley, Judge of the Court;

Frank E. Hinckley, Clerk;

Arthur Bassett, District Attorney;

Orvice R. Leonard, Marshal.

Judge Wilfley is now about to sail for China, to put the Court into operation.

I request you to advise your Government of this new tribunal for the exercise of jurisdiction over American

Sir Chentung Liang Cheng, K. C. M. G.,

Minister of China.

American citizens. It is my hope that the establishment of an American Court of this high character, besides being acceptable to the citizens of this country resident in China, will also be regarded by the Chinese Government itself as an indiction of the solicitude of the United States for the worthy and impartial exercise of the judicial functions reserved to it under our treaties with China.

I feel confident that the officials of this Court may rely upon the cordial assistance of the high authorities of China in the performance of their duties in accordance with the treaties.

Accept, Sir, the renewed assurance of my highest consideration.

(signed) Alvey A. Adee

Acting Secretary.

Enclosures:

Two copies of the Act
above described.

附件二

附片

譯件

照譯美署外部大臣愛地來文 光緒三十二年九月二十五日 西一千九百六年十一月十日

為照會事照得本國議院議定建設美國駐華裁判所限其管轄之權一例 西六月三十號 中五月初九日 奉大伯理璽天德批准當即將建設該所事宜一切遵辦茲本國政府派定

衛理夫禮為該所察司

衛吉禮為書記官

巴變提為律司

練訥為司獄官

衛察司不日將啟行赴華開辦所事查本國政府設立駐華裁判所管理美國人民訟案於旅華美民固有便益而美國按照條約設官聽訟務求公平慎審之意亦為

貴國政府所見信本大臣深信各該員等必蒙

中國地方大員之襄助俾得恪遵條約行其職權也所有美
國派員開辦駐華裁判所緣由理合照會
貴大臣請煩查照轉達
貴國政府可也須至照會者

二二一

閏

十二月廿五日

唐

光緒三十二年十二月二十五日三點鐘美館

儲譯衛理到部

大人接見衛袖出美柔使照會一件云現接漢口美總領事電稱美聖公會文華書院之教習劉家運被地方官指爲叛黨於西正月十六日被拏曾請地方官派令派員觀審地方官不允所請且用刑逼供頗係有違於律等語柔大臣以爲派人觀審領事實有此權應請貴部電飭該地方官將此案再行審訊並派領事派員觀審因恐地方官將劉家運立置典刑要求將照會親自送來以免遲延答以當與本堂商酌電詢湖廣總督飭查審訊情形再行函達衛遂去

二二二

欽差大臣太子少保陸軍部尚書都察院都御史辦理北洋通商事務直隸總督部堂袁　為

咨呈事據山海關道梁如浩申稱光緒三十三年二月二十八日准直隸賑撫局咨開案查光緒三十年夏間美國人伊斯洛被奉天防兵疑匪誤斃一案經外務部議䘏銀洋二萬五千元奉北洋大臣督憲袁　批飭先由敝局照數挪撥俟營口交收後再由關稅內提還等因當經敝局按照市價折合賑公砝化寶銀一萬八千五十三兩六錢七分解交天津銀號查收並咨准貴前道查照辦理上年春間經敝局咨請貴前道將前墊之款尅日籌撥歸墊復准貴前道文咨覆應俟營口收復再行籌還各在案茲查營口地面早已

收回貴道經徵關稅自必有可撥還所有敝局前解郵款亟應
收回歸墊以符原案相應再行咨催為此合咨貴道請煩查照
希即照數提撥尅日匯解來局俾濟要需而清案款幸勿再延
望速施行等因准此查此項墊款文前升道任内迭准該局咨
催因營口未復無憑籌解茲准前因自應如數籌還惟查地面
初復關稅收數無幾仍屬無從動撥而款關歸墊未便再稽現
經職道暫由日本交還關稅項下照撥公砝化寶銀一萬八千
五十三兩六錢七分批交號商匯解該局兑收歸墊以清款目
除備具文批咨解並申報
軍督憲查核外理合申報查核轉咨

外務部核銷等情到本大臣據此相應咨呈

貴部謹請查照核銷施行須至咨呈者

右咨呈

外務部

光緒三十三年十二月　日

應　之件

右參議楊　樞　月　日

二二三

和會司

呈爲咨行事。准義國博使函稱：去年東單牌樓二條胡同洋賭局一事，曾蒙飭將各賭局閉歇，曷勝感佩。惟今訪得該處所有舊賭局一所，於三月十五日前復擅行開局，該局主係美國人杜貴納。事關重要，應請轉行民政部訪察，如果實有其事，務請照章辦理等因前來，相應咨行

貴部查核辦理，並希見復可也。須至咨者。

民政部

光緒三十三年四月　日

二二四

代辦使事駐美二等參贊官吳壽全為申復事竊照宣統元年正月初七日
伍使憲承准
大部文開光緒三十四年六月准南洋大臣文稱美國遊歷人德門內在雲南
維西廳槍斃喇嘛補更弄一案前經四川總督將該犯德門內送交重慶
美領事移送上海美按察司裁判經滬道委縣觀審未及照約辨駁而美按
察遽將德門內釋放無論為有意殺無意殺美公堂既不擬罪又不議卹事
關人命殊不足以昭公允迭由本部照會美使而復稱上海設立之按察衙門
有獨立裁判之權非使臣所能干預查此項裁判之權在國內國外有無不同之
處尚須研究惟准滇督來文內開補更弄家屬控稱補更弄一身為父母妻子
所倚賴之人一旦無辜慘斃實絕闔家生命應請申雪如能將德門內拘回另
審情願赴堂質訊並稱德門內擬允死者父母隨其所欲且能担任其各事在
麗江府堂訊時供明在案惟揆度案情德門內既經上海美按察釋放勢必始

終偏護不如與議卹款俾得轉圜彼邉民亦可稍伸其寃憤等因前來除照會
美使外相應錄全案咨行向美外部磋商應如何定案議卹以重民命而彰公理
並希將商定情形隨時聲復等因當經
伍使憲晤商美外部未據答復旋赴祕國嗣於四月二十一日參贊奉
大部馬電開美人德門內鎗斃喇嘛補吏弄一案前於正月間咨請向美外部
磋商定案議卹迄今未准咨復茲復准滇督電稱現據補吏弄家屬以大寃未
伸並謂補吏弄一身為父母妻子所倚賴無辜慘斃實絕闔家性命呈請作主請
催他處迅速提詢等語希即查照前咨與美外部磋商定案償卹以重民命並即電復
等因奉此當經切實照會美外部乃久不答復迭經催商均以事關法律未敢輕
率為詞旋准送來節畧內稱德門內鎗斃喇嘛補吏弄一案在上海美公堂審
判時有中國政府所派代表在座觀審有中國證人到堂供證業經該公堂按
詧司按照美國律例公平判斷定為誤殺將被告釋放彼時中國政府以為不

然曾請將被告再審查美國憲法修正條例第五條內載凡人之生命或肢體不能因同一之罪名而受兩次之危害若德門內釋放復將其逮捕重審即屬與美國法律之原則相背設竟以同一之罪名將業經受審釋放之德門內逮到重受審判彼不難據重加危害以為伸辯而再審一事必歸無效所以中國所請不能照辦中國政府又曾提議公堂應設法賠償該喇嘛親屬但查此案係殺人致斃之刑事案件並非以疏忽為詞控請賠償之民事訴訟本國業經據以答

釋貴大臣又請本國政府將死者親屬酌加償卹或飭德門內實踐其自允賠償死者親屬之言給與銀兩此兩層本部均不能照允至以為款第一層本國政府不能因一私人之行事而担任賠償該喇嘛之親屬第二層按照本國律例政府實無法可以强逼一私人踐行其所許諾外國人民之言云云參贊當以被告既經釋放逃回美國原告遠在中國從何控告照請切實見復旋接復稱被告歸國後不知下落容俟查明知照似此諉卸迄無賠償之日事經日久理合照譯往來

文件先行申復爲此具申

大部謹請察核施行須至申者附呈譯件

右

申

外務部

宣統元年九月初拾日

應之件

署右參議吳錡 十一月 日

附件

附16　伍前駐美使事　十一月廿一日收

譯件

譯吳代辦函致美外部節畧　宣統元年四月二十二日　西一千九百九年六月九號

案查　伍欽差前接　外務部咨開美國游歷人德門內在雲南維西廳屬鎗斃喇嘛僧補吏弄一案經川督將該犯德門內送交重慶美領事移送上海美按察司裁判經上海道委縣觀審未及照約辦駁而美按察司遽將德門內釋放無論有意故殺無意誤殺美公堂既不擬罪又不議罰事關人命殊不足以昭公允迭由本部照會美使而復稱按察司有獨立裁判之權非使臣所能干預現准滇督文開補吏弄家屬控稱補吏弄一身為父母妻子所倚賴無辜慘斃應請昭雪如能將德門內拘回另審情願赴堂對質並稱德門內擬允死者父母隨其所欲且能担任其各事在麗江府堂訊時供明在案現在德門內既經美公堂釋放中美邦交素篤未便為難惟請美外部設法議罰或令德門內迅速賠償以重人命而彰公理

譯美外部答復節畧　宣統元年六月十三日　西一千九百九年七月廿九號

上畧　德門內鎗斃喇嘛僧補吏弄一案在上海美公堂審判時有中國政府所派代表在座觀審有中國証人到堂供証業經該公堂按察司按照美國律例公平判斷定為誤殺將被告釋放彼時中國政府以為不然曾請將被告再審查美國憲法修正條例

第五條內載凡人之生命或肢體不能因同一之罪名而受兩次之危害若德門內釋放復將其逮捕重審即屬與美國之法律之原則相背設竟以同一之罪名將業經受審釋放之德門內逮到重受審判彼不難據重加危害以為伸辯而再審一事必歸無效所以中國所請不能照辦中國政府又曾提議公堂應設法賠償該喇嘛親屬但查此案係殺人致斃之刑事案件並非以疏忽為詞控請賠償之民事訴訟本國業經據以答釋

貴大臣又請本國政府將死者親屬酌加償卹或飭德門內實踐其自允賠償死者親屬之言給與銀兩此兩層本部均不能照允至以為歉第一層本國政府不能因一私人之行事而担任賠償該喇嘛之親屬第二層按照本國律例政府實無法可以强逼一私人踐行其所許諾外國人民之言今為補更弄親屬計惟有一法可以得美國法權之助即本國駐滬總領事奉本部訓令於本年四月廿四號轉告上海蔡道台可據疏忽為詞照民事賠償訴訟案控告德門內一法是也此等民事訴訟如該死者親屬以為致斃之由實因被告之疏忽而被告可在上海美國公堂或其他公堂法權轄境內踪跡而得即可起訴本部深信此案經如此解釋後能期

貴國政府明白本國對於其事所處之地位及本國政府於如何方可以控告德門內之處實已竭盡其

合例之方法而該受屈之中國人民欲求伸理惟有以上所云以民事起訴控德門內於案耳

譯致美外部文 宣統元年六月十八日 西一千九百九年八月三號

為照會事照得美人德門內在雲南省鎮甦喇嘛補吏弄一案　貴部上月廿九號送來節畧如查得被告德門內在上海美國公堂或其他公堂法權轄境內即可據疏忽為詞照民事賠償訴訟法控之於案等語本代辦查被告之人既經釋放逃回美國原告從何控訴此案如何了結請　貴部明以相告並將查明德門內之下落知照本代辦可也須至照會者

譯美外部復文 宣統元年六月二十六日 西一千九百九年八月十一號

為照復事案照　貴代辦本月三號來文以美人德門內被控在雲南省鎮甦一喇嘛欲查其下落俾原告得以控訴等語查德門內已經上海美國公堂審明釋放至其在上海被釋後一切舉動本部全然不知日後若有所聞再行知照　貴代辦可也須至照會者

二二五

欽命二品頂戴山東撫提部院節制全省軍務兼理鹽政監督臨清鈔關孫　為

咨呈事案據開缺登萊青膠道徐道撫辰稟稱敬稟者案查美國人卓斯在煙台開平碼頭槍傷杉板人甯海州民宮慶因傷身死一案業將在煙會同副總領事衛家立詢供情形稟報在案迨西歷四月二十九號即宣統元年三月初十日美國按察司蔡雅儒由上海率同律官柏錫脫並派捕押解卓犯到煙審判其時職關所延律師羅禮士亦同時來煙當將初訊情形及供證傷單各件飭令譯員詳告羅律師並由職道會晤美臬及美領事照章在美領事署開正式堂審職道率同印官繙譯各員前往觀審於

三月十一十二十四等日堂審三次被告僱律師傅蘭明出為辯護並延西人在場者數人作證幾翻全案幸經華民證人張寶林李執等當堂供明在場目擊宮慶被傷情形眾口僉同始終如一並由職道商同律師羅禮士相錫脫援律辯駁按約爭持至三月廿四日未刻始訊明美臬判定卓斯以故意放槍殺人監禁十年之罪即行定案之日起解赴上海美領事處監禁亦經電稟各在案查此案初起即經職道將全案供證傷單檢備齎全當美領事預審時即已宣明奉其駐滬總裁判電文定以故殺之罪此次判為故意殺人似與原電稍有出入復經職道據以

詰難即准美領事聲稱原電洋文本有實出有心一語故
意即是有心定以故意殺人之罪與此次定案並無出入
查美律故殺係指有事故而言如積憤積讎謀財暗殺等
類仍量其情節定罪輕重重者勦斃輕者監禁其無事故
可指臨時起意者亦分有心無心兩種此案卓斯有意殺
人故定為監禁三年之罪因其與宮慶並無深仇宿怨與
謀而後動者自不相同判以監禁三年在美律已屬重罪
等語質之律師栢錫脱羅禮士所引律法暨所論案情亦
均相符查中西律例不同輕重互異此案卓斯槍傷宮慶
致死堂訊數次辯論多端謂其有故致死則固中外證人

所不能實指其罪第其無故逞兇慘斃人命遇有可爭之處亦不憚筆舌伸辯以儆效尤故於此案初起之時及結案之日疊經職道查敘條約援引成案照會美領事請其轉致美臬務宜秉公辦理一面傳齊要證訊取實供延訂律師推闡例案觀審之日又復商同律師逐款指駁竭力辯爭多方籌備而因應之蓋以民命至重

國體攸關東省歷年辦理交涉命案多至十數起悉因供證參差一訊即釋無有一案辦罪者此次供證確鑿毫無罅漏傷單全備無可改移始經美臬定以監禁三年之罪當其定案之時尚呼卓斯至前垂涕泣而道之語及三年二

字幾於梗不成聲觀審兩人亦多於邑推其大意以為旅居兩人犯有命案兩定罪者近已不數數覯耳若於定案之後猶復較量輕重任情指駁作無益之辯論徒傷感情無裨事實則又非職道之所敢出也理合將此案始末訊判情形暨全案供詞分別繕印成冊稟請查核訓示并請

分咨

外務部查考立案實為公便又據另單稱敬再稟者查本年四月間議代事主延聘律師到堂申辯曾奉

前北洋大臣直隸督憲楊　電諭所有延聘律師費用准其報銷等因嗣經職道函託江海關蔡道代聘律師羅禮

士議明需費洋一千元所有川資房飯酬勞等項在外均由職道籌款墊發再加以傳到事主見證多人並經職道飭員伴守留養以備質訊此數月内一切日用火食來往川資等費概由職道籌發案結後又爲宫慶老母籌給卹賞綜計全案約共用洋四千三百五十元有奇統由職道捐廉彌補不敢造册報銷合併陳明等情到本部院據此除稟批據稟已悉此案經該道多方籌備因應咸宜使卓犯無可避就按照美律監禁三年洵屬辦理有方克昭炯戒另單稱延聘律師暨卹賞等費需洋四千餘元統由該道捐廉尤堪嘉尚仰候咨呈

外務部查核立案並候分行司局查照繳華洋文册均存

印發並分行外相應咨呈

鈞部謹請查核立案望切施行須至咨呈者

計咨鈔清册肆本

右　　咨　　呈

外　　務　　部

宣統元年捌月拾伍日

應　之件

附件一

外務部

譯呈美國副領事官豫審美人卓斯槍傷華人宮慶全案供詞判詞清冊傷單附

譯西歷壹千玖百玖年叁月貳拾叁號美副領事署第壹次堂訊

副領事衛家立問被告卓斯云前禮拜六即西歷叁月貳拾號下午約四句鐘時汝槍傷華人宮慶係出有心汝云有罪否

被告答云無罪

醫官顧林森誓言貳拾日申刻承衛副領事所召並交我以華人一名我將伊帶到醫院後知其為槍所傷其子係由左邊背後打入及向前面將子掏出甚易當時收傷者似無甚險狀且欲離院後經攔阻忽於昨日病勢增劇即此數日間亦難決其再無更變槍子在此請驗之

衛副領事答云貴醫生亦欲留此子以為將來過堂時之證據乎

顧醫生曰然

見證人李保仁供稱該舢舨係屬孫姓的伊等正在彼處候連陞船進口攬客此時我立於碼頭被告招呼舢舨舢舨不來是以被告抽出手槍放了一响此係我目覩之事放槍後遂見宮慶伏於舟内呼云被槍所傷其夥伴孫七即將舢舨靠岸我們即置渠於小車上送至美副領事處由彼轉送至醫院所供是實

船夥孫七供稱當被告在碼頭招呼舢舨之時我却同宮慶在一舢舨内正擬開往連

顧醫生曰然本醫官已於上次堂訊時曾將此子呈驗矣不幸該槍子兼别物同放衣袋内偶於上船時失足落水致將袋内一切物件失落其子查係比啤布郎之類槍子掏出時離臍若干遠

顧醫生曰約二寸許近臍左邊説完顧醫官親筆簽押

見証人李秋供稱中歷叁月廿玖日下午約四句鐘時我同孫七在碼頭適有華人到覓舢舨我等方各欲争攬而客人已隨孫七而去此人即下舢舨方擬開往連陞並由彼攬客而回忽值被告行至碼頭以手招該舢舨該舢舨不應被告旋轉行數步招呼别人舢舨亦無有應者被告復回原處由衣袋内取出手槍對宮慶施放旋見該舢舨駛回我問孫七何以去而復返孫姓答云伊夥宮姓被洋人槍傷繼問我可否將該洋人擒獲答曰不可不可恐其再放也應即往告美領事為要我們即將受傷者送往彌子房隨即遇美副領事於小車上美副領事令將宮慶交顧醫官帶往醫院

律師問曰槍發時該舢舨離岸若干遠

答曰三步

當時舢舨上有幾人

答曰三人一客與宮孫二人

此時宮姓在舢舨何處

答曰在舢舨後左邊　此係寗海人之慣習　正預備開駛孫七亦於此時將纜放好以

便搖使

洋人有怒氣否

答曰舢舨招之不來洋人發怒

汝何以知之

答曰洋人面帶怒容

洋人説何惡話

答曰無之

復又如何

答曰洋人仍立碼頭及我們將宮姓帶去後則不知其所之矣

當時亦有許多舢舨在傍否

答曰有於該舢舨開往時有數舢舨在傍

洋人放槍疾速否放後作何狀

答曰洋槍後即將槍復裝入袋内

陞接客聞槍响即見被告將手插回衣袋内即由我們將宫慶送至美副領事處

所供是實

見證人李秋供稱我立於碼頭時有一華人許給我二百錢渡伊至連陞輪船隨見被

告來至碼頭招呼舢舨繼而施放手槍一响該舢舨既已離岸復又駛回我問其何

故據宫慶稱已被槍傷其舢舨係宫慶孫七二人所駛的所供是實

被告並無話説

衛副領事對被告云按以上各供乃係初次堂訊已足證汝所犯之罪應歸美國公

堂審訊如受傷華人有速愈之望本領事自當代為電請准汝取保出獄候訊

現暫交本署總巡捕看管

大美國派駐煙台副領事官衛家立簽押

大清國登萊青膠道東海關監督徐撫辰委派　署登州同知張秉澤　繙譯委員候選縣丞馬應緒　觀審

譯西歷叁月叁拾號美副領事署第二次堂訊

兹承駐華美總裁判之命將汝卓斯判定故殺之[illegible]

出有心致該華人宫慶因傷斃命汝云有罪否

被告答曰無罪

顧醫生先誓而後言曰本醫官乃著名醫士在煙台習業已十三年矣

美副領事曰請貴醫官即將案内所悉情形明以告我

顧醫官曰西歷叁月貳拾號承衛副領事之名驗看一被槍所傷之華人本醫官

將該華人帶在醫院隨即見槍子係由背後左邊脇下而入直穿腹内遂於前面

肚皮左邊將子掏出受傷者初猶不甚驚覺且擬離院就醫復經衆勸始行作罷

過了三十六點鐘忽腹内發熱如是數日或輕或重於貳拾柒號早四點鐘身死是早

午承東海關道憲徐道台諭將死者驗看腹膜熱甚槍子穿腸數處此其斃命

之緣也

被告所延律師泰羅問曰槍子穿腸乎

顧醫生曰然

貴醫官存有槍子否

汝有舢舨否

答曰有

汝之夥計何在

答曰亦在碼頭

伊現在何處

美副領事接曰當時華人之在碼頭者不少似不宜再傳多人作證徒使口供重複

汝之夥計何名

答曰李保仁　李秋親筆簽供　衛領事及書記同簽押

船夥孫七供稱我們與宫慶同一舢舨貳月廿九日下午四點鐘時有華人到碼頭擬往

連陞我們即行載伊前往適有洋人到碼頭以手招呼我們回轉惟我們已有了

華人未便再應其招宫慶當時祇知使槳我在後亦預備搖櫓忽聽身後槍响

宫慶即時伏於舟上以手摩其肚及回視即見洋人正將槍放袋内我隨將舢舨

駛回岸上議將洋人捕獲彼等云恐他再放槍是[illegible]

醫院就醫並赴官署呈報

美領事問放槍時舢舨離岸若干遠

答曰三四步

律師問後來洋人如何

答云見洋人乘别舢舨往别船而去

洋人面帶怒氣否

答曰洋人發怒

美領事問汝何以知其怒

答曰洋人招呼我們不應自然有怒氣　美領解其理以折律師之問難

律師問汝見此槍否此何式槍

答曰我只見洋人將槍放入袋内乃一小槍惟不能説其長若干

律師問舢舨内之客人又何如

答曰我們既不能去祇可任他自便了　孫七親筆簽供　衛領事及書記同簽押

見證人李保仁供貳月廿九日下午四句鐘我立於碼頭一華人來雇孫七舢舨往連

陞時有一洋人來在碼頭以手招其舢舨該舢舨已開駛且因有客在内不肯回轉

美領事問洋人招呼孫七舢舨不來隨後再招呼别人舢舨否

答曰有洋人發怒徘徊數步即以槍轟擊宫慶乃宫慶之舢舨回岸時我問其

回來之故答云宮慶被洋人槍傷我云必此洋人也他雖在此放了一响我們議當時
將洋人拏獲惟見伊有槍在懷未敢遽行只得報知美副領事我們將受傷者
送至美領事後即發往醫院矣
律師問汝斯時在何處
答曰在碼頭
問汝先時曾見過此人否
答曰曾經見過
美領事問因何洋人雇舢舨如是之難
答曰洋人所雇舢舨向不給價
律師問認識接攬被告之舢舨人否
答曰雖未其姓名惟時常見其往來是以見面便認識
律師問放槍時宮慶離岸若干遠
答曰約三步　李保仁親筆簽供　衛領事及書記同簽押
律師云按以上各供此人與舢舨人無甚冤仇本律師敢請貴署將被
告所犯之罪改故殺為悞殺已足蔽辜
美副領事曰本署已奉駐滬總裁判之命判
律師又請曰取保開釋可乎
美副領事曰不可
美署判云按以上各供汝卓斯於此次初訊已足証汝所犯之罪宜歸駐華美公
堂審判現奉駐滬美總裁判諭將案暫停解汝到滬監禁明日即交本署
總巡捕乘景星輪船起解此案現特為汝告知須俟至五月初旬在滬審訊
大美國派駐烟台副領事官衛家立簽押
大清國登萊青膠道東海關監督徐撫辰委派　署福山縣知縣姚贊元　署登州同知張東澤　繙譯委員候選縣丞馬應緇　觀審

譯西醫官顧林森驗明華人宮慶因傷身死詳單西歷三月廿九號
中國舢舨人宮慶係於西歷一千九百九年三月廿柒號下午四句鐘身死
察其病係因槍子穿肚後腹內血湧即於是日下午經中美各員會驗本差
該傷之結局卒以腹內血湧大發而死槍子穿腸數處
醫官顧林森親筆簽押
大美國派駐煙台副領事官衛家立委派洋員會驗
大清國登萊青膠道東海關監督徐撫辰委派　署登州同知張東澤　署福山縣知縣姚贊元　会驗

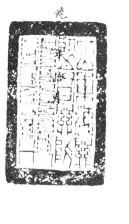

宣統　年拾　月

山東東海關監督登萊青膠道徐撫辰

附件二

外務部

譯呈美國按察司會審美人卓斯槍斃華人宮慶一案判詞清冊

譯美國臬司堂判美人卓斯槍斃華人宮慶壹案西歷壹千玖百玖年五月四號在烟台結案

原案詳稱美民卓斯於西歷壹千玖百玖年叁月貳拾號在中國烟台境內抱怨逞兇槍擊華人宮慶所傷甚重該華人遂於月之貳拾柒號因傷隕命實係卓斯抱怨逞兇將宮慶殺死疊經東海關道徐道台照會請按律柬公嚴訊按律重辦

照美國法律若犯在本國政府有裁判全權之境內其罪係在公律故殺之首列與國律故殺之罪相同

此案業經東海關道徐道台照會駐烟美副領事衞家立貳次提訊在案該副領事以故殺之罪詳請本臬司判斷乃於壹千玖百玖年四月拾四號由美國郡縣司律官詳請歸案究辦於堂訊時被告供稱無罪

此案之全情已為醫官顧林森所稔悉宮某被槍傷後未幾即經該醫生驗看將槍子掏出留院就醫直至該華人身死之日

該華人死後即於是日下午四句鐘經東海關道徐道台派該醫生前往察驗在案杢該華人係於西歷壹千玖百玖年叁月貳拾柒號早四句鐘身死

該華人之傷確係因槍子穿腹後因傷致命已無須審問供內所可爭辯之處
祇有數端其詳細列下
所供該死者於受傷時在舢舨內正靠開平碼頭係衆人上落之區固無可辯論
惟於該華人受傷之時其舢舨之確實地位下文另有分鮮宮慶受傷之時其
舢舨內有華人壹名不詳其姓氏與其船夥孫七亦在其內均係實供又云該華
人於受傷之際見其捧腹呼叫伏於舢舨內其舢舨即於斯時駛回碼頭旋有同夥
多人將伊抬上小車送往彈子房本擬找尋美領事隨即於該處見之彼等之
所以先尋該領事者以兇手係美民理宜送交美國駐烟領事究辦此實情也
再被告係於叁月貳拾號下午在碼頭靠近北梯手持小槍壹枝名小兒紅槍
內裝有彈子於其握槍在手時壹子忽然爆發亦均屬實醫生由死者腹內將
子掏出云此子名小兒紅乃壹小槍之子也
醫生初次堂供謂曾將此子示人皆謂不能致命復據其稱伊曾習識槍枝
各等因又查此案所錄之供此子確係宮慶受傷身內之子無疑且亦係卓
斯槍內所發之子
被告所供各節如果屬實似可免其故殺之罪然[illegible]其律節當時亦認宮
某之傷係於是日是地被卓斯手持之槍發出壹子所傷且當時附近亦無
別人放槍所以宮某之傷確係由被告槍內發出之子無疑
按本臬司之意以供內未言明放槍究在何時[illegible]
供稱係約在四句鐘時見此受傷之人旋又云約在五句鐘之間亦未能將確實
時刻記準即各証人亦均未說出壹定時刻多云約在四句鐘而已
被告供稱伊到碼頭之時已在五句鐘之後自有見証在此按被告各証人所供
其時又與被告所供較晚然此項爭辯均屬細微即原告各証人亦並未說出
壹准時刻總之當堂兩造証人所供彼此均有不符之處被告或於此處稍
有大意以致其証人所供均不可靠
至詢及死者於受傷時其舢舨究在何處據各華人所供又有可疑之處即
如有供稱在宮之舢舨者有供稱在碼頭者又有供稱在送被告往燈船之舢
舨者本司已承郡縣司律官之請同被告所延律師傅蘭明齊到碼頭踏勘
處地段及附近壹帶等處此兩碼頭以目測之相去約拾丈之譜壹在北首壹在
南首其牆向裏灣入第壹名証人孫七供稱於放槍時宮之舢舨已離了南碼
頭畧駛至北碼頭之南與碼頭相去頗遠約有公堂之寬在拾伍尺之間其舢舨

正與碼頭平對此人與宮同壹舢舨云第貳名証人李保仁供稱其時伊在碼頭
上槍响之際伊離北碼頭僅兩叁步而宮之舢舨則在北碼頭之南於橫訊時答以
該舢舨駛出碼頭僅兩叁步耳第叁名証人李秋於被訊時並未曾供述及此
據云放槍之時伊與被告相去僅伍陸步又宮之舢舨離碼頭不遠是以見其受
傷伏於舟內第四名証人部保山於槍响時並未看見宮之舢舨在後始行見之第五
名証人王三元即係送被告往燈船之人供稱伊靠北碼頭不遠且宮之舢舨亦
靠他之舢舨不遠畧在南方云
據被告供稱伊到碼頭時並不見有舢舨在貳拾步或叁拾步內伊之所見者祇有送伊
往燈船之壹艘而已此舢舨亦在伊到碼頭幾分鐘後方見之當時並無別人舢
舨靠近該處其供又與各華証不符此數華人所供被告放槍情形與其所以放
之之故並其當時之手勢各節均屬直言不諱足表下文之的確矣被告到碼
頭時以手招宮之舢舨內有其夥孫七及華人[illegible]此舢舨[illegible]南碼頭或在北
碼頭之南該舢舨不顧其招被告回步招呼別人舢舨亦無有應者被告因而將袋
內掏出手槍伸手放出壹子照宮之舢舨施放後隨即將槍裝回衣袋內孫七
原與宮慶同舟放槍時其背正朝著被告[illegible]响方回首見被告[illegible]槍在衣袋內
所見之槍原係壹小槍僅見在被告手內露出寸許而已
第貳名証人李保仁其時立於碼頭正靠北首離被告僅兩叁步見被告以
手先招宮之舢舨繼而又招別人舢舨容怒[illegible]有毆打之狀將手插在右
邊衣袋內掏出手槍向宮慶舢舨施放
第叁名証人李秋於槍响時亦在碼頭離被告約數步亦見被告招呼舢舨
貳次無有應者被告怒形於色以右手由衣袋內掏出手槍照宮慶舢舨
施放槍响後復見被告將槍收入衣內
第四名証人部寶山於槍响時亦在碼頭立於被告之後約貳拾步之遠僅聞槍
聲未見其形又聞有人疾呼謂此人受傷伊即時行近碼頭及受傷者抬上南
岸時被告已由北碼頭乘別人舢舨駛去矣
第伍名証人王三元係於槍响後方將被告送往燈船者據稱既聞槍聲且見其
將手伸出此數華人皆供稱在南碼頭見宮慶受傷或於其回岸時見之
被告供稱是日下午伍句鐘後到碼頭擬到牛莊燈船訪友當日過午早已出門遊蕩未
出門之先其槍已放在右邊衣袋內以防瘋狗回店時又忘却將槍掏出及到碼頭
始覺其槍尚在衣袋內被告即將槍取出意欲掏出槍膛內所裝彈子數枚此係

被告於未落舢舨之前慣有此節當時亦甚小心不料於掏子時壹子忽然爆發亦不明其所以然之故惟放槍時該處壹帶並無舢舨且見其子打在水面約離碼頭陸拾尺或玖拾尺之遠至云伊僱壹舢舨殊屬不易且無有答應者伊概不招認且稱並不見槍子之下落伊所乘之舢舨即其初次招呼者且不知當時傷及人身按被告原供則謂槍响之時宮慶之舢舨不在碼頭近處似在陸拾尺或玖拾尺之外在槍路之左勢必因此子打在水面再向左跳以致擊傷宮慶云如被告之供果可作准則此伍華人之供實在有意說謊而據被告律師固已力辯其誣矣其所辯之宗旨有叁

一此伍華人所供彼此甚相符合其預備在前顯然可見

二此數華人之見以為所供如是不能不取信於公堂

三獨有華人之供似係預為教授固有如是之妥協大有令公堂不能不取信其供者

以上各款立案離奇以此離奇情形置諸美國[illegible]法律[illegible]如從該律師之辯則須牽動美律之基礎[illegible]憑供判斷公堂自無中美之歧視以其所供符合即應信以為實本臬司斷不能以種類之殊而分厚薄亦不能以該律師之請而別等差更不知出於何律而竟有此分別也

本臬司素知此數華人駕駛舢舨係華工之[illegible]者雖係愚民然亦各具天性或善或惡其心地與別國鄉僻之民無異則其[illegible]有殊別

至云彼等言過其實本臬司斷難聽信然彼等所供各節公堂自有權衡固不能盡信彼等之言亦不能以彼等之言目為無據

此數華人之供其中不無稍有錯誤彼等當時且驚且亂難免於此驚急無措之際忽駭交加之時忘却被告如何動手如何放槍惟彼等當時確見此槍亦係實在情形再無可辯之處蓋彼等均供此乃壹小槍當時不過見其槍頭在被告手內露出少許而已顯係被告當時所持之槍係壹特式小槍形甚短小是以入衣袋頗易按此壹節此數華人之供斷非由教授得來且此槍係壹新式手槍按被告以熟識槍械自居又曾在水師學習槍炮更兼時常出獵尚供不諳用法然則彼等之不識此槍之形也明矣再烟台壹區未必有此項華人或華官特用此槍預為指授令彼等到堂供說也縱有此節則彼等所供衹可供係尋常之式或比此畧大而已觀此壹節及彼等所供當時舢舨之地位與宮慶受傷抬回碼頭各情形可見被告所供皆屬有意說謊希圖狡避

判至此處本臬司不但自有權衡且不待明言亦可知被告所供之底蘊矣再被告所供其如是之背理其如是之反常在公堂斷不能作為案內實據如被告云於其掏子出槍時壹子忽然爆發等語此情間或有之然以壹熟識槍械之人此項偶然之事殊為罕見被告說此愚供尚未心足又稱於槍子爆炸時彼頗覺驚駭然則按當時情形而言被告之驚疑必不可達之於言語間也忽又稱當時伊並不以為異且目能急視見其子打在水面離伊所立之處約陸拾尺至玖拾尺之遠試問心地明白之人能以此等供詞為可信乎

衆供均謂此槍其力甚大壹經發出其子之擊力不小若論打在陸拾尺或玖拾尺之遠影響相隨其疾速幾無形可見本臬司料此槍壹經爆發不待被告神定其子已不知去向矣再本臬司所難信者被告橫訊之供也

問據汝所見槍子向何方落水

答云子向前打去我在碼頭上該處附近並無舢舨各舢舨俱在右邊

問子落水面離汝若干遠

答云約貳拾步或叁拾步我當時未及量度

問衆舢舨離汝若干遠

答云約拾伍步或貳拾步之譜

問然則槍子之落水究比舢舨之離汝又較遠矣

答云是也且其方向不同

觀此則被告先云槍子落水之處不在舢舨停泊之淺水界且過其界外若使此子能傷宮慶此子必須在該處跳離水面約玖拾度之叁角形方可濟事公堂斷不能以此出常之理為然蓋此子確已傷宮慶矣觀被告之供其放肆不慎之處自以為所供得法亦在本臬司洞鑒之中惜乎此供終難逃法網也本臬司無須再評其供矣所供如此之類不壹而足不過擇其大概而言之本臬司現嚴定其所犯之罪秉公處斷惟細查其供不得不念及此節本公堂並無陪審人員固不能不量予矜恤苟有可原之處亦無不代為寬解務使其供至無可寬解地步為止俾該犯甘受其罰退無後言本臬司業經宣告在先謂此數華人之供原無可疑彼等本係當時目覩情形實非虛偽所差者不過當時片刻之間未必究能確見被告如何放槍如何手勢耳際此倉猝之時無論彼等如何虛智如何誠實胥已驚惶失措是乃常情其到堂所供或

因彼時匆遽傷人未及細察事後姑作揣度以符當塲情景似亦在所難免
據本臬司之見以為被告之罪按此即可畧減横訊時詢及被告放槍是否
將手伸出各華証多云其手如是而伸倘被告當時確係將手伸出則本臬
司祇有按美國公律定其故殺之罪照郡縣司律官暨原告律師所請壹
樣辦法惟據被告云於掏子時其槍偶然爆發誠如是言則被告當時之手
勢又何如乎若欲將子掏出勢必用隻手於其握槍在手意欲取出其子
忽然壹响爆發當時誰能説出其如何手勢乎其手可以不必伸出槍子方
向亦難定准即旁觀者此時亦被此响所驚已無暇及此且未悉被告此時
究作何事難免與被告壹般錯誤是以此等情節於是案大有性命關繫
按律理宜柬公核斷再本臬司於被告放槍時其手之伸出與否實無確
証判及此處本臬司亦未見供內指明被告當時曾否發怒即各華証於當
時亦未有聽見供内祇云被告以舢舨不應其招面滯慾容而已無供其怒係因
壹時忿激所致情節較輕不致得故殺之罪以此[illegible]
臬司已有判斷之限祇可决其槍傷宮慶雖[illegible]
致被告已知此槍之利害且以識槍自居又係慣[illegible]
未識用法何能辭咎耶況伊在此衆人上下碼[illegible]
兇器内掏出其子以致爆發擊傷宮慶因而[illegible]
實則有心以行此不測也
本臬司現判卓斯所得之罪應在上海美總領事署監禁叁年由西歷壹千
玖百玖年伍月肆號起算
大美國按察使駐華總裁判官蔡雅儒簽押
大清國山東登萊青膠道東海關監督徐撫辰會同觀審

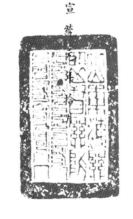

宣統元年拾月
日山東東海關監督登萊青膠道徐撫辰

附件三

外務部

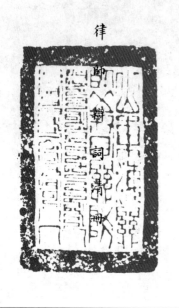

譯呈柏律師辯詞清冊

譯柏律師堂辯 美人卓斯槍傷華人宮慶命案

一被告所舉出之證人無非欲證其到碼頭之時及其放槍之時已近五句鐘惟各華證與顧醫生均供約在四句鐘或畧晚些各華證當時亦不過揣度而言此節本無可置議惟被告證人士班那供稱五點四拾五分時見被告仍在酒店内而被告則稱五句鐘時伊已不在店矣各華證均直稱不能說定何時被告所舉各證人均知在何時遇見被告其情甚可疑也

二被告原供曾在美國水師演習槍炮因事被革可見被告實知此槍之利害與其用之之法也况被告所呈之証據皆係謂伊善諳槍械者誠如是則此槍苟非隻手照常施放斷乎難以發子况用此槍之法必須將其火門收回以指攀其機再用手推其後掣方能施放如欲將子掏出頗費周折惟被告供稱於掏子之際槍子忽然爆發誠如被告之言則該槍之回力必傷其手或其空子必鋇在槍内二者俱無可見所供不實再被告站在證見箱位内比試此槍時毫不費事而且巧妙之極及其當堂試演掏子時槍口朝上迨臬司詢被告是日掏子是否照現時一樣情形被告頗費力始能將槍子掏出其槍口又畧爲朝下

三被告云掏子時該槍忽然爆發且見子打在陸拾或九拾尺遠落水而没誠如其言

則被告當時勢必驚駭目注其槍斷難兼顧其子之打在何處子之出没幾與槍
响同時歸盡況在風霧交作之際試問被告能否於陸拾至九拾尺之外而見此子落水
乎再如此子果打在陸拾貳九拾尺外則宮慶之舢舨正在被告與子落處之中靠被
告甚近按各華證所供均云宮慶之舢舨確在原供之處此皆實事顯係被告有意
説謊無疑矣各華證均説宮慶之舢舨於被告到碼頭之時駛離碼頭不遠惟被告
不招認且云伊所乘之舢舨係其初次所招者又云招此舢舨後方行放槍惟該舢
舨人供稱伊招呼他的舢舨係在槍响之後

四衆華證供稱被告右手持槍將手伸出始行施放放後隨將槍入於右邊衣袋之内
被告供云槍响後伊將掏出之手放入左袋其槍則放入右袋槍子爆發時手上之子
無一遺落亦未被回機所傷等因如此供果確殊屬奇異之事其最忍心害理者乃
被告之舉動也

五宮慶既被槍傷而被告殊不介意夫豈不見其受傷在目前乎當孫七將宮慶
送上岸時被告既不往觀其如何受傷亦未幫同送往醫院竟敢逍遙法外
行若謂被告不知宮慶受傷此乃謊言蓋被告已知傷了宮慶視人命如螻蟻視國
法為兒戲是以潛往燈船在彼用膳至晚始返希圖躲避其忍心害理不顧天良已
可顯見況復巧言掩飾謂見槍子落水不料復能傷人無非以偽滅真欲減其罪
而已查當時宮慶之舢舨實在其前面理應見槍子之下落而被告之不肯相助受
傷者蓋因伊係有意施放此槍故急於逃遁耳

六舢舨人雖係愚民而所供均係清白正直之供被告所供均屬不在情理駕舢舨
人等熟識被告且常見之彼等於被告放槍後本欲當場擒獲惟因被告係外國
人未敢遽行暴動隨有勸彼等呈控被告者又有勸彼等報知美領事者維時情
急無暇計議祇有將宮慶置一小車上送往該管領事驗明後由領事轉送醫
院再請華官照會領事拘犯辦罪其舉動光明正大實未有過於此者

七被告於壹千九百叁年所犯之案已顯其猖狂野蠻之手段伊放槍後竟昧良心
寔由品性所出無論其有意與否既犯此法竟能悍然不顧設法逃逸其立心
險詐實與豺狼成性相同

八假令華證所供不實則被告之供或可作信惟查被告之供不獨預備於犯
法之後且已預備於原告伸控之前作為全案之領脉在被告本欲設法辯其
放槍之時不在彼處惟以事屬不易祇可辯其悞殺而已

九總而言之被告如此之狠毒猖狂於叁月貳拾號來至碼頭招一舢舨該舢舨
因已有客不及招接隨又招别隻亦無應者被告遂逞一時之怒奮率爾掏
出手槍有心向該舢舨施放料
貴臬司亦必定以故殺之罪也

宣統叁年拾月

日山東東海關監督登萊青膠道徐撫辰

二二六

駐檀香山領事官梁國英秘密謹此叩稟

為檀香山革命黨事。竊領事查檀香山革命設自由新報館、華文學堂、革命軍政部。自由報鼓吹革命，華文學堂教授革命新書，軍政部辦軍械運回香港。孫汶胞兄孫徽在九龍種植，接收外洋軍械，供給土匪。

檀香山商董余蘭芬等稟稱：華人無公立學堂，將來少年讀革命新書（揚州十日記、革命自由、創世英雄、世界平權）等等書目，為害不淺。求領事倡辦華文義學。迴想此舉非得十餘萬美金實欵生息，不敢云創辦華人公立學堂，事甚籌躕。稟請

欽差大臣札諭籌華人之財辦華人之事。檀香山向無

抽收華人公項不辦將來讀畢業西文考有憑照深染
革命資格者到部考試授職其性格自幼習染則防無可
防其革命色藏巨深實為深慮祇有勸商董想法辦理
撫李啓輝禀檀山務學會前建有房舍本是學堂無
經費功竣尚未開學愿將全間地皮房舍撥出公立學
堂於是會議凡華人每年捐學堂經費一員但恐革命黨
反對請存案如抗捐有子弟入學堂收書金每月四員
開捐之後自由新報大造謠言革命黨故然抗例不樂從
認捐者不滿百人之數焉能舉辦商董再會議請領事監
督革命黨既反對則是逆匪禀

欽差存案凡華命黨與美國籍民不肯捐學堂經
費者不准回國入內地村鄉居駐秋洛粵省關卡
兩廣總督部堂各州縣鄉村公局紳耆嚴查檀山
華命混跡內地查華命入美國籍回鄉强買强賣
引盜搶劫擄人勒贖坐地分肥遇有案件恃美籍
稟美領事干涉往往激出變故如此不得不嚴禁春
間逆首孫汶來檀林雲、許發、譚亮、曾長福、盧遜、梁
海、梁于譚、達梁、長雷、官晋、雷官爵、溫雄飛等接納
借華人戲園設席唱戲歡迎每人收銀五員親自簽
名入會播戲園人約計滿座三四千人之外自由新報特

書華命總統孫汶其日在某處戲園演説檀山民主

例不禁自由言論領事官卑職小自愧無才於有秘會

欽憲

兩廣督部堂

香山縣正堂查拿

孫汶 孫科（之子） 孫徽（之兄） 香山縣翠坑村人

林雲香山縣大洲坑村人　許發香山縣洋洲村人

梁海梁于梁長香山縣石岐人　曾長福歸善縣人

雷官晋雷官爵香山縣埗頭村人　溫雄飛盧遜粤人

譚亮譚達香山縣涯口村人

事實理合備稟須至者伏祈

外務部王爺中堂尚書恩准察核施行

宣統二年九月十三日

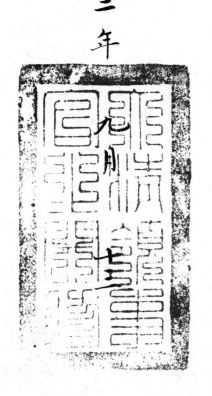

二二七

其一　宣統二年十一月初十日　禮拜六日　第壹千五百十二號報紙　一千九百一十年十二月十號

新中國報

Sun Chung Kwock Bo Ltd.

No. 49 Cor. of SMITH AND HOTEL STREETS HONOLULU, T. H. P. O. BOX 1022

Tong York Manager
Dr. K. F. Li Editor

…is paper is issued
T… times a week,
…sdays, Thursdays, &
Saturdays.

……$ 1.25
……$ 2.50
1 YEAR……$ 5.00

Entered at the Post Office of Honolulu as second class matter

CABLE ADDRESS
Sunchung Kwockbo

本島全年報費五元半年二元五毫一季一元二毫五美國各埠全年六元半年三元一季一元五毫此外各國酌加郵費俱照美金算賜閱請惠上期

記者李啓輝　司理唐玉

本館在檀山正埠荷梯盧夾士蔑街角門牌四十九號　信箱一千零二十二號　每逢禮拜二四六日派報

December 10, 1910. NO. 1512

專有。。吾不知所謂君主專有之文義……來。。日前既以本報所錄美國憲法。。爲剿襲彼說。。美國憲法。。不啻成于温雄飛之手。。今又將憲法大綱。。君主有發交議案之權。。加入專有二字。。然則憲法大綱。。亦成于温雄飛之手乎。。無怪乎于其報內。。大言不慚。。以爲才大如海也。。夫温雄飛能引憲法大綱。。則于原文。。罔嘗寓目者也。。吾今別徵引一條。。以見非君主亦有發交議案之權者。。温雄飛其合十乂手。。五体投地。。長跪諦聽。。憲法大綱。。附議院法要領。。于第二欵有云。。

議院提議事件。。須關乎全國公同利害者。。不得以一省尋常地方之事提議。。

有提議則有議案。。此温雄飛自下之鉄板注脚也。。有議案則可建議。。亦温雄飛自立之確定前提也。。吾不知所謂提議事件者。。得謂之議案否。。既曰提議矣。。得謂之建議否。。提議事件。。而其上冠以議院二字。。仍得謂之君主專有否。。温雄飛才大如海。。或有特別之解說。。

鍾宇盧藻恃有叔姪有弄使館當參隨，檀山華黨使其暗中運動，據華黨云有金何患其清奴不聽我命令相殺其奴隸

其二

宣統弍年　　檀山新中國報　　十一月初十日

金山轉電

◉十月三十日香港專電云、、新會縣屬石步墟慘遭大火災、、共燒去商店三百餘間、、損失甚鉅、、

按石步墟、、在新會縣屬西方、、近白廟河村、、李族丁戶甚繁盛

◉又專電云、、澳門葡兵變起、、全埠商民震恐、、罷市奔避、、經澳督極力安撫、、現已平靜無事、、商塲已復開市、、

◉又專電云、、粟署粵督增祺、、恐澳門兵變擾及、、特派新軍八百人、、馳赴前山駐守、、以資保護、、

◉十一月初二日、、北京專電云、、北京國會同志總會、、聯合各省分會、、簽名上請願書於資政院、、請速提議具奏、、實行開黨禁、、並上書於軍諮大臣濤郡王、、濤邸已允力助、、

檀山近聞

◉稟批照錄　自梁領事移會香山縣、、查拿革命黨發現以來、、經在中華會館議事、、惟迄無結果、、茲查得本月七號晚、、各代表到領署遞稟、、及八號領事發出稟批、、而是晚中華會館議事、、決議在張欽使及北京外務部兩處、、稟控領事、、蓋至是而該稟所謂官商衝突之勢成矣、、茲將該稟及領事批詞、、照錄如下、、

具稟中華會館代表趙蔭榮鍾宇古雲開余蘭芬劉景濚、、稟爲按關黨獄、、盡人可危、、聯懇移咨祖國、、將案註消、、以維大局而服人心事、、竊香山旬報、、七十六期所登駐檀香山領官梁、、文行到縣、、據稱邑屬石岐人、、林雲梁海粱于粱長、、崖口村人、、譚亮譚葵、、泮沙村人許發、、翠坑村人孫文、、在檀香山倡言革命、、開設自由報、、運軍械供土匪、、孫文胞兄孫眉、、逃混回九龍新界、、種畜爲名、、接濟外洋軍械、、窩聚土匪爲實等語、、邑令准此、、恐其混回內地、、有碍治安、、已飭營札屬、、一体嚴拿矣云云、、全體僑民聞之、、呼號悲憤、、異口同聲、、人盡寒心、、慘無天日、、殊不意文明世界、、立憲時期、、有此劈頭之大紀念也、、迺者全體僑民、、一再集議、、勢將決裂、、商等竊以官商衝突、、有碍治安、、又據許發等投訴、、伊等七人俱係埠中營業商民、、並無運軍械供土匪等情、、今無辜獲罪、、心實不甘、、聲勢洶洶、、風潮頗烈、、迫得聯懇移咨祖國、、將案註消、、以維大局而服人心、、公便兩便、、切赴正領事大人台前察奪施行、、宣統二年十一月初七日稟、、

據稟香山旬報七十六期登本領事移會到縣查拿革命黨存案一事、、本領事到檀、、目擊孫汶春間來檀、、林雲接納、、駐在自由新報、、即晚在新人和當席演說、、打刼謀逆、、復借華人戲院、、招人簽名入黨、、發賣革命票、、自由新報言論悖逆、、鼓吹革命、、已明目張膽、、今中華會館代表趙鍾等、、具稟懇請註銷、、該代表何異與黨爲朋、、顯有恃衆滋事、、着商董等勸解華僑、、安分營生、、如有悔改前非、、商董查明確實、、具保甘結前來聽候、、倘仍恃衆聚議、、妄自暴動、、本領事定必嚴懲重辦、、決不寬貸、、批抄發、、宣統二年十一月初八日、、

檀香山庚戌年十二月初六日中華會館趙蔭棠 鍾宇 盧信 黄亮 楊耕焜 古今福 張慎謀 盧燧 古伯荃 杜黄

發起大集議對待梁領事仇對檀山革命黨事當場所派傳單及自由新報所登 檀山春秋

根本問題

〔盧信〕

列位今日在呢處地方大集議。小弟好喜歡得呢個機會。同我地同胞講吓一個問題。我今日見列位咁熱心咁踴躍黎抗拒一個官。小弟十分歡喜。點解呢。我地中國人向來最怕官。官要殺頭就任佢殺頭。官要抄家就任佢抄家。今日列位能够唔怕殺頭抄家。敢膽同一個官黎抗拒。可見得中國人心進步。民智日開。實係一件最好嘅事。但列位經過呢件事之後。更要認眞做愛國求自由嘅功夫。因爲驅逐領事一件事。卽使能够達你地嘅目的。仍然不能還你地嘅完全自由。點解呢。有兩層道理。

第壹層現在嘅滿清政府實在不能倚賴嘅。凡人民想咁樣。政府一定要反對。好似近來有人入北京請開國會。点知政府吩咐民政部趕佢地出北京押解回籍。呢件就係至近嘅事。可以知到呢個政府實在靠唔住。倘若滿清政府係好政府。同美國政府一樣。咁就所有大小官員個個都好嘅。卽使有一個唔好。但係人民有權。得法律保護。官固知唔敢欺我地人民。如果欺我地人民。政府時時查察官吏。官吏一有唔妥當嘅。就立刻革職。倘若借注册題目。每年勒每人收一元二五。咁就唔止革職。一定要坐監添。你地話梁國英注册勒捐誣陷商民。就要開全埠集議。請政府革佢嘅職。但係細想起來。你地如果得一個好政府。呢件事幹駛乜鬧成咁大。你地今日冇法律保護。祇打一封電上一張稟。請政府調去個個領事。但係滿清政府與別國政府不同。別國政府唔係好人唔做得官。滿清政府凡係越唔好人。越有大官做。你睇滿清官吏。有邊個係好嘅。況且你地係政府嘅奴隸。領事係政府嘅伙記。滿政府斷唔信奴隸嘅說話。就立刻趕去一個伙記。你地想下。凡係文明國政府。被人控告。亦要開堂審過。方能定罪。今梁國英控告你地係革命黨。廣東總督聽佢一面說話。唔再查審吓。就立刻行文到各處。照梁國英嘅法子黎壓制你地。你話政府如果可以倚賴。邊有咁野蠻嘅。故此我地大家要知到呢個滿清政府唔能倚賴嘅。

第式層滿清政府就係可以倚賴。照你哋意思。立刻調去梁國英。但係滿洲官吏個個一樣。趕一個梁國英。別個梁國英又來。今日對待梁國英。明日又對待別個梁國英。你話煩唔煩呢。我地須知到官之唔好。因爲政府唔好。政府唔好。因爲人民唔知自己係主人。樣樣事都倚賴政府。政府因此乘勢黎苛制人民。所以我地如果想得好官黎代我地辦事。必要先得一個好政府。想得一個好政府必要自己知到我係主人。樣樣事唔好倚賴政府。你地想下昨日梁國英話許發係我子民唔係朋友。点知有民邊有官。歐美各國。人民係主人。官吏係公僕。滿清官吏自己稱作父母官。話我地係佢地子民。点知有我地人民納糧。個的官邊處有飯食。應該叫做父母百姓方合。如果係父母官。應該代我地辦事。豈有請狀師在外國法庭告子民嘅道理。我地明白呢件事。就要自己認明係在乜野地位。如果甘心做官吏既奴隸。樣樣倚賴政府。咁就一梁國英去。別個梁國英來。我地禍無了日咯。故此我地要知到我地係主人。唔應該倚賴政府既。

第三層我地既知到保自己身家性命。須要保到永遠。兼保到子孫。点解呢。滿洲政府野蠻專制。人家都知到。你地在美國地方。得享自由。就係領事壓制你地。你地重可以在亞鴉剌公園地方大集議。反對領事。但係你地要想一吓。倘若你地在中國受官吏壓制。你地敢集議反抗唔呢。我睇你地一定唔敢。就係集衆開會。滿清官員一定派一隊兵嚟亂咁開炮。將你地殺得尸橫遍野血流成河咯。邊處有咁嘅自由。任你集議任你演說咩。你地試想美國人與我中國人同是人類。同是天地生成。點解美國人得咁自由。我地咁受人苛制。至到一個領事出到外國地方。都重令僑民騷擾不堪。你話爲乜來由。唔通我地中國人生成做牛馬做奴隸嘅。你地反對領事。不過好彩在美國地方啫。倘在中國。你地一味吞聲忍氣。任滿洲政府殺頭抄家就算萬幸。但係你地終之要返唐山。一返唐山就唔得自由。你地又有子孫。今日你地或者可以保住個條命。但有咁嘅政府。你地子孫。都難自保。所以我地要想吓自己永遠嘅自由。想吓唐山同胞嘅苦境。想吓子孫嘅將來。咁就要設法子盡我地一分嘅責任。你地千山萬水。都要去搵錢。点有話唔識得搵自由幸福嘅。

列位如果想搵永遠嘅自由幸福。必要研究呢個根本問題。点解叫做根本問題呢。好似一條樹嘅根本一樣。所有枝葉皆由根生嘅。今日我地受官壓制。做人奴隸。係乜野原因。由於滿洲政府唔好。所以累得我地咁悽慘。如果我地得一個好政府同美國政府一樣嘅。我地一定好自由好安樂同美國人一樣。你想我地中國有四千年嘅歷史。有四百兆嘅種族。有四百萬英方里嘅地方。今日被人欺侮至於極地。你話爲乜來由呢。皆因滿洲政府腐敗專制。我地受其禍害。我地大家知到滿洲政府。係滿洲人操權嘅。但我地想吓滿人唔過五百萬。又係野蠻賤種。点解我地四百兆嘅中國人。被佢專制至弍百六十多年呢。所有政治大權。盡被佢揸實。你話奇怪唔奇怪呢。好在近來人心漸醒。我見本埠同胞熱心愛國。知到中國將來一定有望。今日你地反對領事。爲保護自己身家性命計。固知一件緊要嘅事。但係列位要想永遠保得身家性命。一定要齊心合力。做過一個新共和政府。同美國政府一樣。我地大家知到反對清政府係一件危險嘅事。但係反對政府固知危險。反對領事亦係一件危險嘅事。一樣危險。不如做呢件根本問題。咁就一勞永逸咯。小弟因見列位熱心反對領事。知到列位求自由安樂嘅心好急。小弟因講吓呢個根本問題。請列位慢慢想透。勿嫌小弟粗言。總要大家勉力愛國。小弟就十分感激咯。

檀香山春閒孫汶鼓吹革命謀逆事檀山自由新報大書特書人所共見領事不將情形禀告是領事溺職領事既然禀告革命報攻擊　政府不能保護領事反受妄動輕舉張勤捐輸办事操切咎由自取檀山革命得此消息更加鼓譟刻聞梁參贊來檀查办革命已經集議科金運動務使政府驅逐檀領償其心愿達其目的顯其革命勢力從此檀山革命成功　大清不堪切想

趙蔭棠則趙錦吉金福吉重開吉伯奎鍾宇張慎謀楊耀焜黄亮黄燦廷温雄飛盧信盧藻等因想中華會館董值附和革命西歷九月初二日中華會館值期革命黨公舉新董值則順革命黨大集議於公園由會館撥大集議使費壹百金現中華會館董值非革命黨不能當董值

檀香山自由新報

鍾宇恃美使館有后[illegible]
此藻在檀當美律師翻譯　亦有姪在美使館

請看荒謬絕倫之批

中華會館代表趙蔭棠　鍾宇　古雲開。余蘭芬　劉景濼等稟。據稟香山旬報七十六期。登本領事。移會到縣。查拿革命黨存案一事。本領事到檀。目擊孫汶春間來檀（該領除孫逸仙來檀之時。皆盲其目耶。須知爾韃主人。派爾來檀。亦不過保護華僑治安。乃該領僅於孫逸仙到檀之時。始一開其眼。餘外華僑之困苦集告。皆可付之不聞不知）林雲等接納。駐在自由新報（鄉情梓里。周旋接納何害。漢族自然接納漢族。豈配爾韃奴接納耶）卽晚在新人和當席演說打劫謀逆（爾韃奴又非在塲。此打劫謀逆四字。從何得來。老實些將尊頭縮埋罷。不然。我將韃狗當日入關。殺戮漢人之苦況。逐欵問爾。恐爾雖沒盡良心。亦不能答也。揚州十日。廣州三日。定嘉三屠。此又爲誰人打劫。然則韃狗。豈眞爾祖宗耶。）復借華人戲院。招人簽名入黨。發賣革命票。（簽名入革黨。則如是踴躍。不交一元二五注册。則無人過問。不恨煞爾耶）自由新報悖逆（打破爾注册摳丁之荷包。不利於韃奴。自然叛逆）鼓吹革命（代湯武孔孟立言）已明目張胆（老實。自然光明正大。豈效爾韃奴。白晝閉門謝客不敢見人乎）

按此一段不過極論自由新報之革命而已。究竟與該七人有何關係。乃僅以「林雲等接納」五字輕輕一提。以下純是論自由新報倡革命夫自由新報倡革命。豈爾今日始知耶。無法以誣此七人革命之憑據。乃避重就輕。舞文之術巧矣特華僑非盡盲者。

今中華會館代表趙鍾等。具稟懇請註銷。該代表何异與黨爲朋。（此句立意更險。「何异」兩字。幾至無一定之解釋。總之使其箝口結舌。不敢復道。此後被誣之人。如有人代其訴半句。卽可以此句塞之。曰何異與黨爲朋。好批）顯有恃衆滋事（中華之代表。自然是全体華僑人多則曰。恃衆滋事。人少則曰。衆情不附。祇是任爾自講自駁足矣）著商董等。勸解華僑。安分營生。（華僑人人。皆安分營生。何用勸。何用解。）如有悔改前非（人人皆安分營生。何有非處。既無非處。又何悔改之有）商董查明確實具保甘結。前來聽候（既無前非可悔改。又何用具結。一味糊塗發夢）倘仍恃衆集議（野蠻野蠻。不許人集議。昨晚集議。看爾又有何妙法）妄自暴動（與逃犯等叉痳雀。或有暴動。）本領事定必嚴懲重辦。決不寬貸。批抄發。（一派囈語）

此段祇罵中華商董。與黨爲朋。並無中肯之處。雖自稱爲批。其實非批。前段論自由新報之倡革命。後段論中華之類於黨人。純非批駁之語。該原稟內。最要者「又據許發等投訴。伊等七人俱係埠中營業商民。並無運軍械供土匪等情」此數語爲該稟之主腦。純無半句批駁。吾可信該領未嘗寓目該稟也。

◉梁國英奈全體華僑何

昨晚中華會館集議◎○討論禀控梁國英之事○○經大多數決議○○全體簽名禀控梁國英於清公使及清外部○○此禀交張伯詢古今福高覲臣主稿○◎林檻泉參議○○准由思鴉刺船寄去云云呵呵梁國英之批何其强硬○○「倘仍聚衆集議妄自暴動定必嚴懲重辦決不寬貸」吾等試睜大一雙眼○○看你老梁有何本事嚴懲重辦中華會館値理○◎及一般檀山華僑○○呵呵國英好自爲之○○毋令吾等笑汝無能也○○

◉華興報記者程又雄亦說謊

昨日華興報記中華會館代表往見梁國英○○要求消案之事○謂「領事經已允准」哈哈不料程又雄大主筆亦學得逃犯主筆與謀財害命領事説謊之慣技○○檀山報界又多一説謊記者矣

◉日人新設俱樂部

埠上日商等◎○昨組織一社會上交際之會○○名曰「日本人俱樂部」○○昨日開午餐會○○該會現賃舊日之美路學堂校舍○○爲會館○○賃批五年○○月租一百元◎○開始三月○○每月八十元○○

檀山春秋

（笑）

庚戌冬清領事梁國英被審於美國警署○○

庚戌者何○○紀歷也○○不書年者何◎○斷統也○○建虜僭窃○○又從而君之○○恥莫甚焉○○故不書○○

何言乎冬而不言月○○蓋自十五號以來○○無日不奔走於警署受審○○司空見慣○○書不勝書也○○

清領事梁國英者何○○醜之也○○曷爲醜之○○梁國英以炎黄遺裔○○際神州板蕩之時代○○既不能蓄志光復○○振大漢之天聲○○又不能遯跡山林○○草討虜之露布○○乃靦顔事仇○○認賊作父○○甘爲奴隸○◎故醜之○○

不曰控許發而曰被審者。譏之也。譏之奈何。誅爾。何誅。領事之職守。旅民之生命財產是保。既不能保矣。又從而陷之。一元二五之苛例未去。五元護照之酷法又來。然則清領直以人民之膏血爲酒肉耶。故誅之。

裁審者爲漢拿魯爐埠之警署。何以泛言美之警署。所以譏其不知國際公法也。梁國英不知國際公法。在漢拿魯爐埠之警署。可以被審。則何處之警署。不可以被審。世界豈有被居留國法律裁判之領事哉。不知國際公法。而爲領事。其能爲旅民謀利亦希矣。故譏之。

君子曰。春秋之義。貴復仇。梁國英既爲讐效力。固已不齒於此方士夫。乃更復誣陷同胞。以媚其讐。則眞千古之罕聞。人類之希有。其見誅也。不亦宜乎。

皇會居一。。郎謂檀山華僑。◎皆是謂亂党。。檀人得知此事。。大動公。。今夕故開大集議。。以籌對待之。。言畢。。衆大鼓掌。。贊成驅逐梁英之舉。。

梁國英欲取同胞之血以染紅其頂張伯詢君繼起。◎宣讀時敏報所載國英控稟全檀同包之詳文。。並演曰。◎領事之設。。乃爲保護旅民起。◎今梁國英自充領事以來。。未嘗華僑。。辦過一件有益之事。◎不但能保護華僑。。反欲殺盡我華僑。。後心甘。。此等虎狠無道之領事。。洲萬國所無者。。料梁國英之在檀。。爲領事。。不過欲取我二萬同包血來。。染紅其頂子耳。。諸君尙要領事乎。。言竟聽者狂呼。。或云逐出境。。不認他爲領事。。更有呼殺者。。語曰。。衆怒難犯。◎梁國英見情形。◎亦當知機矣。。

檀革之出做必祇然必禍件必又凡回◉。。將並又

國英甚於虎狼蛇蝎　黃主席又請
燿焜君演說○○大意勉勵衆人○○須
心協力以除此害○○又繼言者○○爲
藻廷君○○黃君取洪水猛獸爲喻○○
中國上古時代○○洪水氾濫○○猛獸
入之時○○後以衆志堅齊○○終除禍
○今日梁國英之爲禍華僑○○實甚
洪水猛獸○○其心之陰險則毒於于
蛇虎狼萬倍○○若華僑不協力以除
○爲禍之大不堪設想矣○○時聽者
紛大呼者○○殺他殺他○○怒恨之聲
不絕於耳◎
君說畢○○主席請林鑑泉君宣讀○○
辦梁國英致中華會館之書○◎强迫
也註册事○○該信爲梁親筆所書者
其文理顚倒○○幾難卒讀◎中「可笑
把○曰「該一次自由報○○又犯前轍
事若使官威○○壓我僑民◎○則札
[illegible]

於
國
吾等
欲擅
等
數千
○○五
同句
○○逃
中華
包於
人○○
實賞
或曰
誤耳
◉如
即散
棧夜

◉中華會館中之人物

今夕中華會館於亞鴉刺公園開華僑大集議。。此事已成而幾於不成者。。誰之罪歟。。幾於不成而終得成者誰之功歟。。故檀山華僑不可不知中華會館中誰爲托領事大脚之人也。。去月中華會館已經決議開華僑大集議。。派出値理十二人。。不料選舉新職員之後。。十弍値理於本月三號開議此事。。中有弍値理力持反對之議。。而亞鴉刺公園之大集議幾於不成矣。。後經古趙諸人等決意舉行乃得成之。。當十弍値理議事時（盧藻君等未在塲）議停辦集議事。。托大脚者在街上佈散流言。。謂人言舊任職員托領事大脚。。然尚決議執行大集議之事。。今新任職員已就任矣。。乃竟不舉行大集議。。此等托大脚之人。。一面設法以阻撓此事。。又一面謀中傷趙古弍人。。計亦巧矣。。夫使中華會館而改其招牌爲大清會館。。則本報可以置之不理。。否則排斥奸佞。。亦本報之責也。。

Sunday Adver

VOL. VIII, NO. 1?

CHINESE FLEET HOISTS SUN FLAG

WILL MARCH ON CAPITAL

by Rebels.

THEY HAVE NOW BEEN IN SOME REAL BATTLES

CHINESE IMPERIAL TROOPS IN MANEUVERS

REPUBLIC TOO SOON IN CHINA

David Starr Jordan Thinks People There Are Not Ready for So Radical a Change

REVOLUTIONISTS READY TO MARCH ON CAPITAL

ASIATIC FLEET WILL ASSEMBLE IN YANGTSE-KIANG

REPUBLIC TOO SOON IN CHINA

試署檀香山領事官梁國英禀

為檀香山革命黨煽衆謀逆事竊領事到任以來所見華僑
多安分營生然暗中談革命亦間有所聞領事屢經設法開導
並着中華會館商董善為勸諫檀山無華人學堂有革
命自由新報主筆自作革命新書如革命外交 自由言論 洪秀全演義 楊州十日記
等等新書各腐儒散館張伯純 温雄飛等以為作學童讀本領事勸華
僑籌辦華人公立義學照奏訂章程辦理有明倫學堂華
僑李啓輝具禀開辦擬每人每年收壹員明倫學堂經費二
毫半作經手值理工金通計每人壹員二五領事批准散館張伯純 温雄飛
妒忌以為有碍其生計領事力勸安分將來如果有効可以由
學堂聘請充當教習以期各華僑得教育均明大義去惡從
善乃於本年春三月逆匪孫汶來檀由林鑑泉之姪林雲、梁森之
姪梁海、梁長、梁于、譚亮、譚達、許發、温雄飛、曾長福、盧遜
等接納孫汶駐居自由新報館即晚曾長福林雲等遍請華僑
在新人和酒店同飲孫汶當席演説粤省新起軍叛軍餉未足速
要籌款五千員接濟煽惑各華僑入黨又發賣革命軍債票
又名曰同盟票到各内地小埠演説鼓衆而自由新報主筆温雄飛
專鼓吹革命譭謗
朝廷辱詈官長領事職守所關斷難容忍經已密禀在案又
兩廣總督部堂

民政部

欽差美墨秘古各國大臣又移會香山縣嚴防革命黨混跡緣該華黨演說時謂先由香山起事如官兵勦匪可以聳動澳門香港外人干預等語迨於是月由中國香山寄到香山旬報第七十六期登載領事行文到縣縣已准移營嚴防華黨混跡一則該華黨等深恨領事發其逆謀即日鼓噪威挾中華會館董值開議並舉代表趙蔭榮、鍾宇、古雲開、劉景濚、余蘭芬五人到領署要將香山旬報所登載一案全消領事以其事據確鑿難以空口辯論如果其中有委係被愚受挾誤入華黨剋己悔過准中華會館商董等查明確實具保甘結聽候辦理而商董等以事情重大不允具結該華黨遂又集會館鼓動大衆擬由檀山華黨全體籌欵運動聯名分稟

外務部

欽差駐美大臣將領事革職然後派人行刺領事盡職行事一身生死可不必計惟以華黨兇橫大局所關不得不據情稟陳伏乞

外務部中堂尚書侍郎鑒察恩准備案

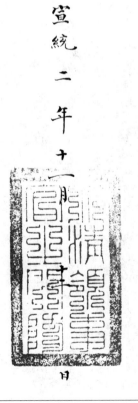

並粘檀山新聞紙兩則

駐檀香山領事官梁國英叩稟

宣統二年十一月 日

附件

◉載洵亦知滿清之將亡

滿洲考察海軍大奴載洵等。回國後。連日載灃任貝載洵奏陳考察情形。極力主張從速組織閣會兩事。措詞極爲痛切。略謂以吾國現形與各國比較。不但陸海軍力相去霄壤。凡關於行政立法等等事。均紛亂異常。美國太統領於晤見時。力言中國危狀。暨各國對待吾國力針。幾有不可終日之勢。再遲一二年後。吾國將無以自存云云。

按近年自土耳其波斯葡萄牙諸國革命告成功。世界之專制獨夫民賊。續漸淘汰。將無復容於二十世紀之新世界上矣。載洵游歷各國。深見各埠華僑近日智識發達。非復如昔日之爲滿人所愚弄。

故有急以中央集權請。。以爲藉此可以愚惑我漢人。。而殊不知滿人自私自利之心。◎無論如何變法。。雖無非爲彼族鞏固勢力計。。而絕不足以阻我漢人更新之舉也。。葡萄牙◎。土耳其等國。。豈非曾宣佈立憲乎。。然終不免於革命。。吾爲滿人不若快退歸長白山下之爲愈矣。。

[illegible]意連屋時屋宇未仙館牛馬傢生什[illegible]車馬牲口及一切利益盡項與余森[illegible]郭潮寬雷祥雷連貴梁帝來徐章力[illegible]伍等承受仍用回祥利園招牌加多[illegible]記二字訂於一九一一年正月壹號[illegible]永生和交易清楚倘日前祥利園舊欠人會揭賬項欠項等項俱歸舊人理不干承受人之事自交易之後生盈虧與祥利園舊人無涉特此佈告

祥利園合記謹啓

大　光　|　本　永　器

新報

◎若一切軍需要品◎○皆賴西北利亞鐵路輸送○○未免陷於危險之地位○○若實行移民政策◎○移民以實遠東一有戰事○○其軍需品固能取給於吾輩云○○基扶之美化檀島○○與菩魯金之移民遠東○○其政策同○○其目的同○○謀國者不當如是乎○○

冊華工之事　夫基扶之政策○○爲美化的○○備戰的○○主張招白工排非工○○則東亞工人○○固不在目

◉反對革命者數千人　昨晚亞鴉刺公園、華人大議事、各舖戶限令五點鐘閉門、一時到場諦聽者、凡數千人、主席黃亮、次第演說者、爲張伯詢楊守毅林檻泉鍾宇盧藻楊鋭等、皆以領事誣陷、而表明全体華僑、多非革黨、當演說時、有人派傳單、標目曰根本問題、署名曰盧信、大抵如日前自由報論說、排領事不如排政府、一樣議論、試思昨晚演說、所據之時敏報、確指領事誣陷、非革黨而以爲革黨、欲斥逐梁國英者、實以報誣陷之仇耳、而盧信傳單、則與大議事之本意、適立于反對地位、請君入甕、乃不先不後、噫異矣、

最奇者彼亦曾充主筆、亦自號爲文墨中人、乃竟以本報禮拜四日之論說、所言梁聯芳查辦之事、誤會爲昨晚大集議之事、公然大聲疾呼、使畧識之無、斷不至誤會若是、又本報謂中華會館、不得不理、而反以爲宜置之不理、此等顛倒是非、蓋曠萬古而不一見者也、

有人謂宜不承認政府所派之領事、宜以西人爲之、由華僑公舉、或上稟美京、此說亦斷難實行、然竟有提出以爲言者、亦一最奇異思想也、

因一二人。。而可以黑白變色　東西易人我之必責成于中華會館經理之者。。以會館而名爲中華也。。既以中華名之矣。。則許發以爲一家之言。。亦不攻自破。。而普告二字。。亦用之而恰合者也。。

又新中國報云。。此事方訴于公使。。又安有轉而排公使之理。。更安有轉而排政府之理。。不認則不訴之。。諸君之本來面目。。與革黨所異者在此。。而不認一二人爲革黨者亦在此。。奈之之何自反其初心哉。。偶一失足。。便是陷坑。。豈獨從井而救人。。且將無辜下井者。擠之永不得出也。。失足陷坑。。從井救人。。**全爲排公使排政府六字說法**。。**並非指排領事而言**。。原文亦甚明白。。彼不甚深曉者。。或以爲相恐嚇。。亦毋怪其然。。奈原文並不爾爾何哉。。

妥而言之。。彼三人駁論之失點。。誤會全在于禮拜四本報。**爲對于禮拜五日大集**

中華開國紀元四千六百零八年　**自由新報**　西曆一千九百十一年元月六號　七

海電

●土耳其斯坦大地震

俄四號俄屬土耳其斯坦打市堅電。俄屬土耳其斯坦大地震。傷害人命。損破產業極巨。本埠屋宇之倒塌者無數。鄉人亦甚衆。傳聞維野尼全埠毁沒。其居民二萬五千人中。死者占多數。

五號又電　據現各地報告。此處一帶死亡者以數千計。傷者數千。在本埠經覓回死屍四十具。死者數百傷者數千。恐糧食缺乏。淒苦猶甚

五號又電　現聞丕利富士克及丕市北式埠。全爲地震所毁。內地山裡傳至之消息。更爲可駭。

●南美界務可望和平了結

四號南美里馬電　益圭多與秘魯二國。今允將爭國界事。交海牙裁判

●禁東亞人購買土地

五號沙架免度電　加剌科尼省上議院。現提議一案。凡不入籍之外國人。概不能在本省購買或批租公地。此案則由於排日人之運動所起者也。日人之在本省。多購買菓園。驅逐白工離去其地。此案一通過成例。則所有非市民之東亞人。俱不能購買土地矣。

●美政府控航業托辣斯

五號紐約電　合衆國政府。昨日在合衆國巡環署。控告航走太西洋之汽船公司十三家。指以犯不法聯合。壟斷載大艙客生意事。被控之公司爲英卡公司　太西洋輪運公司　根匿公司　法人之太西洋公司　咸北亞美利近公司　荷蘭亞美利近公司　德國𠍲公司　士加地尼維仁亞美利堅公司　及白星公司　聞此數公司據有載艙客生意十分之九。每年所獲不下五千五百萬元。十三公司中。外國者居十一家。

●國防問題近聞

今朝嘩盛頓電　國會昨日再提議軍備問題。陸軍卿德建臣。請國會立卽撥七十七萬元。爲購辦野戰砲。以供給國民兵之用。太平洋沿岸代表團。則謁總統力言太平洋岸之乏保護。並請加派潛水艇。在太平洋岸各港。陸軍部又求撥一百七十五萬元。以再敷築巴拿馬鐵路。

EMPORIUM　Hilo　Hawaii

新貨　廣告

本店設在希爐埠位亞奴內及布列治街耑辦蘇杭雜貨衣物靴鞋及食料等物發客並代理金山之加剌寬尼肥料公司

吟波庵厘商店啓

代理燕梳廣告

Theo H Do avis &Co

希盧爹比士有限公司

代理倫頓諾敦保險公司凡欲購燕梳祈至商酌

裕隆泰接收匯單

Yee Lung Tai P.O.B 1017 Honolulu

啓者本店設在檀山正埠士蔑街耑辦唐山什貨耕田器具唐番罐頭伙食麵粉麥糠米糠粟米白米餘未共錄並代收各處梓友金銀書信交到　府上妥收及取回音與付銀人收照如有遺失照原來數給補屢蒙各梓友深信均從時價平順以圖信順爲禱

一香港泰安棧程名譽付交南朗同安銀舖甘康裕代交四大都等處

一香港寶源興金山庄付交澳門晉享銀舖陳邦榮代交恭谷良都斗門等處

一石岐泗和隆銀舖代交附城等處

本店信箱壹千十七號

裕隆泰謹啓

新辦到華人賀年頂上貨物平沽廣告

啓者本號近由歐美新辦到頂上各樣貨物列左

男女各色羊毛遮結葛衫

大小子女各色羊毛遮結葛衫

自定阿打大小童成套絨衫褲

各樣男女底衫底褲

各樣各色男說衫

各色男女靚襪頭

各色靚絲巾各樣巾仔

各色大小靚絲帶

各樣項上草帽毡帽

各樣靚窗門布門簾布

各樣項上各色布草疋頭但各貨大多不能盡錄諸君光顧定必貨美價廉此佈

漢拿魯爐蘇杭公司劉接麟秀春啓

[illegible]之先尤當治病于既起之後藥石之功不可沒也

本葯房體天地好生之德搜羅各種藥水藥膏藥散普濟羣生俾得益壽延年經試用者口碑載道

又有香鹼香水牙粉牙刷凡歐美各國名勝畫圖文房四寶一俱齊備　華友光顧價必平順請祈留心是荷

再本店有一種吉神藥此藥專治一切痲病之症靈效可驚雖症至重一禮拜久可能全愈

電音一五八一

荷梯厘夾怒安奴街　牧野藥舖啓

謹謝隆情

啓者弟於月前適因染病醫藥無資荷蒙　得都寄廬道威利開憲政會計嚕寶昌圍各親及捐助得以入日本醫院調治全愈愧無以答特登報端以鳴謝焉

十二月廿八號　楊灶謹啓

第一藥房

本藥房設在怒安奴及秘利天彌街角常有各種藥水葯膏葯粉發售凡虛寒實熱奇難雜症用之者莫不奏效如神所以遠近馳名消流日廣又有香鹼香水牙粉牙刷療病刀圭棉花剃刀一俱齊備華友賜顧價值極外平順伏祈留心是荷

電音二二〇九

千九百十年十一月廿一號

日人石井藥舖白

八中華開國紀元四千六百零八年 自由新報 西曆壹千九百一十一年元月六號

專件

[illegible]僑民驅逐滿奴張蔭棠記 （非非）

●羅省埠攻張奴之電 （六）

北京農工商部暨外務部鑒。美港醫藉血虫症阻加禍華僑入美。經名醫查無害。公派關鏘庭醫士入美都辯爭。張使容揆不肯帮辦。大失國體。乞向美廷速駁。羅省埠華僑代表□□叩

●沙加免度攻張奴之電 （七）

北京外務部農工商部均鑒。美關苛待。誣我商民染血虫症。刺耳指取血。用水管射入工門。酷驗。苦甚羞甚。請張使容揆力爭。不理。辱國棄民。請撤退。 沙加免度華僑全體代表馬碧池余樂三等叩

●金山埠中華會館攻張奴之電（八）

北京分呈外務部資政院暨報界公會鑒。美港醫以勾虫血虫症。苛驗來美華人。苛驗之法。先以瀉藥令其服。後用水管探入工門取糞。驗蟲之法。則用刀刺手指刺耳珠取血。種種耻辱。不堪言狀。向例舊客免驗眼。今復驗。撥回籍。迫得求使署力爭。並舉代表關景堅入美京協助。奈張使膜視。而容揆尤爲驕悍。反怒代表實屬溺職。乞速換以護僑民。金山中華會館董事。李寶湛。許炳芬。黃商瑚。唐瑞年。胡祝祥。戴協三。雷棟傳。余靈等全體叩。

查各梓里前到中華會館。勸發電回北京。各人願捐助電費。昨晚到座者百餘人。異口同聲。謂電文內。要有速換張容字樣。故將捐欵繳出者多至九十餘人。

●尾利賀華商之函 （一）

中華會館紳商鑒。敬啓者。欽使之設。所以保護華僑也。乃張使自履任以來。迄今將一載矣。毫無建白。尤可異者。近日林社血毒虫之案。關[illegible]利害甚大。爲欽使者。縱無[illegible]呼籲。亦當據理力駁。除苛例[illegible]民困。庶幾上可以副朝廷之寄託。下可以安梓里衆心。今竟不顧大局。各報皆謂成使聽信容某。不爲之理。商等得聞之下。不勝駭異。憂憤交迫。伏望我同胞急籌對待之法。迅卽電禀北京軍機及外務部。務去尸位素餐之官。以免辱國誤民。則我華喬不至絕迹於美洲也。

十一月十一日 尾利賀衆梓里字頓

●卡士固連地埠梓里之函 （二）

大同日報列位先生鑒。清公使張蔭棠參贊容揆。不爲華喬人美境力爭。有負厥職。請代轉致中華會館。電清政府籌對待。西十二月十四號 亞拉笋拿省卡士固連地埠梓里叩

●甯陽會館之攻張奴 （一）

甯陽會館者。旅居美洲新甯人士之團體也。惟歷任主席。均由公使發護照回國聘請。詎此次張奴。不允發給。說者謂他別有用意。然不能知也。今因此事。全埠鼓噪。該會館亦乘舊衅卽開大集會議於該會館中。人情洶洶。衆怒如火。堂無隙地。門限爲穿。當時皆主張立卽禀攻。隨有人謂不如俟關君回埠後。開全體大會於中華會館。以全體攻之。較之我甯陽一部分之攻擊。更爲有力。遂決議。乃該埠領事黎榮耀。則四處運動。欲破壞其局。此奴死心爲主。亦可哀矣。

●仲公理會之攻張奴 （二）

仲公理會。爲該埠之志士所發起。因於昔年梁林之案而發者也。今回因張奴貽害華僑。該會亦决議具禀北京政府。詳叙張容兩大奴之無狀。冀達撤退之目的。現已起稿。俟謄正後。由總值理署名外。復由各商店聯給圖章。然後郵北京云。

●僑民全体之攻張奴 （三）

●趣妙畫圖之諧謔

自張蔭棠不理血虫案風潮發生以來。劇烈情形。畧見各報。最妙者。有畫師繪圖多幅。張帖通衢。用意深婉。諧謔趣妙。聞二埠亦有人帖此畫云。

（甲）繪出闊佬懶理情景。維肖維妙

（乙）繪出一翎項小人。托兩翎項大人之脚。其脚卻非常之大。以示大奴不遠千里來接濤洵兩酋之意

（丙）繪出僑民無數。各持掃管。追逐一翎項之人。中有一人。以長掃管從後挑撥翎項者飛向空中去。翎項如飛絮。見者捧腹。

●詩詞白鈔之陰毒

旬日來。睡罵之白鈔。滿街滿巷。如秋山飛落葉。其中最陰毒者。惟解員氏七絕三首。有云「天河水莫洗腥羶。次柳文章遇偶然」閱者莫知其故。有識者曰。天河乃該大奴鄉名。正喻夾筆也。次柳先生。乃爲該大奴中舉之槍手也。不知是否。姑照錄之。以質本人。

報界之攻張奴 （四）

報紙者。代表輿論者也。金埠有日報四。少年中國晨報。中西日報。大同日報。與世界日報也。自此事出現。各報記者皆操筆直書。毫無廻護之意。其言論驅風捲雨。立海垂潮。全文難盡載。載其論說之題目。於以見三千毛瑟之力。並羞本埠報界記者自負爲代表輿論。而實如婦女之羞人答答。禁（旁口）不敢言云者。

（甲）少年中國晨報之論題

（一）張蔭棠不如禽獸說

（二）駁黎領事爲張蔭棠廻護之言

（三）宣佈張蔭棠之罪狀

（四）滿奴張公使容參贊欲滅絕美國華僑之眞意

（五）冷評諧文班本數種

（乙）大同日報論題

（一）關醫生之報告斷定張蔭棠之罪案

（二）張蔭棠容揆實爲華僑公敵

（三）張蔭棠怠玩容揆昏昧

（四）關醫生回埠宜同胞開歡迎會

（丙）中西日報論題

（一）張公使爲容揆傀儡耶

（二）張公使果欲貪天之功以爲已力耶

（三）異哉張公使容參贊眞膜視華僑

夫人民之交報費而閱其報者。原欲報館之代爲之謀也。金門報界。發達如此。誠可謂不負其天職矣。特不知本埠收人五元報費一年之報。果足以盡其職否。非非曰統計美洲此次驅逐張蔭棠之役。爲電攻者八。爲禀攻者三。文明公衆之團体主動者四。各埠華僑之主動者八。報界文攻者十一。其餘詩詞白鈔妙趣畫圖之諷嘲者。更不知幾許。壯哉美洲之民氣也。 三續完

中華會館投筒廣告

茲將本會館一千九百十一年正月二号投筒公舉當年董事芳名列

正董事 趙 錦 英書記 葉桂芳

副董事 古今福 華書記 高覲宸

正管庫 何 寬 副管庫 楊廣達

三年連任値理

鍾 宇 盧 藻 古伯全 楊廣達

葉桂芳

投筒主席劉登趙錦仝啓

◎欽使來電文照譯
檀僑代表張慎謀等電禀梁領設册陷
商壞學該電是否由會館公發希將詳
情禀明以憑核辦
◎中華會館電覆照錄
電悉會館並未預電容詳墨禀商董余
劉叩

律。即或有之。國會一以不信任之
決議。即得使大臣去職。固無俟此
制度也。就採政黨内閣制之國之大
臣對於國會之□任而論。國務大臣
對於國會之□任。在政黨内閣制
之國。最爲完全發達。如英法等國
是也。盖政黨内閣制。其國務大臣。
以由下院多數之政黨中選任。爲習

二三〇

敬稟者自中國湖北兵民肇亂以來檀香山華僑附和革
命黨者日多已占全數八成各處皆懸民國旗發行民國
金幣情形異常猖獗兹將報紙載有革黨鈔票者剪呈
伏祈
察閱肅此恭請
各位憲台大人鈞安
檀館通譯官李光亨謹稟 九月初二日

FEATURE SECTION
Pages 1 to 8

Sunday Advertiser.

FEATURE SECTION
Pages 1 to 8

HONOLULU, HAWAII TERRITORY, SUNDAY, OCTOBER 22, 1911.

Sun Yat Sen--The Honolulu Boy Now in World's Limelight

"THEN some day we may hope to hear of you as President of the Chinese Republic?"

Seven years ago in Honolulu this question was addressed to Dr. Sun Yat Sen, whose name was flashed over cable and telegraph wires a week ago as the probable President of the newly proclaimed Republic of China. If history moves in periods of seven years, even as seven-year periods are believed to mark the changes in the development of man, then the inspired prediction of an Advertiser reporter, in the above question, has practically been established.

For nearly twelve years Doctor Sun's name has been repeatedly brought before the people of civilized nations, first as leading the forlorn hope of a small revolutionary army against overwhelming imperial forces in Southern China, then as a fugitive, then again mysteriously appearing in an inland city to lead a new revolt only to retreat after capturing a city; again as the prisoner of the Chinese minister in the London legation, when, for a time the act threatened to bring on international complications, now in hiding to avoid death after a price of $500,000 taels was placed on his head by the Empress Dowager and the viceroys of various Chinese provinces.

Eventually, Doctor Sun found his way back to Honolulu, for in this city Doctor Sun received his early education, and it was in the Hawaiian Islands that he first saw the light of day, circumstances which have had a powerful influence on his life and career. Although born of Chinese parents he is an American citizen by reason of the specific conditions in the Organic Act and later congressional acts which admitted all who were citizens of the Republic of Hawaii as citizens of the United States.

When Hawaii became part of the American republic and its citizens became citizens of the Greater Republic, Doctor Sun first began the remarkable propaganda which was based on the ideals he learned of Republican forms of government under the American flag, ideals which at first merely smouldered and threatened to be extinguished because the fuel was green and unseasoned. Doctor Sun, with his co-worker Leung Chi Tso, fanned the smouldering embers into a blaze which is now sweeping across Central China.

The writer has interviewed Doctor Sun several times in the last few years and on each occasion found the man, now become suddenly famous, retiring and modest, not given to bombast and only inclined to tell of his plans and those of the party which he has labored to create into a strong organization when pressed for reasons why such a revolutionary movement as the complete overturning of the Manchu throne was necessary. Then the doctor, quietly but earnestly gives the reasons.

China's weakness among other nations was one cause for the new propaganda, the weakness which permitted foreign powers to step upon China's shores, hoist their flags and declare such territory under their shadow to be under the domination of their various governments; the weakness which permitted a supine government, swayed by the personal prejudices and interests of its officials, as opposed to national development and pride, to be overreached by the diplomacy and overridden by the armed forces of nations which carved a slice of the Empire of the five-clawed dragon.

But it was the passing of Manchuria over to the control of Russia which was the last straw to the progressive Chinese and then Doctor Sun, Leung Chi Tso and numerous other powerful men of the rank and file, undertook to fan the embers of discontent into revolution, and caused them to put armed men into the field in conflict with the imperial forces. For ten years Doctor Sun's one hope has been to overthrow the Manchu dynasty, believing that any other government set up by the Chinese would be a source of power and cause other nations to respect not only the government but its citizens.

Only a year ago Doctor Sun slipped quietly into Honolulu and was here for a week before the news of his arrival had spread. He visited with the family of Chang Kim and Chang Chan, relatives, with whom he always makes his home when here. Between their home and the office of the Liberty News, the organ of the local revolutionists, there is always a well beaten path. If he is not at the home of his friends he is the center of an interested circle in the office of the Liberty News. At the time of his last visit Doctor Sun outlined clearly the plans of the revolutionary party, expressing the hope that within a short time the opportunity would come to turn the Imperial army against the throne.

The crux of the interview which Doctor Sun at that time accorded The Advertiser, was, that the army was to be composed of a large number of divisions, each division to comprise 15,000 men and within a few years China expected to have a million men under arms and ready for the field. This army would be ninety per cent Chinese, with Manchu officers. At the psychological moment, when the throne was to be attacked, Doctor Sun expected that the army, being Chinese, would flock to the revolutionary standard and aid in ridding the land of its Manchu masters. He expected that the red flag with its small blue field and sun design would replace the great dragon flag of the Manchus at the head of many drilled regiments. His expectations are being fulfilled, for, exactly as he planned, Chinese troops are now deserting the Imperial standards and rallying around the red flag of the revolutionists—the flag which is now seen floating over dozens of Chinese buildings in Honolulu.

While Doctor Sun may be termed a soldier of fortune he is not the swaggering, swashbuckling type with personal ambition overtopping the ideal which he has set up for the great nation of Chinese. He is quiet, unassuming and philosophic with just a [illegible] trace in his makeup, the determination of a Washington to overcome apparently insurmountable obstacles, a [illegible] people and a Franklin in the efforts he has made to obtain aid for his cause in foreign lands.

Even in the land of his birth he was denied admittance after an absence of several years, but the United States Department of Commerce and Labor saw no reason why he should be denied admission to Hawaii, for he was recognized by the United States government as a full-fledged citizen. It was on April 6, 1904, that he arrived at this port on the Pacific Mail steamer Korea, but was not allowed to land except under bond, under the belief that he was a Chinese without right to land. The matter was taken before the Washington government. The department worked over the case and finally presented a conclusive set of facts as to his right to receive the protection of the United States government.

The department found that he was born at Kula, Maui, Hawaiian Islands, on November 24, 1870. When about four years of age he accompanied his parents to China. When about ten years old he returned to Honolulu with his mother (his father having died in the meantime), remaining about seven or eight years.

While in Honolulu he attended Iolani College, conducted by Right Reverend Alfred Willis, Bishop of Honolulu, who personally taught him. He was an excellent scholar, became proficient in English, history and literature. He never wore a queue and was always, even from that standpoint, in the class of the progressivists. On June 10, 1896, he was admitted to San Francisco as a student and traveler on

DR. SUN YAT SEN.

[illegible] presented by him in China, and after traveling in the United States and Europe, he returned to the Hawaiian Islands, [illegible] Hongkong. His family resided [illegible] Maui [illegible] Doctor Sun's head [illegible] Japan, [illegible] hovered about them hoping [illegible] opportunity to kidnap and convey the family to China, where they [illegible].

[illegible] his claim of American citizenship, Doctor Sun, [illegible] certificate [illegible]. He claimed [illegible] after the annexation of the Hawaiian Islands a registration was taken of all the Chinese and that he was then registered as a Hawaiian-born Chinese, and that he then took the oath of allegiance to the United States.

The United States government did not feel that the fact he had once offered a certificate of the Chinese government was an act of renunciation. He happened to be living in the Chinese Empire and desiring to travel as a student, secured from the Imperial government a certificate of his residence.

That has settled Doctor Sun's status as a citizen of the American Republic.

He was one of the leaders in the plot of 1895 to seize and control Canton, but it was then regarded as a mere riot. Some of the plotters were executed, but with his usual good fortune, Doctor Sun escaped. He then went abroad and began to disseminate the new propaganda. He enlisted the aid of college students who grasped the ideals quickly and became active adherents. He went to England. While in London he was kidnapped by employes of the Chinese minister and held a prisoner in the legation. Sir Halliday MacArtney was then serving as counsellor to the Chinese legation, a position he had held for about thirty years. It was the only time that he came in conflict with his British friends, for the kidnapping of Doctor Sun threatened to bring on international complications and finally the doctor was released. The Chinese hoped to spirit him away to China, where he would have been beheaded.

In January, 1907, the Chinese minister in Paris telegraphed to his government suggesting the arrest of Doctor Sun who was then traveling from Hanoi to Yunan. The doctor was not taken.

In 1906 he personally led the first real revolt against the throne. This was in a province in lower China and at the head of only 600 men he attempted to bring about the overthrow of the throne and establish occidental ideals of government. Four thousand Imperial troops were sent against him and his force were defeated. Later he led a new force and captured two towns.

Many of the plans of the present uprising were hatched in the editorial office of the Liberty News, Honolulu, in April and May of 1910, on the occasion of Doctor Sun's last visit to Honolulu. In all his utterances during this visit Doctor Sun stated with more positiveness than usual, that the time was then almost ripe for a general uprising. While there might be sporadic armed protests against the government they would be untimely if they occurred earlier than this fall, he said.

Later one night in April, 1910, Doctor Sun was found in the editorial office surrounded by an admiring group of young Chinese, all queueless, representative of a modernized and progressive China. Doctor Sun looked less a Chinese than any in the group. He wore a suit of white linen, of the cut any style seen all through the Orient and particularly in the Philippines, with the collar made military fashion and fastened in front by two gold studs, just such a suit as any American in the Philippines wears. His face, a trifle broad, his eyes set wide apart and steady in their intensity, his upper lip adorned with a small black mustache, gave him the appearance of a Mexican, a South American, or Spaniard, and it could easily be understood how he could pass in various parts of the world without being known as Doctor Sun, the famous Chinese revolutionist.

This man, with a price of nearly $500,000 on his head, looked the fearless leader he is. The writer interrupted what was afterwards learned was an important conference on future plans for a few days afterwards, the revolutionist departed on a mission which was to extend all around the world, and to terminate in the present uprising.

To the writer Doctor Sun stated positively that the Manchu dynasty was weakening and that the Chinese were preparing to rise and drive the Manchus out of the Empire. Upon the ruins of the Manchu throne he hoped to see erected a Republican government. "The Chinese regard the Manchus as our conquerors," he said. "They have never been able to affiliate with the Chinese, but the latter, for some reason or another, have never been able to rise and overthrow them. If the way is shown them to overthrow these foreigners—the Manchus—I believe they would accept whatever new form of government was offered them, if it were a Chinese government."

At that time The Advertiser announced that Doctor Sun was quietly preparing for his next visit to China, "A trip which he now believes will be fraught with history, a history in which all the powers will be interested." The Advertiser further added: "Six years ago Doctor Sun sat in an other editorial office and told for The Advertiser readers his hopes and some of his plans. In those six years that have passed Doctor Sun has labored unceasingly in his system of education among the Chinese of the Empire undermining the Manchu government wherever and whenever possible. Doctor Sun may be called a dreamer, an idealist by some, but he is practical. He points to the movement of the Young Turks in Turkey, and states that the movement which he heads in China is identical in spirit and plan with that which caused the overthrow of Abdul Hamid and the establishment of a modernized government, lacking the weaknesses of the absolute power once possessed by the fallen sultan."

Doctor Sun stated that there was more danger to the Manchu dynasty from its own weaknesses than the Imperial government imagined. "The Manchu dynasty believes that it will popularize itself with the Chinese people if a hostile sentiment is fostered against Europeans and Americans. At present the Manchus are raising a great army and putting it on a modern basis. It plans at once to spread thirty-six divisions of all branches of the armed service over China. This means nearly a million men. But," and Doctor Sun half closed his eyes and smiled, "that army cannot be all Manchus. They may put in many Manchu officers, but the bulk of the army will be Chinese.

"When the Chinese government expects to use the army to popularize the government the army may roll back upon the usurpers and crush them. To my mind this is what will happen, for we will not be asleep during this time, and a sentiment will be fostered among the Chinese troops that will cause this vast armed force to be used against the government instead of for it.

"I am for a Republican form of government when the usurpers are driven out and crushed. I am for a president of the Chinese people. I am for radical changes in the development of the great country."

OFFICE OF THE LIBERTY NEWS.

At this Hotel street printing office, where the flag of the Chinese Republic was first hoisted in Honolulu, Doctor Sun planned much of what is now taking place in China.

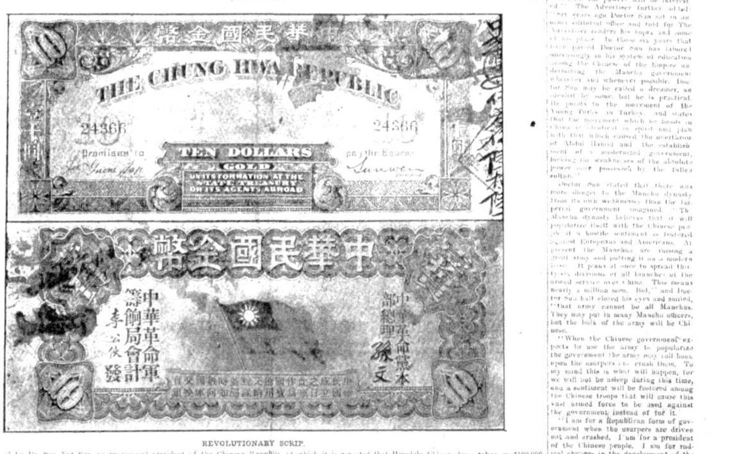

REVOLUTIONARY SCRIP.

Money issued by Dr. Sun Yat Sen, as provisional president of the Chinese Republic, of which it is reported that Honolulu Chinese have taken up $100,000 at fifty cents on the dollar.

The Whaling Empire of the Pacific

BY DAVID LORING MACKAYE

It seems unfortunately probable that when our savants have resurrected ancient glory, portraying that of Egypt, for instance, that we might visualize Pharoic processionals and the ceremonials of the time, that we will have forgotten empires nearer the present and of our own building, as truly imperial in their elements as was that earlier one, but unhappily recorded on nothing more substantial than the surges of the Seven Seas. The greatest of these, beyond a doubt, has been the whaling realm of the Pacific, and yet although it is hardly four decades since the last New England whaler crept around the Horn into the oblivion of some New England inlet, her deeds and the life of which she was a part have been all but forgotten. Fitful memories exchanged about the docks of New Bedford and New London are alone the substitute for the continuum of this portion of our national life. It is strange that America, in recording her history, could have overlooked this fruitful source of tradition and discarded the great moral benefits she might have derived from a clear knowledge of the achievements of her marine pioneers.

The beginning and end of this empire are shrouded in the mists of unrecorded events. When Vancouver crept cautiously into the Pacific to survey the northwest, he met the first of the American whalers sailing blithely over the routes of the Spanish Navigators as if this realm was inherently theirs. The drawing rooms of the old world were still being entertained with anecdotes of the savagisms of this region when the New England sailor was pillaging the kanaka homes with a good-natured alcoholic sang-froid that endeared him to all hearts to the end of the whaling windjammer. The missionaries, carrying their message to those same thatched

A RESCUE AT SEA.

huts, are greeted by the boisterous halloos of the men of New Bedford and her sister ports chasing whalers in ships outrageously incompatible with the dignity of this good-natured ocean. The American whaler had become a part of the Pacific and was to remain so for seventy years to come, carrying the banner of adventure to the uttermost ends of its world.

The First Whaler.

According to a short article in the New Bedford Mercury, early in the forties, the first American whale ship that ever visited the Pacific was the Rebecca, a vessel of 185 tons which was, at that time, considered a ship of good size. She sailed from New Bedford in September, 1791, under command of Captain Joseph Kersey and after an absence of fifteen months returned with a full cargo of oil obtained off the coasts of Chili and Peru. It is certain that the fleet increased with comparative rapidity and there were already large numbers of the craft in Pacific waters at the time the missionaries first formed white settlements in Polynesia in 1819 and 1820. The coast of Baja California and the waters intervening between the mainland and Hawaii were the favorite haunts of the pioneers, but ten years later when the industry had reached more imperial proportions, the beach settlements from Papeete to Raratonga knew him and were known by him. Still later the fleets had penetrated into the Arctic fastnesses and from there crept down the East Asian coast into the sacred waters of Japan itself.

The fleets that assembled yearly off Honolulu and Lahaina in the Hawaiian Islands therefore brought the most exact knowledge of the entire Pacific region, an intimate acquaintance with it, indeed, that has never again been recorded since the whaling fleets have gone. The Russian company governors of the Aleutians became characters known by their familiar names all over the South Seas and the degree of hospitality evinced by each were matters of moment wherever two ship-captains happened to meet. And in the same way the hardy masters chatted with their northern friends of the kanaka chiefs as they drank each other's healths by these far fireplaces.

The whalers, as their confidence increased, spread first over the whaling grounds westward of the Hawaiian group and among the shoals and rocks that trend off a thousand miles northwest from Kauai to Midway Island. This district thus became the first scene of adventure and remained a fruitful source of sea tales as long as the fleets were existent. From here they traveled southward until the common route of the whalers on the southern cruise resolved itself from Honolulu to lower California, to the Tahitians and northward again to the central grounds and back to port to prepare for the cruise in the Behring waters.

Mishaps.

On May 24, 1846, to illustrate the continual misadventures reported from the shoals in the rocky groups north of Hawaii, the whale ship Konohasset ran ashore on Pell's Island, striking the reef shortly after midnight seventeen miles from the place where the Eben Holden had been wrecked three or four years previously. The Konohasset became a total loss and the crew, after remaining alongside in boats all night, pulled for the shore where they discovered the after decks and the cabins of the Eben Holden half buried in the sand. Here they quartered themselves while they constructed a small sloop out of the timbers saved from their own vessel. In this sloop of eight tons, which they christened the Konohasset Junior, a few of the men made Honolulu, leaving twenty-four of their companions on the island with only forty pounds of meat as provision. At Honolulu another whaler was met who at once spread sail for Pell's Island, reaching it forty-two days after the sloop had left. Eventually the rest were saved. Quick action and ever-ready resource has, on similar occasions, saved hundreds of American sailors from death by starvation on the uninhabited islands of the sea, far out of the ordinary routes.

The full roster of wrecked ships would be too long to mention, but for the most part the crews escaped with a miraculous regularity. Tales of the greatest privation were common and more lives lost through hardships on the barren islands or adrift on the ocean than in the stormy moments of the wreck. The whale ship Francis, Captain Smith, of New Bedford, after three seasons of successful cruising, was lost in a hurricane off the coast of New Granada, one hundred and twenty miles south of Buenaventura, in the late '30s. The captain and four men were lost but First Mate William Sherman and two of the crew escaped in an open boat drifting for sixteen days under the tropic sun with neither provisions or water. When picked up, one of the men was insane and the others nearly dead from exhaustion.

The America of Sag Harbor arrived in Honolulu in July, 1846, reporting Captain Pearson, her skipper and three of the crew killed by the blow of a whale's tail, two kanaka seamen who were in the boat at the time swimming two miles back to their ship. Damage done by whales, was often reported, and although some of the tales were doubtless greatly exaggerated danger from the giant prey was always imminent. They did not confine their attacks to their common enemy, the whalers, but on frequent occasions were responsible for disasters to trading vessels. An incident of this occured in '49 when a whale carried off the keel of the brig Frederick, Captain Spinola, off Porto Anna, Nicaragua. The vessel sank twenty four hours later.

Some ships gained a hoodoo reputation which they literally never survived, having to be either sold or broken up. The brig Hawaii, Captain Rabe, was one of these, arriving at the island port in 1857. He had not been out of port more than a few days, according to his log book, when he sprung his main-topmast, finding later that its head was rotten. In Shantar Bay on the first of September his first officer was killed by a whale and several days later the same fate met several of his crew as they were working on a carcass. Two months before they reached port Captain Rabe was stricken with paralysis and eight days later the ship sprung a leak. For the rest of the cruise the crew was continually at the pumps, doing seven hundred strokes an hour.

South Sea Wrecks.

The southern whaling grounds were the richer in adventure, although the tales of the north which were being added to the gossip of this watery realm were not lacking in spice and variety. The charts of the southern islands were far from perfect and were formed chiefly of notes exchanged among the whalers themselves. Wrecks were consequently numerous and every season saw many of the whalers end their careers on the atolls and reefs. One of these was the American whaler Marie Helena which broke up on the reef off Christmas Island in '48. The crew remained on the island, a mere dot on the map below the Hawaiians, for four or five months, subsisting on yams, sweet potatoes, and wild pigs all of which had been introduced on the island by Captain Cook on his memorable voyage of 1777, in anticipation of just such an occurrence. Such instances were frequent and the foresight of the old pioneers, English particularly, saved hundreds of lives in the after years. The crew of the Marie Helena were afterwards rescued by the French ship-of-war [illegible]racelle which made a special trip to Honolulu for that purpose.

A curious analogy between American colonial history and south sea adventure is presented in the log of the Alabama of Nantucket, to which was transferred Captain Spencer and the crew of the unfortunate whaler Triton. The men had been picked up by chance by the frigate United States, then on on its way to Japan, from Sydenham's Island. Early in 1847 the Triton had stopped off the island and Captain Spencer, with a boat's crew, went ashore to purchase stores from a Portuguese trader named Manuel. Having completed the trade, the whalers returned to their boat after dark to find that the natives had taken the oars away. These they secured after a struggle, and fighting their way through the crowd of kanakas, pulled out. The tide, however, was too low and they were compelled to put back. They were seized and placed under guard. The following morning Manuel, with a dozen of his kanakas, rowed out to the Triton on the pretense of coming after the water casks for Captain Spencer. He was to remain aboard the ship over night, at the mate's invitation, while the casks were made ready, but after the crew had turned in, the natives rose and murdered all. Manuel proved to be a fiend but was himself killed by the third mate as he was backing up the cooper.

For several days, the skipper and the few other survivors on land lay bound in a native hut, being told that their companions had been murdered and their ship despoiled. They doubted the story, however, as they could see the vessel standing off the coast at intervals, but were finally convinced by the arrival of several canoes laden with the Triton's spoils. They were then told that it was their turn and they were taken to a small island nine hundred feet or so from shore. Here a burly native was in the act of beating out the skipper's brains, when the chief woman sprang forward and declared them under the tabu, that mysterious rite of the kanaka nations. Spencer was christened Cogio by his deliveress and permitted to wander about, the natives, owing to the tabus upon him, fleeing from him at sight. Finally the United States anchored off the cove for water and the men were rescued.

In the Arctic.

Contrasted to the wild and sometimes sanguinary adventures of the whalers in the south seas, the privations of the north Pacific had a different appeal, seemingly cold and uninviting, but as many lives were sacrificed to the spirit of this icy region as to the lure of the palm-fringed, treacherous shores of "the line." Probably ten years after the Triton massacre at Sydenhams, the whaler Natchez, Captain Bellows, furnished an example of what the adventurers on the Siberian coast had to look forward to. The Natchez's crew prompted by the mistaken desire which has cost hundreds of lives, remained in the Okhotsk Sea long after the remainder of the fleet was beating towards the Japan grounds and home. The vessel consequently met the inevitable gales that disturb this region in autumn and finally, almost totally dismasted, had to seek safety in Potter's Bay. The Natchez was assisted to a position of safety by the Harmony which had returned to seek for her and the captain and all but four of the crew were taken aboard the latter. Those who remained, Isaac Wrisley, third officer, John Lockman, fourth officer, Charles Ripney, boatswain, and Isaac Bunce, carpenter, prepared to spend the winter on the hulk for the sake of a share in the salvage, and bade their mates good bye as the captain, departing over the rail, cried that tragic formula of the high seas, "I abandon the ship to the winds and the waves."

The four men remaining immediately pulled for the shore after anchoring the hulk. But it was too grim and inhospitable for the hearts that dared it in the first flush of enthusiasm and they returned to the ship and stayed there until November, two months. One black November night the Natchez was struck by a north easter and blown

AMONG THE ICEBERGS.

five miles out to sea. For three days they drifted about unable to gain the shelter of the land and fearing that the wretched hulk would go to pieces any moment. They made several attempts to land and leave the vessel to its fate but could not until finally it drifted close enough to the ice pack to permit them to take this advantage. Once on shore they built a miserable cabin of stripped boughs where they could watch their late home. The Natchez continued to drift about for the next ten or fifteen days and finally became jammed in the floe some distance up the coast.

For four months the men lived on the meager allowance of rations that they had, occasionally killing hares to vary the menu. Late in the season they were overjoyed to see a Cossack and an Indian making their way over the pack with mail for the town of Nicolaesky. The Cossack greeted them, but after a short stay, pushed on towards the north. Fifteen days afterwards he returned with a letter from the Governor reading:

Town of Nicolaessky,
River Amoor, Dec. 22.

The Governor of this place, having heard that a whaleship has been cast away near the Okhotsk Sea and that there are a portion of her crew yet alive, sends by these Indians warm clothing and food and if you are disposed, you can follow them to this settlement, about 150 miles from where you are. Here you will be cared for.

N. A. KHITTROVO,
Secretary of Imperial Russian Governor.

The letter was addressed to the crew of any whaler cast ashore near the Okhotsk. Lockman accepted the invitation and paid a visit to the Governor, but the others decided to remain and keep dismal ward over the hulk that contained their hopes of fortune. The Governor told Lockman that as the ship had been found deserted by the Cossack, it was the prize of the Russian government, at which the sailor's heart sank within him, but the official finally, on his own initiative, permitted the vessels stores to be taken away.

Lockman returned to his companions and proceeded to wait for the coming of the summer season. Winter was late that year, and the floe showed no signs of breaking, even by May. In June, Bunce, who had been for twenty days sick of the fever, died in delirium and the position of the survivors became lonelier than ever. At last, however, when their provisions were gone and they were ready to journey to Nicolaessky, the whaler Italy arrived to take them off and after ten months of privation they were enabled to return to Honolulu. Their share of the salvage of the oil and bone of the Natchez ran into a figure which they considered to well repay them for their privations.

Gales and Pirates.

In 1846 the whale ship Bengal reached the rendezvous after an eventful trip, during which it had rescued from Behring's Island, lat. 56N, the crew of the whaler Baltic which went ashore in a gale on June 10. This crew had remained on the island from that date until they were taken off by the Bengal on July 5, snow being forty to fifty feet deep notwithstanding the season, if the story brought back is to be believed. On another leg of her cruise the Bengal touched at the Kings Mill group where the ship Columbia had been lost some time previously. The Baltic landed her men and made a raid inland in the hopes of rescuing the survivors from the unfortunate vessel but discovered that they had been ransomed for a few plugs of tobacco by another whaler just as the natives were going to cook them.

About this time the trouble with Mexico and shortly afterwards the gold rush to California became the chief topics of discussion from one end of the Pacific to the other. The former had a serious effect on the whaling industry for the Mexicans fitted up privateers, little more than pirates, and hung around the coast of Baja California, which had been a favorite cruising grounds for the whalers since 1830. Small colonies had sprung up along the coast, usually one or two white renegades and a few natives who made a sparse living supplying wood and water and stealing whatever they could from the men who visited them. According to a report brought to New Bedford by the whaler America, Captain Nash, which had been chased by privateers in Margarita Bay, three hundred seamen had been captured by the Mexicans and were kept imprisoned on the peninsula, the value of the ships taken aggregating $300,000.

The report of the gold fever and the California Eldorados were a source of continual annoyance to the whaling captains as their men were deserting at Honolulu at every opportunity and shipping to the gold fields. At one time the situation became so tense that the seamen set fire to the vessels rather than be taken back over the long cruise to New England, according to their signed articles. Two whalers, at least, the Tobacco Plant and the Mercury, were destroyed in this manner as they rode at anchor beyond the reef, fearing to enter the harbor lest the crew leave the ship in a body and take to the hills until such time as they could return without fear of arrest.

At this time the whaling industry was in its prime. The adventurers were reaching into corners still more remote from the understood world and there were few captains who would not turn off their way for the chance of a little excitement.

WHALER BACK FROM THE ARCTIC.

The Cruise of the Inez.

Probably the cruise of the Inez, of New Bedford, a well-known whaler under command of a Captain Jackson, was as typical of the ventures of these marine pioneers as any. This vessel arrived at Honolulu, November 18, 1848, after spending a year and a half on the northern cruise, an unusual length of time, with but occasional interims in port to refit. A laughable incident which, it is safe to say, Captain Jackson was never permitted to forget, initiated this voyage. The ship at the time it occurred, was standing off some islands in the neighborhood of 60N., the captain being on shore in an effort to sign some recruits for the rest of the trip. A steady breeze was blowing and the day from a mariner's standpoint, was perfect. Every sail on the vessel was set and, with the expectation of soon standing out to sea, no effort was made to drop anchor.

The skipper had not been gone long before the officer in command, believing himself to be in deep water, was disagreeably surprised to feel the vessel strike on sunken rocks and remain fast. For some inexplicable reason a panic ensued and the remainder of the crew took to the boats and pulled lustily for shore. No sooner had they touched the beach, however, when they turned to see the Inez, under full sail, headed for the open sea and bowling along, without man or master, at a fair rate of speed. The captain's feelings are not recorded; only the long, hard pull that ensued, the crew in three boats bucking down to as unique a chase as there is probably recorded in the annals of this whaling empire. For sixteen hours they strained every muscle in the wake of their departing ship and it was not until the streaks of the dawn of the following day had appeared that a calm took mercy on them and permitted them to reach the errant vessel.

A few months later Honolulu was shocked to hear that the French whaler Fanny, Captain Delande, had been found a total wreck off Europa or Company's Island. Captain Hoxie, of the whaler South Boston, had spoken the unfortunate vessel off Krinel's Island earlier in the season, afterwards finding the wreck and reporting that the crew was either drowned or lost on one of the islands among the Aleutians. Hoxie, who thought himself the last man "down" proved not to be, for the Inez had extended her northern cruise up to the very time the ice compelled her to leave and had happily discovered the wreck crew under the care of the Russian governor of the Aleutians, M. Goborotf.

Still having no desire to return to the autumn rendezvous, Captain Jackson retreated slowly before the ice, and assisted by the rescued crew was able to make one of the largest seasons yet reported. April found him in the Straits of Matsuro, well into land, with the mysterious shores of Japan stretching invitingly before him. For a month he cruised in Japanese waters, meeting several junks and experiencing fairly good luck, sufficient, at least, to give him an excuse to linger in hopes of making a landing in this strange realm. Finally he did so, and on May 5, according to his log book, stood in for a sheltered cove to escape an increasing gale from the northwest. He rode at anchor within plain sight of a village on the shore, for some time, and as soon as the weather permitted, lowered a boat and went ashore. Here he was met by several samurais with a detachment of soldiery and was welcomed, but from the first received very little encouragement to prolong his visit.

With the Japanese.

"I tried to barter with them," he says, "and offered to give them several articles, but they would accept nothing from me nor let me have anything of theirs except when I made signs that I wanted something to eat and they brought me a basket of large radishes."

He was not permitted to go into the village until he started to return to the boat, when he noticed that several of his crew were missing. The Japanese had paid little attention to them, although they watched the captain closely, but permitted him finally to go to the village under guard to search for the stragglers. This gave him an opportunity to take many observations, all of which he has left and it is remarkable how complete and accurate they proved to be, when compared with later knowledge. He then returned to the ship for the Ensign, accompanied by one of the younger Japanese officers who had evinced a desire to see the vessel.

"He was very curious in examining the ship," records the captain, and I think he had never seen glass before for I took him into the cabin and he was very much surprised at the windows; and when I gave him a piece of glass he accepted it and showed himself a little roguish at once. He pulled off his clothes, ripped them open and put the glass, a silver dollar, a small map of the world and some other small things in them. He then placed his hand on his mouth to me as much as to say mum."

Captain Jackson afterwards observed that as soon as his visitor had landed he knelt down and stripped to show that he was not smuggling any foreign articles into this sacred land. The Japanese appeared to understand other items shown them and were perfectly accustomed to the use of firearms. They evinced the greatest curiosity concerning the world from which they were barred and showed a great deal of acuteness in putting questions and receiving answers through the medium of signs. But curious as they were they would not let the American remain and compelled him, the same evening to hoist his anchors and sail back into the wider world from whence he had come.

The Inez continued to cruise and it was not until November that she returned at last to Honolulu with her

(Continued on Page Three.)

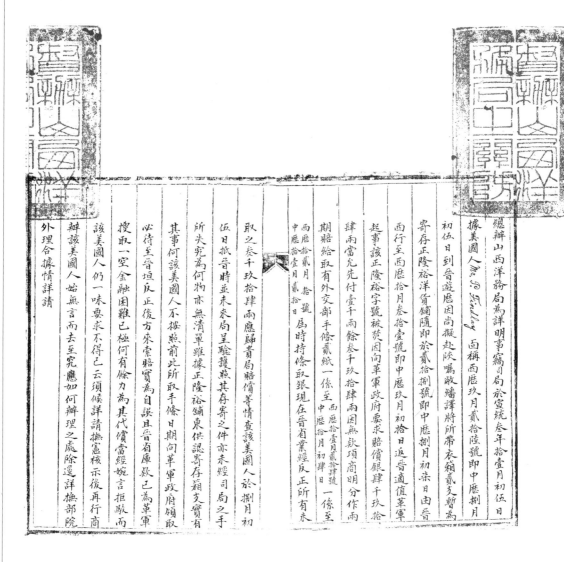

總辦山西洋務局為詳明事竊司局於宣統叁年拾壹月初伍日
據美國人Mr. P. Findlay面稱西歷玖月貳拾陸號即中歷捌月
初伍日到晉遊歷因尚擬赴陜囑敝繙譯將所帶衣箱貳支暫為
寄存正隆裕洋貨鋪隨即於貳拾捌號即中歷捌月初柒日由晉
西行至西歷拾月叁拾壹號即中歷玖月初拾日返晉適值革軍
起事該正隆裕字號被焚因向革軍政府要求賠償銀肆千玖拾
肆兩當允先付壹千兩餘叁千玖拾肆兩因無款項商明分作兩
期賠給取有外交部手條貳紙一係至（西歷拾壹月貳拾肆號 中歷拾月初肆日）一係至
（西歷拾貳月拾號 中歷拾壹月貳拾日）屆時持條取銀現在晉省業經反正所有未
取之叁千玖拾肆兩應歸貴局賠償等情查該美國人於捌月初
伍日抵晉時並未來局呈驗護照其存寄之件亦未經司局之手
所失究為何物亦無清單雖據正隆裕鋪東供認寄存箱支實有
其事何該美國人不按照前此所取手條日期向革軍政府領取
必待至晉垣反正後方來索賠實為自誤且晉省庫款已為革軍
搜取一空金融困難已極何有餘力為其代償當經婉言拒駁而
該美國人仍一味要求不得已云須候詳請撫憲核示後再行商
辦該美國人始無言而去至究應如何辦理之處除逕詳撫部院
外理合據情詳請

示遵施行須至詳者

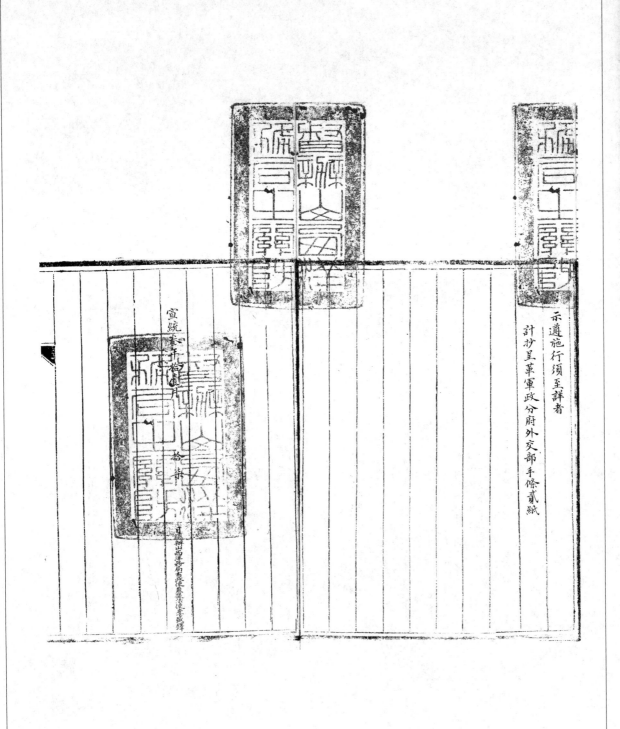

計抄呈革軍政分府外交部手條貳紙

宣統叁年拾貳月 拾柒 日總辦山西洋務局布政使兼署提法使李盛鐸

逕復者：十一月二十一日接准

來函以革軍如有向美國借款之事，請阻止美國商

民勿允此借款等因。本大臣現已查明美商於革軍

並無欲借款及已商訂借款等事，相應函復

貴部查照可也。此復，順候

日祉。附洋文

嘉樂恆啟 十二月十三日

美國使署

附件

169

The American Minister has the honor to acknowledge the receipt of a communication from the Ministry of Foreign Affairs dated January 9, 1912, wherein he is requested to prohibit Americans from making a loan to the Revolutionaries, and he has the honor to state in reply that he has not been able to learn from inquiries instituted by him that any Americans are, or desire to be, the negotiators of any such loan.

Mr. Calhoun avails himself of this opportunity to renew to the Ministry of Foreign Affairs the assurance of his highest consideration.

Peking, January 31, 1912.

Proclamation

By the President of the United States

Whereas, the convention between the United States of America, German and Great Britain, to adjust amicably the questions which have arisen between the three Governments in respect to the Samoan group of Islands and to avoid all furture misunderstanding in respect to their joint or several rights and claims of possession or jurisdiction therein, was concluded and signed by their respective Plenipotentiaries, at the City of Washinton, on the second day of December, 1899, the original of which Convention, being in the English and German languages, is word for word as follows; The President of the United States of America, His Imperial Majesty the German Emperor, King of Prussia, and Her Majesty the Queen of the United Kingdom of Great Britain and Ireland, Empress of India, desiring to adjust amicably the questions which havearisen between them in respect to the Samoan group of Islands, as well as to avoid all future misunderstanding in respect to their joint or several rights and claims of possession or jurisdiction therein, have agreed to establish and regulate the same by the Governments of German and Great Britain have, with the concurrence of that of the United States, made an agreement regarding their respective rights and interests in the aforesaid group, the three Powers before named in futherance of the ends above mentioned have appointed respectively their Plenipotentiaries as follows

The President of the United States of America, the Honourable Jhon Hay, Secretary of State of the United States.

His Majesty the German Emperor, King of Prussia, His Ambassador Extraordinary and Plenipotentiary, Herr von Holleben; and

Her Majesty the Queen of Great Britain and Ireland, Empress of India, the Right Honorable Lord Pauncefote of Preston, G. C. B., G. C. M. G., Her Britanic Majesty's Ambassador Extraordinary and Plenipotentiary;

who, after having communicated each to the other their respective full powers which were found to be in proper form, have agree upon and concluded the following articles

Article I

The General Act concluded and signed by the aforesaid Powers at Berlin on the 14th day of June, A.D. 1889, and all previous treaties, conventions and agreements relating to Samoa, are annulled

Article II

Germany renounces in favor of the United States of America all her rights and claims over and in respect to the Island of Tutuila and all other islands of the Samoan group east of Longitude 171° west of Greenwich.

Great Britain in like manner renounces in favor of the United States of America all her rights and claims over and in respect to the Island of Tutuila and all other islands of the Samoan group east of Longitude 171° west of Greenwich

Reciprocally, the United States of America renounce in favor of Germany all their rights and claims over and in respect to the Islands of Upolu and Savaii and all other Islands of the Samoan group west of Longitude 171° west of Greenwich.

Article III

It is understood and agreed that each of the three signatory Powers shall continue to enjoy, in respect to their commerce and commercial vessels, in all the islands of the Samoan group privileges and conditions equal to those enjoyed by the Sovereign Power, in all ports which may be open to the commerce of either of them

Article IV

The present Convention shall be ratified as soon

as possible, and shall come into force immediately after the exchange of ratifications. In faith whereof, we, the respective Plenipotentiaries, have signed this Convention and have hereunto affixed our seals.

Done in triplicate, at Washington, the second day of December, in the year of our Lord one thousand eight hundred and ninety-nine

John Hay
Holleben } Seals
Pauncefote

And whereas the said Convention has been duly ratified on the part of each Government and the ratifications of the three Governments were exchanged in the Cities of Washington, Berlin and London on the sixteenth day of February one thousand nine hundred, in the following manner to wit, each Government handing to the Ambassadors of the other two, at its capital, its ratification;

Now, therefore, be it known, that I, William McKinley, President of the United States of America, have caused the said Convention to be made public, to the end that the same and every article and clause thereof may be observed and fulfilled with good faith by the United States and the citizens thereof.

In witness whereof, I have hereunto set may hand and caused the seal of the United States to be affixed.

Done in the city of Washington, this sixteenth day of February, in the year of Our Lord one thousand nine hundred and of the

Seal. Independence of the United States the one hundred and twenty forth

By the President; William McKinley
Jhon Hay
Secretary of States

附件

光緒二十六年二月二十日美國繙譯格士送洋文一件
當交馬繙譯首廷賁照譯存案 附洋文

大美國伯理璽天德麥金麗 為
出示曉諭事窃美德英三國因欵和衷商辦在
薩摩阿群島彼此交涉事宜並免將來在該島
因要索各項利權致啟爭端爲此商訂條約業
経各國特派大臣於一千八百九十九年十二
月二號在美京華盛頓畫押其原约英德文字

照錄於後 大美國 大伯理璽天德 大
德國 大皇帝 大英國 大君主兼顧
將此彼在薩摩阿群島交涉事宜和衷商辦並
免將來在該島要索各項利權致啟爭端自應
互相妥訂專约辦理又因彼此政府願將在該
島利權詳爲訂明是以 大美國特派執政大
臣赫卓笙 大德國特派欽差大臣胡理邉
大英國特派欽差大臣潘士佛各將所奉
敕賜全權之命互相比較均屬妥善現將會議
商定各條開列於左 第一條 一一千八百
八十九年六月十四日三國所訂通例暨向来
辦理該島和约專條合同等項即行作廢 第

二條　一德國現將特台辣島暨枚連尼比西經一百七十一度以東薩模阿所屬各島一切利權全行棄去以厚美国英国亦將以上各島中原有利權棄去以厚美国而美国則將汝普路薩瓦依兩島暨枚連尼比西經一百七十一度以西薩模阿所屬各島一切利權全行棄去以厚德國

第三條　一商妥訂明立約之國在薩模阿島所享商務商船一切格外利權當與該居主國無異若另行開口通商一律均沾

第四條　一訂明條約趕緊批准將批准互換後即行照辦彼此欽派大臣先將約文三分在華盛頓先行畫押蓋印用示信守

一千八百九十九年十二月二號

又因此約業經各政府批准並於本年二月十六號此国將批准之約文與彼兩国駐紮此国使臣收執作為互換之據本伯理璽天德為此特將原約照錄出示曉諭仰美国人民一體遵守勿違用是親行畫押蓋印国寶以昭慎重特示

降生一千九百年即美国自主一百二十四年二月十六日　示

伯理璽天德畫押

執政大臣畫押

二三四

第十號　二月初三日收

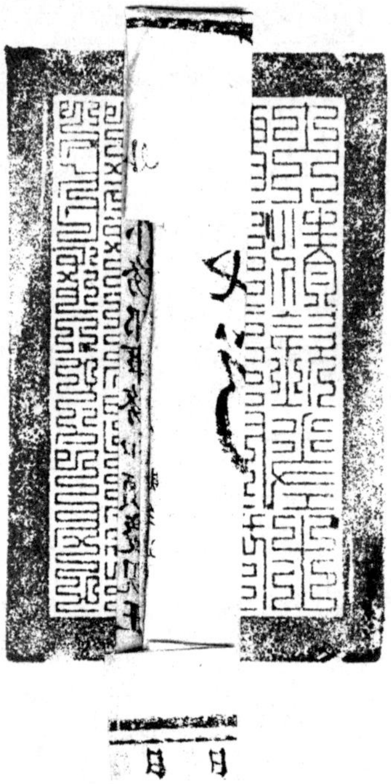

欽差出使美日秘國大臣伍　為

咨呈事光緒二十七年十月三十日承准

貴部咨行本年九月二十一日准美國康使函稱茲接本國紐約可倫比亞大學堂總教習函稱該堂內現值添設中國之學擬分學問言語儒釋道教工藝等為四門意欲備一好處所俾本國人盡得通曉中華學業要總教習

以為如此辦理將來中美必致格外相睦必應彼此於所學考究一切本源囑
請轉達外務部茲按其所囑者代為函達該堂現擬購聚中國書籍存於學
堂並集中華百工所精製各物陳於博物院貴部如何設法俾可廣集中國書
籍或有何書籍與百工精製何物送與該學堂等因前來應由貴大臣將應
購書籍並百工製造各器廣為購備送交紐約可倫比亞大學堂總教習查收
除咨行外相應咨行查照可也等因承准此查紐約可倫比亞大學堂既添設
中國之學分門學習俾國人通曉中學考究本原所有中國書籍並百工精
製各器自應酌購致送除俟購備書籍器物送交該大學堂另文咨呈外理
合備文先行咨復為此咨呈
貴部謹請察照須至咨呈者

右咨呈

欽命外務部

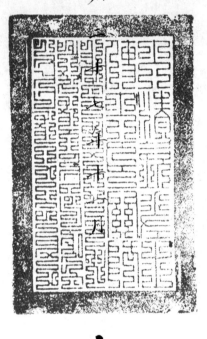

光緒二十七年十一月十六日

二三五

收

美人李佳白先生痛陳利弊書

溯自中外立約和好歷有年矣本大臣奉
命總理各國事務得與
貴大臣因公來往辦理交涉事件迄今日久彼此相見以心本大臣耿耿愚衷顧全大局欲求
中國有益亦不願和好各國有損此心如鏡可
鑑而
貴大臣知之為最深誠以
貴大臣居心平允識見洞達其用意所在每與
本大臣有兩相印合者而本大臣之欣且佩亦職是故也今有事關中國之大利害即係和局之大利害既為和局之大利害即為
貴國之大利害者特為
貴大臣詳切言之其一在鴉片之貽毒從前犯者科罪極嚴未敢明目張胆而為此也自立約以來載入稅則而中國於此開禁其毒人也小者誤其經營大者戕其生命夫人而知之也中國明知其害而洋藥既許進口則吸食鴉片者無可禁矣外國可售之中國則中國之種罌粟

者為有詞矣
貴國有吸食鴉片之禁而不禁罌粟之種專為
中國之售豈欲利己而害人哉萬國公法所謂
揆之以情度之以理斷不肯存是見也向與
貴大臣言及以為鴉片之害甚為不淺則
貴大臣之不肯以此貽害可知也始謂洋商財
貨以洋藥為大宗中國至今未便更議耳而
貴大臣言及洋商各貨均可販運亦不願運售
洋藥則
貴大臣不必以此為利可知也且兩國交誼在
信與義即於商有利而以
貴國所利之一端欲為中國所害之最甚友睦
之邦豈忍出此中國豈不能執吸食鴉片者盡
人而刑之臨流而止其飲羣奔而縶其足中國
所不為也是以嚴申其禁不如先清其源中國
川陝之田凡種罌粟者皆奉
上諭禁止一律播種五穀然禁中國之自種而仍納
外洋之販運彼將有詞謂驅人而吸洋藥轉為
洋商專其利也此其禁之不能盡也今本大臣
因
貴大臣之美意而厚望於
貴大臣之果行務念此事深為中國受害之處
並非本大臣好為更張之論通飭
貴國所屬與中國一律嚴禁栽種罌粟是以絕

鴉片之根更勝於嚴申鴉片之禁去中國吸食鴉片之大害咸知
貴國商人不販烟土不害中國之盛名和好大局益堅洋商貿易日隆利源亦日厚久之鴉片消絕人登仁壽中外皆知此事由於
貴大臣之盛舉而並以見本大臣之　苦心名與實皆係乎此知
貴大臣之必決然行之也其一在傳教之流弊行教本以勸善為事
貴國教士亦有體而非欲與中國民人為難也乃換約以來歷有年所不見中國民人信從之眾轉啟民教齟齬之端揚州則有戴教士之案台灣則有馬教師之案地方官欲保護之而不及保護之衙門欲安輯之而無可安輯
貴大臣欲扶掖之而未能扶掖其故何也泰西各國奉教者專有此途則善良之輩咸入其教至於中國堯舜禹湯文武周公孔子之教自洪荒甫闢以迄於今日用倫常人人依歸唯知聖人之教中國民人之良秀者盡服而習之即如佛教仙教為之宗者何必非卓絕非常之士而人之歸於儒者十之九歸於佛於仙者不及十之一且既儒矣而猶有為佛之說為仙之學者以為佛為仙之無大背於儒非若耶蘇天主教之不祀祖先不拜神位之必去乎彼而後可入

乎此也其專事佛而為僧人專習仙而為道士者既無所禁亦無所强僧道有罪則地方官治以齊民之法亦未聞主乎僧者為僧庇主乎道者為道庇也今欲於儒與佛與仙之外而為耶蘇天主教又必棄其為儒為佛為仙不祀祖先不拜神位而為耶蘇教天主教人亦無幾矣而良善者未識傳教者勸人為善之心望望然去之於是歸其教者半多不逞之徒無賴之輩既入其教而恃其教以與平民爭平民亦與之爭設主教者能如佛與仙之不與物競徐待人之信我與否原可安然無事而主教者又從而護庇之夫主教者之心本不願收有罪之人而始

則朦蔽以圖入教繼而有恃以凌壓平民非教迫民之興教水火既形地方官維持大局遇事周旋而教民以為未能滿意平民以為偏徇教民衆怒難犯激成事端勢必至於法不能制力不能禁及至萬無可為則因小債大積怨成讐恐教民無可容之處而和好有嫌隙之生釁者教禁之弛原以議和也設以傳教之開禁而轉致和局之有碍如兩家相好交情極篤因一二臧獲遷成衅隙揆之大局豈不可惜豈不可慮

貴大臣洞悉華情明白大體本大臣非欲違棄條約以傳教為不可行正欲善保和誼使教之無妨於行今願與

貴大臣通籌全局妥議善策如主教傳教者悉
歸地方官約束與中國編氓自然相處而安外
國主教猶中國士人也中國不能因優待士人
而不隸於籍中即不能因保護教士而縱之於
法外如是則地方官既有管束之權始得行其
保護之實教與民無異民於教亦無疑此為第
一善保教士之法即為久保和局之法至於育
嬰堂之設中國地方官紳每有此舉教中各有
本分之事不必為越俎之謀各傳教士自有可
行之善何必以此啟局外之疑應令無庸設堂
致滋異說此外則姓氏有考生死有報著之冊
籍隸諸地方有罪者屏之勿收涉訟者聽之勿
庇一切詳議妥當條規以期永遠安處此誠事
之不易行行之而必有益者其於交誼所裨豈
淺鮮哉以上兩事本大臣不惜盡言相告望
貴大臣亦不吝盡力以籌或謂此事裨益於中
國者多而不知其增美於
貴國者更不少也唯
貴大臣詳察而力行之幸甚幸甚

李擬

二三六

三月初三日收

咨呈

欽差出使美日秘國大臣伍　為

咨呈事光緒二十七年十二月二十五日承准

貴部咨開光緒二十七年九月二十一日准美國康使函稱接本

國紐約可倫比亞大學堂總教習函稱該堂內擬購聚中國書籍

並百工精製各物陳於博物院當即咨行南洋大臣並貴大臣查

照在案兹准南洋大臣咨稱擬以圖書集成一部備送美國學堂
至百工製造各器購不勝購美商在華通商已久中國製造各器
如該學堂有應需用之物自可由該商量為購辦等因除由本部
咨復南洋大臣飭屬備辦寄交貴大臣轉交紐約可倫比亞大學
堂總教習查收並函致康使查照外相應咨行查照可也等因承
准此除俟南洋大臣寄到圖書集成一部即行轉交紐約可倫比亞大
學堂總教習查收外理合先行聲復為此咨呈
貴部謹請察照須至咨呈者

右咨呈

欽命外務部

預用

空白

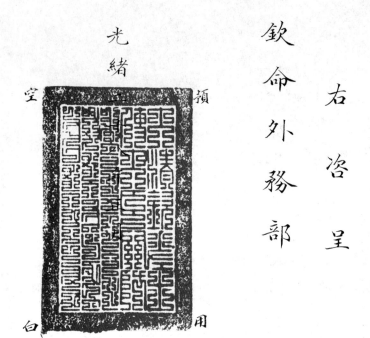

光緒二十八年五月初五日

二三七

逕啟者西上年十一月初三日准
貴部函復云已咨行南洋大臣及盛大臣、住美京伍大臣、囑其
將中國書籍、搜輯選購、送至紐約可倫比亞大學堂所添設之華
文學堂、本大臣准此函後、即行轉送本國外部、請其轉知該大學
堂總教習俾知
貴國有此美意、現准本國外部轉送到該總教習來函、内云
現有紐約博物院羅先生、寄寓北京、被甚樂助
貴國各大臣選購本學堂有用之書等言、查該教習繕此函時、
係尚未接本大臣二次轉寄之函、二次寄函、係將西上年十二月
二十六日所准
貴部函據南洋大臣咨、擬將圖書集成書一部、備送大學堂
一事、既經

貴國已選送此美備要書，羅先生自不必再行幫同選購，羅先生係最有名之士，專門東方語言書籍，將來貴部恐不免與之商送此書，以及他事，是以囑本館衛參贊偕同羅先生於明日下午一點半鐘前赴貴部拜謁，並將該大學堂總教習甚爲感激貴國送此要書之意面爲轉達也。特此即請貴部王大臣查照，順頌日祉。附送洋文

名另具 正月二十七日

附件

F.C. No.

LEGATION OF THE UNITED STATES OF AMERICA,
PEKIN, CHINA.

March 6th. 1902.

Your Highness and
Your Excellencies:-

I have the honor to remind Your Highness and Your Excellencies that on Nov. 3d. 1901 your Board sent me a note saying that you had written to the Superintendent of Trade for the South, to His Excellency, Shêng, and to His Excellency Wu, the Chinese Minister at Washington, charging them to select and purchase some of the most important Chinese books for a present to the newly established Department of Chinese at Columbia University at New York. Immediately on receipt of your Board's note, I wrote to the State Department, asking them to acquaint the President of the University with your generous offer, and I am now in receipt of a despatch from the Secretary of State, inclosing a letter from the President of the University, saying that Dr. Laufer of the Natural History Museum of New York City is in Pekin, and will be glad to assist the Chinese Government by suggestions as to the books that will be of most use to the University.

When the President of the University wrote this letter, he had not yet received my second communication with regard to the gift, in which I quoted the note from your Board of Dec. 26th. 1901, saying that you had received a report from the Superintendent of Trade for the South, proposing to present to the said University a set of the "Tú Shu Chi Ch'êng". As the books have been already selected, and since no better selection could have been made, it will not be necessary for Dr. Laufer to give any advice on this subject, but, as Dr. Laufer is in Pekin, and is a distinguished scholar, who has made a special study of Oriental languages and literature, it may be that your Board would like

To His Highness, Prince Ch'ing, President,
and Their Excellencies, the Ministers
of the Board of Foreign Affairs.

to consult him in the future, either with reference to the shipment of the books mentioned or on other matters, and I shall send Mr. Williams, the Chinese Secretary of this Legation, to accompany him to your yamen, that he may pay his respects to the members of your Board, to-morrow at I:30,P.M.

I beg to say further that the President of the University expresses his high appreciation of the very generous offer made by your Board.

I avail myself of this occasion to renew to Your Highness and Your Excellencies the assurance of my highest consideration.

Envoy Extraordinary and
Minister Plenipotentiary of
the United States.

二三八

逕啟者、頃接前駐京議和大臣柔來函、以現有德國士人石拉根都埃特、奉上德欽差一稟、內附藏字信函一件、請該國欽差轉致
貴親王設法代致藏中、交達賴喇嘛登收、該前大臣聞藏字文義、因有古書目錄、係論釋教史記之事、此書向存藏中喇嘛廟、希轉知達賴喇嘛、將目錄送交該德國士人為要、況該前大臣云石拉根都埃特信內亦曾道及柔某之意、與渠相符、為囑達賴喇嘛允將目錄賞讀、故請轉致
貴親王多為費心、將該信送至藏中、該前大臣不勝心感、並請飭令駐藏大臣速行見覆、即希轉致等因、該前大臣所稱、實足擴人學識、故本大臣樂為轉致、即
貴親王亦必允為飭送、相應函達
貴親王查照、即希見覆可也、此布、順頌
爵祺、附送洋文

名另具 四月十六日

附件

F.O.No. 384.

LEGATION OF THE UNITED STATES OF AMERICA,
PEKIN, CHINA.

May22nd, 1902.

Your Highness:

I am in receipt of a letter from the Hon. W.W.Rockhill, in which he states that a Professor of note, an eminent Orientalist of Zweibrucken, Germany, is sending to the German Minister in Pekin a communication in Tibetan, which he is anxious to have transmitted to the Dalai Lama of Tibet.

This communication is simply a request that certain lists of old books, bearing on the history and literature of Buddhism, and of Tibet, and which have been kept in some of the great Monasteries of the country, be communicated to Dr.Schlagintweit.

Mr. Rockhill further states that his name is mentioned in the Address, as being also interested in this question, and that he jointly with the Doctor makes this request of the Dalai Lama.

He would consider it a personal favor if Your Highness would see to it that the Address is transmitted to Lhassa, and the Chinese Resident there be requested to secure an answer to it.

As Mr. Rockhill's request is purely in the interests of Science, I forward it with pleasure, and feel sure that Your Highness will give the order for its transmission, and that an answer be secured.

I avail myself of this occasion to assure Your Highness of my highest consideration.

E.H. Conger

To His Highness
Prince of Ching.

Envoy Extraordinary and
Minister Plenipotentiary of
the United States of America.

二三九

庶務司

呈為劄行事光緒二十八年十月二十六日據文稱美國人瑞貝稟控當商陳鳳儀等對明認還借款至期不歸一案查美國人瑞貝因追索李希蓮欠款李希蓮即以陳鳳儀馬冠卿欠伊之銀一萬一千兩對還今已押追十月訊供二十餘堂始終支吾不還陳鳳儀等所欠李希蓮銀兩訊係該當鋪亂時被搶一空李希蓮希圖搪塞欠款將陳鳳儀等所開長泰當鋪借銀一萬一千兩對還瑞貝以致轇轕不清自應各歸各案辦理等因查該府尹所擬辦法甚屬妥協應由該府尹將此案迅即照此訊結以清積訟可也須至劄者

右劄順天府府尹　准此

光緒二十八年十月　日

二四〇

榷算司

呈爲劄行事光緒二十九年五月二十八日據總稅務司申稱粵海關稅務司馬士呈稱准香港輔政司文送中外商船互相碰撞之新例一本但此項管理華船章程不能在香港擅行訂定應由中外政府互相定立爲是呈請核奪等語總稅務司溯查前數年曾有此項船隻免碰章程由美國西大臣送請照行嗣於光緒二十三年春間亦有須發通行之事惟總稅務司案卷被燬倘部内存有先後兩項案卷希擲交一全分以便憑中國已認照行之章劄復該稅務司遵辦等因查本部案卷經亂亦多散失現檢查存檔美國西大臣任内並無照送船隻免碰章程舊案惟光緒二十二年准美國田大臣英國竇大臣先後送到洋文改訂行海船隻免碰章程於是年七月九月譯交總稅務司核議據復通行有案未知總稅務司所稱通行之案是否即係此件相應抄錄前項劄文照會並刷印章程劄行備核至香港輔政司所送新例據馬稅務司呈稱各節於華船行海權限有無妨碍應由總稅務司詳核劄復並申復本部可也須至劄者 計文稿三件 章程一本

右劄總稅務司赫 准此

光緒二十九年閏五月 日

二四一

逕復者、六月初十日、准
貴親王來函、以上海租界拏獲革命党犯六名、謂其意係欲
敗壞公家、並錄中美通商條約第十八款內列之言、論中國逃犯、
用何法捉拏送回、又錄上海租界會審之章數條、並云是約章
所載條款、均甚明確、今該犯等犯案重大、案中並無洋人牽涉、自
應按照條約章程、交歸中國自辦、且各犯若得早日懲治、亂萌亦
可漸息、更於大局有益、請即電知駐滬領事、轉飭將所獲之六犯
交出、歸上海道解省審辦等因、查
貴親王所錄南洋大臣初次之來電云、經上海道約會各國領
事、並商工部局簽字拏獲人犯六名、但未將如何約會之意敘
及、該約會係上海道情願約明、若於所出捕票上簽字、拏獲
各犯、並願在租界內審訊、如係有罪、並在租界內科定罪名、發落

懲辦、按此約會之意、係已在租界、開有審問此案之端、乃忽由
南洋大臣來命、阻其在租界審訊、似係遵奉
貴親王之意、論此案本國政府、並無他意、惟按約內所言辦
理、然所聞已經認罪之二人、若上海道尚未與領事有此約會、
恐未肯承認其作書之罪、
貴國政府、似欲將上海道之約會廢棄、不准照辦、如定有廢
棄所約之意、不必乘該犯因倚靠此約會、而有此承認之言、
即定其為有罪之人、請交出辦理、至論其餘四犯、仍應詳核
証據有無犯有輕重之罪、與應否交歸上海道辦理也、特此布
復、即頌
爵祺、附送洋文

名另具 六月十三日

二四二

逕啟者，茲有韋伯思得爾英文字典三部，係美國梅理安印書
公司情願進呈
大皇帝一部，奉送
貴親王及外務部各一部。此書係於一千九百年送交於李
佳白，因亂存於上海，未得運京。迄今由李佳白轉送前來，請本
大臣按照梅理安公司之意轉爲分送。茲甚樂將該書三部
差送
貴親王查照，代爲進呈，並按照該公司之意分别
哂收轉送是荷。特泐，即頌
爵祺。附送洋文外，差送書三部。
名另具。九月初四日

附件

F.O. No.

Legation of the United States of America,
Pekin, China.

October 22d. 1903.

Your Imperial Highness:-

I have the honor to send to Your Imperial Highness herewith three copies of Webster's Unabridged Dictionary, which the publishers, Messrs.G.&C.Merriam & Co.desire to have presented as follows; one copy to His Imperial Majesty, the Emperor, one to Your Imperial Highness, and one to the Board of Foreign Affairs.

These dictionaries were sent in the first instance to Rev. Gilbert Reid, D.D. to be forwarded through this Legation to Your Highness, and arrived in Shanghai in 1900 during the troubles of that year. As it was impossible to deliver them at that time, they have been lying in Shanghai ever since, and are now forwarded to me by Dr.Reid, with the request that the original intention of the publishers may be carried out. I have much pleasure therefore in handing them to Your Highness and trust that you will forward them as desired by the donors.

I avail myself of the opportunity to renew to Your Imperial Highness the assurance of my highest consideration.

U.S.Minister.

To H.I.H.Prince of Ch'ing,

Chinese Foreign Office.

二四三

卟

照會

大亞美理駕合衆國欽命駐劄中華便宜行事全權大臣康　為

照復事八月二十八日准

貴親王照會將

貴國所定商旂式樣繪就圖式一紙照送查照轉致

等因查所請係欲將此商旂圖式轉送本國外部本
館必致無此圖式存案應請
貴親王再將商旂圖式另行繪送一分可也為此照
復須至照會者　附送洋文

右　照　會

大清欽命全權大臣便宜行事軍機大臣總理外務部事務和碩慶親王

一千九百三年拾月貳拾叁日
光緒貳拾玖年　　初肆

二四四

敬啟者現有駐滬西人名易華斯者函稱有一美國
人藏有墨寫兩書（未言明係兩部或兩本）係庚子年亂時所得現
聞中國
内廷尋覓此書請函詢赫總稅務司當如何繳還等語
並附有此書皮面照像一紙前來總稅務司詳閱照
像此書名
大清世祖章皇帝本紀大約係庚子年所失應如何收回之
處未敢擅擬惟該西人如此致函其美國人是否欲
將此書報效抑或索價均屬難定且此兩人為誰亦
不熟識合特備函並照像一紙一併附呈
鑒核應如何辦理希
示復為荷專此佈泐順頌
升祺
附原具照像一紙
名另具光緒叁拾年捌月貳拾肆日

二四五

逕啓者昨日晤談烟台擬修水垻一事兹據駐烟台美國總領
事官耒函內附有美商函請願包修此項工程之做法單請
代轉達等情本大臣兹將兩原函照録轉請
貴親王詳細查閱並請轉屬該管此項工程之官詳加核
奪該商之做法准其投遞承修攬單是荷此泐順頌
台祺 附洋文抄件
名另具 五月二十日

柔克義

二四六

逕啓者，兹接本館武隨員連都司那得函稱，奉美國兵部大臣、飭其將一千九百六年、美國現行營制兵籍名册一部、轉送中國練兵處

王大臣查閲，復接連都司來函，係奉本國偵訪各國兵政大臣、請將一册附送中國練兵處、偵訪各國兵政營中備查、各等因，本大臣相應備函將册二本、送請

貴部大臣查照，轉交練兵處查收存閲，是荷。此泐，順頌

日祉。外附册二本。

名另具 五月十四日

柔克義

二四七

逵啓者兹接有紐約基督先鋒報主人柯拉士來函請轉送
貴親王書信一件特為舉荐石森内教士已来北京該教士並
代柯拉士將書一部轉送
貴親王查收此書名曰游陜紀畧係前數年美國内克司所著
因一千九百一年
貴親王極力帮助内克司前往陜西其曾在基督先鋒報中

倡集款項賑濟該省荒年現柯拉士深盼
貴親王哂存是書以爲申謝之意故本署大臣備函將原書
附送並盼允於收閲仍希
見復爲荷此頌
爵祺 附送洋文及荐信
並外附書一部
名另具
九月十二日

閏立之

附件一

LEGATION OF THE UNITED STATES OF AMERICA,
PEKIN, CHINA.

To F.O. No.
W.

October 29, 1906.

Your Imperial Highness:-

I have the honor to send inclosed a letter from Mr. Louis Klopsch, Editor and Proprietor of the Christian Herald of New York City, introducing Rev. J. Sumner Stone, D.D. who has just arrived in Peking, and who brings from Mr. Klopsch to Your Imperial Highness a copy of Mr. Francis H. Nichols' "Hidden Shensi", which it is hoped Your Highness will consent to accept as a slight token of Mr. Klopsch's high appreciation of the generous assistance given to Mr. Nichols on his journey to Shensi in 1901 with funds raised by the Christian Herald for the relief of the famine in that province. I have the honor to transmit the book mentioned under separate cover, and trust that Your Highness will be pleased to accept the same and kindly acknowledge receipt.

I avail myself of the occasion to renew to Your Imperial Highness the assurance of my highest consideration.

John Gardner Coolidge
Chargé d'Affaires of
the United States.

To His Imperial Highness, Prince of Ch'ing,
President of the Board of Foreign Affairs,
etc. etc. etc.

附件二

TELEPHONE CALL:
910 EIGHTEENTH ST.

CABLE ADDRESS:
KLOPSCH, NEW YORK.

THE
CHRISTIAN HERALD

PRESS ROOM BINDERY
MAILING & SHIPPING DEPT
LEXINGTON BUILDING.

ESTABLISHED A.D. 1878.

LOUIS KLOPSCH, EDITOR AND PROPRIETOR

B.J. FERNIE — ASSOCIATE EDITORS. — G.H. SANDISON.

91 TO 106 BIBLE HOUSE
EIGHTH & NINTH STREETS-THIRD & FOURTH AVE'S
NEW YORK CITY.

BUSINESS OFFICES
AND
EDITORIAL DEPARTMENT
BIBLE HOUSE.

To His Imperial Highness

Prince Ching.

This will introduce Rev. Dr. J. Sumner Stone, now making a tour of the world, who will endeavor to express to Your Highness my great appreciation of the kindness shown to Mr. Francis H. Nichols, our representative during the famine in the provinces of Shansi and Shensi, when The Christian Herald, in response to a cablegram from His Excellency Li Hung Chang sent $100,000. to relieve the suffering.

Mr. Nichols, who died in 1904 on his way to the interior of Thibet, often told me that but for the generous and kind cooperation of Your Highness he could not have succeeded in his mission and that your gracious helpfulness enabled him to traverse the country with ease and comfort.

I have long desired to have my heartfelt gratitude for this very kind assistance expressed to Your Highness but not until now was it possible for me to secure a fitting representative. Dr.

THE CHRISTIAN HERALD

Stone, an old friend of mine about to visit China has kindly consented to carry out my wishes and I gladly avail myself of his very kind offer.

Your Highness and I may differ somewhat in our religion but we are evidently agreed in the matter of charity and I am so grateful that Mr. Nichols found such a generous heart to beat responsive to his own. May God bless and reward Your Highness a thousand fold for all you did for him -- a stranger in your great country on a mission of charity that knew no creed, color or nationality.

Please accept the assurances of my profound esteem and believe me

Your Highness'

Most obedient servant,

Louis Klopsch

二四八

榷算司

呈為照復事光緒三十二年閏四月二十七日准

柔大臣照稱奉本國外部文囑禁止莫啡鴉一事

應係中國先事自辦美國外部方允設法議為定

例禁止莫啡鴉運進中國此係按照一千九百零三年

中美商約第十六條所定至所云中國先事自辦之法

一係中國應請各國亦當一律允准如此例禁二中國

須禁止國內鋪戶製煉莫啡鴉或製造此項之鍼

三中政府聲明應在禁止此項以前預先布告並

言明為醫治所必需者應照約所定辦理等因

前來查此事本部已先於三月間照會未經新

訂商約各國請允禁莫啡鴉及藥針販運來華

現各國已大半應允惟尚有數國未見復除由本部

照催外相應先行照復

貴署大臣查照俟各國一律應允再請轉達

貴國政府照約施行須至照會者

美莫署使

光緒三十二年十月

二四九

復美柔使

逕復者，接准

函稱，有美國人畢沙珀生前備有研究玉石書一套，遺囑俟印成後裝飾呈進，茲寄到該書兩本，備函附送，請代爲呈進等因前來。本部業經代爲進呈

御覽

相應函復

貴大臣查照，轉知畢沙珀之後人可也。此復，順頌

時祉

全堂銜

光緒三十二年十二月　日

二五〇

照會

大亞美理駕合衆國欽命駐劄中華便宜行事全權大臣柔　爲
照會事、一千九百零五年九月十八號本大臣函以所請
貴國政府設立交换書局、願中美兩國將每年所印書籍
互换一事、催請見復等因、旋於是月二十四號准復稱已

咨行南洋大臣核辦、隨接南洋大臣電復、兩江擬以江寗學務處爲換書總局、以蘇州上海兩處洋務局爲分局、中美兩國如有各種新書、均請交上海洋務局接收、云云本大臣已按照來函轉達本國政府各在案、茲准美國交換書局叅議大臣函稱、本局已按貴大臣前次來函擬將美政府所有成案滙集成書、送往中國、是以三次修函寄送上海洋務局、此三函有二函係於一千九百零五年十二月間封寄、有一函係於一千九百零六年寄發、直至本

年五月十四號迄未接有洋務局復函查所定彼此換
書之法係與兩國人民及學堂互有裨益相應按照該
參議所請照會
貴親王查照希將洋務局迄未答復之意轉飭查明
並請將換書章程設法妥定更正可也須至照會者附送洋文

右　照　會

大清欽命全權大臣便宜行事軍機大臣總理外務部事務和碩慶親王

一千九百柒年陸月貳拾壹日
光緒叁拾叁年伍月拾壹日

復美柔使

逕復者：上年接准函送
貴國官立考查地質石層局員維理士所繪地質
石層圖册内云，俟所著之書印就續送等因。現該書
印出，首部照前轉寄復承
貴大臣分送一部，本大臣現已收到。查該書考據
詳晰，圖畫精工，具徵該員地學頗有心得，不勝欣佩。
相應函達
貴大臣，即希轉為致謝可也。此復。順頌
日祉。

袁宫保銜

光緒三十三年八月　日

二五二

光緒三十三年月廿四日三點鐘美館
參贊馬到部，唐大人接見。賀云：美國人
何尔路思係因謀騙官地被拏人犯，並非國
事犯可比。逃往奉天，駐奉美領事認
護該犯，貴署大臣深恐其逃往別處搬
該貴部迅即電致奉省地方官將該犯先行拏
獲，此一端也。至應否交付美國，可俟貴部
查明案情再議交犯，此又一端也。若不先發
一電，深恐離開中國境內更難找尋。貴
部如允發電，我們即可派人前往奉天，以期接洽。究
竟貴部是否可以發電，請於明日見復。答以
當代回
堂憲，先諭發電與否，均可擬文答復。賀隨交出
照會存件又取出卷宗洋文一厚本，並云
此件我仍帶回查閱。遂去

二五三

外務部 上

[illegible] 為

咨呈

咨復事案准

貴部咨准美柔使照稱美國交換書局將美政府所有成案滙集成書三次函寄上海洋務局至今未接復函等因飭查上海洋務局是否接有美國書局寄來書籍函件何以三次並未答復

迅即聲復以憑轉復該使等因到本大臣准此當經札飭上海
道查明詳復去後茲據該道呈稱伏查美國請中國設立局所
將每年所印文冊書籍彼此互換代為分送曾於光緒三十年
二月奉魏前憲札飭查明辦理經袁前升道轉詢駐滬美總領
事將如何互換章程辦法查示迄未見復旋奉周前憲札兩江
擬以江甯學務處為換書總局以蘇州上海二處洋務局為分
局美國如有格致各種新書交上海洋務局接收轉寄分送江
南如有新出書籍文冊亦當互換交上海洋務局收存即經袁
前升道呈復遵辦在案茲奉前因細查卷內祇有三十一年冬間
美國華盛頓格致書院洋文函一紙內開將該院前半世紀紀略

及總理造呈之報册並互換史各一分另摺送閱等語查檢各書
無着此係前道之事職道任內並未接有前項互換書籍理
合具文呈覆仰祈憲台俯賜察核轉咨寔為公便再斜橋北洋
務局現既作為中美換書分局自應派員駐局收發遇有美國
寄來及本省寄交各種書籍分別接收隨時禀道互換以專
責成而免貽誤除札委陳丞世光妥慎辦理仍俟
學部咨行換書定章到道飭知遵辦外合併陳明等情前
來查此案現准
貴部電催業經明晰電復請轉復美使前項書籍寄至上
海關斜橋北洋務局內中美換書委員交上海道查收轉寄

在案除批示外相應咨復爲此咨呈

貴部謹請查照施行須至咨呈者

右　咨　呈

外　務　部

光緒叁拾叁年捌月　　日

咨復事

二五四

戌

花翎二品頂戴江南分巡蘇松太道呈送美京運到交換書籍十六箱並請　察收聽候核辦由

花翎二品頂戴江南分巡蘇松太道爲呈送事。本年七月十四日奉

兩江總督部堂端　批：職道詳美京寄到交換書籍作何辦理，録摺呈請示遵由。奉批：據詳已悉。

卷查光緒三十年二月

魏前部堂准

外務部咨稱：美使函請交换公文書籍一案，其原函係注重格致書院等書，爲分送學堂之用。

現在美京寄到書籍十六箱，查核該道譯開書名，除户口册十四卷、地圖、土地肥磽攷、耶蘇德行各一卷外，其餘八百六十卷盡屬議院文件，於學堂無甚用處，俟譯成漢文後送部，則卷帙繁冗，累月難畢。解省轉送亦多周折，應由該道逕行派員賫呈

外務部察收，應否轉咨

憲政編查館擇要繙譯，或送

學部圖書館庋藏之處，聽候

外務部核辦，除咨明

外務部查照外，並候咨請

學部訂定換書章程咨復，飭遵仍候札行南洋官書局，選擇各種史書及有關政法之書

呈備换送，暨咨請

各省督撫部堂院轉飭官書局，將新出書籍文册可備换送者，酌量發局轉送可也。仰即遵照繳。

摺存等因。到道奉此。職道伏查此案先於本年四月二十七日奉

督憲轉行

大部咨准美柔使照稱中美互换官書事本國局員已將初次所運官書十六箱送滬局查收請飭

滬局於收到美書後分置各處應用並照章將中國應換往之書亦行運送等因咨行轉飭

滬局核办並將美局送到之書如何分置詳復本部以憑轉復等因遵即行查去後旋據上海

中美换書局委員陳縣丞世光復稱本年四月十三日准美國華盛頓斯密沙寧院寄到書籍

十六箱逐箱開視其書共分十三種計八百七十七卷開具書目本數清摺呈閱前來當查摺開

各書均係洋文必須譯方能查閲且每種祇有一分均係議院報告文件應否解呈

憲政編查館備核抑解

督轅飭發編譯局譯存分送具詳請示並聲明中國换往之書查無奉發到局擬請分

别咨行將中國新出書籍文册可備换送者酌量發局轉送在案奉批前因合將前項書籍

十六箱開具書目本數清摺具文呈解仰祈

憲台俯賜察收核辦實為公便為此備由呈乞

照驗施行須至呈者

照驗施行須至呈者

計呈送書籍十六箱清摺一扣

右 呈

外務部大堂

光緒叁拾肆年柒月貳拾伍日

滬道蔡乃煌

附件

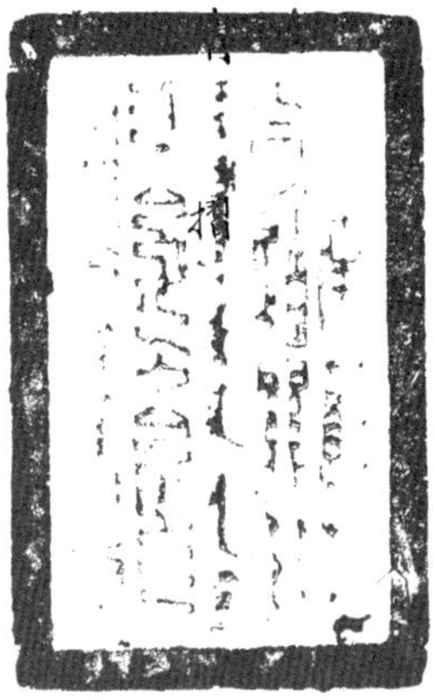

謹將美國華盛頓斯密沙寓院换書所寄來書籍名目本數録摺呈請

憲鑒

計開

第一箱 議院文件 六十九卷 計六十九卷

第二箱 上議院文件 十六卷

議院文件 四十二卷

議院報告 八卷 計六十六卷

第三箱 户口公署特别報告四卷

議院文件 十一卷

第十二次户口簡冊 一卷

美國第十二次户口冊 十三卷 計二十九卷

第四箱 議院文件 四十八卷

上議院文件 拾卷

議院報告 三卷

上議院報告 五卷 計六十六卷

第五箱 議院文件 四十五卷

美國地界圖 一卷

上議院文件 一卷 計四十七卷

第六箱 議院文件 四十四卷

上議院文件 十卷

上議院報告　九卷
議院報告　三卷　計六十六卷
第七箱
上議院文件　六卷
議院文件　三十一卷　計三十七卷
第八箱
議院文件　三十卷
上議院文件　五卷
議院記　三卷
上議院記　二卷
上議院報告　一卷　計四十一卷
第九箱
議院文件　二十五卷
議院記　一卷
議院報告　一卷

上議院文件　十二卷
上議院記　一卷　計四十卷
第十箱
議院文件　四十四卷
上議院報告　三卷
上議院文件　十六卷
議院報告　四卷　計六十七卷
第十一箱
又　二十四卷
土地肥磽考　一卷
上議院文件　十二卷
議院記　二卷
上議院報告　五卷
上議院記　一卷　計四十五卷

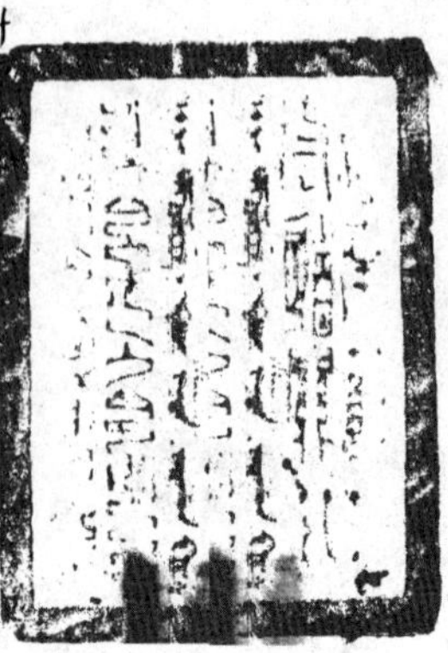

第十二箱　議院文件　三十四卷

上議院文件　六件

上議院記　一卷

議院記　一卷　計四十二卷

第十三箱　議院文件　三十六卷

上議院文件　二十三卷

上議院報告　四卷　計六十三卷

第十四箱　議院文件　四十卷

上議院文件　二十卷

議院報告　一卷

上議院文件與畫　一卷　計六十三卷

第十五箱　議院文件　四十一卷

上議院文件　二十卷

議院報告　六卷　計六十七卷

第十六箱　議院文件　六十卷

議院報告　二卷

上議院報告　三卷

上議院文件　二卷

上議院記　一卷

耶穌之德行　一卷　計六十九卷

共計八百七十七卷

[illegible]十九

光緒叁拾肆年柒月　日呈

二五五

逕啓者：茲接尚賢堂總理李佳白寄到轉呈
貴部王大臣稟函一封，暨將其自著書籍報告四種合
五部，請仍按照去歲六月初三日成章，願由
貴部代為進呈
皇太后一部，
大皇帝一部，
貴親王一部，
貴部哂存一部，轉送學部一部。想
貴親王定悉李佳白在華有年，素為士庶所推重，
並知該博士每以輔助中國即時興起為心，是以本大
臣甚願代送此書，由部進呈
御覽，並
貴部與
貴親王存留二部，再將一部轉送學部為荷。此泐布
復，順頌
日祉。附送洋文稟一件 書五包

柔克義啓 九月十八日

附件一

AMERICAN LEGATION,
PEKING, CHINA.

To FO NO. 454.

October 12, 1908.

Your Imperial Highness:

On the 19th of July, 1907, I had the honor to forward to Your Imperial Highness copies of books written by the American Dr. Gilbert Reid, which Your Imperial Highness graciously received.

At Dr. Reid's request I now forward copies of the following books, written by him:

"China's Treaties with Foreign Powers containing Citations and Notes", 2 volumes.

"A Comparative Study in Geographical Terminology".

"Helpers of China".

"Report of the International Institute for 1907".

Dr. Reid requests that one set of these books may be presented to Her Imperial Majesty the Empress Dowager, one to His Imperial Majesty the Emperor, one to Your Imperial Highness, one to the Board of Foreign Affairs, and one to the Board of Education.

I have the honor to enclose a communication written by Dr. Reid himself addressed to the Board of Foreign Affairs.

I avail myself of this opportunity to renew to Your Imperial Highness the assurance of my highest consideration.

Enclosure: One letter .

To His Imperial Highness, Prince of Ch'ing,
President of the Board of Foreign Affairs.

附件二

美國博士李佳白

為呈遞書籍事

美國博士李佳白謹呈
外務部衙門
中堂王爺大人鈞座為進書事竊佳白於光緒三十三年請本國駐
華公使代送所著書籍計列國政治異同考籌華芻
言和好要言三種旋由公使寄示
貴衙門覆函內稱准貴大臣將原書五部送到業經本
爵大臣等查閱代為進呈
御覽並分別存留轉送矣特此函覆即希貴大臣將本爵致
謝之忱轉達李博士等語恭誦之下感激莫名伏以佳白
末學無才
中朝托庇昔依
畿甸今處海隅掌故未諳方愧芻聞之獻
齒芬下逮親承
藻翰之頒
賁寵無涯旅懷彌慰邇者
大皇帝勤求憲政慎重外交

百度維新萬邦咸仰惟是時機迫切交涉繁多退讓既係主
權紛爭又關睦誼兩難相值一是宜衷佳白曾採約
章重編述要提綱挈領敢云隱括靡遺別類分門庶
或簡明易擇間參按語時寓危言略迹原心諒
俯察憂思之鬱結懲前毖後冀
預籌先事之防維茲特裝訂成函並附中外聖賢事蹟
叢談中外地名合璧表尚賢堂報告仰求
賜鑒如無違礙可否仍前
代為進呈
聖德高深原無待壤流之補助羈臣論著或仰邀
日月之照臨佳白不勝屏營惶悚之至所有屢次冒瀆
中堂王爺大人清聽及感荷下忱理合隨書聲敘伏乞
鈞裁祇請
政安統維
霽鑒並候
訓示李佳白謹呈

二五六

廿

咨呈

欽命尚書銜專使美國大臣奉天巡撫部院唐　爲

咨呈事竊前奉

大部頒發圖書集成一部致送美國等因本大臣抵

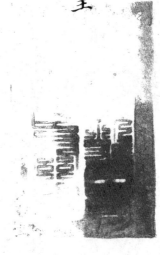

美後當經送至美國藏書樓如數點交旋據美外部

聲稱囑代致謝前來相應咨呈

大部謹請查照須至咨呈者

右咨呈

外務部

光緒三十四年十一月十八日

二五七

于德濬譯呈

美館副漢文參贊斐克孜 梁大人函 一千九百九年十一月六號

敬啟者本月二號會晤時

貴大臣面囑將未結各案案情詳細開送等因茲奉

柔大臣諭遵將本使館與

貴部往來照會開具節略案由送呈

鑒核即請

查照是荷順頌

公祉

附件

外務部與美館未結各案節略 一千九百九年十一月四號

一 西江貿易章程

二 一千九百零七年廣東晨星船教案 即官窑案

三 廣東黄秋爭訟案

四 美孚洋行在長沙開設分棧案

五 山東河南直隸等省征收美國煤油不合例之釐捐案

六 南京征收美國煤油不合例之稅捐案

七 上海美亨洋行案

八 四川教士購地案

茲將關於各案來往照會案由詳列於左

第一件西江貿易章程

一 一千九百七年六月十九號美館致外務部照會 請將此項西江貿易章程改

為與長江通商章程一律

二 一千九百七年七月二十七號外務部致美館照會 此項章程與長江

通商章程相同無須更改

三 一千九百七年九月五號美館致外務部照會 仍請更改此項章

程

四 一千九百七年十月八號外務部致美館照會 稅司已飭將各項洋

貨於抵口時征一進口正稅並一半稅

五 一千九百八年十月二十三號美館致外務部照會 稅務處札飭並

未遵守實行並因由廣州所運之貨物受虧損切實分辯

第二件廣東晨星船鬧事案

一 一千九百八年三月三十號美館致外務部照會 照知晨星案詳細

情形並請賠償銀洋二千三百二十九元三角並請調開知縣謝先模

二 一千九百八年四月四號外務部致美館照會 奥賴巡檢司懲辦

地方官知縣曾極力保護不能懲辦 教士不應在船上宣講 此案宜

由本省了結

三　一千九百八年四月十號美館致外務部照會　粵省所稱全係得自
不實之指告復將（行申明）詳細情形仍請懲办知縣（地方官）並請賠償
款減二銀洋二千二百九十八元二角五分

四　一千九百八年四月二十三號外務部致美館照会　駁復美館照会
粵省稱教民程根美總領事因（教民程根一案）為誤報仍不允懲辦知縣（地方官）

五　一千九百八年六月一號美館致外務部照会　重行申明此案情
形開具實據以證粵省所報之不確仍請懲办知縣（地方官付給）賠償款

六　一千九百八年六月二十六號外務部致美館照会　粵省報稱知縣（地方官）竭
力盡職所開損失浮冒（甚為）美總領事亦無輕信太甚

外務部與美館（議言）未結各案節略　一千九百九年六月四號

一　西江貿易章程

二　一千九百零七年（十月三十號）廣東晨星船教案　即官窑案

三　廣東黃秋爭訟案

四　美孚洋行在長沙開設分棧案

五　山東河南直隸等（各）省征收美國煤油不合例之釐捐（金）案

六　南京征收美國煤油不合例之稅捐案

七　上海美亨洋行案

八　四川教士購地案

茲將關於各案來往照會案由詳列於左

第一件西江貿易章程

一　一千九百七年六月九號美館致外務部照會　請將此項（西江貿易）章程改
為與長江通商章程一律

二　一千九百七年七月二十七號外務部致美館照会　此項章程與長江
通商章程相同無須更改

三　一千九百七年八月五號美館致外務部照會　仍請更改此項章
程

四　一千九百七年十月八號外務部致美館照會　稅司已允將各項詳

七　一千九百八年七月五號美館致外務部照会　指明粵省所稱各
節含有美總領事不稱其職美政府與美館信用不得其人
之意粵省一味巧飾其情將六月一號（本館）所開證實左證概
置不問並將前要索（仍請）懲办知縣（地方官）付給賠償

八　一千九百八年九月五號美館致外務部照会　六月三號照会未邀
賜復甚為切盼請當面議商

第三件廣東黃秋爭訟案

一　一千九百八年六月十號美館致外務部照会　美國籍民黃秋
財產被奪地方官不肯按照約章審辦

二 一千九百八年九月六號外務部致美館照会 黄秋並非美籍
亦未被虐 此案應由地方官按照華律判結
三 一千九百八年九月十九日美館致外務部照会 黄秋實係美國
籍民 雖不應置有(買)田地 惟例准承受祖遺產業(並祖遺產業所置之價) 今查
黄秋華業購買地因產 惟(不過)以地作抵 為擔保 出借款項 此係
須按照一千九百八年北京續約第四款審辦
四 一千九百八年十月十五號外務部致美館照会 黄秋案 按照一千九百八
年續約第四款審辦一節 已達粵省辦理
五 一千九百八年十月三號外務部致美館照会 粵省稱現有
實據證明黄秋在廣東買地並曾交納稅項 外務部力
稱(黄秋)背棄美籍 自認為華民
六 一千九百八年十二月十四號美館致外務部照會 十二月十五號來照
所稱各節與省并未照行 殊為詫異 仍證明黄秋為美籍
從未背棄
七 一千九百八年十二月十八號外務部致美館照會 黄秋背棄美
籍之證據如下 (一)購地納稅 (二)由光緒三十年至三十六年在
內地常居 (三)在地方官衙門直接遞呈 黄秋既自願以上
復回華籍 證據不能認為美籍

八 一千九百八年十二月二十號美館致外務部照會 按照美國法
律 黄秋並未背棄美籍 其證據如下 (一)黄秋不認有購
地之事 並云因為出借款項 曾經以地作為擔保 然無論如
何 此節產只可名為(否有)購地之權 並不與國籍無涉 (二)黄秋
曾將暫居內地之故 呈報美國領事 (三)在地方官衙門呈
遞呈一節 係屬誤 與此案并不干涉
第四件 美孚洋行在長沙開設分棧案
一 一千九百八年八月四號美館致外務部照会 請准美孚煤
油公司照約在長沙開設分棧 惟該處紳民反對此舉
二 一千九百八年八月六號外務部致美館照會 長沙地窄人稠 礙
難允准開設油池分行 該口開埠通商并無准開設油池明文
三 一千九百八年九月五號美館致外務部照會 來照所言不能
作為了結 請定期面商
四 一千九百八年九月二十二號外務部致美館 告知照美館謂若不
順輿情 恐生事端 請俟機會再行商辦
五 一千九百八年十月八號外務部致美館照会 紳民反對甚力
美孚洋行必須靜候
第五件 山東河南直隸各省征收美國煤油不合例之釐金案

一 一千九百八年八月二十二號美館致外務部照會 美孚洋行煤
持有運照在山東河南直隸運載煤油經各處征收不合例之釐
金
二 一千九百八年九月二十三號外務部致美館照會 此案查山東省
閱該行在山東有不遵約章之處
三 一千九百八年十二月十號外務部致美館照會 河南亦無違背
約章之處該行時有有意偷漏之處
四 一千九百八年十二月二十一號美館致外務部照會 各處征收不合例
之釐金一節駐津美總領事確有証據請速行核辦

第六件 南京征收美國煤油不合例之稅捐案
一 一千九百六年（似是七年）九月二十七號美館致外務部照會 南京征收美國
煤油落地稅與約章均不符
二 一千九百六年十月二十號外務部致美館照會 此項稅捐係某
意輸納
三 一千九百七年十二月六號美館致外務部照會 申辯此項稅捐
係強迫輸納決無樂輸之理
四 一千九百七年十一月二十號外務部致美館照會 並無勒捐之事
此項稅捐係華人貨交所輸納於洋商並無干涉

五 一千九百七年十一月二十六號美館致外務部照會 美領事報
稱運煤油商人二名被拿受懲罰商人不敢購買美國煤油是
則並未遵照約章所載貨物無論在洋商或華商之手等
語
六 一千九百八年四月四號外務部致美館照會 已咨行南洋
大臣
七 一千九百八年三月三十號美館致外務部照會 再行申辯違
約收稅事
八 一千九百八年四月七號外務部致美館照會 已咨催南洋大臣
速復文已咨催速復矣
九 一千九百八年十二月二號美館致外務部照會 已逾六個月
尚未接有答復

第七件 上洋美孚洋行案
一 一千九百八年八月十五號美館致外務部照會 美孚洋行控
告裕真行一案上海會審公堂委員並未按照判斷賣行
二 一千九百八年九月十四號美館致外務部照會 上海美總領事
報稱美孚案暨并尚有數案會審委員均未照判斷賣
行照請核辦

二五八

照會

大亞美理駕合衆國欽命駐紮管理全權事務大臣費　爲

照會事，接本國外部來文，轉准本國度支部咨稱，前有由歐羅巴赴紐約之輪船，該船員有勾通外國駐美領事署所用之人，將私運貨物冒充寄送該領事署之箱包夾帶進口，業經本國訊明此案，是以本度支部咨請轉達各國政府，嗣後如送箱包至各該國在美所設之領事署內，請將箱包件數知照輪船局，該局即能將該箱包數目開列於船貨單上，運至美國口岸，即可按一千九百零八年稅

則章程免稅入口至該箱包內物件則無須登列只須將箱包件數聲明即能阻止冒充官物之商貨入口云云囑

本署使達知

貴國嗣後如有物件寄送駐美中國領事署即請按本國度支部所定之辦法辦理可也須至照會者。附洋文

右　照　會

大清欽命全權大臣便宜行事軍機大臣總理外務部事務和碩慶親王

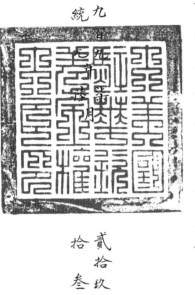

一千九百九年陸月貳拾玖日

宣統元年[illegible]月拾叁日

附件

AMERICAN LEGATION,
PEKING.

To F. O. No. 557.

July 28, 1909.

Your Imperial Highness:

I have the honor to inform Your Imperial Highness that I am in receipt of instructions from the Department of State transmitting a communication from the Treasury Department of the United States which states that an officer on a certain foreign steamship plying between New York and Europe, and an employe of a foreign consulate situated in the former place, were recently convicted of smuggling goods through the medium of packages addressed to the said consulate. The Treasury Department requests, therefore, that the various foreign governments having consular offices in the United States be requested to furnish steamship companies with a list of the exact number of packages forwarded to their consular representatives in America, in order that the same may be noted upon the steamer's manifest and passed free of duty as provided for in the Customs Regulations of 1908. It is not desired that the contents of the packages or mail bags be specified, but only that the number of packages be stated in order that the importation of merchandise under the guise of official

packages

To His Imperial Highness
The Prince of Ch'ing,
President of the Board
of Foreign Affairs.

packages may be prevented.

In commending this matter to the attention of Your Highness' Government I avail myself of the opportunity to renew to Your Imperial Highness the assurance of my highest consideration.

Henry P. Fletcher

Charge d'Affaires.

二五九

函復美費署使海關税則暨條約已由税務處飭送請將美國相等官書互换由

外務部左侍郎聯　正月十九日　行

外務部右侍郎鄒　正月十九日　行

復美費署使函

逕復者：上年十一月初五日接准

函稱本國政府囑請貴政府將所列各書〻每部賜予二册，倘貴國

亦願得有本國相等之官書，即可奉送互换，并囑代詢數事等因。

當經本部以各項書目暨所詢數事均係有關税務，咨行税務

處查核去後。茲准税務處復稱：查美國大臣函開各項書目第一

新出海關稅則第三中國與各國所定各項條約此兩項均有關板官書本處業已飭署總稅務司就近送交美館至第二辦理海關章程中國各海關征稅辦法大致皆以條約為準繩未經另訂有章程第四指定外國地方減稅章程中國并未有指定外國某地方運來之貨許以減稅之事第五外國食物及畜類進口章程并查考屠肉與各食物章程中國除各口遇有防疫事宜隨時就地施行外未經特別訂有前項章程第六出口貨物蒙政府褒獎或賞賜各章程中國出口各土貨未有何項蒙政府給以獎勵金之事第七出口貨物納稅及禁止貨物出口各章程中國禁止出洋之貨物各米穀銅錢等項均載在條約之內所有以上各章程均未有成書應無庸檢送又所詢二節一中國欲更改貨物進出口章程如何辦法并改訂章程之期限一土貨免稅藉助行銷以抵洋貨各章程查

中國於進出口貨物除照條約辦理外如因某項貨物有特別情形須改訂特別章程者皆隨時酌核辦理不必有一定期限至土貨免稅現有機器製造麪粉一項暫免稅釐又機器仿造各洋貨征值百抽五正稅一道不再重征亦均係意在藉助行銷以抵洋貨然皆屬暫行試辦之法未經定有永行章程等因前來除海關稅則各國條約兩書業已由稅務處飭署總稅務司檢送外相應函復

貴大臣查照并希轉達

貴政府請將美國海關稅則暨美國與各國所訂條約各送二份以為相等互換之書可也此復順頌

日祉

全堂銜

宣統二年正月　日

逕啟者據本國博士羅佛禀稱現帶來西藏產生之
犬三頭擬送與中國北京萬牲園收養等因本大臣
當即函達
貴部查照即希轉行農工商部是否需用此犬如肯
收受未悉送交何處請將辦法
示復以便飭知該博士遵照可也此佈順頌
日祉 附送洋文

嘉樂恒啟 八月十三日

美國使署

附件

AMERICAN LEGATION,
PEKING.

To F. O. No. 35.

September 16, 1910.

Your Imperial Highness:

I have the honor to state that Dr. Berthold Laufer, the scientist who has come to China on behalf of the Chicago Field Museum, desires me to inform Your Highness that it is his wish to present the Zoological Gardens with three Tibetan dogs, the said dogs being of a species not found in this region. He has asked me, therefore, to inquire through Your Highness' Board as to whether these Tibetan dogs will prove welcome additions to the animals in the Zoological Gardens and if so how the presentation may be accomplished. The reply to these inquiries I shall be most happy to transmit to Dr. Laufer.

I avail myself of this opportunity to renew to Your Imperial Highness the assurance of my highest consideration.

W. J. Calhoun

American Minister.

To His Imperial Highness Prince Ch'ing,
President of the Board
of Foreign Affairs.

GRAND HOTEL DES WAGONS-LITS, LIMITED
TEL. ADDRESS: WAGONLITS CODE: 5TH EDITION A. B. C.
MANAGER WILH. TRENDEL

Peking, Sept 27/10

The Ministry of Foreign Affairs
Peking

Your Excellencies

I want to thank you for your subscription of one thousand dollars to the Special China number of the Overland Monthly. I appreciate

one thousand Copies
of this Special number.
I also want to say
that we will always
be glad to do every
thing possible for
you. With kind
regards to you I
am

Sincerely

O. E. Ferguson

Your kindness
fully and shall
do my best to carry
out my work in
such a way as
will please your
people I will be
glad to send you
as partial return
for your subscription

附件一

Established 1868

OVERLAND MONTHLY
Founded 1868 Bret Harte
San Francisco

Office 773 Market Street
San Francisco Sept 27th 1909

Received of Wai Wu Pu

One Thousand Dollars

for Subscription to Special China Number

to be published in OVERLAND MONTHLY.

OVERLAND MONTHLY COMPANY

Per O. C. [illegible]

附件二

照譯大陸雜誌主筆福開森上外務部

列堂函

敬啟者承

賜銀洋壹千元作爲預付特刊叢报之費收領之餘感謝無既僕當悉心編輯以冀有裨於

國家俟該叢报出版時當照送壹千份嗣後遇有可以効勞之處更當盡力爲之專肅叩謝敬頌

日祺

福開森謹啟 西九月二十七號

二六二

敬稟者，西歷九月三十號巴黎日報載其紐約訪事專電，謂美國太平洋艦隊現奉其華盛頓政府命令預備戒嚴，因美國駐北京公使格爾豪（Calhoun）電其政府，謂中國將復有拳匪之亂，於外國人性命至為危險，故有此舉。其他一面，於菲律濱之馬里爾所駐之陸軍亦同時得戒嚴之命令，而美國之教士及商人在中國者現極恐慌云云。自此電宣布之後，歐陸各報轉鈔，一時風聲鶴唳，殊足惑人觀聽。今午遠東通信社特發傳單辨正，略謂紐約專電所述美國駐京公使電告其本國政府，稱中國不久將再有拳匪之亂，而美政府已命其太平洋艦隊及菲律濱陸軍同時戒嚴云云。此種新聞，本社不得不亟為更正。中國情勢在前數月雖微有不靖，然皆出於飢民窮餓，並非往年拳匪可比。至於現在已大平穩，決無意外之變，況近來政府復有強大之陸軍，即使萬一不測，遇有匪亂，頃刻之間即可平定，亦決非往年所可同日而語云云。茲特將巴黎日報紐約專電原文及遠東通信社辨正原文附呈於後，專此。恭啟

附件一

巴黎日報紀行專電

...applaudies.

Les troupes sont allées ensuite s'embarquer dans l'arsenal, à Missiessy.

LES BOXERS PRÉPARENT LE MASSACRE DES ÉTRANGERS

NEW-YORK, 30 septembre. (*Par câble de notre correspondant particulier.*) — La flotte américaine de l'océan Pacifique vient de recevoir de Washington l'ordre de se tenir prête à appareiller.

Cet ordre a été adressé à la suite d'une communication reçue du représentant des Etats-Unis à Pékin, M. Calhoun, qui annonce qu'un nouveau soulèvement des Boxers est imminent et que la vie des étrangers est en danger.

Des instructions analogues ont été câblées à l'armée américaine à Manille, aux Philippines.

Les amis des missionnaires et des commerçants américains en Chine sont dans l'anxiété.

ACCIDENTS D'AUTOMOBILES

CHARLEVILLE, 30 septembre. (*Par dépêche de notre correspondant particulier.*) — Avant-hier soir, vers cinq heures, la fillette de M. Grégoire, concierge à l'usine Givet Saint-Hilaire, reve-

崇安伏乞
慈照不莊　王慕陶謹上

Agence d'Extrême-Orient.

NOTE

Une dépêche de New-York dit que le représentant des Etats-Unis à Pékin aurait prévenu son gouvernement que des troubles provoqués par les Boxers étaient sur le point d'éclater en Chine, en suite de quoi, le gouvernement américain aurait donné l'ordre de renforcer immédiatement l'escadre et les troupes américaines.

Nous croyons devoir démentir cette nouvelle en ce qui concerne la situation en Chine. Il est vrai qu'il y a quelques mois, des troubles, non pas provoqués par les Boxers, mais par l'antagonisme entre Jeunes et Vieux Chinois et par la famine, étaient à craindre. Mais actuellement le calme est revenu. La position du gouvernement, à la tête d'une bonne armée, est excellente, et toute tentative de révolte serait immédiatement arrêtée.

Agence d'Extreme-Orient.

附件二

松花江航業問題，俄政府於西八月四號聲言，中俄兩國於西七月三十號已將此項交涉在北京議結，重新另訂條款，其條款節目雖未宣布，然俄外交界及輿論上均極滿足，其感情已較前此為融洽矣。俄報均謂此為俄日協約之效力矣。以去歲兩國特派委員研究磋商，直至三月而不能得頭緒者，今乃以三星期內了結之，其情勢相去為何如乎。然自他面觀之，則此問題原限以八月一號為最後期間，而直延至七月三十號始行議定，則非中國之有所顧忌可概見。是此問題之結果，倘無協約通過，亦烏足以阻此。其普通持論之點，大率如是，亦足表現最近俄人對我之心理也。莫斯科斯拉俄為全俄第一之大報，日前著論謂：俄國與中國重要交涉，松花江航業問題既結，所懸擱者僅有哈爾濱管理問題耳。往時管理之權本為俄所全有，戰後至今則為東清鐵路總理哥瓦大將與中國官吏合管，此種辦法最易滋事，如去歲九月條領事之衝突，稍有不慎，即足惹起國際之戰爭，殊於平和有礙，今後亦望能速結云云。惟彼

得便日報，又謂中國外交現似大有進步，前此與俄抵觸，幾至決裂者，至是忽
為一變，而彼此交誼感情復油然興起，正不得謂非當局者之補事也。當俄日
締結協約時，比利時之遠東通信社攻擊最力，實足代表中國國民之意見。俄
人已大注意，而同時郡王載濤方在聖彼得堡，其隨從各員接見報館記者談
論之間，亦極表中國憤懣之意。於是一面復有陸軍部尚書蔭昌聘德國將官
為中國訓練陸軍之新聞，因此數事，俄人震恐，均以為中俄將即於戰，其勢不
可終日矣。乃中國於七月二十二號之答復，竟承認俄日協約，惟於千九百五
年約中主要之點，尊重中國主權，開放滿洲門戶二語，一再致意，敦請遵
將此次協約範圍收縮，變廣大為狹隘，成兩國協商之効力，然在俄日亟設法以收
對之。彼知俄日之敵愾而不敢言也，則於此而為之特疾，今後僅八日，遂將
松花江條約鐵定，了去中俄間一極困難之交涉。雖曰時迫勢迫，亦未始非有
意悔禍，因以減殺俄日之聯合力也云云。諸西亞報所論略同，特其中有數

諸報關於要求蒙古問題是也。彼謂中國於蒙古，亦與俄起競爭，此亦足慮矣。蒙古之為俄人目的物，因無需詳言，今敢述莫斯科俄商頗覺中國經營蒙古銳進不止，而俄之商務則大退敗，蒙人貨品之輸入於俄國者，實已倍於俄國貨品之輸入於蒙古也。俄商進出不能相抵，非設法平均，則俄之商務必將無偉。因此之故，俄人欲保其西伯利鐵路枝線，須注意於水運，俾衣底克及衣里色區之間交通便利。現方計畫一新線，即由衣尔枯斯基經過衣尔枯斯江流及馬抗加衣陸地。此線若成，則俄蒙交通必更利便，或可挽救從前之失。惟中國政府亦從事經營蒙古，其尤棘手者，在由內地移民至該蒙古各地，實行其殖民政策，是又俄之一大阻力云云。巴黎時報於外交上因法俄同盟之關係，夙覺於俄，此次對松花江交涉，亦屢著論謂中俄邦交實視此為關鍵。在彼之意以為俄僅得其權利中所應有者，並無意外之侵奪也。何以證之，千八百五十八年五月二十八號愛暉條約，其第一條原謂中俄於黑龍江、松花江、烏蘇里江同有航權也。是時滿洲一隅尚僅有俄之勢力，並無第三國起與相競。千八百八十一年二月二十四號聖彼得堡條約第十八條重行聲明愛暉條約第一

條之義意，而較之以約曰中俄彼此應有交換之利益，其詳細章程，當俟議
定。後此擱置，終未妥協，而俄船亦自由航行於松花江，中國與之亦何必耳。至一
千九百五年日俄戰爭之後，樸斯茅斯條約將此予條束盡，此條約之第三
條，聲明俄在滿洲不得有特別利益，對於中國不得有特別權利而致有所防
損於中國之滿洲主權，是否實暗中取消前此璦琿條約及聖彼得堡條約也。
中國海關遂按此條以徵收俄船航稅，與他國商船無異，而俄之北京代表於
終爭持，其去年始由中國總稅務司裴式楷與俄國代表興賀斯多維也議
定暫行簡章，此章曾於去年十月俄商所願，加以海關檢查俄船者，維得須深
夜追捕俄人，大惑彼等，俄政府固不能不承認裴式楷所定暫章，惟其
航稅僅允納交於道勝銀行，不肯直接納於中國海關，海關不承認中國有徵
船稅之權，並令時聲明此項暫章僅於今年八月一號為限，此中須另行訂
議定，仍遵一千八百八十一年二月二十四號聖彼得堡條約之趣旨，而中國與
詞以難之，就是以俄對松花江交涉，俄所爭持根據於條約，實在情理之中云云。
此又言現對此事之輿論也。

Peking
Hsia Kung Fu
5 Jan. 1911.

已復

P.S. Book will be sent tomorrow [illegible]

Dear Dr. Yen,

I send you herewith the promised report. I have made it as short as possible, so as not to throw too much work on the translator but any points that require further elucidation will be willingly explained by me. I may say here, for private information, that the journey cost roughly between Tls 5000.00 & Tls 6000.00. (I am waiting for the passbook from London before I can calculate the exact figure). I received Tls 2500.00 from the Board, as you know, & the fees which I was paid amounted to somewhat between Tls 500 & Tls 1000.00 in total. The rest of the money came out of my own pocket.

As I said to you last week, I do not really care a bit so long as I make both ends meet. At the same time that I am assisting China in having her case laid properly before the world, I am continuing my own work and adding to my own small reputation: therefore I could not possibly think of asking anything from the Board, save a relatively speaking small & legitimate monthly fee which would assist me to cover my travelling expenses. I want to go Manchuria & Korea in a month or two when I have completed some work I am now handling then I want to go on to Canada & America again in the

I know nearly everybody in England & America it will be much easier to push on the work with much better results than the initial campaign as you can notice for yourself. Public opinion is changing; & from all sorts of quarters I am getting requests for

autumn & commence again the campaign. £300 a month is the figure which I venture to request that you lay before the Board as a fixed contribution so long as the Board desires to deal with this work. I think seeing the amount of good that is done — & the great effect it may have in modifying the future for China — this will be held very modest. Now that

7

amount of energy for one man to attempt to cover both England & America, but I think I can do it!

With many thanks for your good offices,

Believe me,

Yours very truly

B. Lenox-Simpson

special information. What I want to do is to bombard the Chambers of Commerce in England — & especially the Manchester Chamber — with facts which will make them worry our own Foreign Office, & thus force a new China policy. I can tell you it requires an immense

附件一

照譯辛博悌致章京顏惠慶函西千九百十一年正月五號中十二月初五日

逕啓者簡明報告一册兹特送呈

台閱該報告係删繁就簡擇要從事倘有未盡明晰之處僕可再爲詳解今有不能不瑣陳者此次旅費合計五六千金惟收支簿未由倫敦寄□細數不能記憶除前領

貴部銀二千五百兩又收到各處演説著論酬銀約自五百至一千兩外其不敷之數悉由僕墊付在僕區區之意祇求敷用不求其他業於上星期面達

清聽況僕此行半爲中國公事半爲私事更不敢非分

外過求倘能得一酌中津貼可資旅費私願已足僕并
擬俟經手事件料理清楚在一兩月間前往滿洲高麗
等處一遊然後於秋間再往坎拿大美利堅各處續辦
一切津貼一層擬按月以三百金為請若以成蹟計之此
數似非太過現在歐美當道幾於無不相識此次再去
必較初次事半功倍也歐美輿論今已幡然改觀諒
閣下亦已見之各處來信向僕探聽特別消息者絡繹
不絶僕之宗旨欲借運動英國孟哲斯德商會或其他
商會俾與英外部纏擾不休迫其改變對清政策而我

得坐收其利此事獨力辦理頗費心力顧僕雖不才尚
能勉爲其難耳
費神種種心感萬分專此順頌
日祺　　辛博惕簽名
附報告一册　　機要股股員徐善慶譯呈

附件二

CONFIDENTIAL REPORT ON A LECTURE-TOUR
IN ENGLAND & AMERICA.

@@@@@@@@@@@

The undersigned begs to submit the following detailed account of lectures and conversations of political value to China.

The writer arrived in Paris in August, and published at once there in the New York Herald a full account of the position in the Far East dwelling with great vehemence on the increasing danger which Japanese domination and the non-activity of the European powers in assisting China to regain her proper autonomy, was steadily bringing. (a copy of this report duly despatched to the Waiwupu, Press Bureau). This account was reproduced in many continental papers and was summarized in London. It met the eye of many statesmen.

Some time was spent by the writer in drafting several lectures in such a vein as seemed suitable most to impress people in England. On arriving there the writer lost no time in getting into close touch with newspaper circles, so as to be able to measure properly the strength with which Japanese interests are always protected in London, and Chinese interests steadily ignored.

The following facts, which were gathered by him on the spot, may be accepted as incontestable.

It may be said that the Japanese have the most powerful hold on the English press---but especially of the London press---because of the relations which they have with The Times newspaper and Reuter's Telegraphic agency. The cablegrams of these two services virtually supply all England with its news of the Far East; they are reproduced almost universally in England and as they give the Japanese case, and seldom---or never---the Chinese case---they have done much grave harm in the past.

As is well-known, the Japanese Government has at its disposal the yearly sum of Two Million yen for Secret service money. It is a very heavy subscriber to Reuter's agency in the form of a regular payment for an exclusive daily telegraphic summary of European political news to Tokio at a figure calculated so as to give the London agency a handsome profit. The actual figures were promised to the writer, but at the last moment his informant in London became nervous and refused to give exact information.

The case with the Times is most peculiar. There seems to be no doubt that the Japanese Government subscribed to a publication called the Times Encyclopedia to the extent of yen 200,000, as a convenient form of subsidy, placing copies of this encyclopedia in all public places in Japan.(1) Copies of this bulky work may be found even in the Railway Hotels of the South Manchuria Railway. Apart from this there are hints of other transactions of a similar nature. It is well-known for instance that the salary of the Tokyo correspondent of the Times is paid by the Japanese Government through the Nippon Yusen Kaisha steamship Co's head office. It is thus clear that The Times has benefitted pecuniarily from its constant advocacy of Japan.

---

(1) So far as the writer can learn, this transaction was completed a year or two ago.

The formation of The Times into a company, (1) at the head of which was Lord Northcliffe, proprietor of the Daily Mail, made a virtual alliance between the chief London paper and many other papers. "The Daily Mail", which has the largest circulation in the world, has been steadily buying up other newspapers in England, and therefore opinions dictated in London are reproduced in all parts of England,

The so-called "Times" policy is therefore reflected from day to day in many parts of England.

For the next biggest newspaper "The Daily Telegraph" the writer had prepared a large series of articles at great labour showing the exact nature of Japanese domination in Korea and Manchuria, and advocating a drastic change in British policy [in the Far East]. The Hon. Harry Lawson, son of the proprietor and general manager, personally informed the writer when these articles were completed and actually set in type, ready to be published, that it was impossible to publish them, as

---

(1) This also took place a year or two ago the capitalists who assisted in the formation of this company, are the same capitalists in the city of London who have a virtual monopoly of the Japanese loans.

publication would be accepted by all as a sign of the fact that the British Govt. was about to change its policy. Payment was offered to the writer all the same ---which he refused unless publication came too. The proprietor remained stubborn in his refusal not to publish, and the matter was abortive.

The writer afterwards discovered, that it was mainly owing to the fact that the Jewish financial house of Rothschild,(1) having played the leading role in making Japanese war-loans---and being committed, it is said, to having the monopoly of future Japanese loans in the event of trouble with America or any other country---influence was brought to bear some time ago, to prevent the publication of criticism of Japan in papers having Jewish proprietors or connections.

The Daily Telegraph belongs to one of the richest Jewish families in London. This point, trivial though it may seem, is specially mentioned so that it may be clearly understood in Peking, how powerful are the

---

(1) These facts will assist in showing the Board that Japan, by borrowing such immense sums in London has succeeded in attaching to her those capitalists who have made very large commissions out of her.

forces which Japanese interests control, and in what a curious manner things work.

Nevertheless the writer persisted in his policy of sounding all the editors and proprietors of London newspapers---discussing every aspect of the Far Eastern problem and often leaving with them memoranda and data proving the validity of his arguments. By the end of September everything being complete, he delivered his first big speech in Manchester before the Manchester Chamber of Commerce. The newspaper summaries of this speech which was fully reported all over England were duly forwarded to the Press Bureau of the Waiwupu---but the writer would like to add the following remarks.

The gist of this speech which lasted nearly two hours and was adopted by a resolution of the Chamber of Commerce---the centre of the trade between England and China, was

(I) that China was being crippled through the lack of consideration shown her and the false policy of the Anglo-Japanese alliance.

(2) That Japan cared nothing for England and showed this in her new proposed tariff which was designed to kill the Manchester trade-

(3) That it had therefore become imperative for powerful commercial bodies like the Manchester Chambers of Commerce, to protest and to continue to protest to the British Government against such a condition of affairs, being maintained in the Far East

(4) That if nothing were done in the near future the markets of China would be lost as the markets of Japan were being lost-

This speech produced a great impression. The writer lost no time in interviewing all the editors of Manchester newspapers as well as many correspondents, insisting again and again on these views, On that day the writer talked for more than fourteen hours---

On the return to London at the beginning of October, he delivered several small talks, and on the

5th October he had an important interview with Lord Morley, Secretary of State for India.

In this conversation at the India Office, the writer attacked the question from a new point of view. He laid down the proposition that if the Japanese were allowed to become the unchallenged dominant power in the Far East sooner, or later, the British position in India would be more radically affected than anything which had happened for a century; and as it had been partly on account of safeguarding India and the Indian frontier against Russia that the system of Japanese alliances had been inangurated, it was self-evident that the time had come when the government of India must interest itself in the designs of Japan. and the problem of Japan in the Far East.

Lord Morley was much surprised at this line of argument. He said that Chinese military activity in Tibet and the capture of Lhassa had occasioned much anxiety in India where many experts believed that Chinese troops had become a real factor of importance on the Indian frontier ie. might become a menace-

The writer ridiculed these views. He showed how the position in Tibet had long been intolerable to the Peking government, and how the military advance on Lhassa was merely the resumption of a position which had been held by China for much more than a century. Furthermore he insisted that the larger view which he had advanced was the one which statesmen should now study---no longer listening to inspired Japanese statements.

In answer to the direct question of the writer as to whether there was any possibility of the present Japanese alliance being renewed in 1915, Lord Morley became reticent, but finally said that the question had not yet been officially considered nor could it be officially considered for several years to come, since the decision had only to be made in five years' time: in 1915. From other conversations with minor government officials in London, the writer has every reason to believe that this statement is absolutely accurate: on the history of the next four or five years the fate of the Anglo-Japanese alliance will hang--

Finally before leaving Lord Morley, the writer begged that his views be repeated to the other members of the cabinet and the seriousness of the position be not lost sight of. The writer has every reason to believe that his statements have carried some weight. Had he remained in England another month or two, interviews would have been arranged with Mr. Asquith, Prime Minister, Mr. Lloyd George, Chancellor of the Excheques and Mr. Winston Churchill. But as his friends assured him that the subject had been sufficiently wellventilated for the time being, the writer decided not to wait but to cross to America without further delay.

In America it was necessary to use new arguments, new points of view, and new material. This threw a great deal of fresh work on the writer.

Soon after he arrived in New York an exhaustive

interview was published in the newspaper "The Sun" (copy forwarded to Press Bureau, Waiwupu). Through the Laffan agency and the Associated Press agency this was telegraphed all over America. It was said that this was repeated 180 times. Following the first interview came a second article dealing with the 50 million gold dollar loan, and the necessity of America persisting in the policy of independently assisting China (copy forwarded to Waiwupu). As a result of these interviews many letters reached the writer, with invitations to speak at many universities as well as an invitation to come as soon as possible to Washington.

The writer proceeded first to Boston, where he supplied the newspapers with data, then returned to New York in time to be present on the publication of his new political book "The Conflict of Colour" (copy now forwarded to the Waiwupu) on the Ist. November.

This book has been received with many comments and will engage public attention for many months. The main argument, so far as China is concerned, is that it has become vitally necessary to establish a balance of power between China and Japan in the Far East---that id to say that China must be so strengthened by the action of the European powers that of her own strength she is made the military equal of Japan and that the policy of nominally guaranteeing her independence by paper treaties (such as the false Anglo-Japanese Alliance) be exchanged for the new policy of directly building her up, so that before it is too late she may be in a position to resist Japanese aggression.

The writer personally handed copies of this book to the editors of all the great New York newspapers and then proceeded to Philadelphia where he gave an address at the university of Pennsylvania which was very largely attended and fully reported in the papers (copy to the Waiwupu).

Going on to Washington the writer lost no time in getting into touch with the State Department. A few days after his arrival President Taft received him and discussed the Far Eastern question. The President did not hesitate to say "that he regretted very much that England should be so tied up to certain other countries that she had showed herself hitherto unable to endorse the American policy in the Orient", and that he trusted a change might come. The writer replied that he himself had insisted on this view to his utmost capacity in England---that he had embodied these views in a new political volume just published in England and America; that he would continue to insist on them without ceasing, and that he had no doubt that the American attitude would finally be accepted.

The President was good enough to pass some flattering remarks on the writer's books which he stated he knew well, and to request him to see Mr. Knox, Secretary of State, as he 'himself being busy' preparing to go to the Panama Canal had but scant time free.

The next day the writer had pleasure in sending the President a copy of his new book "The Conflict of colour". He was given to understand later that the President read it on his way to the Canal Zone. As this book emphasizes in the very strongest language the necessity of America actively curbing Japan, this action was not without value--

A few days later the writer had a long interview with Mr. Knox, Secretary of State, in which Mr. Knox talked with the utmost frankness saying that America was determined to do all she could for China, but that a great stumbling-block was England and the Japanese alliance. The writer then detailed what he had done in England to show this very view, and then ventured to suggest that there was one diplomatic move of great importance which Washington might make to weaken the British alliance with Japan. If Canada, now negotiating a commercial reciprocity Treaty with the United States, could be induced sooner or later to make a formal declaration in company with America regarding the necessity of "the open-door" across the Pacific, the influence on England would be very considerable. The writer returned to this point again and again, and though Mr. Knox carefully refrained from making any statement, the writer has reason to believe that the suggestion has been fully noted. Mr. Knox promised to give full attention to the arguments in the writer's new book, and thanked the writer for the publicity he was attracting to the Far Eastern question in America. The writer subsequently saw and discussed at very great length, all these points of view with the Secretary of War, Mr. Dickinson, the Chief of the Staff, General Leonard Wood, (1) Mr. O'Brien, the American Ambassador to Tokyo (just about to return to Japan) and many military and naval officers. He is able to report that there is an absolute unanimity of opinion is Washington on the Far Eastern question---so much that every nerve is being strained to hasten the completion of the Panama Canal so that the American fleet may become a vital factor. There is no doubt now that the the canal will be ready early in 1914 i.e. in four years' time, and that it is hoped in Washington that

---

(1) An important point in the writer's new book is the manner in which he exposes the military weakness of America in the event of any armed conflict with Japan. This point was the one which attracted the most attention in Washington.

this fact alone will profoundly modify the attitude of England towards Japan.

Interviews now appeared in the Washington papers with the writer's views---the interview in the semi-official Washington Post being of especial importance (copy forwarded to the Waiwupu)

The writer, having done all that was possible, in Washington took train for Chicago, and on the 22nd. November delivered a big lecture there entitled "America to the rescue in the Orient". In this lecture he announced publicly for the first time the necessity of Canada which was building her own navy, falling into line with America on the Pacific question, and thus forcing England to abandon her small views. He dwelt on the danger of Japanese armaments, and the manner in which Japan would prevent China becoming strong, unless the English-speaking powers were united in their policy.

He insisted that before 1923 (when the Port Arthur lease nominally expires) Japan would show her hand against China, unless China in the meantime had been made a strong power. This speech attracted considerable attention, and was copied into all the Canadian papers. The writer gave several more interviews, and at the beginning of December embarked at San Francisco for China. He had been asked to speak at many universities but expenses were very high and the writer felt that as much had been done in his publicity campaign as was for the time being neccessary.

It would be best to allow an interval of half a year or so to pass, and then to return to the charge with fresh facts and fresh arguments, because of too much noise were made all at once, it would defeat its own object. Such was the official opinion in America.

The writer submits this short report feeling that he has done his best though it is not very much. But he was working without ceasing for four months, talking and writing, and it was necessary to show no little ingeniuty in finding the right arguments in each new place---in impressing both the people of England and America in ways that appealed to them. In many cases his pro-Chinese views were not only attacked, but he was personally attacked, and attempts made to pick to pieces his statements. It required no little pertinacity to return to the charge every day with something new to say. He is now busy preparing new articles and it is his intention to return to America during this year and to go to Canada as well. The importance of pushing this question energetically during the next few years is self-evident---it is necessary to make it impossible at least for England to renew the Japanese alliance, on the present terms. Take the support of England away from Japan, and her aggressive policy must cease to a very large extent. The writer believes that a great deal has been done already to modify the relations between Japan and England, as well as to show the world how little consideration China has received. He personally will continue the work he has been doing on his own account for eight years and he trusts he will have the requisite support, ---knowing personally as he now does how to push this campaign---

B. Lenox-Simpson.

(B. L. Putnam Weale)

Peking: 5. January. 1911.

附件三

照译辛博惕游说英美机密报告

谨将有裨中国政治之演说会晤详细情形造具
报告恭呈
鉴核
窃自八月行抵巴黎印具说帖送交纽约希鲁报登载
详陈远东大势并言日本侵略欧洲列强袖手旁观
不助中国恢复主权之意直远东隐患日增一日等语
报外务部 此说一出欧陆各报转登伦敦报章
亦经摘录各国报纸当道见之
适□颈备演词以备英人能阅英国立刻身
报侦察所获日本利益及顾中国利益之
实情其势力之厚今以就地查得事
实缕陈之
日本可谓有操纵英国报界之大力而最大者则
伦敦报界皆因伦敦泰晤士报与路透电
局之关系故也盖远东消息概由该两家海电转
递而英国全国报纸所登彼等传日本事件而不
传中国事件其为害于中国已非浅鲜

日本政府每年年拨二百万圆作为秘密侦探
费是人皆知其津贴路透电也则将欧洲政治新闻
每日择要电寄东京给以重资钜款俾伦敦总
局藉获厚利以调剂之该社实鼓六经其
尚初许相告设东瞻不敢宣泄
泰晤士报馆日私通之法尤觉离奇日本政府将
该报所刊一种报纸名曰泰晤士百科总录所给
之款系日金二十万圆藉资津贴百科总录
系日本全国各处公地散布所编印南满铁
路旅馆中亦能见之且闻此外尚有他种方法与
此亦复相类已历一二年矣且闻尚有他种
方法与此大同小异设如泰晤士报东京访员之薪
水系由日本政府转嘱日本邮船会社总局发
给故泰晤士报得此厚资而常为其附和
辩为日本辩护之报也
自泰晤士报改组改为公司以来伦敦著名报馆
与其他数报馆互相联合已有讨盟一二年其投资
赞助之人即系伦敦城内之资本家公司总理名
亦即垄断日本借款之一党也

日郵報館主人瑪史克之夫世爵也每日郵報銷
路之廣幾徧天下并經迭次收買國中其他報館
故能主張倫敦輿論而英國全國隨聲傳播鍼
隨聲附和此之謂泰晤士政策英國通都大邑
其日之影響及之
第二大報爲每日電報余曾大費心力著作論說多
篇詳陳日本經界韓滿確實情形并力主張英國
應改變遠東政策急宜大爲改革等語該館
主人兼任總辦之子勞生告余曰君所著論說本
館原欲照登將字模排好付印忽
念此論一經刊登恐人將認爲有心攻擊美政府
有意表顯美政府有改其政策之
趨向故不登爲是著論酬銀當照付余
習以况不利於美復再四終不肯
作罷
嗣採得其故蓋因猶太富豪羅斯查爾之銀行實爲
日本軍費借款之主動者并經議定將來日本設
與美國或他國因事開衅而借款彼可得專利

按此事日本由于在倫敦借外此鉅款故資本家得其厚利而日本遂藉此爲之援
是以近來禁止阻報館之猶太人爲館主者或
與猶太人有關係者均不得登載評論日本之
說
每日電報館亦猶太富家之一此事由表面觀之似乎
微細不關緊要然余所以特之提出者欲使北
京深悉日本利益所在操縱勢若何其大
若何其論當注意而毋忽視也
雖然余仍堅持初志百折不撓倫敦各報
主筆館主務達目的遠東實在情勢九
月下旬諸事就緒乃往並哲斯德重要商會
此商會乃中英貿易之樞紐
宣講兩次長大演說一篇經英國報紙登錄
盡情登載此篇演說宣講兩小時之久並
哲斯德商會閱之隨即議決採用數條如下
一 中國因他國及英美日協約政策之影響
一 日本於英國漠不相關心即就其新訂稅
則觀之即可見其擯斥並哲斯德貿易之心
一 勢力擴張之商團若並哲斯德商會者宜

英政府现今远东一切措施急宜坚持反对主义
一 倘不思挽救之策则中国市场行将
坐失与前此之失日本市场无异
此次演说听者大为感动余随即会晤孟塔斯
德君报之笔访员等与之反覆辩论上之
各条之意见一日之间计谈十四小时之久
十月初驰回伦敦首发小册数次电初五日晤
印度部大臣摩礼未世爵谈判与开办重
要之谈判
此次至印度部中内余另用他法开言陈说略
谓英国继续维持日本在远东之势力则迟早
之间印度必受百年未有之大祸原夫联盟日本
之初志本为防御俄国以保印度疆土起见然时
至今日印度政府实不能不关心日本之远东计画
之势矣
毛氏悚然动容乃谓中国兵进西藏据守拉萨印度
颇为焦虑识者佥谓华兵将为印度边疆之害
余力驳其说非因将藏事者何败坏北京政府忍无
可忍

可忍其进兵也特以恢复其数百年固有之权及复申说
后言最要之著执政诸公所应详察者乃不再续订英日
本之盟约也
至于一九一十九百十五年是否续订英日盟约茅氏
默然良久乃言此问题尚未经官场议及且
为时尚久现在未便议及一千九百十五年距今尚有
五年之久方能定夺今为时尚久未便议及
潜探次级官员口气则茅氏所言甚为确凿于以见
英日盟约之续订当在此四五年间定其可否
余复请茅氏将意见转达内阁各大臣采纳并请
陈说利害常注视而勿失也查此次谈判效力颇
为重大若再留伦敦一两月则首相度支大臣等皆
拟设法谒见但经友人劝说此事办到非易亦云可
矣宜暂置勿提余从之遂渡大西洋去而之美
因美国情形不同英国非另拟议论见解资
料不足以动美人余是以不得不用新思想以警之
事实
行抵纽约之日即有一长篇会晤问答刊登太阳

根抄件寄呈外務部機密股印由拉番電局遞根界聯合社通電
美利堅全國議報合計抄登一百八十次云繼著論
說一篇由中國借款五十兆金元借款一案並言美國應堅持獨
立助華政策 抄件送呈外務部 共數後接書札
邀往大學堂演說者有中東請速赴華
國聯者云
余先往卜士頓而以資料寄送該處各報館
仍回紐約適遇所著政治書補譯者出版時
當為十一月初一日也
此書曾經各報讚頌而為大衆所注意其大旨演
於中國一方面者則謂中國与日本遠東勢力務
須設法以平均之蓋言中國須賴歐洲列強
贊助輔以強盛而于中國自己兵力須有陸軍
足与日本相頡頏也如美日盟約保全中國主權之紙上空談
精并日聯合假定美國之新政策以俾直
接輔其強之如此則中國尚可抵禦日本
或他國侵犯也
余曾親送此書与紐約各大報主筆 繼後往

費城德飛省而至本西偉尼大學演說報者甚
衆其稿由各報登載
至華盛頓時即往外部接洽不數日間蒙總
統由塔虎脫接見議論遠東問題總統
捷於言曰美國以附某國以致不能贊成美國東方政策
殊為可惜歎余深悉其政策宗旨乎 余即答以前至英國
曾將此意竭力鼓吹并至新著政治書中屢及討論
在倫敦時曾精心竭慮以圖其務達目的而未能使英國
贊成美國改見而致之一日也
總統謂此書余甚不勝欽佩以巴那
瑪運河之事頗形忙碌不暇久談深為歉余往見外
相諾克司
翼日余即將新書面呈種族競爭總統嗣聞總統將
此書携往巴那瑪而至途中閱看此書于美國制
伏日本一層言之最切故總統深見此書于事實
上頗有價值
數日後謁外相諾克司談甚久諾言論爽直一無隱秘之
其態彼謂美國決意竭力援助中國但美日同盟

实为美大之阻碍。余乃详述五美所为一切，
并献计日：华盛顿可施一极大之外交手段以弱
英日盟约，使英大宪与美国商订互利商约，想彼必
能请英伐令与美国同宣布开放门户之必要，太
平洋东岸必需开放门户之要义。若此，则影
响则美国必大受影响。诺氏虽慎守缄默，不表
意见，然察其神情，似颇赞成，首肯时时。余并将所著书所拟
议论，彼面许详为揣摩，加以披阅，云嗣晤
陆军大臣秋狄金生、参谋总长伍德，驻日本大使
瓯伯拉时，将及其他海陆军官与之讨论。继见华
盛顿对于远东问题舆论一致，均甚注意巴那玛运
河。美政府使美国海军速成动旅，查运河至四年
之内即西历一千九百十四年必可告成。由此一端，美
国对于日本之态度自当改变。
以上会晤问答及余所发意见，均经华盛顿各报
登载。其最要者乃半官华盛顿邮报所登一则
也。抄件一并寄外务部
继往美加高于十一月二十二号发一长篇演说，其题

为美国救援东方。至此演说内，余初次声言于今
大既自主海军，须与美国合力同守太平洋，而破
英国其浅见，彼复加陈日本军兵力可畏，及
其抑制中国不令自强情形，因倡议英法
同文各国，允协定政策，同心戮力，不足以制日本。此
外又若云一千九百二十三年旅顺租借期满之
时，倘中国未能保国，则日本必将动手负云云。
此说一出，闻者大为感动，于拿大各报亦偏登
传登。
嗣经大学堂多处相邀演说，余以费用昂贵，
且已作之事足救当时一时之需，遂于十二月初由
旧金山乘轮赴华。拟俟半年之后，再在美国
用新资料新议论，续办前事，盖援美国
官界之意，若一时言论太多，反无益而有损也。
谨按此次报告，虽所成无多，而心力交瘁，余办事
日夜不接济，四月无休歇，因说笔书所难者
至揽索相当言论，以激动英美两国人之心，
且一日有一日之言，日日不同，颇费斟酌也。余助华政

見横被攻擊[illegible]者已屢見非一見矣今正另

著論說以備[illegible]年內再往美坎也[illegible]鼓

年之間余擬將此遠東問題[illegible]大聲疾呼

冀阻美國與日本續行現訂盟約斯為最要

日本若失英國之援則其野心庶可稍斂歟

竊觀此次經金游說而來美國足以激變美

日交涉[illegible]者良多而亦足以使昭示寰球各列

國於之關切中國者甚少也[illegible]將自己起見

續請前筆八年[illegible]知餘[illegible]

敬啓者：俄美邦交向稱輯睦，朴資茅斯之約，俄得美助實多。近因俄領事對於美國所給美籍猶太人之護照不肯承認，美遂大傷感情。由下議院員舒爾柔 Sulzer 君倡議廢棄一八三二年俄美通商行船條約，以為抵制。衆相贊和，立將舒君之議通過。駐美俄使雖即謁見總統，起而反對，然未幾上議院亦將該案通過。有痛詆俄之專制，謂不應將美國給有護照之人分别人種宗教而加限制者；有謂一八三二年條約本與美國體面有損者；並有謂美國亦應將蒙古種之俄人禁其入美者。美總統遂電飭駐俄大使正式聲告，惟詞氣改從和平，以該約過舊，不適於今日之用為詞，並預留續訂新約之地步。此間美大使遵照訓條，於俄歷本月十五號文告俄外部，該約之效力自一九一三年正月一號為始，即須停止。俄雖未有正式之答復，然輿情極不滿意，謂美人之自由平等不過大言欺人，如不准華人入籍、禁止華工入境等事，平等何在？自由何在？下議院古屈谷甫 Goutchkoff 並已發議，謂應將美貨加倍抽稅，以為報復。此後風雲變幻，正不可測。查俄領事不肯承認美國所給猶太人之護照，以俄律論之，並非過舉。緣該猶太人本係俄人，而入美籍，在俄國籍法並無准人出

駐俄使館

籍之文。是以美雖視為入籍，然俄尚未認其為出籍。俄美本無國籍條約，而俄之限制猶太人本極綦嚴，不過該領不應以宗教人種為辭，遂致美人大憤，牽及商航條約，而兩國際更多一轇轕。且於吾國不無間接之影響，尤為可厭。蓋俄日之交親，為諾克司鐵道中立問題所激而成。此間比國公使前與徵祥密談，言之猶為太息。若此後俄美交惡，則必更謀與日本親密，而且欲損美利，則於我滿洲問題必更易滋爪葛。至於美國方面，雖政策上或可稍為吾助，然欲其為吾而以實力與他國相角，決所不能。翹企前途，良懷隱慮，未識蓋見以為何如。茲將美國駐俄大使文函及巴黎時報議論一篇一并譯呈，姑備垂詧。專此。祇請勛安。

陸徵祥頓首 十一月初四日

俄字第三號

駐俄使館

再封函待發，適見此間新時報載有北京來電內傳北京半官報消息，接中國駐俄公使報告，謂俄國派兵入蒙問題業經詢問沙外部，據稱此次派兵並無他意，只為保護俄人利益等語，甚為詫異。不知該項消息是否果係北京半官報所載，當即向報館聲明此間並無該項報告，亦無因該問題與沙大臣談判。旋俄官報亦同時聲明，謂俄並未派兵入蒙，沙大臣亦無因該問題與中國公使談判云云。查此等消息及其詞氣與外交實有關係，倘係民間報紙亂傳尚屬不可，況半官報更為人所注意。可否請

飭設法以後稍加留意，是所至荷。合并附陳，再頌

日祺

徵祥再頓首　十一月初四日　附俄字第三號

駐俄使館

敬再啓者，此次波斯以沒收廢王之弟財產與俄轇轕，俄竟一再送哀的邁敦書，始則要求波外部向駐波俄使謝罪，繼又要求撤退所聘財政顧問之客卿及此後聘用客卿須先商允俄英政府。現俄兵將抵波京，據聞波政府亦已復允，英亦竭力勸波。强權世界本無足異。該案前後顛末業於秋季報告詳叙，茲姑撮要附陳，以備

冰鑒。再頌

蓋祺

徵祥再頓首　十一月初四日　附俄字第三號

駐俄使館

附件一

照譯十二月廿四號巴黎時報論俄美紛爭

富矣哉一九一一年國際之轇轕也俄美交好迄今不計年期朴次茅斯條約訂結以後邦交益固迺今者以區區之護照問題使兩半球兩涯之國生出困難之交涉矣位尊者占優勢古諺不誣此次作俑者實為美國溯美洲忿忿不平於美國猶太人遊歷俄國而生出之阻力由來已久而此次將近美國選舉總統時代有俄美轇轕之發見亦屬會逢其適蓋吾人不能忘一九零八年塔孚脫之被舉為總統猶太人之票力占其多數現美國共和党仍擬率循舊軌也今姑將選舉問題置之弗問十二月十二號美下議員舒尔柔君Sulzer攻擊俄國之語尚稱詳切受下議院全部之拍掌歡迎俄國對於外國人之非有俄領事蓋印之護照者不得入境而俄領事抗拒猶太人之生為俄人入美國籍而未經俄政府預准出籍者華盛頓之人即以此為傷損美國子民之權利不容寬忍俄人謂各國均可禁止某項人民入其境土美亦未嘗不尔美以残酷之行為驅逐亞西亞洲人其間隸俄籍者實繁有徒且俄對於美國猶太人之辦法業已從寬按照俄國現行法律規章凡外國猶太人之非

商界之店主或其夥伴一律禁止入境以商店之夥伴為名而入境者其護照亦祇准三月之居留俄領事所以不肯對於入美籍之俄國猶太人稍加遷就者因美國一則不照各國通例將入籍之例改正再則此項在自由美洲之子民大抵為俄國之所厭惡也（按此暗指虛無黨）舌辯筆戰言論頗高實則此事甚可請海牙公斷法院斷決而美人以大選舉期漸倡末之思及十二月十二號美下議院幾以全部通過對於俄國不甚謙和之議案即廢棄一八三二年俄美商約之議案是也該約規定俄美兩國之通商暨此國人民在彼國之權利兩國奉為圭臬八十年相茲美總統塔孚脫急欲了結此事又知俄國對此問題甚有關係遂以靈敏之手段竟解結其困難自十二月十五號美國駐俄大使咨照俄國政府謂美國政府願將一八三二年之老朽條約廢棄但毫不涉及護照問題並稱美國極願與俄國賡續交好是毫無觸犯俄國之性質也美國上議院全數贊成當其討議之時上議員勞特君謂當時美利堅大合衆國對於俄籍之亞西亞人亦未免有虧人道美人大驚異之然則今日者兩國毋庸再事爭論另行磋訂

一新商約可也而磋商之難則不容疑慮蓋一九一三年正月一號一八三二年之舊約即將停止實行而一九一二年十一月內則美國行選舉大總統之禮美國政府勢難兼顧倘俄則開罪於猶太人故苟有議約之舉美政府不論自己甘心或不甘心必堅持護照之條款而俄則必不肯使他國干涉其內政抑亦可知又安可簽一正式無期之約現俄下議院已由極有勢力之古臣格甫 Goutchkoff 發議研究一關稅報復之草案將使美貨加倍抽稅是關稅戰爭之恐嚇竟隱見於雲霧之中雖然論者竊以為兩國不若親之為愈免致他日追悔莫及俄美商務之關係不相上下即如一九一零年之統計歐俄之輸入美國貨物值一千六百十九萬六千一百五十四美圓而輸出之數為一千六百七十八萬九千九百三十美圓至亞俄輸入及輸出之數一為一百十八萬一千零五十八美圓一為一百零三萬九千八百八十一圓是兩國買賣之數適相等也準此情形則關稅戰爭必使兩虎俱傷一無疑義即美人所謂一刀兩截者是已美人之應熟計及此自當更甚於俄選舉之關係自屬匪輕而白宮左右之人亦應計及他日英德兩國坐收漁翁之利否耶

附件二

節譯駐俄美大使致俄外部文

奉本政府訓條本政府以為一八三二年俄美通商行船之老朽條約不適今日之用致兩國政府時有抱歉之事故願將該約廢棄

附譯同時致俄外部函

本國政府甚願另訂一友好之通商行船新約俾適宜於今日兩國之利益本國總統極盼與貴國賡續交好并下次議約必使兩國邦交益加鞏固

二六五

照錄美國領事照會

為照會事昨今兩日駐本鎮各領事官聚會敝署公議保免本鎮疫症以杜傳染其最酷者惟發熱一症由申來漢之輪船中如有此症未知貴監督係用何法保免傳染本鎮上年西七月初七日定有此項保免章程貴處曾否行於鄱陽江孚江永江寬亞地三各輪船此各輪載來客人未經醫士驗過如何可以准令上岸請煩知照敝處各領事官是望上年章程係免發熱症傳染本鎮茲各領事官又定一章程較上年所定者尤加詳細今隨文呈上請即迅交江漢關極力施行各領事官並請將逐日查驗清單送交敝署更祈印送各領事官各商行各輪船並張貼江漢關門首緣此事極為緊要醫士一員恐或不及應請添聘一醫助理消患無形豈非美事相應照會貴監督請煩查照望切施行須至照會者

計粘章程五條

保安章程係免長江一帶疫症

一條無論何輪船來漢如內有人於未到漢口之前十日或有病或病故者該船頭桅桿上須懸掛黃旗此黃旗須由醫生允許方准下旗更只准在德租界外之下抛錨亦俟醫生允許方得上泊埠內

二無論何輪船來漢泊在灣船處所其懸掛黃旗抛錨江心者無論何人皆不得擅自上來須醫生驗過允許方能上岸下船

三如先本無病及船到灣泊處所時始發病者須訴知大副大副即告知醫生或再抛錨下邊埠外

四治病全權悉由醫生掌管船上人或病或死一任醫生指使並灑除病藥水於船上

五無論何國人如有破壞此章程者定由其該管官懲辦

A SERIES OF DOCUMENTS ILLUSTRATING THE DIPLOMATIC RELATIONS BETWEEN CHINA AND FOREIGN COUNTRIES IN THE QING DYNASTY

CORRESPONDENCE BETWEEN CHINA AND UNITED STATES

VOLUME VIII

THE CONSOLIDATED

THE FIRST HISTORICAL ARCHIVES OF CHINA
PEKING UNIVERSITY, CHINA
LA TROBE UNIVERSITY, AUSTRALIA

Editorial Name List of Volume Ⅷ

Military Affairs

The Concession of Territory

Charitable Relief

Security and Parties

Others